VIRTUAL PEDOPHILIA

VIRTUAL
PEDOPHILIA

SEX OFFENDER

PROFILING

AND

U.S. SECURITY

CULTURE

Gillian Harkins

DUKE UNIVERSITY PRESS
Durham and London
2020

Designed by Matthew Tauch
Typeset in Minion Pro by Tseng Information Systems, Inc.

Library of Congress Cataloging-in-Publication Data
Names: Harkins, Gillian, author.
Title: Virtual pedophilia : sex offender profiling and
U.S. security culture / Gillian Harkins.
Description: Durham : Duke University Press, 2020. |
Includes bibliographical references and index.
Identifiers: LCCN 2019041100 (print)
LCCN 2019041101 (ebook)
ISBN 9781478006831 (hardcover)
ISBN 9781478008118 (paperback)
ISBN 9781478009153 (ebook)
Subjects: LCSH: Pedophilia—Social aspects—United States. |
Pedophilia in mass media—Social aspects—United States. |
Online sexual predators—United States. | Computer crimes—
Investigation—United States. | Mass media and crime—United
States. | Sex offenders—United States. | Internet and children—
Social aspects—United States.
Classification: LCC HQ72.U53 H355 2020 (print) |
LCC HQ72.U53 (ebook) | DDC 306.77—dc23
LC record available at https://lccn.loc.gov/2019041100
LC ebook record available at https://lccn.loc.gov/2019041101

Cover art: Marga van Oers, *Jumping Fox*.
Courtesy of the artist and StoryTiles.

CONTENTS

ACKNOWLEDGMENTS

This book has proven more educating than elucidating. I learned more than I could have anticipated, but in the end I am not definitively clearer than when I began. The reality of interpersonal, institutional, and structural harm is far beyond the scope of a single academic study, and I hope my efforts are received as part of this larger movement. My thanks go to those who have worked before and alongside me across campus, community, and carceral contexts. First thanks to Staci Haines and everyone who worked with Generation Five, including collaborators across Creative Interventions, INCITE!, and Critical Resistance. At University of Washington's English Department in Seattle, Carolyn Allen, Eva Cherniavksy, Laura Chrisman, Stephanie Clare, Kate Cummings, Tom Foster, Habiba Ibrahim, Carrie Matthews, Chandan Reddy, Sonnet Retman, Caroline Simpson, and Alys Weinbaum have either read portions of the manuscript or helped me struggle through its ideas in conversation. Department chairs Brian Reed and Anis Bawarshi have supported not only this work, but also my less publishable efforts in public humanities. At the Walter Chapin Simpson Center for the Humanities, Kathy Woodward, Miriam Bartha, and Rachel Arteaga have been crucial advocates for connecting individual and collective research. A well-timed Simpson Center Society of Scholars research fellowship, along with multiple grants supporting public scholarship in the humanities more broadly, helped make this book possible.

Through University of Washington and its community partners more broadly, key collaborators in anticarceral projects have included Chris Beasley, Dan Berger, Angélica Cházaro, Annie Dwyer, Tanya Erzen, Megan Ming Francis, Oloth Insyxiengmay, Moon-Ho Jung, Devon Knowles, Ileana Rodriquez-

Silva, Stephanie Smallwood, Shajaunda Tate, Lee Ann Wang, J. M. Wong, Megan Ybarra, and the staff, sponsors, and leaders at University Beyond Bars (UBB), Freedom Education Project Puget Sound (FEPPS), and the Black Prisoners Caucus Taking Education and Creating History (BPC-TEACH). Beyond this regional conversation, scholars and activists who have shaped this work across drafts, conferences, and invited lectures include Kadji Amin, Lisa Duggan, Jane Elliott, Joseph Fischel, Saidiya Hartman, Emily Horowitz, Eng-Beng Lim, Erica Meiners, Katrin Pahl, Todd Sheppard, Emily Thuma, Karen Tongson, Sabina Vaught, Catherine Zimmer, and audiences at Johns Hopkins University, St. Francis College, Seattle University, Cornell University, and Duke University in the United States; King's College, York University, Cambridge University, University of Kent, University of Westminster, and University of Keene in England; University of Humboldt, Friedrich Schiller University, TU Dresden, Leipzig University, and Martin Luther University of Halle-Wittenberg in Germany; and Uppsala University in Sweden. Friends who have supported, cheered on, and hoped for the end of this project include Eli Briskin, Dale Carrico, Shelley Halstead, Dena Healy, Emily Johnston, James Salazar, Lisa Stewart, John Zaia, and the crew of a wider world. Finally, Maureen Wall, Blake Howard, Gaby Carbone, Jack Mystkowski, and Leslie Brooks withstood many outbursts on this topic across occasions and seasons: thank you.

I would be remiss not to name again those superstars who read specific chapters or the entire manuscript (often multiple times) to offer their expertise and insight: Annie Dwyer, Jane Elliott, Joseph Fischel, Emily Horowitz, Habiba Ibrahim, Erica Meiners, Naomi Murakawa, Jack Mystkowski, Chandan Reddy, Sonnet Retman, Emily Thuma, Lee Ann Wang, Alys Weinbaum, Megan Ybarra, and Catherine Zimmer. In relation to the publication of this book, my thanks go to Ken Wissoker, Joshua Tranen, Toni Willis, Susan Deeks, Liz Smith, and the staff at Duke University Press. Ken was very patient as I announced the imminent completion of this book for several years. Anonymous reviewers for the press made my arguments more precise and determined; my thanks in particular to the reader who offered an extraordinarily helpful line-by-line commentary. For research assistance, I thank Safi Karmy-Jones and Ester Garcia, the latter for help with the *Hendricks* case reading in particular. My final thanks for permission to reprint earlier versions of chapter 4 originally published as "Documenting the Pedophile: Virtual White Men in the Era of Recovered Memory," *New Formations* 70 (2010): 23–40, and "Virtual Predators: Neoliberal Loss and Human Futures in *Mystic River*," *Social Text* 31.2 115 (Summer 2013): 123–43.

INTRODUCTION VIRTUAL PEDOPHILIA

> The finer feelings of man revolt at the thought of counting
> the monsters among the psychically normal members of
> human society.
> —RICHARD VON KRAFFT-EBING, *Psychopathia Sexualis*

Calling out the pedophile as monster is a contemporary cri de coeur. Such
calls descry a monstrous sexuality lurking among the denizens of allegedly
normal humanity. Pedophiles lurk "everywhere online," the Federal Bureau
of Investigation (FBI) declares, while police "pedo squads" track this menace and the public is placed on high alert for potential pedophilic harm.[1] Yet
even as more and more resources are dedicated to tracking and punishing
this threat, fewer and fewer certainties exist about what actually threatens.
The pedophile is notoriously difficult to identify, with both police and popular
culture lamenting the limits of diagnostic or forensic profiles to capture this
particular predator. As the pop guru Malcolm Gladwell summarized this phenomenon in a *New Yorker* article in 2012, "The pedophile is often imagined as
the disheveled old man baldly offering candy to preschoolers. But the truth is
that most of the time we have no clue what we are dealing with." The pedophilic predator does not have a typical profile. Even as he bears within him
all the malevolence and grotesquerie of a sexual monster, on the surface he
masquerades as an average Joe. He may read as a little abnormal—nearer the
far poles of the normalcy spectrum, either a little too charming or a little too
odd—but he is unlikely to appear beyond the spectrum of visible norms. He

may be middle-aged, or he may be younger or older. He may be well dressed or disheveled, professional or working class, ensconced in the suburbs or loose in the city. But he is almost always white and is invariably male.

This book asks how and why the pedophile emerged as a white male whose apparent normality makes him elude typical profiles near the end of the twentieth century. How did "pedophile" come to signify all dangerous threats against children, and through them society at large, at the turn of the twenty-first century? After all, this declared threat of white male predators stalking innocent children is not entirely new. We have seen this character before — or, at least, people have tried to see him as he lurked on the fringes of various social imaginaries. The Austro-German psychiatrist Richard von Krafft-Ebing first named him a pedophile in 1886, inaugurating a new diagnostic category at the birth of forensic psychiatry in *Psychopathia Sexualis* ([1886] 1965, 371). In the United States, he was declared a white slaver exploiting innocent youth around the turn of the twentieth century before becoming a sexual delinquent weakened by eugenic degeneracy in the century's early decades. At mid-century, he became known as a sexual psychopath, mentally ill and criminally driven to rape and murder the children of strangers, then briefly appeared in the late 1960s and 1970s as a child molester more prone to misguided touch than murderous violence. Across these earlier twentieth-century figures, the adult who sought out sex with children was mostly imagined as a creepy itinerant, someone outside the social core who lurked around playgrounds and parks to lure children with offerings of money, candy, or toys.

Since the late 1980s, however, the adult seeking sex with children has traveled under different and more thorough cover. In place of the obvious creep driven by greed, deviance, or lust, the late twentieth-century pedophile combines all these monsters into a predator in shepherds' clothing.[2] This pedophile is a new kind of monster who passes easily among the white men at the center of societal norms and institutional trust. Why did this pedophilic figure loom so large only in the 1980s, when the pedophile has existed as a forensic psychological type since 1886? Is this a genuinely different figure from the white slaver, sexual delinquent, sexual psychopath, and child molester who came before? Or is this a new name for an old foe? This book argues that the late twentieth-century pedophile is neither wholly new nor merely a recycled figure from earlier periods. Over the turn of the twenty-first century, earlier diagnostic and criminal categorizations of men seeking sex with children were transfigured to create new regimes of preventative prediction. The pedophile was presented as a predator stalking the space and time between potential and actual crime, always just about to appear if only the right information could be gathered to reveal him among the normal population. The pedophile as virtual predator did not replace earlier figures of child sexual predation, nor did such figures simply assume a new guise. Instead, the pedophile built on and re-assembled earlier figures of child sexual predation to make structural adjustments of safety and sexuality into a modified logic of sexual security. This logic of sexual security declared outdated, yet simultaneously revived and required, the resources of allegedly residual and at times archaic regimes to make virtual threat manifest as actual predator.

The pedophile emerged over the 1980s through the 2010s as a novel kind of virtual predator. The rise of the virtual predator connects new information technologies with modes of mediation that supplement prior regimes of representation. Virtuality describes predators who are alleged to exist in a liminal state combining potentiality, information, and prediction. Potential threat becomes more important than actual danger. The only way to identify this threat, since it does not yet exist, is by gathering information that can predict future action. This is what Eric Janus (2006) describes as the move from crime to risk, a logic of policing focused on potential predation rather than existing harm. Some critics have suggested this shift from punishment to prediction revealed pedophilia as the target of sex panic: exaggerated sexual threats enable predictive policing to expand the effects of empirically validated punishment. Other critics have argued that the shift to prediction elides the historical formations of sexual harm from which the pedophilic figure emerged: the structural, institutional, and interpersonal exposure of young people to sexual harm (as a tactic of colonial occupation; of genocidal projects; and of normativity).

This book builds on these two approaches to ask how the pedophile both *amplifies* fears of virtual dangers and *misdirects* care from the actual targets of sexual harm. I focus on the 1980s–2010s figure of the pedophile to ask how both the demand to police pedophilic predators and reactive declarations of sex panic have come to be recognized and incorporated into security regimes that reproduce relations of harm along familiar historical—and increasingly future-oriented—axes. Of particular interest to me is how this transpired without clarifying either white male culpability for sexual harm, or broader adult patterns of sexual violence against children.

My aim is to disinter the figure of the pedophile from its periodized commonsense moorings to clarify its function within processes of securitization. My approach disaggregates the existence of men who perpetrate sexual harm against children from the creation and circulation of the pedophile as a cultural figure. I argue that the 1980s–2010s pedophile functions as (1) a virtual figure for sexual threat connecting residual modes of policing to new information technologies; (2) a cultural formation assembled from existing, if residual and archaic, materials to justify needs for biopolitical security; and (3) a mode of common sense that extends forensic expertise from now pronouncedly old-fashioned disciplinary and state authorities to the general public. The virtualization of the pedophile figure has enabled an elaboration of sexual security that protects few while increasing harm for many. Thus, I risk seeming to diminish the threat of pedophilia—actual human beings within this diagnostic category may very well commit sexual abuse, although the diagnosis and the act are not persuasively correlated—to show readers how predicting pedophiles came to function as a flawed prophylactic against very real dangers.

My argument takes us into the cultural archives of the turn-of-the-twenty-first-century United States, gathering materials from law, psychology, television, and film to argue that the figure of the pedophile creates a mode of common sense expanding the jurisdiction of public opinion. Starting in the 1980s, the peculiarly unprofileable pedophile came to dominate a particular imaginary of social threat. As the journalist Judith Levine explains in *Harmful to Minors*, pedophiles "look like Every-man or any man" and yet as white men remain "still strangely invisible" (2002, 22–23). The elusive pedophile marked the horizon of visual culture's capture of a newly mediated reality, a raison d'être for television crime shows such as *Law and Order: Special Victims Unit* (1999–) and *To Catch a Predator* (2004–2007), as well as vigilante citizen websites such as Perverted-Justice.com. The pedophile as white child sex predator was depicted on the hunt and as the hunted in films such Todd Solondz's *Happiness* (1998), Michael Cuesta's *L.I.E* (2001), Clint Eastwood's *Mystic River* (2003), Andrew Jarecki's documentary *Capturing the Friedmans* (2003), Greg Araki's *Mysterious Skin* (2004), Nicole Kassell's *The Woodsman* (2004), Todd Field's *Little Children* (2006), and Peter Jackson's *The Lovely Bones* (2009).

Across proliferating cultural texts, audiences were increasingly enjoined to hunt for white male sexual predators lurking among the otherwise protected classes of society. The diverse cultural media of this period worked in tandem with psychological and policing mechanisms to produce a seemingly novel function for figures of pedophilia. I use the term "pedophilic function" to convey the imbrication of figure (the representative) and mechanism (its delivery) in modes of representation that shift relations among domains such as law, science, literature, and film. Existing protocols of interpretation, detection, diagnosis, and analysis were declared increasingly out of date or Luddite in the face of new virtual threats. In their place, a proliferation of political, professional, and cultural materials claimed to teach lay audiences how to look for the ultimate code, clue, symptom, or signifier of virtual sex predators against children. As the virtual pedophile circulated more and more across cultural media as a primary figure for elusive threats to the status quo, state policing and psychological prognosis were depicted as less and less able to protect against its danger. These cultural texts depicted a danger whose profiling and protective registration by science and the state proved ineffectual. The best way to detect and detain this predator was to spread responsibility for virtual surveillance to the widest possible swath of social agents. This virtual predator could be anywhere, in any body, and viewers were expected to be constantly patrolling for his potential presence.

Audiences were trained to have amplified sensitivity to virtual threats, learning how to match information to image in order to discern which white men embody this adaptive and expansive threat. But even as the public was charged with identifying the pedophile, it, too, was constantly disqualified from achieving any modicum of control. No amount of information could conclusively map virtuality to actuality. No process of identification could finally align images with off-screen realities. For every time someone who committed actual sexual harm was revealed in the signs of seeming normality, every time the so-called predator was located on-screen, the pedophile seemed to slip further into the recesses of virtuality. This is the magic of virtual predation: it can never be fully contained. Because the pedophile resides in potentiality, no specific encounter with an actual pedophile would prevent the wider threat of dangerous potentiality lurking in every man. The best way to catch the pedophile might be to predict his next move through informational assemblage, but each time he was forced to appear in image or body, the potentiality of threat moved elsewhere. Sliding easily across cultural domains, the potentiality of the pedophile recurred as a virtual predation always to be sought, yet never permanently found.

This resulted in an unprofileable figure that moved through whiteness without ultimately challenging whiteness as right to state protection rather than persecution. The white pedophile's unnatural nature could pass as normal whiteness, problematizing whiteness as invisible norm for audiences asked to detect monstrosity on its surface. The whiteness of the virtual pedophile, precisely as a statistical outlier among the psychologically normalized and the legally criminalized populations, justified the shift to a security logic of the potential rather than the probable. This worked in tandem with the sexualization of other virtual predators such as the "terrorist" and "illegal immigrant," who affirmed and expanded regimes of criminalized racialization alongside retrenchment of antiblack, antibrown, antiindigenous and antimigrant policing.[3] Newer virtual profiles supplemented long-standing visualizing and territorializing profiles the historian Kelly Lytle Hernández describes as "aligned on the arc of conquest and, more specifically, settler colonialism" (2017, 7). Together these profiles assembled security logics in which renewed commitments to colonial occupation, racial domination, and imperial expansion could appear as protective defense against future rather than historical threats. The pedophile participated in this racial assemblage by reworking whiteness as a biopolitical average of safety, even as security logics came to erode "safety" as a fundamental biopolitical agenda. The development and dissemination of virtual pedophilia reaffirmed the otherwise mental and moral health of white masculinity as statistical average and actuarial safeguard, even as such safeguards were refunctioned for the structural adjustments of sexual security.

This leads us to the strange puzzle created by this undeclared war on the pedophile as Sexual Predator Number 1: the white men depicted as its most likely profile were not criminalized as a gendered and racialized *population*.[4] In other words, the white man existed as a criminalized figure in the form of the pedophile even as white men continued by and large to escape mass-differentiated profiling as a group.[5] There are two major approaches to this puzzle: the first treats the pedophile as a sex offender; the second, as a sex panic. In the first approach, expanded definitions of sex offenses, specifically targeting offenses against children, broadened the net of policing and caught more white men than other carceral projects targeting drug use or violent crime. But there is little empirical evidence to support claims that pedophiles are in fact subject to increased rates of arrest, arraignment, and conviction. And while white men are directly impacted by this system, studies show they are not disproportionately impacted and that, in fact, men of color tend to be overrepresented in the registries.[6] In the second approach, critics debate how the actual vulnerability of young people to sexual harm relates to an alleged panic over pedophilic predators. Those focused on the reality of sexual harm have very different assessments of its scope, but they concur that the current system does little to mitigate the problem, and perhaps much to exacerbate it. Those concerned with the system's punitive effects point out that isolating people who commit sex offenses from other criminalized populations exceptionalizes whiteness and tacitly legitimates mass incarceration to treat social ills. Those concerned with the experience of victims insist that individualized predator analyses do little to address imbalances of power at the institutional and structural level. In all of these cases, the hunt for pedophiles is understood to inflict more harm—including sexual harm—than it redresses across the spectrum of those most impacted.

As Sex Offender

There is little doubt that the hunt for the pedophile fueled dramatic increases in the incarceration rates of people identified as sex offenders, as well as the inauguration of the Sex Offender Registration and Notification (SORN) system.[7] This system built on earlier efforts to reform the Model Penal Code to criminalize a wider range of acts than those historically named "Forcible Rape" by adding the category "Other Sexual Assault," which included crimes such as "statutory rape, lewd acts with children, forcible sodomy, fondling, molestation, indecent practices, and other related offenses" (Greenfeld 1997, 18).[8] This system also sought to track and publicize the movements of people convicted of such offenses. A widely cited Department of Justice report from 1997 names the targeting and incarceration of newly defined sex offenses the second biggest driver of increasing rates of incarceration between 1980 and 1994.[9] Certainly, the number of people incarcerated for sex offenses spiked during this period, as did numbers of people registered as sex offenders after release or through plea bargaining.[10] Statistics reported by the National Center for Missing and Exploited Children (NCMEC) suggest consistent growth in this population since 1997. Numbers of people registered as sex offenders reached 386,000 in February 2001.[11] These numbers hit 747,408 in 2011 (NCMEC 2012, 32). As of June 2018, NCMEC reports a total of 904,011 registered sex offenders in the United States and its territories, or a registration rate of 274 sex offenders per 100,000 people (figure Intro.1).[12] This is a 33 percent increase in people registered as sex offenders since only six months prior.[13]

Describing those most impacted by this expanded system of policing and punishment, the 1997 Department of Justice report summarized the average sex offender as "older than other violent offenders, generally in his early thirties, and more likely to be white than other violent offenders" (Greenfeld 1997, iii). Ongoing demographic studies concur that white men are more likely to be impacted by this system than by other criminal justice regimes, which means that the numbers of white men incarcerated for sexual offenses are

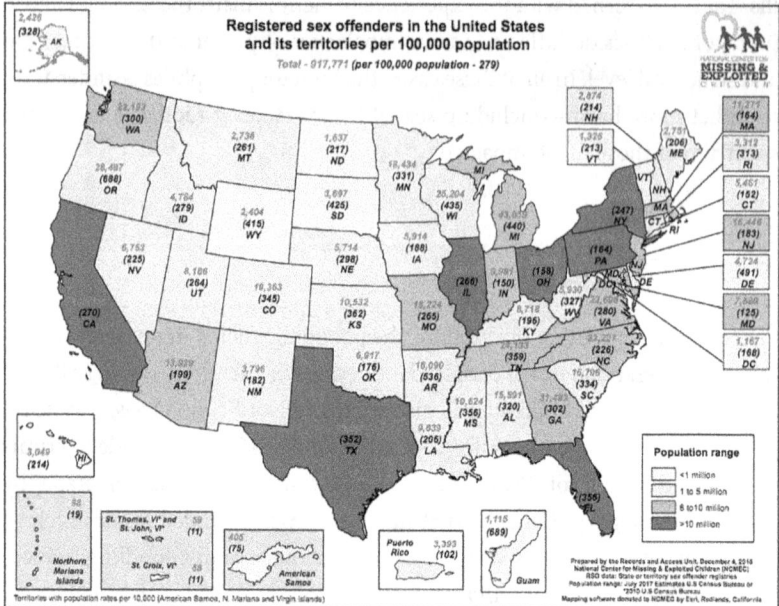

FIGURE INTRO.1 Map of registered sex offenders in the United States, Records and Access Unit, National Center for Missing and Exploited Children (December 4, 2018). The original image with data annotation is available at https://api.missingkids.org/en_US/documents/Sex_Offenders_Map.pdf.

more proportionate to their percentage of the general population. This makes the category an outlier among other criminalized populations, which consistently overrepresent people of color disproportionate to their percentage of the general population (Sentencing Project n.d.). Since 1997, criminologists and political scientists have undertaken studies to ascertain precisely how the sex offender legal system works and whom it most directly affects. Studies have found consistent racial disproportionality registering African American men, belying the correlation of white rates of incarceration with the actual impact of the sex offender management system as a whole. And registration for sex offenses committed by minors remains among SORN's most charged proportionality controversies.[14]

Surging rates of people incarcerated and registered as sex offenders do not, in other words, easily translate purported profile into proportionate impact. While the race, gender, and age demographics of "sex offenders" are not readily available, public messaging continues to conflate pedophiles with

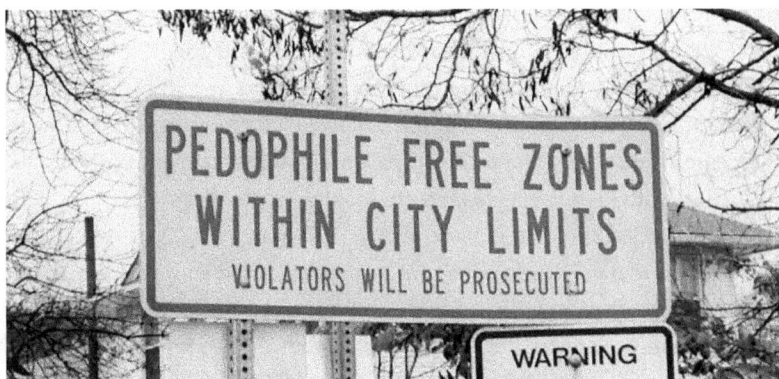

FIGURE INTRO.2 Untitled digital image, in "Sex Offender Statistics," Statistic Brain Research Institute, April 1, 2017, http://www.statisticbrain.com.

those rounded up by SORN. On the website StatisticBrain.com, for example, a seemingly comprehensive and yet easily consumed list of sex offender statistics is placed below an unattributed photograph of a street sign prohibiting pedophiles (Statistic Brain 2017) (figure Intro.2). This conflation of pedophiles with sex offenders can generally be situated within the broader political, economic, and social transformations of the post-1970s period. Scholars concur that the focus on adults seeking sex with children increased between the 1980s and 2010s, a period associated with widespread carceral, neoliberal, and biopolitical reform in the United States.[15] These arguments by and large point out that the detection, detention, and permanent surveillance of alleged white sex predators against children facilitated the U.S. carceral development and biopolitical restructuring more generally associated with the dismantling of the welfare state, commodification of social life, and mass incarceration of people of color.[16]

This period is best known for its suppression of people of color and the poor through the Wars on Drugs, Crime, and Terror, with their collateral policing of borders and bodies through anti-finite mechanisms of racialized profiling, policing, incarceration, and enforced precarity. These wars involved a retrenchment of long-standing modes of racial profiling, with mass-differentiated harassment, detention, and terrorization of people identified as black, brown, indigenous, and noncitizen subject to routinized surveillance and assault.[17] This carceral turn has been linked to counterinsurgency efforts to quash revolutionary activity among race radical, anticolonial, and socialist domestic and international movements gaining ground in the 1960s and 1970s.[18] In this period criminality historically tethered to visual logics of racial identification, and the hyper- and invisibility of blackness in particular, was recalibrated for new information technologies.[19] Criminological data, with their empirical documentation of the past, were supplemented by forensic information, with its speculative prediction of the future.[20]

Scholars often situate this carceral turn within broader shifts toward neoliberalism, a market-driven economic policy conjoined with political strategies to deregulate capitalism and "shrink" government.[21] Increased rates of incarceration were correlated to deindustrialization within many regions of the United States, destruction of urban infrastructures, and increased human displacement, alongside increased regulation of human movement within and across borders. Within the United States, economic privatization and the shift of governance to shadow-state collaborations created modes of individualized entrepreneurial activity coupled with broader distributions of mass-differentiated disposability.[22] During this same period children were increasingly treated as subjects whose valorization or disposability was routed through logics of human capital.[23] A focus on childhood's capacities made their careful cultivation a central concern in what I short-hand as this period's structural adjustment of sexuality and safety into a mode of sexual security.[24] Many scholarly arguments explore how punishment and political economy have been situated among changing regimes of life and death, with a specific focus on child sexual protection as a biopolitical ambition.[25]

The pedophile stands out as a white male profile in an era when crime was predominantly racialized and territorialized as black, brown, indigenous, and noncitizen. The racial profiling of this era, across carceral and security apparatuses, certainly swept up large numbers of white men in its wars on drugs and the nonwhite world more broadly. But white men were not generally profiled as a threatening *population* or circulated as the visual target of police and military procedures. The stereotypical white male serial killer has never galvanized serious security resources, and the statistically significant profile of the white male mass shooter has been viewed primarily through colorblind frameworks. Daniel Filler (2004, 1539) uses the concept of a "'white' narrative frame" to explain how sex crimes committed by white men against white children are made sensational yet exceptional. What Filler (2004, 1588) calls "white-on-white crime" is treated as a violent sexual aberration among stereotypically safe populations, amplifying isolated threat to catastrophic outcome through the racialization of risk. White children's deaths at the hands of presumed pedophiles were memorialized as laws against future catastrophes, including as the Jacob Wetterling Act, Megan's Law, the America's Missing: Broadcast Emergency Response (AMBER) Alert, and the Adam Walsh Act.[26] This cluster of legislation and its increased rates of arrest, charging, incarceration, registration, and indefinite postcarceral detention whitened the iconography of sexual threats to children in ways that justified the punitive turn and buildup of the carceral state. At the same time, focus shifted from white victims to white predators as a threat to all children without somehow disproportionally impacting actual white men.

The sheer scope of the transformations associated with the pedophile's exceptional yet catastrophic threat bears noting. Summary terms used to describe SORN include "containment" to describe the increase in criminal detention, "banishment" to describe the residency and work restrictions redlining sex offender registrants to specific spaces, and "branding" to describe the stigma sex offender registration imposes by making populations exceptional to due process.[27] During this period, registrable sex offenses publicly associated with pedophilia came to include allegedly gateway offenses such as public urination, indecent exposure, underage sexting, and "Romeo and Juliet" crimes between consenting teens, although these offenses are not consistently policed and charged and may themselves be overestimated among the drivers and impacts of the SORN system.[28] In addition, the sweep of incarceration and institutionalization were not tethered exclusively to punishment for a crime but could include preventative detention on the grounds of poorly defined actuarial categories. The U.S. Supreme Court found that people could be sentenced to indefinite civil confinement *after* they had completed their criminal sentence, even if no further crime had been committed, if they exhibited a "mental abnormality" perceived as "dangerous" to the general public.[29] Scientific and legal studies of pedophilic desire, sex acts against children, treatment protocols, and recidivism prediction grew exponentially without ever leading to conclusive answers as to what constitutes the alleged mental abnormality of those seeking sex with children or the dangerousness of those with desires that had never been enacted.

Despite this body of scholarship on sex offenders across the 1980s–2010s, in other words, the specific way pedophilia as a categorical innovation fed into or fostered extensive carceral, neoliberal, and biopolitical regime change remains undertheorized. In fact, a specific account of pedophilia as a diagnostic, forensic, and cultural category within broader state sex offender regimes is pretty hard to find. There are certainly studies of pedophilia as a diagnosis (Okami and Goldberg 1992). And there are studies of sex offenders as a criminal class and sex offenses as a juridico-legal domain (Wright 2009). One might readily find governmental and professional publications on the subject (Wiseman 2015), debates about statistical averages and actuarial predictions (Finkelhor et al. 2008), and squabbles over survey instruments and research protocols for data collection (Hanson and Morton-Bourgon 2005, 2009). Yet consistent data about the state's role in the hunt for predatory pedophiles do not seem to exist. This holds true for demographic data about race, ethnicity, gender, sexual orientation, and class for diagnosed and detained pedophiles.

One problem is that data have not been gathered that subdivide people arrested, charged, convicted, sentenced, and registered for sex offenses into offense categories against children younger than thirteen, the age range designated the diagnostic criteria for pedophilia. Nor do statistics exist that indicate the race and gender of clinical subjects seeking treatment for sexual interest in children younger than thirteen who do not interface with the criminal system. Sex offenders—a criminal category that includes, but is not defined by, adults seeking out, watching pornography about, or engaged in sex with children—technically describes only those interfacing with state policing and punishment systems. Yet increasingly desires, fantasies, or potential actions are described as sex offenses in ways that extend the interface among people, publics, policing, and punishment. The term "sex offender" enfolds diagnostic categories and actuarial prediction into a regime that depends on yet seemingly disqualifies the exclusive power of the state or the psy- professions over the pedophile's political or disciplinary function.

This makes it difficult to determine why pedophilia emerged as an organizing figure in this era. The actual role of pedophilia within the carceral, neoliberal, and biopolitical regimes of institutional life remains murky. As far as I can tell, a diagnosis of pedophilia may occur clinically without leading to carceral containment (if no action has taken place), while criminal charges may be filed without a diagnosis of pedophilia (if no psychopathology is found). Clinical assessment may happen through carceral processes, such that post-arrest psychological evaluation becomes part of amassed evidence or preparation for sentencing. Assessment may also happen on entrance to or release from incarceration to dictate level of security, assignment to treatment, or potential threat after release. A diagnosis of pedophilia is itself irrelevant to a finding of criminal culpability, but it may be more central to civil incapacitation or involuntary commitment (Testa and West 2010). Yet the term "pedophilia" remains central to public, and often juridical, discourses of sex crime against children. As the psychiatrist Fred S. Berlin (2014, 404) explains this problem, "Although from a psychiatric perspective the term Pedophilia is intended to define a recognized clinical entity, in the collective consciousness of contemporary society, the term has become a demonizing pejorative." The relationship among the figure of the pedophile, adult sexual harm of children, and carceral and medical interventions appears to be unclear even to those tasked with defining this relationship. It is instead very much in the "collective consciousness" that the threat of pedophilia takes shape.

As Sex Panic

Many critics have pondered this puzzle, trying to assess why this particular figure took on its central role in the late twentieth century and what actual danger is posed by pedophiles, versus their profiling. This calculation has proved difficult, if not impossible, given the lack of clear data and the complexity of data as a metric of harm. Is the number of people caught in a dragnet designed for exceptional offenders the measure of harm? What about the number of people living with the aftermath of childhood sexual abuse? If we center those most impacted by this system, is it those branded for life as offenders or those with a life sentence of surviving unwanted sexual contact? Is there a differential impact between violent assault ("forcible rape") and unwanted overtures ("lewd acts with children")? How does an inappropriate neighbor relate to a violent stalker? How does statutory rape fit in, and what does it mean that underage sexting can be treated as trafficking in child pornography when the pictures in question are of one's teenage self? I have spoken informally to many people across a wide spectrum about these questions, from those currently incarcerated to those on the registry, those living with the traumatic aftermath of childhood sexual abuse to those who feel minimally impacted by such experiences. And I have spoken repeatedly, of course, to those who have given little thought to the reality behind the slew of pedophilic images they consume across popular media. Such anecdotal evidence, the sheer span of perceptions and experiences of those directly and indirectly impacted by this system, does not rise to the level of data. And even if it did, it would be no more clarifying.

One major cluster of responses to this confusion is to view the hunt for pedophiles as a classic sex panic. As was the case in earlier phases of expanded policing associated with white slavery, sexual delinquency, and sexual psychopaths, the 1980s–2010s period is alleged to be in the throes of a moral panic using sexuality as a distraction from more substantive social and political issues. In general, sex panic is understood to work this way: in a situation in which underlying structural conditions are precipitating social, political, or economic crisis, public discourse taps into the intense affect created by destabilization. This affect is then assigned an objective correlative in a specific moral threat that can be resolved through social or legislative reform agendas. Sexuality is among the most powerful moral threats because it heightens already existing affect with its own reservoir of intense feelings. As Roger Lancaster (2011, 2) summarizes the general logic of this analysis, "Sex panics give rise to bloated imaginings of risk, inflated conceptions of harm, and loose definitions of sex."[30] Declarations of sex panic about adult-child sexuality have tended to dismiss claims about widespread sexual harm as "paranoid" (Lancaster 2011, 186), a sentiment echoed across James Kincaid's (1998, 12) claim that pedophilia creates a "Gothic story" to distract from more "structural social problems," Lee Edelman's screed against the repro-normative Child in *No Future* (2004), and Lancaster's own identification of the pedophile as folk devil in *Sex Panic and the Punitive State* (2011).[31] In *Harmful to Minors*, Judith Levine (2002, 32) summarizes this argument succinctly: "The cold war was melting into detente; for the first time in living memory, Americans were bereft of national enemies and native subversives." She explains, "At times like these, the child-molesting monster can be counted on to creep from the rubble" (Levine 2002, 29).

While I agree with much in these arguments overall—in particular, Lancaster's analysis of economic restructuring and white middle- and working-class biopolitics and Levine's focus on juvenile sexuality—I depart from them in my approach to affect and in my conclusions (Harkins 2013).[32] Lancaster (2011, 205, 212), for example, argues that we live in a broader U.S. culture that has "learned to love trauma" and a leftist politics defined by "fixation on injury," a phenomenon attributed to a punitive and then neoliberal turn valorizing individual suffering as politics. This is a claim familiar from feminist cultural studies of the late twentieth century such as Wendy Brown's *States of Injury* (1995) and Lauren Berlant's *The Queen of America Goes to Washington City* (1997). But Lancaster's (2011, 205, 244) proposed solution—to adapt the "age old wisdom" of "getting over it" into at least the possibility of "the forgetting of trauma"—is a very limited redress for the politics of grievance that allegedly define this period. The idea that moral and political recognition of harm works uniformly across institutions and actors is simply false. Neither loving nor forgetting injury and trauma addresses the complex conditions in which recognition and harm are distributed through interpersonal or institutional modes; nor do they get us very far in understanding how managing affect came to be both cause and solution for this problem.

A second major cluster of responses view the hunt for pedophiles as a misdirection from children's actual vulnerability to sexual abuse, as well as from actual distributions of sexual harm more broadly. These responses argue that pedophilia directs concern toward individualized pathology and away from the interpersonal and institutional networks where the vast majority of sexual abuse takes place. All academic study and much news reporting confirm that stranger danger in particular is the least likely scenario for childhood sexual harm. As Kim Brooks reminds readers in "Motherhood in the Age of Fear," published in the *New York Times* in July 2018, "Statistically speaking, according to the writer Warwick Cairns, you would have to leave a child alone in a public place for 750,000 years before he would be snatched by a stranger." Predatory behavior is statistically and anecdotally acknowledged as least likely as a result of the abduction, assault, and murder featured in the most notorious cases and as most likely among interpersonal or institutional networks. Sexual abuse, in other words, often takes place within a social fabric rather than pitted against it.[33] Focusing on individualized psychological pathology or criminal intention obscures the conditions in which children's uneven structural or situational vulnerability may expose them to sexual harm, including in the home and through contact with so-called opportunistic offenders who have no prior history of sexual abuse or proclivity to sexualize children as such.

The problem posed by the contemporary pedophile figure might be better understood in terms of amplification as misdirection. This is a mix of amplified fears over less likely threats, coupled with a misdirection from actual threats that are themselves *also about sex as a structural social problem*.[34] In other words, the focus on pedophilia is not so much paranoia about sexual harm that directs attention away from apparently more legitimate structural social problems (as Kincaid and others suggest) as a minimization and denial of sexual harm *as* a structural social problem tethered to broader systems. Harmful gendered and sexual experiences are already embedded in interpersonal, institutionalized, and structural frameworks that minimize, accept, or even support those practices. Historically, this process has justified the domination and terrorization of populations racialized and territorialized through modes of sexuality and across the making of genders.[35] An enormous body of scholarship and activism document the interdependence of interpersonal, institutional, and structural violence, both historically and in the present.

Interdisciplinary scholars such as Andrea Smith (2005), Beth Richie (2012), Dian Million (2013), Sarah Deer (2015), Dean Spade (2015), Allison Hargreaves (2017), and Andrea Ritchie (2017) document racialized and gendered inflictions of sexual harm through dominant social structures, including the foundational sexual violence institutionalized through settler colonial and racist state systems. The organization INCITE! Women of Color against Violence has gathered diverse scholars and activists in statements such as "Gender Violence and the Prison Industrial Complex" (2001) and anthologies such as *The Color of Violence* (2006) to demonstrate the dangers of isolating individualist approaches to sexual harm from the broader interpersonal, institutional, and structural conditions that produce them.

Even more troubling, additional harm is often inflicted by the very interpersonal, institutional, and structural mechanisms allegedly designed to mitigate it. Many critics have argued that efforts to elevate the voices and experiences of those directly impacted by sexual harm are often co-opted or redeployed in ways that reproduce or exacerbate that harm. As Million (Tanana Athabascan) explains, indigenous women's representation is often mediated by broader institutional dynamics: "Our suffering is highly mediated, its representation to ourselves and to our relations locally, nationally, and internationally form, interrupt, and constrict larger discourses that create power in our time" (Million 2013, 24). The representation of sexual harm is mediated in ways that create power, but infrequently for those who directly experience that harm. Rather, representations of sexual harm are often appropriated and misdirected to build power for systems that themselves may have been the cause of or may inflict additional harm. Million (2013, 23) elaborates that "unspeakable acts of violence against Indigenous women effectively police them and their communities, but rarely the perpetrator," a situation that holds across gender and sexuality-based violence and its state correlatives. In her study of interpersonally, institutionally, and structurally vulnerable black women and children, Beth Richie (2012) points out that their experiences of sexual harm are often treated as evidence of the need for increased community policing and punishment, often doubling back to target most forcefully women and children themselves.

The logic of sexual security built up through SORN is not, in other words, merely sex panic dressed up in the emperor's new clothes. The emergence of the predatory pedophile does have many components of a sex panic. And there are certainly sex panic analysts who would concur that amplification by misdirection negatively impacts both those targeted as offenders and those recognized as victims. But the mediations introduced in and through the offender-victim binary are not universalizing, and the uneven articulation and effect of these mediations makes sex panic a limited framework. In other words, declaring a sex panic does not complete the analysis, and in the case of pedophilia I have found that declarations of sex panic more often than not operate as part of the dominant logic of mediation (rather than its corrective). Interdisciplinary scholars of gender and sexual liberation movements such as Kristin Bumiller (2008), Christina Hanhardt (2013), and Emily Thuma (2019), for example, have explored the way dominant logics of mediation shape the impact of antiviolence work. Antiviolence activism has been unevenly enfolded into rape law reform, the Violence against Women Act (vawa), and antitrafficking programs in ways that are often antithetical to its aims, as studies by historians, political scientists, sociologists, and legal scholars including Leti Volpp (1994, 2011), Nancy Whittier (2009), Elizabeth Bernstein (2010, 2012), Rose Corrigan (2013), and Lee Ann Wang (2016) demonstrate. Suggestions that victim discourse or an advocacy of injury built the sorn regime are oversimplified, and declarations of sex panic can obscure the more complex ways mediation appropriates and unevenly distributes the effects of diverse efforts to represent sexual harm.

This is the problem seemingly ignored by some sex panic analysis: *every* effort to critique institutional and interpersonal systems of sexual harm is highly mediated, including the declaration of sex panic. The insight of sex panic analysis can seem somewhat obvious to those familiar with institutionalized dynamics of appropriation and denial (what Elizabeth Povinelli [2002] calls "the cunning of recognition" or Jodi Melamed [2011] calls "represent and destroy"). Of course dominant institutions will use moralistic discourse about sex to amplify unjustified fears and distract from actual distributions of harm. This is familiar to anyone who has tried to control the mechanisms through which harm is recognized and redressed. Just because moral panics about sex exist does not mean their effects are universal or even universalizing, or that that such panics are not misdirecting from other forms or instances of actual sexual harm, or that the relation between amplification and misdirection takes familiar or recurrent forms. It certainly does not mean that demands for an injury-transcendent politics would be universally helpful (or new). Missing from these analyses are often the corollary discussion of how alternative and resistant modes of power are built by those directly impacted by sexual harm, such as Million's (2013, 27) discussion of the "often agonistic struggle for life itself in an age of self-determination" sustained by indigenist women's vision, and Richie's (2012, 3, 18) elaboration of activism against a "prison nation" that uses "the power of law, public policy, and institutional practices in strategic ways to advance hegemonic values and to over-power efforts by individuals and groups that challenge the status quo." Without substantive focus on the uneven terrain of mediations and efforts to resist their appropriation, declarations of sex panic can end up participating in what Susan Bandes (2007) shorthands as "institutional denial."

Much of the puzzle comes down to whose voices are centered, and how, as well as who mediates the story those voices are allowed to tell. Such issues of selection and mediation impact both the collection and the analysis of data, as well as the generation of narratives intended to soothe or excite. Raising these questions of method begins to take us away from empirical studies and into the terrain of cultural studies, where the majority of this book is situated. Entering this field of study is daunting. There are few rhetorical positions not already mediated through binary logics of panic and denial, paranoia and reason. But the binaries are not neat, and the realities are not tidy. The populations defined as victim and offender are, for example, highly intertwined, and the high rates of incarceration for both defy the logic of SORN, as well as sex panic analyses that separate victim advocacy from offender demonization. In addition, sexual harm is often de facto part of a prison sentence for people convicted of sex offenses, as it is for all people caught up in the carceral system. Twenty-four-hour surveillance and prohibitions on sexual expression reduce sexual liberty, while routine strip searches, pat downs, and incidents of sexual assault induce sexual harm. It really should not take a news comedian such as John Oliver to remind people that jokes about rape as punishment belie beliefs that incarceration reduces sexual harm.[36]

Questions of method in turn open up questions about which definitions of gender and sexuality organize the distribution of harm and recognition, as well as whose liberty and whose liberation are centered in movements for sexual freedom. I follow in the footsteps of scholarly work demonstrating how sexual entitlement to the bodies and experiences of others is often distributed through white supremacy, male supremacy, nationalist empires, and a hierarchical class system, as well as activist work seeking self-determination and collective determination for those most impacted by those systems. My own involvement with the child sexual abuse prevention organization Generation Five and higher education programs in Washington State prisons is an ongoing reminder of these stakes.[37] And yet this study of pedophilia takes me paradoxically back into a focus on whiteness and masculinity—in particular, the exceptional whiteness of the virtual pedophile and its puzzling failure to become legible as profile or population while being obsessively, if virtually, figured as such. The book's willingness to center alleged white predators of white children is meant neither to demystify a panic nor to demonstrate a threat, although both demystification and demonstration are part of my project. My focus here is on the white pedophile's centrality to dominant mediation in the post-1980s period. In the best-case scenario, a closer focus on the white male pedophile will help explain how and why virtual predators were used to securitize sexual politics in the wake of more radical movements for sexual and gender liberation, including movements that would better serve those of us who have experienced harmful sexual abuse yet remain critical of existing systems of redress and repair.

As Virtual

Virtual Pedophilia centers cultural materials in the production of the pedophile as a figure and mechanism for the structural adjustments of sexual security from the 1980s to the 2010s. My selection of primary materials (popular media, government publications, television programs, and film) and preferred methodology (a blend of descriptive and hermeneutic reading) limits my capacity to argue causation. While I do not consider cultural materials epiphenomenal or superstructural, I do not think the specific materials I study here, or the way I study them, provide an adequate archive for robust historical argument. My archive is culled almost entirely from dominant cultural forms and media. This makes my claims about common sense more akin to a dominant cultural genealogy of the present than the social or subaltern cultural studies or historiography undertaken across disciplinary and interdisciplinary fields. These limitations direct the focus of my argument toward mediation rather than the reality mediated. My hope is that attending to the mediation of virtual pedophilia will make this problem's broader significance for studies of contemporary sexuality and criminality both clear and compelling.

My readings of cultural materials argue that the virtual pedophile functions as both figure and mechanism in late twentieth-century transformations of criminality and sexuality in the United States. Through the cultural mediation of the pedophile, something both more and less definitive than containment, banishment, and branding emerge as central functions in the SORN era. Across these decades, the spatial logic of control, with its regimes of embodiment and containment, shifted to a logic equally predicated on temporal diffusion: the potential to become a threat existed in all bodies and spaces, rationalizing a shift from targeted policing to total surveillance as the charge for sexual security. The late twentieth-century pedophile expanded the range of referents and type of sleuths for sexual criminality by seeming to shift from analogy to virtuality. During this period, the mask of the white man seeking sex with children itself changed. In the late twentieth century, the white mask of normalcy, associated with analogic modes of representing sexual deviancy, became what I will call the veil of virtuality. This veil combines three components of virtuality—potentiality, information, and actuarial prediction—into a screen that hides unnatural deviance on the surface, rather than in analogic depths.

Earlier political and cultural modes of profiling operated primarily through analog representation, in which the sexual predator was "like" a beast, a savage, a fiend, or a monster. Analog figures were produced when early twentieth-century biological and sociological experts used eugenics and environmentalism to explain how degeneration and deviance created monsters among white men who were otherwise deemed normal. Their white masks of normalcy covered a rotten interior, which could be represented through analogy to monsters more visible on the surface. By the 1940s, FBI Director J. Edgar Hoover could easily shorthand "degenerate sex offenders" as "depraved human beings, more savage than beasts" who roamed public space like "wild beasts [who] break out of circus cages" (Hoover 1947, 32). Across the mid-century, white normalization occurred through the professional psychiatric and police differentiation of façades and interiors, as well as the cataloging of behaviors that indexed surface to depth. Meanwhile, lay capacities to navigate this spectrum were created through popular dissemination of what Hoover in 1955 called "common sense," a capacity to discern the white beast among men that could be developed by studying analog media such as news, books, and film (Hoover 1955, 101). The FBI forged a substantive raison d'être across these earlier periods, from the Mann Act's proclaimed fight against white slavery (as blueprint for "vice" legislation) in 1910 through Hoover's own multi-decade (1924–72) reign as federal moralist-in-chief and champion of populist fears of a Red, Black, or Pink planet.[38]

In contrast, late twentieth-century calls for revised and revitalized common sense eschewed such easy analogies to visible threats. In place of popular writings by the FBI, we find the leadership of the crime novelist, lawyer, and FBI consultant Andrew Vachss, whose series of articles in *Parade Magazine* popularized the phrase "predatory pedophile." Vachss's declaration that sex offenders "study children as carefully as any psychologist, and their camouflage is our unwillingness to see the shark in our swimming pool" does not propose a search for sharks masquerading as something else (psychologists perhaps) (Vachss 1989). The pedophile's potential predation lurks *on the surface of norms*, not behind or beneath them. The sharks aren't camouflaged; our eyes are. We are unwilling, or perhaps even unable, to see their looks as predatory. This new form of camouflage does not mask reality but rather participates in it *as normalcy*; a kind of unnatural normalcy changed the function of looking itself. If normal behaviors such as looking at children can themselves *be* an unnatural threat, rather than its cover, how can actual predators be discerned? To do so requires a shift in perception. New technologies were needed that move away from the surface/depth model of normality and instead pierce the veil of virtuality that makes potential threat invisible to the naked eye. Psychologists and police, watchers from a dwindling world order, were presented as ill-equipped to fight a virtual battle with their analog arsenal of perpetrators' photographs and psychological profiles (and perhaps even guilty of their own deviant looking)

The veil of virtuality signals a complex array of meanings and conditions—potentiality, information, and actuarial prediction—not always drawn together as a composite apparatus. The term "virtual" culls its first set of meanings from the European philosophical tradition of Baruch Spinoza (1677), Henri Bergson (1912), and Gilles Deleuze (1991, 2002), which proposes virtuality as the condition of potentiality imminent to all actual phenomena. "Virtuality" names that which might be but is not yet or not ever, a kind of potentiality manifest in all life's matters. The philosopher Brian Massumi (2002, 30) offers a succinct definition: "The body is as immediately virtual as it is actual. The virtual, the pressing crowd of incipiencies and tendencies, is a realm of *potential*." This more philosophical approach differs from the second set of meanings: virtuality as a condition of technologically produced reality that appears through information patterns. The cultural scholar Katherine Hayles (1999, 13–14) defines "virtuality" as *"the cultural perception that material objects are interpenetrated by information patterns*. The definition plays off the duality at the heart of the condition of virtuality—materiality on the one hand, information on the other." This second meaning suggests that binary code, digitality, or information constitute matter in new ways. With the advent of late twentieth-century technological revolutions, virtuality was no longer merely a philosophical concept for potentiality but also a historically specific concept referring to technological mediation.

The veil of virtuality associated with the late twentieth-century pedophile references both these meanings. "Virtuality" names that which is beyond material instantiation (as potentiality) but that might be said to precipitate it (through information). Virtual pedophilia—or the pedophile as a virtual figure—emerges from these conditions as an assemblage of the inhuman or the unnatural beyond either psychological diagnosis or criminal profile. The pedophile, always already potentially slipping into or out of his predatory habits, existed in a conditional tense in which the potential, the probable, and the actual were indistinguishable. It required new kinds of information to make it appear as an "actuality" (Massumi 2002, 43) or "material object" (Hayles 1999, 29). This brings us to the third meaning of "virtual" I develop here: its forensic signification of potentiality as actuarial prediction. The virtual pedophile is part of a broader actuarial turn in which statistical calculation predicting probabilities and providing risk assessment became a dominant tactic of crime prevention. Here the virtual differs from earlier iterations of phantom, folk devil, or monster by insisting that these are not fantasy objects (made up, fake, imaginary) but actuarial averages (realizable, measurable, modifiable). Actuarial information can predict the presence of a pedophile before his crime has been committed or materialize his presence in a body otherwise too normal for notice.

Through this process, the three referents for virtuality—potentiality, information, and prediction—seem to transform the category and capacity of the sexual norm, as well as the relationship between normality and nature for sexuality writ large. Emerging in the wake of late twentieth-century movements for gender and sexual liberation, the pedophile's unnatural nature might pass as one of those more benign sexual variations such as homosexuality or kinkiness now making their way into acceptable zones of abnormality. The white man on-screen might appear normal, or a familiar and acceptable kind of abnormal, but in fact a virtual potential for grotesque or unnatural sexuality lurked as the surface of his white masculinity the whole time.[39] To distinguish the predatory pedophile from garden-variety gay or quirky sexual fetishist, audiences needed help discerning virtual monstrosity within changing distributions of normality across wider ranging human natures. This procedural function situates the pedophile within the era's broader counterinsurgencies. The mediating function of virtual pedophilia captured and redirected insurgent efforts to redistribute sexual harm and pleasure. A widened swath of the population was seemingly empowered to challenge state and disciplinary power by taking self and community protection into their own hands. Yet this empowerment was redirected into a vigilante populism that slightly modified while shoring up existing hierarchies as sexual security.

This is my answer to pedophilia's puzzling emergence as a dominant figure for sexual harm: the pedophile is a virtual assemblage beyond psychological diagnosis and criminal profile whose threatening potentiality expands processes of securitization. First, the proliferation of imprecise information is coupled with a dearth of actual images. The public is told to look out for pedophiles but never given an example of what one looks like. Websites, for example, frequently provide maps and slogans and images of children, but images of pedophiles or predators are almost entirely absent. Second, images are produced through aesthetic media such as television and cinema to present a possible—but not actual—image of the pedophile. These images are analogs for predatory presence, never capable of actually penetrating the virtual realm of pedophilic potentiality but promoting audience common sense as a medium through which analog images can be translated back into forensic information.[40] This explains the centrality of images—from their absence to their inadequacy—to capture an actual pedophile. The cultural mediation of virtual pedophilia produces a process of *insecuritization*. People are made insecure when information promises prophylaxis, surveillance provides the mechanism of informational retrieval, and visual analogs are the only medium through which to match information with image.

Let us turn briefly to the WikiHow.com page "How to Identify a Pedophile" to demonstrate the first step in this process. The page begins with standard clarifications that (1) "not all pedophiles are child molesters, and having thoughts about children is not the same as acting on them"; (2) "anyone can be a child molester, so identifying one can be difficult"; and (3) "there is no one physical characteristic, appearance, profession, or personality type that all child molesters share."[41] No profile: check. But this lack of profile does not mean you can stop trying to identify predators. Instead, the absence of a profile means "you should never dismiss the idea that someone could be a child molester out of hand." So there is potentiality hiding in normality, and pedophiles could be practically anywhere. The page promises, however, that you can "learn which behaviors and traits are red flags, what situations to avoid." Multistep instructions are presented as if they provide information to help identify and prevent pedophilic behavior. But those steps focus primarily on extending surveillance to include accessing the U.S. Department of Justice National Sex Offender Database, using a nanny camera in the home, overseeing children's extracurricular activities, and online safety planning. Instructions to increase surveillance, in other words, are treated as if surveillance is actual information that can guide action. People are then encouraged to assemble this surveillance as information into their own predictive images in the hope that they can map it onto an actual body given the chance. Yet the more technology is used to amass and distribute information about the pedophile, the more difficult it becomes to see him in actuality and the more people at large need information technology rather than professional experts to help them.

This circular process does not yield the protection it promises, however, and people need more and more—information, surveillance—to identify less and less.[42] The virtuality of the pedophile results in a self-reinforcing process of insecuritization and instigation to technological vigilance that has no external limit. This lack of external limit leads to step two: the closed circuit of information and surveillance requires an aesthetic supplement to make the virtual pedophile appear as actual image. Across the screens of television crime procedurals of the 1990s and 2000s, the virtual pedophile created an aura that can be grafted onto any actor's behavior through serial and narrative programming. White male actors carried with them an aura of potential pedophilia that frequently eluded detectives and psychiatrists on-screen as much as the home viewer. Only by learning how to decode these various cultural texts could viewers learn to assemble information into image and identify the predator on-screen. Documentary and narrative films complete this circuit in their capacity to cull images of sex predators from early twentieth-century cinema and transfigure them into avatars—such as wolf, vampire, extraterrestrial, or undead—for explicitly virtual threats.

Across these texts, the hunt for pedophiles was presented as a seemingly liberatory experience that redirected popular energy toward the reproduction of specific social, political, and economic orders. By capturing the pedophile, people could revive their normalcy—often in the form of comparative respectability—in the aftermath of its articulation to fading rights and entitlements. This helps clarify why these cultural texts draw on such a surprising range of source genres. The majority certainly draw on Orientalist, anti-Semitic, and antimigrant genres of detection and surveillance (naturalism and noir rank highly). Yet some also draw on queer, African American, and Latinx genres that counter the racial politics of surveillance.[43] Sometimes presented in the language and visual codes of working-class resistance, in its modes of both white entitlements and black and brown radicalism, these texts rather surprise me as a group or an archive. Certainly, sentimentalism dominates the mass cultural idiom, but a rather curious countercultural thematics and stylistics inform enough of the material to draw my attention here. Thus, we get sequences of suburban white middle-class panic, *Little Children* exemplary among them, but also a knowing and resourceful discernment operationalized through working-class, queer, and minoritized perspectives of sousveillance, *L.I.E.* providing one counterexample.

My readings of these texts suggest that people otherwise threatened with ever more hegemonic disposability through overt and covert necropolitical agendas of the same security era were proffered the branch of life through agency that targeted reprehensible monsters. The white middle and working classes were certainly a primary target for this recruitment, promising agency in the wake of normal life's dwindling promises. But people across a far wider historical and legal spectrum were also enlisted to serve as this arm of public policing. The white pedophile's virtually monstrous nature drew a new line between socially defined crime (the purview of politics) and moral monstrosity (the purview of nature). Through a diverse range of cultural texts, guarding this line was presented as the sine qua non of popular empowerment. Liminal status might be corrected by incorporation into this new base of lay recruits targeting those unnatural monsters beyond the pale of criminalization articulated through racial assemblages of black, brown, indigenous, and noncitizen profiling. Hunting for the unnatural normalcy of the pedophile among them, good people protect a threatened biopolitics associated with white settler supremacy—and expand its domain to include new multiracial agents of security—with just a few strings attached: permanent insecurity and only a vigilant(e) common sense to guard against the forces of structural adjustment.

Chapter Overview

In the first two chapters, I provide a genealogy of the pedophile's late twentieth-century emergence from what I identify as key moments of transition or transfiguration in sexual typology and criminal profiling. Chapter 1, "Monstrous Sexuality and Vile Sovereignty," situates pedophilia as a psychological-forensic category in relation to the rise and fall of various other figures for child sexual predation: the white slaver, the sexual delinquent, and the sexual psychopath. This twentieth-century genealogy begins with Krafft-Ebing's coinage of *paedophilia erotica* ([1886] 1965, 371), whose distinction between psychopathology and criminal intent was immediately tested across the rapidly urbanizing zones of Europe and the United States. During the early and mid-twentieth century, various figures of child sexual predation shuttled between the poles of illness and criminality. The pedophile only reemerged as a central figure in the wake of late twentieth-century popular and biopolitical struggles over relations among the disciplines, the state, and the people. This genealogy reveals the twentieth-century U.S. operation of what Michel Foucault (2003a, 12) calls "vile sovereignty," a mode of power that expands its reach through the definition and discrediting of sexual monsters.

Chapter 2, "Profiling Virtuality and Pedophilic Data," explores how these late twentieth-century struggles produced pedophilia as a central figure for securitization through vile sovereignty. Insurgent movements for gender and sexual liberation challenged the pathologization and criminalization of nonnormative practices, while counterinsurgent activists insisted that all homosexuals were sexual predators with children as their central targets. Struggles in the 1970s over adult-child sexuality, including the emergence of the North American Man/Boy Love Association and Anita Bryant's adversarial Save Our Children campaign, turned in the 1980s to a nearly exclusive focus on childhood sexual experience as harmful when instigated by adults. Across the 1980s and 1990s, various strands of sexual advocacy split focus between normalization of homosexuality and the criminalization of pedophilia. Adult-child sexuality was transformed into predatory pedophilia as criminal conduct, even as that conduct would unfold under a veil of virtuality that required new systems of detection and deterrence. The hallmarks of the SORN era would emerge from this conjuncture, making data collection and dissemination key to the preventative detention and expansive management of pedophiles as sex offenders.

The next two chapters demonstrate the cultural mediation central to new modes of common sense vital to the expansion of sexual security. Chapter 3, "Informational Image and Procedural Tone," attends to television as a cultural medium disseminating common sense in this period. In the 1990s and early 2000s, the white sex predator against children was central to the rise of popular forensic procedurals such as *Law and Order: Special Victims Unit* (1999–) and *To Catch a Predator* (2004–2007). Security protocols were dispersed through new modes of common sense that produced an "aura" for virtual pedophilia that is detectable only when information becomes aesthetic. Aura accumulates to analog figures whose potential predatory nature exceeds their surface signification; they are haunted by a virtual reality that can never be fully represented on-screen. Through readings of *Law and Order: svu*, I explain how procedural tone works to train audiences to exercise aesthetic interpretation as forensic common sense. Aesthetic interpretation reads the aura as sign and returns it to its analog signifieds: code, clue, and symptom. Audiences are tasked with learning how to read "procedural tone" so they can develop a common sense capable of complex aesthetic, forensic, and diagnostic discernments and determinations.

Chapter 4, "Capturing the Past and the Vitality of Crime" takes up two films to engage this procedural tone as it is adapted through documentary and narrative cinema. Andrew Jarecki's HBO documentary *Capturing the Friedmans* (2003) explores one family's real-life response in the late 1980s to accusations of, investigation into, and incarceration for child sexual abuse. The documentary suggests that men whose historically liminal whiteness would have subjected them to sexual surveillance in earlier decades became targets for late twentieth-century sexual security. Focused on the persecution of Jewish masculinity as sexually aberrant, *Capturing the Friedmans* treats late twentieth-century pedophilia as a visual lacunae that virtualized white men as targets of criminalized sexuality. Clint Eastwood's Oscar-winning Hollywood film *Mystic River* (2003) explores how this mediation of white masculinity is rebranded as a resource for white working-class resilience in the face of encroaching structural adjustment and surplus disposability. The film uses hard-boiled and noir genres to recraft a nostalgic representation of residual Irish working-class resistance to earlier modes of governance. By juxtaposing white working-class criminality with the unnatural virtuality of the pedophile, *Mystic River* revives white masculinity as a vital resource for agency in the newly securitized world.

In the final chapter and conclusion, I move toward queer encounters with the assemblage of sexuality and security articulated through SORN and its aesthetic mediations. Chapter 5, "Capturing the Future and the Sexuality of Risk," considers the queer outcomes of SORN's temporal and spatial entanglements through a reading of two narrative films. Gregg Araki's *Mysterious Skin* (2004) tracks insurgent countercultural sexualities as they are enclosed within 1980s and 1990s discourses of trauma and risk. *Mysterious Skin* follows two white boys' divergent experiences of childhood sex with their white baseball coach—one interprets it as love; the other, as alien abduction—to reframe the 1980s as a time when the range of possible sexual acts was constrained by futurist ideologies of sexual threat. Nicole Kassel's *The Woodsman* explores the aftermath of this 1980s switch point, when the pedophilic function of the sex offender made the virtual predator into potential queer. *The Woodsman* presents a known pedophile on-screen by following Walter, a white, middle-aged registered sex offender as he is released from prison and seeks to become "normal." As Walter navigates run-ins with the police, his mandated therapist, family members, and coworkers, the film critiques the forensic commonsense logics of risk and trauma that enclose all sexual possibilities in the threat of virtual dangers and reimagines those logics yielding new zones of queer life.

The conclusion, "Exceptional Pedophilia and the Everyday Case," meditates on the atmosphere produced by virtual pedophilia and the politics of its resistance. Broader approaches to dismantling or reducing the sex offender management system have been on the rise in recent years. Proposals to reduce sentencing and to remove registry-based penalties have often appealed to highly racialized and gendered frameworks of common sense: young white men whose only crime is sex with a consenting nonadult (younger than eighteen) should not suffer permanent stigma. In a brief review of emerging political efforts to dismantle SORN, I explore the dangers and possibilities of culling political futures from the aftermath of sex offender management without adequately calling into question its reliance on the pedophilic function. If the pedophilic function helped enclose white vitality and queer potentiality in sex offender management and its cultural modes, it must be directly addressed to make the aftermath something other than a harmful extension of its origins.

ONE

MONSTROUS SEXUALITY AND VILE SOVEREIGNTY

Political power, at least in some societies, and anyway in our society, can give itself, and has actually given itself, the possibility of conveying its effects and, even more, of finding their source, in a place that is manifestly, explicitly, and readily discredited as odious, despicable, or ridiculous.
—**MICHEL FOUCAULT**, *Abnormal*

Ridiculous but powerful spectacles define adult-child sexuality across the twentieth-century United States. The uproar over white slavery in the first decade of the century is now routinely understood as an odious manifestation of white nativism, in which the threat of sex predators was mobilized to police highly racialized international and domestic patterns of migration. Subsequent decades' rallying cries against sexual degenerates are recognizable as a despicable tactic of eugenics, in which the threat of sex predators was mobilized to shore up white supremacy as biological hierarchy. And J. Edgar Hoover's midcentury "War on the Sex Criminal" registers as ridiculous even as its pernicious effects are well documented: sexual psychopathology mobilized fears of homosexuality and other alleged perversions to make sex predators into national threats. Such spectacles from the late twentieth century are even more familiar. The ever-present dangers of the child molester and the pedophile populate millennial media and governance, combining earlier fears of territorial, biological, and psychopathological contamination with emergent fears of virtual terrorization.

These pronouncements of unstoppable child sexual predation, in other words, are derided as often as they are revered. For every person who hears realistic menace, another hears ridiculous fearmongering. This combination of explicit ridiculousness and effective politics is what Michel Foucault (2003a, 12) describes as the operation of "vile sovereignty," a mode of political power that operates through its own odious disqualification. Such power can also be described as "ubu-esque terror, grotesque sovereignty, or, in starker terms, the maximization of effects of power on the basis of the disqualification of the one who produces them." This mode of power operates by disqualifying existing expertise and enlisting more and more people to expand a network of power over which no one seemingly has final charge. In relation to adult-child sexuality, the operations of vile sovereignty can be described very succinctly: two experts collide in their attempts to determine whether an adult who has sex with (or wants to have sex with) a child is sick or criminal. In its nineteenth-century incarnation, the two experts were defined by their institutional roles in psychiatry or policing. Across its twentieth-century modes, the range of experts expanded, as did the effects of their disqualification.

Pedophilia has been closely associated with the workings of vile sovereignty, from the inauguration (Krafft-Ebing in 1886) through the delimitation (Andrew Vachss in 1989) of forensic and psychiatric power. Vile sovereignty helps explain why defeating the menace of adult-child sexuality proved less possible as more power was amassed against it. The more disciplines were developed to detect it and police were empowered to detain it, the less contained the threat of adult-child sexuality seemed to be. Thus, by midcentury we find Hoover lamenting his own FBI's, as well as local police and psychiatric professionals', failures to properly protect against sex fiends and calling for an activated citizenry as frontline soldiers in a sexual battle for the nation's youth. In popular articles in *American Magazine*, Hoover denounced the nation's common sense and demanded a more activated awareness of sexual threat in everyday life. But the more common sense was deputized as frontline defense and the more citizens became trained to spot sexual menace, the more that defense proved ineffective and disqualified from its own populist authority. For some, this required redoubled vigilance against sexual predators and ever more elaborated regimes of popular detection. For others, it required a return to reason and a renunciation of sex "panic" (Sutherland 1950a, 146) as an irrational fear of sexual threat. This process enfolded a broader range of responses into a binary logic: panic versus reason. Who determined the content of each position became a major battleground over the interpretation of public discourse about sexuality in the twentieth century. The authority of psychological and policing professionals was contested by sociological and criminological experts, while lay people asserted their own common sense as reality's final word.

The seeming paradox of the hunt for sexual predators—more effort, less effect—became central to the mode of power I trace through this chapter. This chapter undertakes a genealogy of the present to locate key switch points where panic and reason meet in the operation of vile sovereignty. The figures I study here are less periodized than situated as having a more or less hegemonic cultural function during specific relationships among the state, professional disciplines, and autonomous social actors. These figures have always gained their power through assemblage or entanglement, each one picking up and modifying, reinscribing, or reviving various elements of the others. Even when figures of sexual predation function to articulate a cut between modes of governance and disciplinarity, they do so in ways that assign novelty to threat as emergent or new, therefore demanding innovations to enhance safety. Such figures assign residual or archaic significance to some forms of sexual danger even as they prefigure threats that are barely discernible on the horizon. Such a genealogy locates late twentieth-century pedophilia as an assemblage of previous sexual figures refunctioned and transfigured to cut through disciplinary and state power and compose new arrangements among disqualified actors and emergent regimes of virtual threat.

Beginning in the twentieth century's earliest decades, a generalized fear that marginal adults would be incorporated into the protected status of whiteness seemingly exploded into what other critics have called the recurrent sex panics of the twentieth century. Successive waves of focus on white slavers, sexual delinquents, and sexual psychopaths sought to determine what kind of adult man would secretly prey on children and what kind of deterrent would predict and stop this undetectable predator. Each predator helped mobilize and regularize relations between emerging disciplinary expertise and state actors by establishing criteria for "normal" whiteness and its internal boundaries. The predators espied passing through white manhood were first identified as not quite white (Bhabha 1994). They were distinct from normalizing white manhood, a separate class of almost-white men derailed by avarice (the greed of white slavers) and atavism (the retrograde animality of sexual degenerates). By midcentury, however, predators were more squarely located within white manhood's norms. These predators could pass as mere abnormals, gaining sympathy and recognition from what Hoover (1947, 102) called the "bleeding heart," but they were always on the slippery slope of sexual monstrous-ness. This was the modus operandi of the sexual psychopath, whose combined sexual greed (avarice) and retrograde animality (atavism) made him both criminally culpable and mentally incompetent in a new elaboration of sexual psychopathology.

What is curious across these spectacles is the absence of the pedophile as a central figure. Although the pedophile was first named as a diagnostic cate-gory in 1886, this figure was not spectacularized as a sexual threat until its dramatic resurgence in the 1980s. This absence is due in no small part to the diagnostic nature of the term. "Pedophilia" was originally coined to name an abnormal desire, an archaic throwback to premodern Greek practices rather than an avaristic and atavistic monstrosity. Monstrousness was reserved for those morally culpable for their actions and therefore subject to criminal charges. Pedophilia entered the field of spectacle in the late twentieth century precisely when abnormality and monstrousness were undergoing yet another dramatic change. Only this time, as insurgent movements for LGBT liberation and against institutional and interpersonal sexual harm pitted acceptable ab-normality against criminalized deviance, counterinsurgency deployed a vir-tual predator to expand the terrain of sexual security. Once again, the actual conditions shaping children's vulnerability to sexual abuse and restricted ac-cess to sexual choice were translated into mediations of the ridiculous and the reasonable.

This is how vile sovereignty operates. It pits diagnostic and forensic ex-pertise against each other in ways that (1) exacerbate spectacular panic and (2) propose reasonable denial as its corrective. This process centers metropoli-tan whiteness as an individualized problem to be treated differently than mass-differentiated problems racialized as nonwhite or territorialized as colonial/im-perial. Through vile sovereignty, adult-child sexuality becomes spectacularized as a problem of aberrant white masculinity in the metropole. Diagnostic and forensic expertise are pitted against each other to answer the following ques-tions: Are white men who seek sex with children predators or patients? Do they deserve punishment or treatment? Are they in fact guilty of any harm, or are they persecuted on the basis of inflamed fears? As white men are centered in these evaluations of culpability and illness, panic and denial, a wider range of people are denied individuality, as well as relevance and access to popular and professional determinations of sexual reason. The spectacle of metropoli-tan white adult-child sexuality, in other words, draws state, professional disci-plines, and autonomous social actors into changing configurations of hegemony, even as racialized and territorialized modes of adult-child sexuality are excluded from individualized consideration. This process narrows the conditions articulated as "sexuality" and militates against social and political actors who challenge existing regimes and demand alternative modes of sexual recognition and redress. A genealogy of vile sovereignty over adult-child sex clarifies how the allegedly new threat of the pedophile legitimated structural adjustments of safety and sexuality as an emergent logic of sexual security.

Of Monsters and Men

My genealogy begins with the psychiatrist Richard von Krafft-Ebing's naming of the pedophile during the late nineteenth-century clash of European expertise over adults who have sex with children. Here we cut into a much longer history, one dated at least in Eurocentric accounts to 1492 and its launching of colonization and conquest as tools of mercantilist and capitalist empire. The contested unfolding of so-called modernity used ideologies of childhood and childlikeness to naturalize colonial relations, racial hierarchy, marital availability, and sexual legitimacy in ways that are far too numerous to summarize here.[1] By the time Krafft-Ebing published *Psychopathia Sexualis: With Especial Reference to the Antipathic Sexual Instinct, A Medico-Forensic Study* in German in 1886, European empires had developed their own discourses of sexuality through encounters with other cultures; exceptionalized dominant-class European sexuality as superior to other modes; and sought to unevenly impose their own discourses of sexuality on much of the globe. Such impositions included efforts to incorporate, exacerbate, and eradicate cultural, social, and political differences in the organization of gender, sexuality, and age across peoples and territories.[2] *Psychopathia Sexualis* enters this field with a narrowly defined focus on sexuality as a domain of psychological abnormality and moral criminality within Europe. In so doing, Krafft-Ebing joins the ranks of European psychiatrists and legal professionals debating how to respond to unwanted sexual behavior within an allegedly homogeneous metropole, rather than in colonized or racialized conditions where sexual behavior was regulated by separate and unequal prohibitions and permissions.[3]

Psychopathia Sexualis is notable as an inaugural text in forensic psychiatry, a field developed to professionalize expertise over psychological abnormality and moral criminality. Krafft-Ebing's contribution was to center pathological sexuality in the annals of criminal psychopathy. His entry on "pedophilia" makes adult-child sex into a unique problem for medico-forensic psychiatry, in that sexual psychopathology is distinguished from criminal culpability by differentiating nature from normalcy. In the section "Pathological Sexuality in Its Legal Aspects," *paedophilia erotica* (erotic pedophilia) appears under "Notes on the Question of Responsibility in Sexual Offences Caused by Delusion." Here Krafft-Ebing ([1886] 1965, 367) argues that pathological sexualities — such as "fetishism, sadism and exhibition" — are illness rather than crime. Such sexual pathologies should be treated by "confinement in insane asylum" (369) rather than confinement in prison, as "the offender is merely an automaton, slave of a driving idea" (367). *Paedophilia erotica* is, however, to be distinguished from these other forms of pathological sexuality, since in Krafft-Ebing's understanding it poses a unique set of problems for determinations of legal responsibility.

The unique problems posed by age makes it difficult to differentiate between natural sexuality and its pathological or immoral deviations. Krafft-Ebing posits age fourteen as the sexual line between adults and children, below which all sexual activity must be either psychopathological or immoral. The law might establish this line, but its interpretation requires the expertise of forensic psychiatry. In the subsection "Violation of Individuals under the Age of Fourteen," Krafft-Ebing ponders the legal problem of those who have sex with children. On one hand, such actions constitute a crime. On the other, they may be the expression of mental illness and require treatment rather than incarceration. In the first instance, he finds cases including "the most horrible perversions and acts, which are possible only to a man who is a slave to lust and morally weak, and, as is usually the case, lacking in sexual power" (369). In the latter instance, he finds "cases in which the sexually needy subject is drawn to children not in consequence of degenerated morality or psychical or physical impotence, but rather by a morbid disposition, a *psycho-sexual perversion*, which may at present be named erotic paedophilia (love of children)" (371). Only the first group should be held legally responsible for their behavior as immoral choice. The second group is diagnosed with *paedophilia erotica*, a "psycho-sexual perversion" expressed as an erotic love of children that marks a "morbid disposition" and that therefore should be treated like other psycho-pathologies.

Differentiating between these two types introduces a struggle between psychiatric and legal authority. The sexual act is not in dispute: this is what brings psychiatry into conversation with law in the first place. Krafft-Ebing is not focused on a diagnosis of a desire or psychological condition *separate* from a criminalized act. He is, rather, focused on the specific expertise psychiatry brings to forensics when an adult has been caught engaging in sex with someone younger than fourteen. He avers that "judgment of the act should ever be guided by the monstrosity and the degree in which it psychically and physically differs from the natural act" (370). The "monstrosity" of the "act" must be measured, psychically as well as physically, by its departure from nature rather than from norms. Psychiatric expertise is needed to correct the law's tacit reliance on commonsense, rather than scientific, approaches to sexual behavior. According to Krafft-Ebing, for most people "it is psychologically incomprehensible that an adult of full virility and mentally sound should indulge in sexual abuses with children" (369). Normal people who retain a moral compass insist that all adults who seek sex with children must be sick, unnatural, outside the bounds of human norms. Faced with adults who have sex with children, normal people experience moral revulsion: "the finer feelings of man revolt at the thought of counting the monsters among the psychically normal members of human society" (370).

When confronted with this kind of criminalized sexual act, legal reasoning is hampered by its own normative assumptions and is ill-equipped to assess human psychology. This brings forensic psychiatry into law as the arbiter delineating nature from norms. Psychiatry, Krafft-Ebing argues, has the scientific distance needed to differentiate the normal, and therefore immoral, from the abnormal, and therefore pathological, case. The law has expertise to determine what sexual acts are unnatural (to set norms), while psychiatry has expertise to treat those who experience these acts as natural (who are abnormal but not monstrous). According to forensic psychiatry, people with erotic pedophilia are *not* monsters; they are enacting their own abnormal nature, or their psychopathology, and are therefore ill rather than morally corrupt. It is normal people whose "injury in the sphere of morality and potency" allows them to act like monsters. But this does not "preclude the moral responsibility of the perpetrator" (370). The normal person who has sex with children is unnatural and must be punished (a monster), while the pedophile is enacting an abnormal nature that needs treatment and correction.

Notable in Krafft-Ebing's distinction between nature and norms is the use of the ancient Greek term *pedophilia*. Krafft-Ebing's Viennese coinage consolidates a longer history of Greek *paiderastia* (pederasty) into a new psychological object of medico-forensic study. Greeks used the term *paedophilia* (παιδοφιλία), composed of child (*paido*/παιδο) and love (*philia*/φιλία), interchangeably with *paederasty*. In ancient Greece, an adult citizen's love of a child/youth (*paedophilia*) was not necessarily distinguished from an adult citizen's sexual activity with a male child/youth (*paederasty*).[4] By 1886, the system of status relations regularizing love among Western Europeans was vastly different from that governing pedophilia's classical Greek meaning. Pedophilia returns in this context at the juncture of legal and psychological power, asserted as forensic psychiatry's specific authority to spot abnormal natures via an archaic Greek intrusion into modern German (itself an amalgam of linguistic and territorial imperialisms). Deracinated, the pedophile entered the annals of forensic psychiatry as a modern abnormal reviving archaic remnants of classical nature. The peculiarly archaic modern pedophile of 1886 appears as pitiable, not monstrous. "Monstrous" was reserved for those successfully modern men who sought out sex with children while in charge of their full faculties or operating at half-mast due to inebriation or other modes of self-imposed moral compromise.

In the period in which Krafft-Ebing published his magnum opus, the distinction between psychopathology and sexual criminality was being negotiated across rapidly urbanizing zones in continental Europe, England, and the United States. In contrast to what Foucault (2003a, 296) labels "marginal adults" centered in mid-nineteenth-century Western European adult-child sex spectacles, this late nineteenth-century problem was no longer a seemingly peripheral or rural phenomena. Instead, adults who seek out sex with children were associated with the disease of metropolitan urban industrialization and mass migration or displacement of populations. In 1880s England, for example, moral activists such as Josephine Butler and W. T. Stead worked to raise awareness of young people's vulnerability to sexual abuses (Jenkins 1998, 28). Periodicals such as the *Pall Mall Gazette* published articles such as Stead's "The Maiden Tribute to Modern Babylon" (1885), specifically citing the city's anonymous public spaces and displaced labor forces as a recipe for sexual exploitation called "white slavery."[5] White slavery focused on young English girls and boys tricked, lured, or seduced into prostitution by predatory adults. In the 1880s, according to Mara L. Keire (2010, 71), the English activist Alfred Dyer decisively "shifted the meaning of white slavery away from the systemic metaphor representing unequal power in the capitalist state to the meaning with which we are most familiar: involuntary brothel prostitution."

This shift deployed tropes of racial slavery (chattelization of blackness) and wage slavery (exploitation of white labor power) but shifted its associations to racially gendered vulnerability as the basis of sex (Irwin 1996). White girls' and young women's sexual labor power could be expropriated because of its added racialized value; they were uniquely vulnerable to exploitation by traffickers who wished to expropriate the sexual valorization of whiteness.[6] In the 1880s and 90s in the United States, new modes of expertise directed public attention to such sexual threats: Charlton Edholm's tract *Traffic in Girls and Florence Crittenton Missions* (1893) and *Traffic in Girls and Work of Rescue Missions* (1899) echoed concerns from the United Kingdom about white slavery; Krafft-Ebing's *Psychopathia Sexualis* was translated into English and circulated in the United States; and the American discipline of criminology was founded. Across these emerging modes of expertise, concern about young white people's vulnerability to sexual predation from dangerous strangers became a dominant focus. By 1896, Krafft-Ebing's ([1886] 1965, 369) observation that "in large cities the markets for these filthy needs are well stocked" seemed prophetic, as urban space became increasingly associated in white-dominated popular and professional culture with the danger of sexual predators exploiting white youth within the destructive nexus of surplus labor, corporate capitalism, and kinship alienation.

In contrast, Ida B. Wells's anti-lynching tract *A Red Record* ([1895] 1997a) pushed back on the popular and professional "expertise" that justified racial terror through appeals to white sexual endangerment. Advocates and intellectuals such as Wells and Mary Church Terrell documented the gap between hyperbolic threats to white women and children and actual threats to black people across age and gender. Their work drew attention to white sexual endangerment as a process of amplification as misdirection, which replaces actual sexual threats with amplified fears used to direct attention away from the real distribution of harm. Actual violence against black, brown, indigenous, and noncitizen peoples was transfigured into the threat those populations posed to white innocence. Wells (1997a, 1997b) tracked this process as the myth of the black rapist used to justify antiblack terrorization and lynching in *Southern Horrors: Lynch Law in all Its Phases* (1892) as well as *A Red Record*. The historian Nayan Shah (2001) shows how the specter of Asian prostitution and perversion was used to justify migration exclusion and spatial containment in the period 1875–1965. And numerous other activists and scholars have traced how ongoing colonial warfare against indigenous peoples, emerging military and market strategies of imperial expansion, and intra- and international urban migration were used to amplify and misdirect threats to white national purity.

Sexual threats to white *children* in particular were slowly and unevenly separated from a broader range of alleged threats to national white purity. Scholars have documented complex and noncommensurate zones of sexual and criminal policing in relation to the making of childhood during this period, limning in particular the ways legal, social, biological, and psychological approaches to maturity conditioned civilizational difference. As wars and treaties carved the United States out of diverse indigeneous lands and in opposition to Mexico and Canada, more than one "frontier thesis" was generated about sexual encounters of and as civilizational borders (Turner [1893] 2007). Sexual threat has been associated with contact zones and border patrol from their beginnings, with spectacularized claims about sexual predators a central apparatus of turning opposition into Other (Kazanjian 2003). Captivity narratives figured diverse indigenous peoples as predators lacking the sexual and marital mores of European settlers, despite the fact that white colonists were far more likely to commit sexual violence against native peoples (Smith 2005). The formation of white supremacy as a legal and social doctrine generally racialized blackness through hypo-descent, although this pseudobiologizing process was central to territorializing agrarian infrastructure (the Black Belt) and capitalist urbanization (the Great Migration) through racial terror spanning postemancipation Black Codes in the U.S. South and the emergence of the Ku Klux Klan (enshrined federally in *Plessy v. Ferguson*).[7]

In the late nineteenth century, the process of naturalizing norms as "white" leaned heavily on the successful dissemination of social Darwinism and various raciologies animated by long-standing antiblack "science."[8] The passage of the Page Act of 1875 and the Chinese Exclusion Act of 1882 mobilized popular fear of so-called Oriental differences of conduct and desire placed beyond the pale of nationalist normalization altogether. The status of science itself, particularly racial and ethnographic knowledges, was subject to Foucault's logic of vile sovereignty when disciplinary expertise was pitted against common sense and legal expeditiousness in the immigration-focused "racial prerequisite cases" beginning in 1878, and the property-focused blood quantum determinations associated with the General Allotment Act (Dawes Act) of 1887.[9] The Spanish-American War of 1898 mobilized discourses of the foreign as racialization—summarized in the famous phrase "foreign in a domestic sense"—even as expansions of U.S. empire into Asia and the Americas diversified discourses of the foreign and deployed them as military and market means.[10]

Across these conditions, nationalist normalization became tethered to childhood as a special phase of life that required the right combination of discipline and care. At the turn of the twentieth century, children and youth were developed as special-status categories, a process in no small part negotiated through the separation of criminalization (racialized as nonwhite in changing configurations) and protection (racialized as white in changing configurations). Between 1886 and 1895, childhood underwent redefinition as protection from pre-mature sexuality when many states raised the legal age of consent from ten to fourteen–eighteen, while the status of the "juvenile" began to carve out a liminal phase of criminality between childlike innocence and adult culpability. Efforts to discipline, regulate, and police relations among sexuality, age of maturity, and criminality were taken up across developing psychological and criminological fields of expertise. Those who preyed on young people were monstrous to the degree that the youth in question could be diagnosed as innocent. This period's practices of child saving (1870s–80s) and invention of juvenile courts (1899) reorganized childhood as a specifically modern threshold for entrance into the bios of politics.[11]

These processes often divided subjects of care from subjects of punishment, a central mechanism of U.S. empire's racial capitalisms and gendered divisions of life and labor (Lowe 2015). The simultaneous institutionalization of child protection and juvenile courts constellate age as status signifying modernity (Ibrahim 2016). Thus, this period coupled the traffic in child saving and child stealing, referred to as orphan trains and Indian boarding schools, alongside the attribution of dependent status via post-1898 occupation of the Philippines, Puerto Rico, and Guam (adjudicated in the 1901–1905 Insular Cases). The distribution of childhood status was weaponized against populations deemed unfit for self-government and in childlike tutelage to the United States as a ward of the colonial state. Nationalized normalization was overall reserved for whiteness, which laid claim to gender and sexuality as individuating concerns that were denied to allegedly mass-differentiated populations. During this period, territory and biology asserted black, brown, indigenous, and noncitizen difference as sexually monstrous by nature, not sexually deviant from a norm.

Given this context, Krafft-Ebing's *pedophilia erotica* might have seemed tailor-made for professional and national elaboration as U.S. boundary patrol. The erotic pedophile could have been used to cut normality—what Foucault (2003b, 255) calls a "biological-type caesura within a population" associated with the appearance of "racism"—in ways that would enable group differentiation and exceptional individuation to be encoded as the nature and normality of sexuality. One might assume that, once Krafft-Ebing introduced this difference into professional jargon, a Greek eruption in psychological categories could productively displace the accepted term for cross-generational homosexual activity (*pederasty*) or the more general criminal terms for immoral sex (buggery, sodomy, rape) with a more clinical diagnosis of persistent desire (*pedophilia*).[12] Pedophilia seemed poised to introduce an explicitly psycho-forensic professional authority over the difference between action (subject to moralization and, potentially, criminalization) and desire (subject only to diagnosis and, potentially, treatment). Pedophiles might have enabled an apparatus that would target white abnormals as having a uniquely archaic nature, different from the bestial nature that denied normalization entirely to nonwhite groups. More like ancient Greeks, pedophiles could be construed as a natural part of European civilization, if no longer in step with its modern norms. This would differentiate them from aberrant monsters who are either normal brutes or utterly beyond Eurocentric norms.

But even though Krafft-Ebing's term was taken up in English-language professional discourse at the turn of the century, placed under the heading "Abnormality" in the English sexologist Havelock Ellis's *Studies in the Psychology of Sex* in 1906, the diagnostic term "pedophilia" did not become central to the U.S.-specific problematization of adult-child sex until much later in the twentieth century.[13] Instead, in the early and mid-twentieth century, the sexual delinquent and sexual psychopath played far more important roles in the spectacularization of adult-child sex. The peripheral threats associated with marginal adults shifted across the twentieth century to the threat posed by successful normalization of white manhood itself. White degenerates and psychopaths disrupted given orders of expertise and regularized new regimes of power that ultimately would become the groundwork for dismantling "normal life" nearer to the century's end (Spade 2015), when the pedophile makes his virtual appearance.

Of Perverts and Psychopaths

At our second switch point in processes of vile sovereignty, the discourse of white slavery was mobilized into a more focused wave of early twentieth-century U.S. state and disciplinary reaction. Across the 1910s, Keire (2010, 87) points out, "the white slavery scare changed the way Americans prosecuted urban vice." This scare shifted focus from the prostitute to the profiteer in ways that "redefined responsibility juridically," as well as socially and politically. The passage of the Mann Act of 1910 revised antiprostitution and red-light abatement laws as the basis for antivice enforcement at the origins of the FBI.[14] White slavers were avaristic or greedy men—frequently figured as "Jewish" and "Oriental" (Keire 2010, 72)—who were perceived as producing a crisis in the value(s) of whiteness. These environmental threats were separated from those attributed to African American men's sexually predatory nature, figured as an inherent criminality. Emerging fields of expertise such as public health and criminology helped differentiate these threats by translating psychology and criminality into environmental and biological terms. As Khalil Gibran Muhammad (2010, 2–3) argues, "New sources of statistical data" from the 1890 census on prison populations were aggregated to racialize crime as black. Crime statistics came to "outpace, at times, many competitors—such as body odor, brain size, disease, and intelligence—in the national marketplace of ideas about, and 'scientific' proofs of, black inferiority." What Muhammad calls the "condemnation of Blackness" through criminology simultaneously exceptionalized whiteness as an amalgam of ethnicity and citizenship that was better explained by environment.

But even as barbaric depravity was exemplified by mass-differentiated discourses of racial biology, and white criminality was exceptionalized by individualized discourses of ethnic environment, seemingly atavistic eruptions of sexual depravity among white men threatened to disrupt this system. As Kali Gross (2006, 11) points out in her comparison of white men imprisoned for sodomy and black women imprisoned for a range of offenses at Eastern State Penitentiary in Philadelphia, "Inherent pathology explained blacks' criminal actions, but this very notion simultaneously disallowed the existence of a native-born white male degenerate."[15] Degeneracy among U.S.-born white men must be explained by other means, not only in contrast to the dramatis personae of European alienage, black criminality, native savagery, and Asian inassimilability, but in its own, unique terms (Bederman 1995).[16] During this period, psychiatrists such as Adolf Meyer and William Healy increased surveillance of metropolitan white manliness for "mental hygiene" amid broader adaptations of social Darwinism and the "positivist criminology" of Cesare Lombroso, often recommending incapacitation over incarceration for white sexual defectives (Jenkins 1998, 21, 44). Thus, we find the disciplinary origins and political necessity of a biopolitical caesura *internal to* whiteness that comes to define the abnormal: a deviation in the "mental hygiene" of a fictively coherent psychological and biological whiteness.

White male sexuality underwent normalization through regimes of diagnosis and detection. The norms governing legitimate whiteness were shored up by regularizing abnormality as sexual exception, a forensic psychiatric determination to be set in motion by criminal investigation. Legal reform shored up this emerging disciplinary and state complex using what Philip Jenkins (1998, 38, 43) summarizes as "the defective-delinquent codes and the eugenics statutes" linking criminology and psychiatry through their joint interest in sexual "*psychopathy.*"[17] This process, however, opened the doors to lay experts, including people living sexual deviance as regular life, to claim their own authority over the meaning of sexual irregularity. If one institution's dangerous defect is another's mere abnormality, subjects caught up in those institutions or living happily separate from them could assert their own expertise in determinations of dangerous perversion versus benign difference.[18] Over the opening decades of the twentieth century, efforts to target and manage aberrations in white male sexuality enabled criminological data gathering, psychobiological diagnosis, and lay assertions of expertise to vie for dominance over the meaning of white sexual deviance. In tandem, earlier categorizations of children were assembled into what the literary scholar Kathryn Bond Stockton (2009, 17) calls modern "genres of children," including the often-studied figure of white innocence and its erotic others: sexual children demonized as predators or spectralized as queer (Ohi 2005).[19]

This configuration helps explain our next switch point of vile sovereignty: the explosion of discourses about the "sexual psychopath" in the 1930s, in response to which the idea of sex "panic" came into broader use to name an upwelling of media and police attention to sex crimes against children. Often considered a key precursor to the late twentieth-century focus on stranger danger, this three-decade period (1930s–50s) produced a wealth of scholarly and popular debate over the myth versus the evidence that children were in significant sexual danger. This in turn sowed the seeds of a data revolution that would introduce vile sovereignty into relations between science and the state at the federal level. Scholars concur that a series of widely reported cases of white child rape and murder created a media firestorm over sexual threats to children from the 1930s through the 1950s (the 1940s are sometimes considered a lull correlated with World War II).[20] During this period, mainstream media reports of child sexual predation rose drastically; even previous cases such as that of Nathan Leopold and Richard Loeb were recast publicly as the work of possible sexual psychopaths. In 1937, the *New York Times* created a new index category for "sex crimes" to name the unique psychological and criminological problem posed by "sex fiends" and "sex psychopaths"; Hoover declared a "War on the Sex Criminal" in the *New York Herald Tribune*; and the New York press reported the child rape and murder crimes of Lawrence

Marks (white, age forty-nine) and Salvatore Ossido (white, age twenty-six), both recently released from prison and both guilty of attacking a white child (Jenkins 1998, 50–52).

The backdrop to these individualized stories of sexually motivated murders of white children seemed to be the mass disposability of children racialized as nonwhite, understood as disabled, or undocumented as wards of the streets. Young people were assigned the category of child unevenly, with race trumping age in many determinations of who counted as a child at all. Black youth in particular was notoriously targeted as sexually predatory (as young as thirteen in the case of the Scottsboro Boys [1931] and fourteen for Emmett Till [1955]), rather than recognized as sexually targeted (as in the rape cases of twelve-year-old Melba Patillo [1954] or eleven-year-old Ida Mae Holland [1955]) (McGuire 2011). Cases that caught the mainstream media's attention as "sex crimes" often alluded to mass or serial sexual abuse of children leading up to a final rape and murder of a white child. When the children harmed en route to this gruesome finale were accorded lower social status, their abuse often went undetected or unpunished by the powers that be.

The 1934–36 case of Albert Fish provides an exemplary case in point. Fish (born in 1870) was arrested in 1934 for multiple crimes of child murder, confessing upon arrest early-onset paraphilia, including homosexuality and sexual play with excrement and urine beginning at age twelve, which led to his work as a male prostitute in New York at twenty and sexual assault of underage boys at the same time.[21] While in an arranged marriage to a woman with whom he had six children, Fish continued to have consensual sadomasochistic relations with young men while pursuing sexual assault, torture, murder, and, ultimately, cannibalism against multiple children younger than eleven. Fish claimed to have committed at least three, and possibly more than ten, sexually motivated murders over a ten-year period (1924–34) and to have molested children in every state. His most common targets were those he believed to be at the margins of society, young boys he identified most consistently as African American or as having cognitive disabilities.

Fish's case seemed to expose every failure possible in the early twentieth-century arsenal of state and disciplinary expertise. The orphanage did not detect his early childhood paraphilias; the police did not intervene in his young adult prostitution; and neither the court, the prison warden, nor the parole officers raised a red flag for potential psychopathology during his later arrest and incarceration for embezzlement. His sexual crimes against African American and marginalized youth remained beneath the threshold of criminal detection, and his sexual psychopathology did not raise enough red flags for psychiatric authorities. Fish was caught only when he mailed a letter confessing to the murder in 1928 of a ten-year-old white girl named Grace Budd to the Budd family in 1934. (This apparently caused him some remorse.) Despite widespread belief in his insanity, Fish stood trial and was electrocuted at Sing Sing in 1936, where he had previously served time. The Fish case raised public alarm about the failures of state and disciplinary mechanisms to detect and deter sexually motivated crimes of this nature. Media outlets raged that no checks were in place to catch this type of psychopathological criminal, who by all reports seemed like an innocuous and kindly man most often likened to someone's gentle white grandfather (Taylor 2004).

These cases dramatized the problem that repeat offenders were either eluding arrest entirely or, when caught by the system, not deterred from committing further crimes that ultimately led to the rape and murder of individual white children. A repeated refrain complained that neither legal nor psychiatric systems protected the public from sexual predators targeting children, a failure that resulted in extensive sexual abuse, as well as exceptional rapes and murders. And, even worse, those systems seemed unable even to calculate the magnitude of the threat, much less predict its occurrence or move to prevent it. One chief complaint focused on insufficient recordkeeping and the lack of centralized data collection related to sexual offenses against children. The Uniform Crime Report, initiated in 1930 by the new FBI, collected state criminological data to compile the first nationwide crime report with the aim of creating reliable statistics for analysis. Yet data on sexual criminality, as well as on psychological risk factors that did not lead to crime but to immorality and vice, resisted the alleged uniformity of crime reporting. As Tamara Rice Lave (2009, 554) points out, during this era there was an "utter void of any and all data on child molestations. The FBI simply did not provide crime statistics on the most feared form of sexual offending: child molestation."

But according to both expert and popular sources, data collection alone would not solve the problem. These new sex predators against children posed a particular diagnostic problem for criminal deterrence. This new type of crime was itself psychopathological and marked by compulsivity; it was not susceptible to deterrence by standard criminological or psychological means. In response, U.S. states began to pass the sexual psychopath laws (1937–67) that would come to define the vile sovereignty of the midcentury. These laws allowed those who committed sex crimes to be tried in criminal courts, but after conviction they allowed discretionary psychiatric evaluation to determine whether mental illness and dangerousness made a particular convict better suited to civil commitment for psychological treatment. As Jenkins (1998, 81) explains, "Sex psychopath legislation built on the positivist precedent of the defective delinquent laws, which meant observing sex offenders in order to determine their mental condition and dangerousness and, where appropriate, committing perverts indefinitely to a special institution for dangerous defectives."

The sexual psychopath laws instituted new modes of vile sovereignty over the racialized and gendered formations of criminality and abnormality. Race and class often determined how male-identified sex offenders were processed through the system. In her study of California sex crime procedures of this period, Chrysanthi Leon (2011, 106) shows that race and class determinations "track" from arrest through sentencing: "The bare arrest data suggest that police officers were more likely to arrest blacks for rape," which, unlike lower-level sexual offenses, usually resulted in prison time.[22] Thus, "decisions at both the arrest and the disposition stage" often "meant prison time for offenders of color" (106), in contrast to civil commitment for white middle-class offenders charged with more psychologically ambiguous offenses, including offenses against children. This matches the racialization of sex crime along differential axes of treatable psychopathology versus violent criminality.[23] The public furor over sexual psychopaths as sex criminals yielded increased power for criminal and psychological institutions while creating a treatable white man neither truly disordered nor violent, just "slightly mixed up" (61) and in need of institutional normalization. The historians Estelle Freedman (1987) and Regina Kunzel (2017) describe this as a dragnet for white men as sexual abnormals that disproportionately targeted male homosexuality and public sex as low-lying threats of greater offense.

The sexual psychopath laws, like the sex panics before them, can be construed as part of containment strategies targeting alternative approaches to sexuality emerging from below. Racialized violence was often justified by claims that people had disrespected or disrupted dominant norms of gender or sexuality, as in the Zoot Suit Riots of 1943 in Los Angeles (Escobedo 2007). In the later portion of period, homophile organizations such as the Mattachine Society (founded in 1950) and the Daughters of Bilitis (founded in 1955) offered cautious normalization campaigns for white middle- and upper-class homosexuals, in contrast to living "in the shadows" of cross-class and sometimes cross-race enclaves for same-sex practices and multigender expression across small and large cities.[24] At the same time, civil rights activists such as Rosa Parks and Fannie Lou Hamer targeted rape and sexual assault as practices of gendered racial terror.[25] Some activists called on respectability as a political—or, of necessity, a survival—strategy. Others criticized norms of respectability devised for white, male, heterosexual, and nationalist supremacy. As multiple strategies emerged in the United States to challenge sexual harm and expand sexual pleasure, some fled to locations abroad perceived as more permissive for same-sex and cross-generational sexual expression. Expatriation by James Baldwin to Europe continued the out-migration earlier in the twentieth century to places where racial segregation and morality crusades (such as Prohibition) were perceived as less draconian. Meanwhile, some white men of means relocated to Morocco or Southeast Asia in search of less repressive climes, including for cross-generational sexuality, echoing and exacerbating colonial patterns in ways that were unevenly articulated to consent and choice.[26]

The media discourse of sexual psychopathy resulted in substantive shifts of criminological and psychological power over the general population and a recalibrated relation among experts, including the rise of explicit authority for a specific genre of lay experts activated as concerned citizens. The status of respectability marked sharp divisions between those hailed by populism and those who became its targets.[27] The call for citizens' common sense as a barrier against growing sexual and gendered threats to public safety once again organized the popular into a populace defined by existing hierarchies of oppression and recognition. The sexual psychopath laws introduced new mechanisms of vile sovereignty that fortified the authority of psychiatry in criminal sentencing while undermining the authority of psychiatry as a research profession. It also promoted state law-and-order agencies associated with policing over other state domains of regulation and control, leading to the rise of new collaborations between law and sociology. Some psychiatric experts complained that media and law-enforcement claims about sexual psychopathy were not grounded in psychological science. Some state actors worried that there was no way to verify claims that sexual predation against children was on the rise and that legislative agendas were being set by the FBI. Empirical data became the rejoinder to media hype, yet such data required new modes of expertise to create reliable and relevant categories of analysis. This ended up requiring an activated populace positioned to interpret data and protect children from threats to sexual respectability as much as bodily harm.

During the period from 1937 to 1967, residual and emerging experts struggled for dominance over this process of identification and detection, even as state and disciplinary experts were declared unable to protect a public increasingly called to arm itself against this ubiquitous threat. Some psychiatrists, such as Benjamin Karpman in his book *The Sexual Offender and His Offenses* (1954), claimed that sex offenses were motivated by abnormal sexual pathologies, while other psychological experts helped shape civil commitment protocols for sexual psychopath laws. Meanwhile, large funding initiatives supported newly respectable research in areas such as sexology, with the Rockefeller Foundation funding Alfred Kinsey's eight-hundred-page *Sexual Behavior in the Human Male* (Kinsey et al. 1948) that advocated for benign sexual variation based on empirical evidence.[28] New collaborations between law and sociology relied on criminological expertise, such as James M. Reinhardt and Edward C. Fisher's article "The Sexual Psychopath and the Law" (1949) and Paul Tappan's "Some Myths about the Sex Offender" (1955). Reinhardt and Fisher (1949, 734) argued that empirical data supported the need for sexual psychopath laws despite the fact that "knowledge of the nature and development of 'sexual psychopathy' is, to say the least, imperfect," while Tappan challenged the evidence supporting the need for such laws by attacking the "myths" of sexual psychopathy as the little-understood basis for widespread sexual crime.

Such heterogeneous approaches to expert knowledge about the psychosexual roots of sex crime are reflected in a multiplication of terms for sexual offending against laws, morals, women, children, society, or the nation (often in combination or outright contradiction with one another).[29] Calls for more and better empirical verification were conjoined with the delimitation of data as an adequate method of understanding this unique psychocriminological crisis.[30] In addition, neither empirical nor psychological expertise was capable of preventing its violence or managing its effects. Instead, more and more experts themselves advocated for popular understandings of the problem to cut through this heterogeneous field of ineffective expertise. Reinhardt and Fisher's "The Sexual Psychopath and the Law" clarifies this point by admitting that empirical data about sex crime cannot be easily correlated to the less-documented phenomena of sexual psychopathology. "It is important, therefore," they explain, "that society make up its mind what kind of perversions it is willing to tolerate and what kind of risks it is willing to take" (Reinhardt and

Fisher 1949, 734). Public opinion plays an important role in helping identify sexual psychopaths among the seemingly normal people around them, since "sexualized 'criminal' monsters do not begin as monstrosities" (Reinhardt and Fisher 1949, 736) and must be detected while in the merely abnormal state, before they become full-fledged monsters. This resonates with critics of sexual psychopathy, as well, such as Tappan or Kinsey, who, however, argue that the empirical studies do not necessarily correlate to the less-documented phenomena of benign sexual abnormality, about which society should also "make up its mind" about toleration versus risk.

Both sides, in other words, argued that predicting criminality through sexuality remained well outside the domain of existing expertise. Public safety in this arena would increasingly be presented as the responsibility of a general populace serving as frontline experts routing out dangerous abnormality in the home and on the street. Having declared "War on the Sex Criminal" in 1937, Hoover used his *American Magazine* articles "How Safe Is Your Daughter?" (1947) and "How Safe Is Your Youngster?" (1955) to mobilize public sentiment against sex crime and expand the public front in this war. Hoover's overarching message is that existing law-and-order approaches fail to engage sufficiently with forensic psychiatry. Sex offenders are treated as mere criminals rather than as the mental degenerates they also are. In "How Safe Is Your Daughter?" Hoover (1947, 32) proposes that, instead of arrest, conviction, and short-term criminal confinement, sex offenders need the same public mobilization that happens when "wild beasts break out of circus cages." They are beasts whose sexual depravity is best understood as mental degeneracy (abnormality) leading to criminal perversion (monstrosity). Thus, for Hoover "sex maniacs" or "sex fiend[s]" can be described as *both* "wrongdoer" and "maladjusted" (32).

Left unchecked and untreated, this unique combination of criminality and psychopathology inevitably leads from mere abnormality to "eventual crime[s] of violence" (32). But because existing police and professional mechanisms do not work together to prevent this inevitability, "degenerate sex offenders" are allowed to run amuck: "depraved human beings, more savage than beasts, are permitted to rove America almost at will" (32). (In 1947, Humbert Humbert had not yet begun his American adventure, although this era had given birth to him by the time of Hoover's 1955 essay.) Hoover proposes "common sense" as the best defense against such bestial depravity: "More can be accomplished in combating the menace of sex fiends through an aroused public opinion than through any other means. . . . What is acutely needed is a realistic viewpoint based on common sense and logic" (102).[31] The nation as a whole must be aroused to "face reality" and prevent "crimes of even greater ferocity in the future" (32). To achieve this end, all "law-abiding citizens" (103) need to adopt a "realistic viewpoint based on common sense and logic" (102), "removing the taboo and recognizing the facts," on one hand, and piercing "a smoke screen of false sentimentality," on the other (102). Such common sense is best learned from the media. "The American press and the radio have turned in a splendid performance as the watchdogs of our liberties," Hoover explains, so now all citizens have to do is shine a "spotlight of publicity on sex degenerates and the cesspools of vice which nurture their development" (104). If they do so, they get to become media advocates who "join hands in surveying the communities which they serve" (104) by "proclaiming to the world the identities of the wrongdoers" (32) and having their own identities protected.[32]

The mode of common sense concocted by Hoover appears to be an explicit expression of vile sovereignty. The state and the disciplines are unable to protect citizens against territorial, biological, and psychopathological sex predators, so citizens must learn from the media a common sense that goes beyond existing expertise. On one hand, recognizing the "facts" is presented as coupling statistics with case narratives that demonstrate a pattern of police and prison failures to deter escalating sex crimes. Readers can use the stories to bring statistics to life as parables of a heretofore unperceived reality, quite literally engaging in sexual sensationalism as a vehicle for "aroused public opinion."[33] On the other hand, culpable denial is presented as the false sentimentality of "sob-sister[s]" and "'bleeding heart[s]'" (102) who excuse or explain away abnormal behavior as benign difference. This bad affective response replaces sensationalism with sentimentality, arousal of the wrong sort that aligns sentimentalists with the perverts they protect. Readers who do not "proclaim to the world the identities of the wrongdoers" are in danger of becoming abnormal themselves and subject to aroused vigilance by others. Thus, readers are given some relatively clear admonitions: men must conform to sexual norms or else face unspecified but draconian sounding "treatment" (103); women must embrace motherhood's mantle as a shield against sexual disrespect and danger; and children must fear public spaces—mostly roads leading to secreted cabins, woods, and basements—where they may meet "stranger[s]" (104) who end up "ruining them for life" (32).

Yet the senses of this common cause remain unclear, as does the media-spotlighted line between vigilance and perversion. Disciplining arousal becomes a central tactic of spectacularization, leading to what later critics will

"The nation's women and children will never be secure . . . so long as degenerates run wild"

FIGURE 1.1 Untitled photograph by Lejaren Hiller, in J. Edgar Hoover, "How Safe Is Your Daughter?" *American Magazine*, July 1947, 33.

call the "pedophilia of everyday life" in which erotic children are presented to audiences who must distinguish between aroused feelings of protective care and those of predatory desire (Mohr 2004). Hoover's 1947 article, for example, is accompanied by a surreal image of an oversize hand reaching over three ter-rified white girls on what appears to be an otherwise empty city street (figure 1.1). The magazine cover, in contrast, features a close-up of a white female child blowing up a red balloon next to the sole headline, "How Safe Is Your Daughter?" (figure 1.2). This seeming contrast—between erotic innocence and shadowy danger—would by 1955 be combined into a single photograph de-picting a more covert danger blending into the land of innocence (figure 1.3). (The 1955 cover makes recourse to a pair of wide-eyed kittens [figure 1.4].) While in both cases faceless predators menace children, in the first that men-ace is announced as distinct from scenes of bucolic pleasure. In the second, the child is no longer able to recognize danger that appears wearing nicely

FIGURE 1.2 Untitled photograph by Edward Patston, *American Magazine*, July 1947, cover.

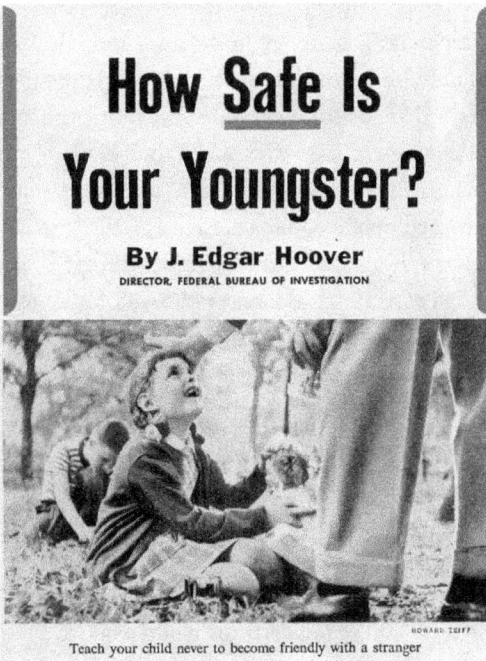

FIGURE 1.3 Untitled photograph by Howard Zeiff, in J. Edgar Hoover, "How Safe Is Your Youngster?" *American Magazine*, March 1955, 19.

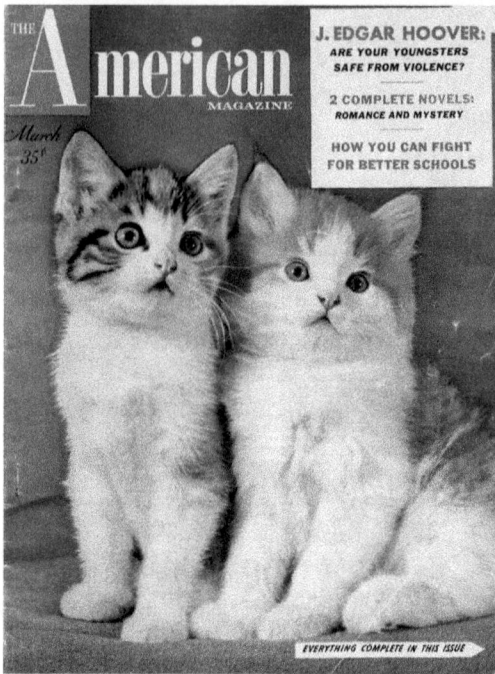

FIGURE 1.4 Untitled photograph by Joseph Rustan, *American Magazine*, March 1955, cover.

pressed trousers in a springtime park. Danger lay in shadows and a lack of proclaimed identification, certainly, but learning to sense that danger requires more than a pedagogy of pants and hands. To suggest that the former images foment faceless terror while the latter eroticize white childhood is merely to point out what has become obvious: in this period, common sense was trained through what Hoover calls "aroused public opinion" to see as "fact" a mass-mediated difference between perverse looking and its loving corollary.

Hoover's writings on the sexual psychopath as threat to the nation's "daughters" and "youth" represent only one emerging discourse consolidating a new mode of popular expertise. Disciplinary experts such as the criminologist Edwin Sutherland (1950a, 142) countered such spectacularizing projects by declaring them a "panic." Sutherland's articles "The Diffusion of Sex Psychopath Laws" and "The Sexual Psychopath Laws" (in the *American Journal of Sociology* and *Journal of Criminal Law and Criminology*, respectively) define such panic as media-induced "bursts into hysteria" not substantiated by empirical fact (144). In "the Diffusion of Sex Psychopath Laws," Sutherland summarizes this process in three steps: "a community is thrown into panic by a few serious sex crimes, which are given nation-wide publicity; the community acts in an agitated manner, and all sorts of proposals are made; a committee is then appointed to study the facts and to make recommendations" (142). Citizen activism resulting from a sex panic is likely to target increasingly unrelated conduct. This might make "condemnation of strip-tease and other lewd shows as stimulating sex fiends" (144) the justification for increasingly draconian measures of protection and punishment, such as castration and whipping. A sex panic might lead the state to appoint expert committees to "determine 'facts'" (145), but such state-dependent expertise can be too easily driven by professional self-interest (psychiatrists are roundly blamed) that leads to the "organization of information in the name of science without critical appraisal" (147). At the end of this cycle, a new synthesis of state power and professional expertise can legitimate unreasonable laws and shoddy science.

This now familiar critique of sex panic sounds uncannily like Krafft-Ebing's explanation of the problem posed by the normalcy of most adults who have sex with children. While Krafft-Ebing ([1886] 1965, 360) thought that "man's finer feelings" revolt against "counting the monsters among the psychically normal members of human society," Sutherland argues that "the ordinary citizen" finds "a sexual attack on an infant or a girl of six years . . . incomprehensible." Sutherland writes, "The hysteria produced by child murders is due in part to the fact that the ordinary citizen cannot understand a sex attack on a child. The ordinary citizen can understand fornication or even forcible rape of a woman, but he concludes that a sexual attack on an infant or a girl of six years must be the act of a fiend or maniac. Fear is the greater because the behavior is so incomprehensible" (Sutherland 1950a, 143). Because a sexual attack on a prepubescent child is so outside the norms of common sense, an ordinary citizen might experience an exceptional level of fear in response to such a fact. This creates a desire to see the culprit as monstrous, a commonsense baseline easily aroused to hysteria by the likes of Hoover. For Sutherland, this commonsense baseline measures monstrosity through its distance from "fornication or even forcible rape of a woman" (not differentiated as baseline norms). Here Sutherland resurrects Krafft-Ebing's definition of monstrosity as measured by "the degree in which it psychically and physically differs from the natural act" (Krafft-Ebing [1886] 1965, 370), now presented as either heterosexual coitus or rape. Sutherland (1950a, 144) wishes to correct the hysterical fears aroused in "ordinary citizens" who can comprehend adult rape as a corollary to heterosexual coitus, but cannot comprehend sex with an infant or female child.

This correction requires a return to reason not via sentimentality ("sob-sisters" are no one's friends in the panic/denial school of proper feelings) but, rather, through engaging "statistical trends in sex crimes." Sutherland counters sentiment and sensation with statistical knowledge: the antidote to arousal is reason. Learning how to interpret data will create a more realistic, and therefore more reasonable, assessment of the threat posed by sexual predators. As he presents this solution in "The Sexual Psychopath Laws," if more people understood how to separate "prostitution, rape, and other sex offenses" in the statistics they read, they would understand how few data exist to support fears of "serious sex crimes" at all (Sutherland 1950b, 544–45). The category "other sex offenses," he points out, includes a laundry list of crimes such as "indecencies with children (generally not involving intercourse), sodomy and other perversions, indecent exposure or exhibitionism, and incest" (544). Statistics on "other sex offenses" are actually cataloguing nonviolent or even moral crimes, he points out, while statistics on rape often combine "forcible and statutory" (younger than sixteen or eighteen) cases (544). Ultimately, even the most seemingly violent of sex crimes—forcible rape—may be inflated statistically by including possibly consensual sex. To return to the conflation of coitus and rape referenced in the previous article, Sutherland argues that "physicians have testified again and again that forcible rape is practically impossible unless the female has been rendered practically unconscious by drugs or injury; many cases reported as forcible rape have certainly involved nothing more than passive resistance" (Sutherland 1950b, 545).

Across the examples of Hoover and Sutherland, the struggle over common sense shuttles between populist paranoia and reactionary reason. First, Hoover's discourse of expert disqualification and popular vigilance takes identifiably ridiculous or grotesque forms. It appropriates actual incidence of harm and uses them to call for more normalizing and normative constraints on sexual behavior. Second, Sutherland's declaration of sex panic criticizes such ridiculous or grotesque mechanisms of power wearing a fool's cap proudly inscribed "FBI" but introduces its own ridiculous reason as corrective. Positioned as a corrective to hysteria, declarations of panic such as Sutherland's often dismiss gendered claims about sexual harm outright and ignore racial and colonial formations of gender and sexuality altogether.[34] Working together, these two discourses of state and professional disqualification create a new zone of common sense regularizing relations among such disqualified actors and institutions. Reason and panic become the binary positions through which new modes of common sense are forged. To be adjudged a lay expert, an "ordinary citizen" must take up one of two modes of reasonable suspicion: of the pervert *or* of the panic. Properly interpreting popularized discourse of child sex predators separates the reasonable critic from the populist dupe (much like the *American Magazine* cover girl is separated from her black-and-white doppelgangers by the faceless menace of normal pants). In neither case does recognizing and redressing actual sexual harm become a mode of "reason," instead aligning those impacted by sex harm (including rape) with "panic" and its activist affect.

Of Homosexuals and Predators

We now arrive at our final switch point, when insurgent social mobilizations of the late 1960s and 1970s sought to challenge this binary formation of common sense across cultural and political spectrums. Such efforts had been ongoing across the twentieth century, but they gained momentum during the formal break with white supremacy marked by civil rights victories in education, employment, housing, and voting from 1954 to 1968, and by marital and reproductive rights enshrined in *Loving v. Virginia* (1967) and *Roe v. Wade* (1973). Growing movements of radicalized activists fought for the end of institutionalized sexual and/as racial violence, the equitable distribution of reproductive rights as justice, and the protection of gender and sexual choice under the sign of consent (Fischel 2016). Discourses of sexual pleasure and sexual harm were under siege from below in what Audre Lorde (1984) and Jacqui Alexander (1997) describe as gendered and sexual liberation and erotic autonomy struggles. Movements for self-defense against sexual and gendered harm included activism against sterilization and reproductive abuse, institutionalization and imprisonment, and sexual assault in interpersonal and institutional settings.[35] Race radical and civil rights struggles brought national and international attention once again to the use of sex crime as lynch law and the failure to treat African American young people as children at all. Even the most mainstream feminists asserted that while workplace harassment, date rape, and intimate partner violence are commonplace, that should not make them common sense.

These movements pushed beyond binaries and insisted on a far broader range of possibilities for recognition and redress than existing circuits of panic and denial. In this period of social upheaval, lay knowledges from below were granted uneven recognition as expertise and even installed in universities and governments as modes of legitimate disciplinary and regulatory knowledge (Ferguson 2012).[36] Summaries of policy shifts of the 1960s–70s describe this era more broadly as the "anti-psychiatry" movement, "the liberal era" (Jenkins 1998, 16), and "the era of rehabilitative debate" (Leon 2011, 13), featuring more open discussion of what abnormalities constitute a sexual threat and what state and disciplinary responses are reasonable.[37] In the sexual liberation movements following the Stonewall rebellion of 1969, for example, protests against the American Psychiatric Association's inclusion of homosexuality as a mental disorder led to changes in the Diagnostic and Statistical Manual of Mental Disorders (DSM)-II of 1974.[38] Meanwhile, the sociologist Robert Martinson's famous study "What Works?" (1974) opened the door to rethinking the aims of detention as rehabilitation or punishment. Efforts to diminish state and disciplinary punishment of nonnormative sexualities and increase protections for racial and sexual minorities against state and vigilante violence emerged alongside claims that diagnosis and rehabilitation were not relevant mechanisms for disciplinary and state responses to such claims.

During this decade, the figure of the "child molester" also appeared as a kinder and gentler predator against children, one who might be stigmatized as abnormal rather than feared as monstrous (Jenkins 1998, 98). This version of the child molester resonates with Foucault's account of adult-child sexuality in his collection of Collège de France lectures of 1974–75 titled Abnormal. At the close of Abnormal (and again briefly in The History of Sexuality, Volume I), Foucault (2003a, 57) turns to the 1867 case of Charles Jouy to explain the emergence of the adult who has sex with children as an "abnormal individual" rather than a monster (see Harkins 2012). In this case, a forty-year-old French man Foucault (2003a, 294) calls the "village idiot" has a "young girl" named Sophie Adam masturbate him in front of another girl. The girl's family calls in outside experts to assess the conduct of Jouy, an unusual turn to external mechanisms to resolve what Foucault calls a "quite everyday offense" in "the depths of the countryside" (293). Foucault argues that as an "internal immigrant" (294) who performs low-status wage work, Jouy would have been a routine part of village life. His sexual contact with a higher-status child is what moves the otherwise largely ignored, "peripheral, floating sexuality that brings children and marginal adults together" (296) into the courtroom. As a result of this cross-status age-differentiated sexual contact, the 1867 case against Jouy inaugurates the "infracriminal and parapathological" (21) realm where psychiatry meets forensics.

This account resonates with the 1970s discourse of child molestation and locates a nineteenth-century European antecedent where it all began to go wrong.[39] Foucault argues that Jouy as abnormal individual may contain within him a "pale monster," but this weakened danger was subject not to criminal punishment but, rather, to neutralization by psychiatric and legal professionals called on to diagnose and detain him. This is similar to the description of the 1970s child molester. He has committed abnormal acts, yes, and he may even be a little repugnant in a "pale monster" kind of way. But he is not a catastrophic predator. Foucault acknowledges that, according to the case file, Jouy may have engaged in penetrative sexual contact with Sophie Adam, an act evidenced by unnamed signs reported by her mother on the girl's clothes. Foucault summarizes, "Something happened: almost rape, perhaps" (292). But his primary focus is on what he perceives as the problematic expansion of power through the investigation of Jouy. This leads Foucault to summarize this case even more dismissively in *The History of Sexuality, Volume I*, where he remarks on "the pettiness of it all; the fact that this everyday occurrence in the life of village sexuality, these inconsequential bucolic pleasures, could become, from a certain time, the object not only of a collective intolerance but of a judicial action, a medical intervention, a careful clinical examination, and an entire theoretical elaboration" (Foucault 1990, 31).

While Foucault sidesteps the question of Sophie Adam's experience of pleasure or harm in both lectures and book, in interviews of the period he expresses concern that children are also penalized by this system. In an interview originally published in *Le Nouvel Observateur* on March 12, 1977, Foucault states that the child "has an assortment of pleasure for which the 'sex' grid is a veritable prison" (Foucault 1988a, 117). By challenging the stigmatization of the child molester, both adult and child would be released from a veritable prison created at least in part by the regimes of sexuality described in *Abnormal*. Foucault's approach to adult-child sexuality echoed contemporary efforts to challenge prohibitions on cross-generational sexuality. Across some areas of Europe and the United States, advocates claimed that adult-child sexuality suffered unwarranted stigma as perversion or abuse. Foucault participated on the periphery of movements to decriminalize adult-child sex and remove the age of consent during the French Penal Code reform of 1977–78. Along with many other scholars, Foucault signed a petition to Parliament in 1977 to change articles in the law regarding the age of sexual majority. In a broadcast in 1978 by *France-Culture* that featured Foucault, Guy Hocquenghem, and Jean Danet, Foucault situates his support for French sex law reform in the context of post-1968 movements: "Things had evolved on such a wide front, in such an overwhelming and at first sight apparently irreversible way, that many of us began to hope that the legal regime imposed on the sexual practices of our contemporaries would at last be relaxed and broken up" (Foucault 1988b, 271).

But these efforts were rapidly declared a moral threat to society and countered by what Foucault calls "a system of information carried out in the press" (Foucault 1988b, 272). He cites Anita Bryant's 1977 U.S. movement Save Our Children as his prime example of media-based activism meant to moralize against the dangers of sexual liberalism. Bryant, a Christian singer turned spokesperson for Florida orange juice, felt called by God to stand up to the moral decline of American values represented by advocates for gay rights. As she explains in her memoir (Bryant 1977, 13), she was motivated to enter politics for the first time "because of my love for Almighty God, because of my love for His Word, because of my love for my country, because of my love for my children"; God called her to resist an ordinance proposed in Miami that would "give special privileges to homosexuals in areas of housing, public accommodation, and employment." The initiative, proposed after lobbying by the Dade County Coalition for the Humanistic Rights of Gays, legally banned discrimination in those areas based on sexual orientation. Bryant's most famous response to the initiative is her conflation of homosexuals with child molesters. She voiced two major concerns about "known homosexual school-teachers": first, they would "encourage more homosexuality by inducing pupils into looking upon it as an acceptable life-style," and second, "a particularly deviant-minded teacher could sexually molest children" (Bryant 1977, 114). Her understanding of "the act of homosexuality" explicitly included both outcomes: normalization and predation.

Bryant's effort to make "homosexual" signify normalized predation of children was successful in the local and, increasingly, the national context.[40] The Dade ordinance was repealed by a 70 percent vote. It drew national attention and inspired similar efforts in other municipalities. Soon St. Paul, Minnesota; Wichita, Kansas; and Eugene, Oregon had passed similar initiatives, while efforts failed in Seattle and in California. The concept of "special rights" as positive legal creation rather than liberal legal dismantling would galvanize new political discourses at the heart of the Moral Majority (1979–89) and religious right in the 1980s, which targeted homosexuality, abortion, the equal rights amendment, and pornography as moral enemies of the nation. In opposition, new organizations and individuals sprang up touting gay rights and legitimacy, from Pride South Florida to the election of Harvey Milk. But even more important, the Bryant revolution drew renewed focus on the dangers of sex crimes against children, now pitched as the predations of "known homo-sexuals." In 1977, twenty-four men were arrested for statutory rape of boys age eight to fifteen in what was widely called a "sex ring" in Revere, Massachusetts, and the district attorney in Boston set up an anonymous tip line focused on teenage male prostitution.

The response included affirmation of consensual intergenerational sexuality and, ultimately, separation of age-differentiated sex from legitimate sexual consent. The North American Man/Boy Love Association (NAMBLA) was founded in 1978 after the Boston Community Church held a conference on intergenerational sexuality.[41] Allied at first with the Gay Liberation Front and other movements for erotic self-determination, efforts to decriminalize or legitimate adult-child sexuality resurrected Krafft-Ebing's understanding of the "pedophile" as a child lover rather than a sexual criminal.[42] This was a strategic shift away from the relatively benign molester—who was, after all, defined by criminal acts—to the erotic pedophile, whose desire, while unusual, was not unnatural. Advocates called up antecedents in ancient Greece and across allegedly "nonmodern" societies to insist that pedophilia was a natural human expression of desire and affection.[43] Evidence of cross-cultural and historical practices of permitted adult-child sexuality often fueled these arguments, with a specific emphasis on the ancient Greek example quashed by a moralistic European modernity. Yet arguments in favor of normalizing pedophilia as a possibly consensual sexual orientation were soon ostracized from broader sexual-liberalization strategies. Organizing for recognition of consensual sexual relations was limited to rational and responsible subjects, excluding children and those deemed cognitively incompetent (Rubin 1984). From this crucible the normalization of various and uneven strands of the L, G, B, T, and Q acronym occurred alongside the demonization of adults who seek sex with children as a meeting ground where left and right can reach consensus.

This genealogy brings us to this project's present tense: the 1980s–2010s period when the pedophile emerged in dominant culture as a figure for virtual predation. The switch points I have traced here produced a spectacularization of adult-child sexuality that centered white male sexuality as its primary problem. This problematization would define the function of pedophilia in the millennial era and predict many of the effects of its virtualization. As my genealogy suggests, this approach to adult-child sexuality minimized or misdirected attention away from the ongoing existence of adult-child sexuality as modern European and white settler colonial practices. In the 1970s, what Kadji Amin (2017, 15) calls "modern pederasty," the age-differentiated and/or status-differentiated male-male sexuality fostered within European modernity, was itself under attack by new models of same-age/same-gender homosexual identity. As a result, modern European pederasty was once again projected onto zones deemed more permissive or more available for sexual practices veritably imprisoned in the metropoles or exceptionalized as a white male deviation from changing metropolitan norms.[44]

The normalization of homosexuality as modern same-age/same-gender love revitalized the discourse of "boy love" long written into various mercantile, colonial, and imperial enterprises of Europe, including Orientalist attributions of child-loving to Muslim or Asian societies. The organization of adult-child sexuality in the European metropole was correlated, as Eng-Beng Lim (2014, xi) has argued, with a "white man/native boy dyad" in the so-called peripheries. In *Brown Boys and Rice Queens*, Lim argues that the "well-known and yet unspeakable love story" (4) of European "pedo-love" (3) actually "point[s] to and pivot[s] on the open secret of the native boy" (3). Lim theorizes the open-secret history of European and white male entitlement to cross-generational sex within and across the colonies as a "colonial dyad" (xi), or what in U.S. contexts names the coercive sexualization of racialized or colonized people regardless of, and sometimes through, the fetishization of age as difference. These "open secrets" existed alongside racialized and colonized appropriations of girls and women, which were also "well known," if not quite so "unspeakable." (Harriet Jacobs's *Incidents in the Life of a Slave Girl* [2000] stands out among stories oft-told and often ignored.) They also include the instrumentalization of white girls in particular to demonstrate or mitigate claims of sexual harm, as evidenced in Foucault's dismissal of Sophie Adam's experience from the creation of technologies of power.[45]

Centering white male sexuality in the spectacularization of adult-child sex normalizes the presumed sexual availability of young people outside the boundaries of whiteness, leaving only white-on-white adult-child sex as a state of vile exception. White male entitlement to adult women and some children—the right to look among these entitlements—becomes through this process the test of reasonable common sense. Simone Browne (2015, 12, 17) theorizes the territorializing effects of "racializing surveillance" as the creation of "public spaces [that] are shaped for and by whiteness" in ways that "abnormalize" specific acts "coded for disciplinary measures that are punitive in their effects." In this instance, racializing surveillance makes the policing or permitting of white male sexual liberty the central—and, sometimes, seemingly the only—concern when differentiating normal behavior from its menacing shadows. This no more serves children assigned higher social status — or "the Child," in Lee Edelman's later summary — than it does those children assigned lower social status and young people denied the status of child at all. It also subjects those identified as white men to strict scrutiny for latent child-threatening perversion, regularizing suspicions that white men who deviate from highly gendered work and domestic practices are perverts likely to prey on children. (Childcare is among the divisions of gendered labor reified here.) As the next chapter shows, these experiences of regulated adult-child sexuality would become the building blocks of a new kind of power, one that sought to replace a veritable prison with a virtual one.

TWO

PROFILING VIRTUALITY AND PEDOPHILIC DATA

> The circus and the audience are absolutely indispensable
> to the hygiene of the State.
> —**JAMES BALDWIN**, *The Evidence of Things Not Seen*

This chapter picks up my genealogy in the 1980s, as the homosexual went the way of abnormalization and the pedophile underwent recoding as its parallel, if denied, twin, the moral monster. The pedophile from the late 1980s onward transformed the rational interest of the white slaver (avarice) into an irrational interest in exploiting children without financial gain; the amoral instinct of the sexual delinquent (atavism) into the immoral choice to act on such instincts; and the aberrant desires of the sexual psychopath (abnormality) into the unnatural nature of compulsive acts. This monster combined irrational interest, immoral choice, and unnatural nature into a seemingly new mode of threat: the virtual pedophile. The declaration of a new threat functioned to expand vile sovereignty by creating virtual zones for its operation.[1] The demand for commonsense solutions to diagnostic and forensic failures familiar from chapter 1 moved populist agency into virtual reality. People were recruited to look for pedophiles and inundated with information to help them discern this predator. But the more this information circulated, the less helpful it seemed to be in revealing the actual pedophile among the seemingly normal white men. In place of the street-level search cultivated in J. Edgar Hoover's mid-century America, activated citizens in this later period were to direct their attention on-screen and online to learn how information could be assembled with images into a composite sketch of predatory dangers.

Chapter 1 left off in the 1970s, with a central shift in U.S. sexual politics in which LGBT advocacy efforts split from movements to dismantle the heterogeneous stigma assigned to adult-child sexuality. Sexual liberation groups quickly began to signal their distance from the North American Man/Boy Love Association and related organizing and shifted to an argument for normalization on the grounds of their difference from pedophilia and other genuinely harmful perversions. Meanwhile, a diverse cross-section of feminists was fighting to show that sex crimes against women and girls were so routine as to be construed as normal, not psychologically deviant. Rape in particular was situated as part of a larger "rape culture" in which the sexual availability of women and girls to men and boys was understood to be normative. Legal reforms to include graded sexual assault attempted to show that harmful sexual conduct was normal and required legal intervention if normal was not to become normative. Across these movements, state and disciplinary actors were shifting rationales for intervention and policing. Abnormal sexual conduct could be non-harmful, while normal sexual conduct could inflict harm. Thus, the state and its disciplinary partners were called to shift the grounds for intervention away from moralities associated with safeguarding social norms (rather than people) and toward the protection of people from harm (including that which may be inflicted by moralistic social norms). By the turn of the twenty-first century, pedophiles would be among the only psychological perverts left in the basket of criminal defectives.

It is at this switch point that the pedophile began to reemerge as a sexual monster. The reassembled figure of the pedophile introduced a crisis whereby professional expertise would once again be subject to the reorganizations of vile sovereignty, only this time normalization itself would be among the targets of its grotesque power. The nineteenth-century Austrian psychiatrist Richard von Krafft-Ebing's forensic diagnostic term became newly relevant as late twentieth-century governance shifted away from normalization and toward grotesque power as a newly hegemonic condition extending beyond psychiatry and the state. Pedophilia picked up the earlier figures of white child predation — white slaver, sexual delinquent, sexual psychopath, and child molester — and created what James B. Waldram (2012, 75) calls a "forensic black hole" in his study of sex offender rehabilitation units. This zone of indistinction draws all dangers and abnormalities into its field and proposes the pedophile as its event horizon. The pedophile became the figure for a virtual predator whose sexuality exemplifies what Michel Foucault (1988b, 281) calls a broader movement away from "a kind of behavior hedged in by precise prohibitions" and toward "a kind of roaming danger, a sort of omnipresent phantom." The pedophile was declared a monster, neither sick nor criminal but an unnatural combination of the two that redefined the psychology and criminology of the sexual predator. What makes the predatory pedophile unique is that it does not appear on expanding spectrums of sexual normality at all. Instead, the pedophile remains virtual, a sign marking one end of this spectrum as the unnatural condition of natural sexuality, a threatening potentiality haunting all forms of sexuality but appearing in no specific or measurable place on its normative scale.

Pedophilia was reassembled in ways that introduced permanent insecurity into childhood as an allegedly universal condition without fundamentally redistributing value or protection across childhood's heterogeneous differences. From the 1980s to the 2010s, the term "pedophile" was used more and more often to describe the threat to children posed by sexual predators, regardless of the diagnostic or even forensic relevance of the term. These new monsters—pedophiles whose predatory nature needed to be discerned among the otherwise seemingly normal population of white men—created an overtly white focus on the legal category of sex offenders and a covert dragnet gathering people of color. During these years, the number of people arrested, incarcerated, committed, or registered as "sex offenders" grew exponentially, second only to individuals targeted in the War on Drugs. Scholars and pundits agree that the vast expansion of sex offense lawmaking, policing, and punishment contributed centrally to the emergence of the prison-industrial complex and its neoliberal corollary, the carceral state. While a large number of white men were identified and enrolled in the new regime of sex offender management—the cluster of conditions focused on sex offender identification, policing, arrest, conviction, incarceration, civil detention, registration, and notification—they were not necessarily the group disproportionately affected by this procedure. Instead, the new focus on sex offenders against children racialized various subjects (including young people), sometimes as group-differentiated and sometimes as individualized exceptions, through regimes of normalization, abnormalization, and monstrosity refunctioned through the virtual pedophile.

Here we enter this book's focal switch point, when adult-child sexuality was transfigured from its early twentieth-century engagement with normalization into the production of monstrous exceptionalism at the century's end.

Across the 1980s, pedophiles came to inherit the predatory association, slowly sloughing off normalized homosexuals and queers of various stripes. The pedophile as virtual menace would expand vile sovereignty into new domains even as it recentered whiteness as the seeming target of explicitly grotesque uses of power. Yet the analysis of this phenomenon has tended to be largely color-blind or to accept the white frame narrative as a reflection of empirical data or statistical averages. This chapter examines how pedophilia is racialized through the transformation of empirical data and statistical averages into predictive information. The capacity to predict pedophilia was linked to the dissemination of information in a pattern familiar from the broader actuarial turn in psychiatry and policing in this era. Information produced by and through channels of state and disciplinary expertise, however, was declared inadequate when it entered the forensic black hole of pedophilia. This dynamic became part of what James Baldwin (1985, 2) calls the "hygiene of the State," creating a moveable circus whose audience participates in the disqualification of expertise across both psychiatric and state institutions. The criminologists, psychiatrists, police, and Federal Bureau of Investigation (FBI) were there merely to gather the data, denounce the mythology, and declare a public emergency for alert citizens ready to act. The state's power to provide for and protect its subjects shifted to a focus on administering the bare minimum and regularizing the remaining redistribution.

Pedophile versus Predator

At the end of the 1970s, the terrain of sexual politics was still uneven and somewhat heterogeneous. Feminist and LGBT efforts to transform gender and sexual norms, if not normativity itself, unfolded alongside liberal challenges to the Model Penal Code that sought to expand sexual assault beyond forcible rape. There was no single figure for sexual threats to children, despite Anita Bryant's attempt to posit homosexuality as de facto child molestation. Nor was there generalized accord about the relation between morality and danger, or between abnormality and harm. It was in this crucible that the disappearance in 1979 of Etan Patz, whom the *New York Times* ("Police and Neighbors" 1979) described as a six-year-old boy with "blond-hair, blue eyes," from a downtown Manhattan street received national media attention and led to a renewed focus on missing children. Patz's disappearance has been made famous by the milk carton "Have You Seen Me?" campaigns, which conflated noncustodial "child-snatching" associated with contested parental rights and the murderous and sexualized abduction of children by strangers.[2] Meanwhile, the Atlanta child murders of 1979–81 recorded at least twenty-six African American children age seven to seventeen kidnapped and murdered while national attention to Etan Patz's disappearance yielded milk carton activism featuring predominantly white children. The Atlanta cases did eventually receive widespread media attention and critical reflection—most notably, in James Baldwin's *Evidence of Things Not Seen* (1985) and Toni Cade Bambara's *Those Bones Are Not My Child* (1999). But these child abductions and murders were not consistently integrated into the hegemonic political or cultural narrative about missing and murdered children developed during this period.

The 1980s did not offer a single consolidated figure for adult-child sexuality, either. This was a period of uneven struggles over the meaning of a relatively new concept, child sexual abuse, in which various feminist, therapeutic, and forensic actors struggled to define the general vulnerability of children to sexual harm.[3] During the 1980s, incest and intimate caregiver conduct was as much the focus as stranger danger in the form of roaming child molesters. Thus, media focus was distributed across many topics: adult women such as the former Miss America Marilyn Van Derbur and the actor Roseanne Barr brought forward stories of incestuous sexual abuse; entire generations of survivors testified to institutionalized sexual abuse at Native American and Canadian residential schools; cross-regional groups exposed the Catholic Church's practices of covering up and condoning sexual abuse by priests; day-care centers were increasingly accused of widespread sexual abuse; and the unsolved kidnappings and murders of children such as eleven-year-old Adam Walsh in Florida (1981) continued the focus on sexually motivated abduction. Institutions such as the family, the church, and the school were targeted as sites where structural dependence of children on adults could be exploited. But this structural exploitation was not consistently understood as gendered, racialized, or economic in nature, with a dearth of popular analysis on how understaffed, poorly regulated, or overtly punitive institutions intersect forms of oppression with vulnerability to sexual violence.[4]

A growing consensus of single-axis feminist and therapeutic voices saw the exploitation of children as an effect of a universalized age differential, in which children were the subjects of "power" misused for adult pleasure (or adult pleasure misused for power).[5] The recognition that child sexual abuse occurs across cultural and social contexts included representation of diverse children as victims. But this recognition did not necessarily include analysis of the factors that differentiate childhoods and children and expose specific individuals and groups to higher likelihood of sexual harm. In her history of child sexual abuse activism, Nancy Whittier (2009) notes that 1970s–90s media coverage tended to take up activist discourses that best aligned with dominant cultural frameworks. Thus, Whittier (2009, 119) points out that "steady coverage" in African American magazines such as *Jet* and *Ebony*, although illustrated with images of "black models," was similar to the coverage in "white mainstream news journals and magazines" in that "both black and white media took a 'race-neutral' approach." Opposing the structural exceptionalism of childhood as universal status, many feminist activists of the 1970s and 1980s situated sexual harm as part of interlocking systems of oppression expressed through dominant institutions. This included an analysis of, and activism targeting, the relations among institutional and interpersonal forms of harm. But in mainstream translation, even activists' focus on interlocking systems often became more individualized stories of institutional harm, which in turn competed with stories of sexually endangered children who were targeted individually outside the home, school, or church.

In 1980s discourse popularizing images and approaches to child sexual abuse, the individualized children who were used to represent the issue were almost invariably iconized as white. This process is consistent across historical periods, from nineteenth-century sentimentalism's Little Eva to Victorian, and then modern, iterations of Alice's adventures (including those through the midcentury looking glass of Lolita). While the Gilded Age renegades Tom Sawyer and Huck Finn may have yielded to Horatio Alger's bootstrap-pulling lads, the iconization of white gender remained a mainstay of hegemonic discourses of childhood across the nineteenth and twentieth centuries. Childhood iconography certainly exceeds this hegemonic frame, as Robin Bernstein's *Racial Innocence* (2011), Katharine Capshaw's *Civil Rights Childhood* (2014), and routine experience demonstrates. But despite widespread recognition of children as complex subjects of representation and resistance, the white child has been continuously centered in white-dominated hegemonic discourse as representative of age-status determinations as such.[6] The 1980s white child returned to innocence after a 1970s dalliance with experience. In the 1970s, sexually knowing white children appeared more consistently in popular culture, from Jodi Foster in *Taxi Driver* (1976) to Brooke Shields in just about everything (*Pretty Baby* of 1978 through the Calvin Klein commercials of 1981). In the 1980s, these sexually agentic white children were replaced with passive sexual innocents. This included efforts to differentiate white children from sexuality, as in the case of Ryan White as the symbol for "innocent" people diagnosed with HIV/AIDS — the white child once again used to demonize through contrast those attributed immoral agency or psychological unfitness (figured as intravenous drug users or homosexuals).[7]

The year 1989 could be construed as a key moment in this switch point between more heterogeneous approaches to childhood sexual vulnerability and a single-axis focus on children as an undifferentiated (iconized as white) group uniquely vulnerable to sexual harm. The year crystallized a number of threads into pivotal news stories: the so-called Central Park jogger case directed attention once again to the alleged danger of sexually predatory black male youth targeting middle-class white women in public spaces (April); Public Enemy's "Fight the Power" was released as a top single for Spike Lee's summer blockbuster challenging the racialized targeting of black male youth in *Do the Right Thing* (June); Andrew Vachss's "How We Can Fight Child Abuse" announced the dangers of the "predatory pedophile" targeting all children in the Sunday circular *Parade Magazine* (August); ACT UP's action at the New York Stock Exchange redirected public attention from HIV/AIDS as homosexual contagion to the financial politics of "letting die" (September); and the kidnapping of the white, eleven-year-old Jacob Wetterling in Minnesota announced stranger danger as a catastrophic threat to individual children (October).[8] As the 1980s drew to a close, cases such as these were organized to support a highly racialized narrative of stranger danger. In this narrative, familiar figures of sexual danger, such as the white pervert and the black rapist, reappear as lone child predators and juvenile gang members, individualized danger and group-differentiated threat. The former demanded child protection, while the latter denied childhood on the basis of race. Representations of "contagion" meanwhile transfigured the predatory homosexual from child molester into criminal and medical culprit for HIV transmission (later to be named a sex crime), while the child molester was declared a pedophile posing newly monstrous danger.[9]

The construction of this narrative required a great deal of amplification as misdirection. The Central Park Jogger case, in which five teenage boys — four black and one Latino — were convicted without physical evidence, was not taken up by mainstream child protectionists, who focused instead on the disappearance of Jacob Wetterling.[10] Spike Lee's outlier cry against the targeting of black youth by white predators would be taken up as itself a single-axis politics opposing racial terror as gendered violence against boys and men. Meanwhile, Vachss's identification of predatory pedophiles as public enemy number one intersected with changing patterns of demonization and normalization of adult male homosexuality. The ongoing racialization of HIV/AIDS as black and Latinx, as well as heterosexual, men who have sex with men (MSM), or intravenous drug-transmitted, intersected with the whitening of homosexuality as an identity category normalized in contradistinction to sexual predation, either medical or criminal.[11] Vachss's translation of child molesters into predatory pedophiles in this moment captured broader intersectional struggles over the distribution of harm and pleasure. Threats to childhood innocence—by black youth (Central Park), by a racist society (Spike Lee), by predatory pedophiles (Vachss), and by either gay men or a homophobic state (ACT UP)—were amplified and misdirected through the case of Jacob Wetterling as dangers posed by "strangers."

Other approaches to gendered and sexual harm, such as those developed in this period by black feminist and women of color feminist and queer thinkers in particular, were publicly elided in this struggle over new disseminations of common sense. Publications such as the "Combahee River Collective Statement" (1977) and *This Bridge Called My Back* (Moraga and Anzaldúa 1981) did not separate children as a special status group exceptional to the "interlocking systems of oppression" that shape racialized gender and sexuality more broadly.[12] The "Sex Wars" of the mid-1980s also drew attention to dynamic and differential approaches to pleasure and danger within self-defined feminist organizing, including the anthropologist Gayle Rubin's proposal to separate gender from sexuality in "Thinking Sex" (1984).[13] Meanwhile feminist and queer involvement with HIV/AIDS activism across communities fought to address structural disparities in health access linked to sexual harm and pleasure, developing collaborative work that resisted single-axis approaches to medical neglect and state-sanctioned violence. These diverse approaches included anticarceral activists and thinkers staunchly opposed to criminalization and pathologization (Thuma 2019). Yet hegemonic accounts of child endangerment and predation have proved recalcitrant in tokenizing or ignoring this scholarship and activism.

Despite the wider range of cases reported in the 1980s, by the decade's end threats to children were frequently represented as abduction for the purposes of sexual abuse. Mainstream child protectionists were at least somewhat complicit in this shift from a focus on interpersonal and institutional sexual abuse—from parents to state-sanctioned or even state-mandated *parens patriae*—to more hegemonic coverage of stranger danger (Bumiller 2008). The 1990s saw an upsurge in reports of child kidnapping, rape, and murder, with the focus almost exclusively on white children attacked by white men. The most famous of these cases include the kidnapping and murder of twelve-year-old Polly Klaas in California and of seven-year-old Ashley Estell in Texas in 1993; the kidnapping and murder of seven-year-old Megan Kanka in New Jersey in 1994; and the kidnapping and murder of nine-year-old Amber Hagerman in Texas in 1996. These specific cases led to a growing public outcry against the presence of serial child predators motivated by monstrous desires left undiagnosed and underpoliced in the general population. In particular, attention was focused once again on the failures of state systems and disciplinary specialists to protect the general public from known—that is, previously arrested—sexual predators. In 1990, Washington State passed the Community Protection Act, the first statewide sex offender registration policy that included community notification requirements, as well as a Sexually Violent Predators (SVP) Act, which enabled the state to indefinitely institutionalize sex offenders deemed still "dangerous" at the end of their prison sentence. And in Washington State (1993) first, and then in California (1994), "three-strikes" legislation made use of violent sex crimes against children to persuade voters that some convicts could not be reformed. These three-strikes laws used high-profile cases to emphasize the dangers of slippery slope criminality culminating in child rape and murder.[14]

As almost every critic on this topic points out, the focus on adult-child sexuality sought to foment concern almost exclusively in cases featuring white children, while equally sensationalized or politicized cases about children of color were not incorporated into a panic framework (unless those children were considered predators rather than victims). Once again, individualized white children were centered, while sexual and physical violence directed against black, brown, indigenous, and noncitizen children was often reported as if it was a mass-differentiated problem not directly related to individualized sexual predation. Thus, this period could include revelations about institutionalized sexual abuse and physical violence in native boarding schools, the Catholic Church, or sports franchises and yet minimize its significance to generalized sexual threat unless white children were involved. The rape and murder in 1997 of seven-year-old Sherrice Iverson, an African American girl from Los Angeles, by Jeremy Strohmeyer, an eighteen-year-old white tourist from Long Beach, in a public bathroom in Las Vegas is a horrifying case in point. The public rape and murder of Iverson did receive national media coverage, but it was not folded into the hegemonic narrative about sex predators targeting children in public spaces. Critical focus on the devaluing of black girls' lives came primarily from the advocacy of Iverson's mother, Yolanda Manuel, who worked to hold Strohmeyer's friend David Cash Jr. accountable for witnessing the rape and murder of a seven-year-old black girl and doing nothing to stop it.[15] Yolanda Manuel's activism foregrounded wider frameworks of white indifference to black violation and death, which both increased vulnerability of children of color to rape and murder and systematically erased epistemological approaches to more structural and intersectional realities of sexual violence (Meiners 2016).

Across the country, cases focused on the abduction and murder of white children galvanized legislative concern about dangerous sexual predators released from prison without public warning or insufficiently policed in the first place. These cases prompted "apostrophe laws" reelevating deterrence of sex crimes against children to a federal priority: the Jacob Wetterling Act (1994), Megan's Law (1994), Ashley's Laws (1995), the AMBER Alert (1996), the Jessica Lunsford Act (2005), and the Adam Walsh Act (2006). In concert, these acts created federal requirements for state-by-state offender registration and state-by-state public disclosure of data via internet registries; enhanced penalties and registration and notification requirements at the state level; and a national registry supporting uniform state registry and notification systems.[16] This legal apparatus built on the sexual psychopath statutes of the 1930s–60s, some of which were still on the books in this era of resurgent sex crime law, and earlier sex offender registration systems (such as the one instituted in California in 1947). Federal laws memorialized in particular the victims of formerly incarcerated men who kidnapped and murdered children after release. They announced the failure of the state's punishment and parole systems to protect children from sexual predators and introduced new domains of state-based restriction to correct this failure.

In the alchemy of the 1990s, white children turned into state laws, and state laws turned into indefinite realms of surveillance and detention. We see the coordination of surveillance as popular reason across the Jacob Wetterling Act's establishment of sex offender registries, Megan's Law's expansion of community notification about such registries, and the AMBER Alert's heightening of public responsibility to spot sexually endangered children. This legislative cluster introduced constitutional states of exception for the registration, notification, and detention of sex offenders upheld by the U.S. Supreme Court against charges that they violate substantive due process, ex post facto, and double jeopardy.[17] As in earlier phases of child sexual protection, sensationalized cases of rape and murder (kidnapping features highly) led to proclamations of failed policing due to limited data and profile information. Pledges to capture the predator focused on increased data gathering and dissemination as a means to incapacitate potential threats. Only this time, the focus was increasingly on preventative criminalization and punishment. Expanding charges for child pornography possession, not production, attest to the expanded domains of sexual conduct considered violent. And indefinite detention imposed for dangerous abnormality by svp laws expanded prevention to include practices recognizable as punishment in any other regime of penalization.

Diagnosis versus Danger

Certainly in the post-1980s period more sex crimes were defined and more punishment was meted out. This included the creation of sex offender registries to keep track of the whereabouts of those released from prison and community notification programs to publicize the identity, location, and probable threat level of people now moving around in public space. But most novel was the move to administer extrastate penalties and redistrict public space through the identification of potential sex offenses. New svp statutes, like the sexual psychopath laws before them, allowed indefinite civil detention on the basis of future threats anticipated through identification of dangerous mental abnormality. This is what Eric Janus (2006, 107) describes as the Sex Offender Registration and Notification (sorn) groundwork of the "preventative state," which shifts away from criminological approaches to safety and toward actuarial approaches to security. Writing on the svp statutes' shift from crime to risk, Janus explains: "Crime solving begins when a crime is reported. Risk assessment precedes an actual crime." Unlike in the early twentieth-century statutes, institutionalization was not alternative sentencing for a crime but *additional* sentencing to be served after the end of a prison term. This new regime focused on permanent incapacitation as the means and ends of management-focused surveillance. More criminalized acts required greater policing, while increased criminal penalty resulted not just in longer prison sentences but also in postcarceral detention, permanent registration and surveillance, and community notification.[18] Despite the demand for heightened vigilance against child sex predators, however, it was not clear what precisely constituted signs of potential sexual predation.

Enter the pedophile as sexual monster, with his immoral interest in unnatural conduct. Seeking to advance community notification practices in New Jersey, Maureen Kanka connected the loss of her daughter Megan Kanka to the problem of undetected pedophilia: "If we had known there was a pedophile living on our street, my daughter would be alive today" (quoted in Filler 2004, 1545). Maureen Kanka's conditional logic—"if we had known there was a pedophile living on our street"—suggests that knowledge about pedophilia can protect children from sexual predation and its murderous outcomes. But knowing where a pedophile is requires first knowing *what* one is. And this has proved most difficult, and most useful, in enabling pedophilia to name that virtual threat that would join power and panic in an emerging mode of securitization. Pedophilia introduced what Waldram, as noted earlier, calls a "forensic black hole" into the heart of the state and its disciplinary apparatus, where efforts to gather data about the prevalence and location of pedophiles as exceptional monsters enabled a burgeoning bureaucracy of sex offender detection, registration, and detention. State and disciplinary expertise foundered in the face of so-called pedophilic threats to children, in part because of inconsistent description and assessment of pedophilia. Efforts to define it—offered by the American Psychiatric Association, the FBI, and a popular crime novelist—resulted in a expansion of possible meanings that included child molesters, serial predators, and sexual perverts.

Official discourses of the psychiatric and psychological professions have offered a somewhat ambiguous definition of pedophilia as a diagnostic category. Pedophilia officially entered the U.S. psychological lexicon via the Diagnostic and Statistical Manual (DSM)-I in 1952 as a subgroup of paraphilia (sexual psychopathology).[19] Pedophilia was given its own diagnostic category in the DSM-III of 1980, included in the "Paraphilias" section of "Psychosexual Disorders" (261–283) with two diagnostic criteria: "A. The act or fantasy of engaging in sexual activity with prepubertal children is a repeatedly preferred or exclusive method of achieving sexual excitement"; and "B.," which specified the age criteria as a difference of at least 10 years between adult and minor (leaving the defining age difference between minors up to "clinical judgment"). The revised DSM-III-R (1987) included three diagnostic categories that separated out psychological from behavioral criteria:

A. Over a period of at least six months, recurrent intense sexual urges and sexually arousing fantasies involving sexual activity with a prepubescent child or children (generally age 13 years or younger).
B. The person has acted on these urges, or is markedly distressed by them.

    c. The person is at least 16 years old and at least 5 years older than the child or children in A.

Criterion A is psychological, including urges and fantasies; Criterion B is behavioral, including conduct either sexual (acted on these urges) or affective (marked distress). While acts are included within this diagnostic criteria, the preceding "Differential Diagnosis" section suggests that acts alone are not a sufficient criterion: "isolated acts with children do not necessarily warrant the diagnosis of Pedophilia" (285) since they may be merely situational, not psycho-sexual.

    Subsequent revisions to the DSM have struggled to clarify the confusion about the necessary relationship *between* criteria A and B as well as the interpretation of the conjunctions (*and/or*) within each criterion. Does the differential diagnosis commentary mean people diagnosed with pedophilia need to meet the criteria of *both* A (fantasies and urges) *and* B (acts or distress)? Or are there cases where A alone is sufficient? Is the diagnosis defined by psychological states (fantasies and urges) or by conduct (acts or distress)? Or do all psychological states such as fantasies and urges threaten to create conduct in the form of acts or distress? The DSM IV–TR (2000) revised criteria only created more confusion:

    A. Over a period of at least 6 months, recurrent, intense sexually arousing fantasies, sexual urges, or behaviors involving sexual activity with a prepubescent child or children (generally age 13 years or younger).
    B. The person has acted on these urges, or the sexual urges or fantasies cause marked distress or interpersonal difficulty.

The 2000 revision moves fantasies, urges, and behaviors into a single criterion (A), but then changes the conjunction "and" to "or"—fantasies, urges, *or* behaviors—muddling the diagnostic sufficiency of each category within the single criterion (see Hinderliter 2011). Criterion B still includes sexual acts, making it part of both criteria, but has added after the "or" not only psychological distress but "interpersonal difficulty," introducing for the first time the diagnostic relevance of social impairment. Additionally, the difference between "behaviors" (A) and having "acted on these urges" (B) raises more questions about what conduct is included in "behaviors" versus "actions."

    A focused effort to clarify the relations among fantasies/urges (thoughts), behaviors/action (conduct), and distress/difficulty (affect) was undertaken for the DSM-V (2013). This included efforts to separate paraphilias overall into two types: a sexual orientation, preference, or interest (understood as a legitimate if unusual sexuality), and a *disorder* meriting clinical diagnosis (understood as a distressing abnormality).[20] The revised DSM-5 section heading for paraphilias outlines the difference between a paraphilia and a paraphilic disorder: "A *paraphilic disorder* is a paraphilia that is currently causing distress or impairment to the individual or a paraphilia whose satisfaction has entailed personal harm, or risk of harm, to others. A paraphilia is a necessary but not a sufficient condition for having a paraphilic disorder, and a paraphilia by itself does not necessarily justify or require clinical intervention." The diagnostic criteria are made consistent across paraphilic sub-categories, with criterion A of a "qualitative nature" (what Blanchard [2010, 305] calls "signs and symptoms") while criterion B measures "negative consequences" ("distress and impairment" [Blanchard 2010, 305]). The term "diagnosis" should be reserved only for those who meet both criteria A and B; otherwise this interest is merely a paraphilia, not a disorder.

These revisions to the paraphilia section overall introduced questions about the diagnostic classification of pedophilia in particular. Could pedophilia be understood as an acceptable condition if the subject did not experience distress about it or act on it? If so, might pedophilia *disorder* result from distress caused by imposed social impairment, such as stigmatization, incarceration, or registration restrictions, rather than distress over the urges, fantasies, or acts themselves? In addition, are all "behaviors" equal, or is there a difference between viewing child pornography and commiting sexual "acts" with a child? These efforts opened debate about what precisely constituted necessary and/or sufficient criteria for a diagnosis of pedophilia as a problematic condition. In a review leading to revision for DSM-V (2013), the psychiatrist Ray Blanchard (2010, 304) recommends upholding the DSM-IV implication that "There is one sufficient condition for diagnosing pedophilia—a history of sexual acts involving children. That is sufficient because sexual acts satisfy the signs/symptoms criterion and the distress/impairment criterion." Behavioral sufficiency aside, however, "There are no necessary conditions for diagnosing pedophilia. Either fantasies or urges can be used to make the diagnosis, provided they are accompanied by marked distress or inter-personal difficulty" (305). The final entry for Pedophilia Disorder left the criteria fundamentally unrevised (although it removed the language of "interpersonal difficulty" from criterion B). The new entry did however add language to its discussion section about the difference between pedophilia as a "preference" and its disorder. Public outcry against the language of preference (understood to undermine criminal culpability) lead the APA to apologize for what it claimed was a "typographical error" in its first print edition, and to replace "preference" with "interest" in subsequent electronic and print editions.[21]

Confusion about the relation between diagnostic categories and criminal culpability continues to haunt the term however. Blanchard's proposal suggests that someone who commits sexual acts involving children (his proposed threshold was three) provides sufficient grounds for a pedophilia diagnosis, a claim disputed by forensic profiles of child molesters more generally.[22] While sexual acts with children younger than thirteen are always criminalized, police profiles do not assume that all adults who molest children can be diagnosed as pedophiles (or experience distress over sexuality rather than punishment).[23] In the 1980s, the FBI turned to the term "child molesting" to underscore the behavioral rather than the psychological focus of its forensic approach to child sex trafficking and child pornography (Adler 2001). In 1986, a collaboration between the FBI Behavioral Science Unit and the National Center for Missing and Exploited Children led to the publication of the first FBI profiling manual on how to identify a child molester. Special Agent Kenneth V. Lanning's *Child Molesters: A Behavioral Analysis, for Law Enforcement Officers Investigating Cases of Child Sexual Exploitation* (1986, 1) begins by trotting out the stereotypical image of a child molester as a pedophile: "For many, it brings to mind the image of the dirty old man in a wrinkled raincoat hanging around a school playground with a bag of candy, waiting to lure little children."[24] Lanning moves on to debunk this stereotype, pointing out that the actual problem of child molestation exceeds the problem of pedophilia, both as it is culturally imagined and as it is more narrowly defined by the DSM.

In 1986, Lanning could already lament that the use of "pedophile" to denounce anyone who has sex with young people under the age of legal sexual consent: "the media now routinely refer to those who sexually abuse children as *pedophiles*. This term is also being used more and more by law-enforcement personnel. It has even entered their slang usage—with some officers talking about investigating a 'pedo case' or being assigned to a 'pedo squad'" (1). Yet official discourses of the state have been no more clarifying in their effort to separate behavioral clues from psychological symptoms. Lanning points out that a child molester or pornographer or murderer is not necessarily a pedophile; nor is a pedophile necessarily someone who acts on their desires. But, he argues, "many child molesters are, in fact, pedophiles, and many pedophiles are child molesters" (2). Ultimately the "Preferential Child Molester" (7), which should be considered "synonymous with the pedophile who sexually molests or exploits children" (7), is the type most susceptible to criminal profiling. While Lanning insists that this is a forensic and not a diagnostic category, the Preferential Child Molester remains the only one that has discernible behavioral patterns. Yet even the state-of-the-art FBI profiling manual provides a mere taxonomy—or, like the DSM, bullet-point list—of signs that become clues only when they are reassembled in a pattern. Like the diagnostic category of the pedophile, the Preferential Child Molester requires expertise to translate signs into a pattern: "*the indicators alone mean little*. Their significance and weight comes as they are accumulated and come to form a pattern of behavior" (11). Signs as symptoms or clues do not become diagnoses or detections until filtered by psychiatric or forensic experts.[25]

The problem with the DSM diagnosis and FBI profile is not only that they are not internally coherent, but also that they do not regularize knowledge across institutions or expertise. Within one field, the same signs may be construed differently to create a specific pattern, while across fields experts may clash over the diagnostic or forensic interpretation of signs as symptoms or clues. Such signs never clearly collate a pattern that will remain coherent across individual or institutional zones of expertise. In place of internal coherence or institutional regularization, the process I have associated with vile sovereignty works to disqualify and extend the reach of power into new domains of preventative deterrence. In their review of the clinical and criminological literature on pedophilia, Paul Okami and Amy Goldberg (1992, 302) find that "Definitional and Diagnostic Chaos" reigns. While there is technically a difference between "child molestation (a criminal behavior)" and "pedophilia (an anomalous sexual preference)" (299), this difference is not clarified in any sector of expertise.[26] Into the breach created once again by the potential clash of professional expertise, and its self-proclaimed limits in domain and scope, we find new modes of expertise seeming to speak for, if not from, the popular front. The crime novelist, attorney, and child advocate Andrew Vachss provides a central example of new switch points introduced among domains of expertise in this period. Starting in 1989 and continuing through the present, Vachss draws on his multisectoral expertise to write popular articles on the problem of pedophilia for the weekly circular *Parade*. Like the *American Magazine* of Hoover's midcentury calls to arms, *Parade* magazine is a middle-brow publication with a wide reach, delivered to homes as a serial newspaper insert. Unlike Hoover, however, Vachss deliberately positions himself as an expert beyond the confines of either state or disciplinary institutions.

Vachss's article "How We Can Fight Child Abuse" (1989) introduced the term "predatory pedophile" to a popular audience. Coining a term that seemed to appear from within but move beyond psychological or criminological domains, Vachss explained: "Predatory pedophiles are clever, calculating criminals. They stalk their victims with great care, working themselves into positions of trust. They study children as carefully as any psychologist, and their camouflage is our unwillingness to see the shark in our swimming pool." The intelligence of the predatory pedophile—long associated with elite white serial killers or child lovers (think Leopold and Loeb or Humbert Humbert) rather than their degenerate doppelgängers (think Alfred Dyer or Fred Stroble)—is here likened to the criminal cunning of psychology. The difference, although mere camouflage, is a sign the public must learn to read, lest children suffer a fate far worse than drowning. The public, implicitly the parents of the swimming pool set, must become the new experts in child sex predation, lifeguards who glue their eyes to the line between safety and danger. Across his numerous popular articles, Vachss (2002) insists that the pedophile is *both* "sick" *and* "evil," a new kind of predatory monster whose illness is part of his morally bankrupt conduct, not its justification or excuse.

Dangerousness versus Risk

From the late 1980s onward, the pedophile became more broadly associated with a generalized danger posed by all forms of adult-child sexuality, whether psychological, behavioral, or through a conflation of the two. Pedophilia came to operate very much like "mugging" in the United Kingdom of the 1970s, as analyzed by Stuart Hall, Chas Critcher, Tony Jefferson, John Clarke, and Brian Roberts in *Policing the Crisis* (1978). *Policing the Crisis* uses a moral panic frame to argue that the late 1960s U.S. term "mugging" was picked up in the United Kingdom and used to differentiate unnecessarily violent street crime from working-class theft as survival or resistance in the face of scarcity.[27] "Mugging" imported an entire semantic field developed to delegitimize and police urban black agency and social worlds in the United States. The term's uptake in the United Kingdom could then "mobilize *this whole referential context*, with all its associated meanings and connotations" (Hall et al. 1978, 23) without seeming to be overtly racist. By stripping it of its context and importing it into a media environment where the term was unfamiliar, "mugging" could mobilize racist sentiment while claiming to describe a transnational phenomenon of social crisis (rather than a moral panic invented by racial and colonial states).[28] In other words, the label "mugging" enabled a *"signification spiral"* (219), or *"a self-amplifying sequence within the area of signification*: the activity or event with which the signification deals is *escalated* — made to seem more threatening — within the course of the signification itself" (220). Setting the terms for moral panic arguments to follow, Hall and his colleagues argue that this process "has done incalculable harm — raising the wrong things into sensational focus, hiding and mystifying the deeper causes" (1).

Pedophilia operated in a similar fashion in the post-1980s United States. The label imported references to legitimate erotic love of children, from ancient Greece through modern Germany, via the stigmatization of crime and pathology operationalized through the hunt for white sex predators against children in the United States. It "mystif[ied] the deeper causes" of the spectacularization of adult-child sexuality, treated at length in chapter 1, even as it "sensation[alized]" the threat of white stranger danger as a crisis in state power. Yet pedophilia also introduced new mechanisms into the logic of crisis associated with vile sovereignty. Laws against sexually violent predators used popular rather than expert reason to justify new carceral logics focused on predicting danger rather than punishing acts. Specialized laws were introduced enabling police to charge misdemeanor or even felony sex offense for practices such as urinating in public and engaging in consensual sex across the law's bright line of age (the so-called Romeo and Juliet crimes). Enhanced sentencing for charges, longer mandatory sentences, registration for lower-level offenses post-plea or conviction, and expanded notification practices led to spikes in registration as well as rates of incarceration. More and more people took plea bargains to avoid prison time, not understanding the resultant lifetime sexual offender registration, while others bargained to serve time for lower-level offenses to avoid such automatic registration, raising incarceration rates for new categorizations of sexual assault. "Sex offenders" were branded and controlled (required to keep 500–2,500 feet away from zones including schools, parks, playgrounds, and day-care centers), while the general public was put on high alert for the signs of potential child sexual predation all around them.[29]

These laws frequently sounded more like Vachss than the DSM or FBI. The Kansas Sexually Violent Predators (SVP) statutes, for example, justified the indefinite detention of sex offenders who had come to the end of their sentence on the grounds of a seemingly dangerous mental abnormality. Kansas's SVP laws, like similar laws across states, introduced new judicial proceedings to determine whether a person convicted of sex offenses had a "mental abnormality" that was "dangerous" enough to public safety to merit that person's indefinite civil commitment. The problem was that mental abnormality is not a recognized psychological diagnosis, and the assessment of dangerousness lacked scientifically validated protocols. Legislation seemed to be creating its own clinical and criminological categories without relying on the diagnostic expertise of the DSM or the forensic expertise of the FBI. As a result, the signification spiral of pedophilia became the subject of judicial cases bringing psychological and forensic expertise into direct conflict with popular reason and legislative power.

This was the focus of the 1997 U.S. Supreme Court case *Kansas v. Hendricks*, which challenged the Kansas SVP laws over the constitutional rights violated through this redefinition of psychological states relevant to criminal acts.[30] In the state trial, testimony by the state psychiatrist offered a diagnosis of pedophilia, and Leroy Hendricks has been cited in the Supreme Court case as stating he was likely to reoffend under stress.[31] The jury upheld him as a sexually violent offender on the grounds that pedophilia counts as a mental abnormality under the legislative act, with subsequent appeals bringing challenges based on violations of substantive due process, ex post facto, and double jeopardy requirements to the U.S. Supreme Court. The Supreme Court's 5–4 majority opinion (written by Justice Clarence Thomas) upheld the constitutionality of defining mental abnormality legislatively; this denied Hendricks's appeal that only "mental illness" provided grounds for civil commitment and that state legislators lacked the psychiatric authority to determine when "abnormality" was equivalent to illness or posed a threat to public safety. The majority also held that civil commitment in this situation did not violate ex post facto or double jeopardy clauses because the confinement does not satisfy a criminal purpose. Justices William Rhenquist, Sandra Day O'Connor, Antonin Scalia, and Anthony Kennedy joined the majority opinion, with a concurring opinion filed by Justice Kennedy and a dissenting opinion written by Justice Stephen Breyer joined by Justices John Paul Stevens, David Souter, and (in part) Ruth Bader Ginsburg.

The *Hendricks* ruling is important for three reasons: (1) it affirmed legislative rights to define psychological threats to public order (the use of mental abnormality over mental illness); (2) it allowed the civil court system to judge the mental abnormality of convicted or accused sex offenders (after initial risk assessment inside criminal justice systems and institutions); and (3) it used psychiatric expertise to differentiate involuntary civil commitment from "punishment" on the grounds that psychiatric debate could not determine whether people who committed sex offenses could be effectively treated. *Kansas v. Hendricks* found that there was no scientifically validated evidence for psychological diagnosis or treatment of dangerous sexual offenders that courts could currently use to determine public risk, which means that in this instance detention is "*potentially* indefinite." This meant that legislatures could use criteria beyond DSM diagnoses, even as civil courts could use criteria beyond criminal law. The lack of scientific consensus on this type of exceptional sexual predation meant that there was "no object or purpose to punish." Thus, involuntary and indefinite civil commitment *after* completing a prison sentence did not punish for the same crime twice (double jeopardy). And since the scientific community could not agree about whether and how dangerous sexual behavior could be changed — or adapted through psychological treatment — such offenders could be institutionalized without having access to the very treatment programs that allegedly differentiate institutionalization (for treatment) from incarceration (for punishment). This meant that the "indefinite" part of a commitment sentence was pretty definite (forever), since no treatment would be provided to resolve the reason for their institutionalization.

The Hendricks case effectively found that state legislatures could set diagnostic criteria for criminalization of specific acts or even fantasies or desires, expanding at the same time the range of behavior that might be subject to forensic review and sentencing. As Justice Kennedy concurred with the majority, specifically noting the unique role of pedophilia diagnoses within these cases: "Notwithstanding its civil attributes, the practical effect of the Kansas law may be to impose confinement for life. At this stage of medical knowledge, although future treatments cannot be predicted, psychiatrists or other professionals engaged in treating pedophilia may be reluctant to find measurable success in treatment even after a long period and may be unable to predict that no serious danger will come from release of the detainee" [521 U.S. 346 (1997), 372]. Kennedy finds the statute constitutional in relation to pedophilia's treatment lacunae but notes its potential limits if "civil confinement were to become a mechanism for retribution or general deterrence, or if it were shown that mental abnormality is too imprecise a category to offer a solid basis for concluding that civil detention is justified" (373). This was upheld even in Justice Breyer's dissenting opinion, which asserted that "the psychiatric debate, therefore, helps to inform the law by setting the bounds of what is reasonable, but it cannot here decide just how States must write their laws within those bounds" (375). The dissent emphasized that lack of treatment during original time served suggested "treatment was not a particularly important legislative objective" and indicated a punitive objective in subsequent civil commitment.[32]

The American Psychiatric Association (APA) was not happy with the expanded powers granted to legislators—rather than court systems in which individual cases may be shaped by expert testimony—to determine mental "abnormality," "illness" and "dangerousness" assigned to predatory proclivities. The APA volleyed by creating a 181-page task force report titled *Dangerous Sex Offenders* (1999) to assert the priority of psychological expertise in the diagnosis and treatment of adults who have sex with children. The report insisted that medical expertise over diagnostic criteria should not be defined by legislators or applied by forensic scientists in judicial systems. As the report explains, "The sexual predator commitment laws establish a nonmedical definition of what purports to be a clinical condition without regard to scientific and clinical knowledge. In so doing, legislators have used psychiatric commitment to effect nonmedical societal ends that cannot be openly avowed" (174). To rectify this "serious assault on the integrity of psychiatry" (173), the report's "Policy Recommendations" (167) focus primarily on supporting psychiatric research on psychologically motivated sexual offending and rectifying laws that try "to cloak their quasi-punitive intent in the language of medical commitment" (173).

Following the *Hendricks* decision, the *U.S. v. Comstock* (2004) case affirmed the federal government's right to enforce the Adam Walsh Act and its move to civilly commit "dangerous sexual offenders" after federal time served. Across state and federal jurisdictions, dangerous sexual interests could be susceptible to profiled risk and involuntary civil commitment, sometimes even when no sexual acts are charged or convicted.[33] Determining the danger of sexual interests or desires produced new zones of expert disqualification and the expansion of grotesque power's coercive effects. A review essay in *Prison Legal News* reveals ongoing conflicts between "private (non-government) psychologists hired by defense attorneys" and Bureau of Prisons (BOP) or Department of Justice (DOJ) psychologists (Gilna 2012). Private psychologists were far more likely to suggest postprison release; BOP or DOJ psychologists were more likely to suggest postprison civil commitment. The psychologist running the BOP's civil commitment program "acknowledged the inadequacy of the BOP's expertise in this area and said that some prison psychologists had no experience in performing civil commitment certifications." In their study of civil commitment procedures, Megan Testa and Sara G. West (2010, 36) point out that "paraphilia, not otherwise specified" is the most common diagnosis used for civil commitment after pedophilia, indicating "catchall diagnoses" that link psychological assessments to the probability of future harm.[34]

Diagnosing and treating pedophilia more specifically introduces new problems for legal and psychiatric evaluation. Testing an adult's level of sexual arousal by children would typically rely on phallometric or penile plethysmographic procedures, which for pedophilia would require breaking the law prohibiting the possession of child pornography (obviously no actual children can be used). Meanwhile, "treating" pedophilia can involve chemical castration, aversion therapy, and physical castration (at least in Texas) to deter what is presented as inevitably compulsive conduct and unverifiable therapeutic impact (Hall and Hall 2009). Both diagnosis and treatment seem to necessitate a turn to newer actuarial instruments to predict both abnormality and danger. Actuarial instruments such as the Static-99 and Static-2002 or the Violence Risk Scale–Sexual Offender Version (VRS-SO) create new relays among actors and institutions beyond existing legal and psychological expertise.[35] These paraprofessional instruments (they do not have consistent protocols for training and use) focus on taxonomies of static and dynamic factors that predict likely future acts. Through the actuarial turn, the pedophile as sex offender creates a problem best solved by administrative expansion, the deprofessionalization of risk assessment, and the extension of sentencing and surveillance beyond the walls of either prison or clinic (Janus 2006).

Instructions for using the Static-99 claim that it is the most widely used instrument of its kind, effective across race and culture despite its test sample being majority white (Harris et al. 2003, 7).[36] Its wide use has placed it "into the hands of primary service providers such as, parole and probation officers, psychologists, psychometrists and others who use the instrument in applied settings" (9). The Static-99 is designed for use with adult men and evaluates as unchanging or static factors correlated to recidivism: (1) being between age eighteen and twenty-five; (2) not having lived with a partner for two years; (3) having a conviction for nonsexual violence; (4) having a past conviction for nonsexual violence; (5) having prior sex offense convictions; (6) having four or more previous sentencing dates; (7) having noncontact sexual offense convictions; (8) having an unrelated victim; (9) having a stranger victim; (10) having a male victim. The other major actuarial instrument, the VRS-SO, has seven static and seventeen dynamic items correlated to sexual recidivism intended to introduce change into the predictive equation, with dynamic variables correlated to cognitive processing, treatment protocols, and behavioral choices (including "sexually deviant lifestyle" and "intimacy deficits").[37]

Such instruments correlate a series of normative assessments, either fixed or changing, to probable reconviction for a sex offense. The Static-99 includes as higher-risk categories not being in long-term cohabitation, having male nonfamilial victims, having a history of nonsexually based arrests, and, surprisingly, *not* touching a victim (pornography possession or other charges). In her study of Megan's Law, Rose Corrigan (2006) points out that these risk assessment protocols define risk in terms of nonfamilial and same-gender contact. They also predict higher risk for those who have a previous history of arrests or who do not commit contact offenses. These risk factors are correlated to higher rates of rearrest and likelihood of coming into renewed contact with the criminal legal system, rather than rates of repeat sexual offending. Repeat sexual offenses are largely untrackable unless the person committing the offense comes into contact with policing or psychiatric mechanisms. In addition, recidivism rates are not necessarily connected to a new sexual offense, since violations of parole or registry restrictions can result in rearrest. A previous arrest history may indeed be correlated to the likelihood of ongoing contact with police. But that does not necessarily mean it predicts greater likelihood of ongoing sexual offenses. The same caveat holds for those seeking sex with children inside their own family, who are at lower risk of rearrest, perhaps, but not necessarily of reoffending.

When such correlations are used to predict risk, a profile emerges that claims to be able to profile a predator before he strikes again. The phrase "Level 3 sex offender" seems unambiguously to denote a sexually violent predator, but this placement is filtered through the risk assessment process I have just described. The highest-risk sexual predator is assembled from the unmarried, same-gender, or repeat-arrest males and those who have expressed desire for or acted on desires with other people's children. Such actuarial instruments are central to determinations of civil incapacitation, post-release registration, and community notification. Based on these instruments, the legal scholar Daniel Filler suggests that increased racial disparities in registration and notification rolls may in fact be related to higher rates of nonsexual felony history or historically racialized rates of arrest for sexual offenses. In addition, some people facing incarceration have been documented as reporting sexual fantasies or even events that did not happen in order to seek placement in facilities where treatment services are provided, rather than a standard prison where services are limited or nonexistent. Such self-reporting occurs across assessment for prison level, in-prison services, postprison civil commitment, and postprison registration and notification (Waldram 2012). This is often combined with information in the individual's file gathered through criminal conviction, which may include diagnostic findings from very different sources. Its composite places people on a scale of dangerousness to the public not necessarily correlated to actual risk of reoffense and infliction of harm.

This forensic and diagnostic "black hole" led to an increased focus on data-collection as predictive information. As Okami and Goldberg (1992, 321) point out, the lack of scientifically validated information about pedophilia is not proof that such information does not exist. It means that no reliable information exists *yet*. Studies based on carceral populations or in clinical settings do not provide a clear and consistent profile. But it is unclear whether this is due to the "intrinsic heterogeneity of pedophilia or from the absence of even a single investigation to use adequate, potentially representative nonclinical, nonforensic samples of pedophiles for study." More than a decade later, Ryan C. W. Hall and Richard Hall produced similar results. Their 2009 article "A Profile of Pedophilia: Definition, Characteristics of Offenders, Recidivism, Treatment Outcomes, and Forensic Issues" reports once again that a "profile of pedophilia" remains underspecified and without expert consensus not only within but across forensic and diagnostic fields, coming to a crisis in particular where they overlap in judicial cases.[38] A clear profile would continue to elude forensic and diagnostic expertise, but this did not mean that efforts to constitute a profile would stop. Instead, a movement to gather information about pedophiles as preferential sex offenders against children expanded focus on prediction as protection and security as the only means to public safety.

The virtual form of the predatory pedophile was beginning to take shape. It did not yet exist—it never would, of course, but here its existence was just beginning to manifest as an official absence. It was a gap in the record, an absence to be turned into aspirational presence through ever-increasing administrative commitments to information as profiling instrument.[39] In 1997, the same year of the Hendricks case, a key Bureau of Justice Statistics report titled *Sex Offenses and Offenders* provided the first presentation of cross-departmental and integrated field data on sexual assault in the United States. The forty-five-page report, produced by the DOJ statistician Lawrence A. Greenfeld and frequently referred to as the Greenfeld Report, attempts to correlate data from across survey instruments and data collection processes that do not have uniform categories, timelines, samples, or intentions. As Edwin

Sutherland complained in 1950, data collection on sexual offenses did not gather consistent and comparable information differentiating forcible rape, statutory rape, and other sexual offenses, including a variety of child sexual contacts and sexualized noncontact conduct. This situation remained relatively unchanged in 1997, despite the increasing number of data collection instruments introduced by the federal government and various public-private research partnerships, including the FBI Uniform Crime Report (UCR), which has provided voluntarily reported law enforcement data nationally since 1930; the National Incident-Based Reporting System (NIBRS); the National Crime Victimization Survey (NCVS), introduced by the DOJ in 1972; the National Pretrial Reporting Program; the National Judicial Reporting Program; the Survey of Inmates in State Correctional Facilities; and the National Corrections Reporting Program.[40]

The composite data created by such disparate sources is just that: a composition. These numbers do not reveal a clear statistical picture. Noncomparable data collection is listed side by side, without the capacity to analyze points of intersection, overlap, or contradiction. Yet the Greenfeld Report's findings have been summarized and repeated to present a seemingly clear portrait of sex offenses in the United States. Takeaway claims include that "in a high percentage of cases, the victims are children" (Greenfeld 1997, iii) and that "imprisoned violent sex offenders [both rape and sexual assault] were more likely to have been male and white than other violent offenders" (21). More specifically, those imprisoned for "sexual assault" rather than rape "were substantially more likely to be white, and they were nearly 3 years older, on average, at the time of their arrest for the offense. While about half of incarcerated rapists were white, about 3 out of 4 prisoners serving time for sexual assault were white" (21). These findings can seem correlated, since elsewhere in the report "other sexual assault" is listed as including "statutory rape, lewd acts with children, forcible sodomy, fondling, molestation, indecent practices, and other related offenses" (18). And since this report tracks "sexual assaults other than rape" increasing almost 16 percent (second only to drug offenses, at 18 percent) in the "average annual percent change in the number of state prisoners, by type of offense, 1980–94," it might seem to indicate a boom in incarceration rates for white men having sex with children. The report also states that this is "a more rapid rate of change than for any other category of violent crime" (18), clarifying that these white-perpetrated sex crimes against children are categorically violent.

Yet data about offenses against children age twelve and younger—the diagnostic criteria for pedophilia—are not gathered across any of these instruments (and at times data about offenses against children younger than twelve are excluded from collection). The category "children" here appear to be those younger than eighteen, and, as a less circulated finding reports, "The victims of sexual assault, like the offenders, were more likely to have been white than was the case among victims and offenders in rape and other violent crimes" (24). In 1997, the lack of consistent data on the interface among victims, offenders, and the entire policing and justice system creates information whose composite picture is a white sexual offender posing violent danger to white children. Such a picture could just as easily testify to the undervaluing of nonwhite children and the increased likelihood of police and justice involvement for nonwhite men beyond the category of "other sexual assault," as has been demonstrated in the earlier sexual psychopath phase of differential incapacitation. Yet neither of these accounts measures incidence of sexual offense—from violent to noncontact—against children younger than thirteen; nor do they clarify how these informational compositions link to broader concerns about pedophilic threat.

Despite this confusion, the Greenfeld Report is most often cited as the source for the idea that sex offenders are "most likely to be white" and its implied corollary that "in a high percentage of cases" their "victims are children" (Greenfeld Summary).[41] In the original Greenfeld Report, this information is presented in the separately authored foreword as a summary of findings: "The FBI's UCR arrest data, as well as court conviction data and prison admissions data, all point to a sex offender who is older than other violent offenders, generally in his early thirties, and more likely to be white than other violent offenders—characteristics that match the information obtained from victims who describe the offender to interviewers in the National Crime Victimization Survey" (3).[42] While the convicted sex offender is indeed "most likely" to be white—white men are the numerical majority in prison and on registries—the use of empirical citation here suggests that the comparison set with other violent crimes establishes a predictive ratio. The slide positions "violence" as a stable carceral index and legitimates the high rates of sex offender detention (coded as "violent" despite wide-ranging offense categories), as well as the seemingly nonracist or color-blind logic of sex offense law. The statistically paradoxical profile of the white sex offender became part of the pedophilic function: such disqualified information was retooled as an actuarial instrument capable of predicting danger rather than a static data set describing completed crime.

Data versus Information

Beginning in the 1990s federal efforts to correct data deficits have increasingly translated into the mandate of providing the public with predictive information. During that decade, a more general trend in informatics used "big data" to describe emerging modes and rates of data collection, as well as increasingly large sample sizes. Originating in Silicon Graphics Products, the term "big data" was popularized in the 2000s to describe the combination of "computer science and statistics/econometrics" to manage increasing volume, velocity, and variety of data.[43] In the context of criminology, big data sought to manage high volumes of evolving information to quantify more effectively what were seemingly more limited qualitative approaches to diagnosis and detection by turning data collection into risk management. Big data was alleged to enable predictive policing, translating mass data about previous crimes to information able to predict their future (Ferguson 2017). By 2010, predictive policing was analogized to earthquake prediction and other statistical modeling paradigms as lending scientific and technocratic accuracy to the messier edges of detection.[44]

After 2001, the late twentieth-century apparatus for dealing with the pedophilic predator was updated for the new technologies associated with the post-9/11 world. The carceral apparatus shifted more explicitly to work hand in glove with an enhanced security apparatus, leading to crises of U.S. state legitimacy associated with the USA Patriot Act (2001), Homeland Security Act (2002), Guantánamo Bay Detention Camp (2002), Abu Ghraib Prison (2004), WikiLeaks (2006), Chelsea Manning's Iraq War Logs (2010), and Edward Snowden's National Security Agency disclosures (2013). The Bureau of Justice Statistics, along with the Office of Immigration Statistics, was placed within the new Office of Homeland Security. Data collection shifted to target "terrorism" and the threat of the "enemy combatant," or U.S. citizens beyond domestic or international law. In his study of Chicanx carceral politics, Ben Olguín (2010, 3) links the post-9/11 profiling of the "dark-skinned Muslim male" to long-standing Latinx criminalization—specifically, the political and social criminalization of Chicanx and Puerto Rican agency. The alleged threat posed by the virtual predators among these criminalized categories supplemented existing modes of racial profiling with forensic informatics, adding new elements to the assemblage of skin color, visibility, and profiling as a process of racialization (such as "Muslim-looking"). Thus, the post-9/11 detention of U.S. citizens as enemy combatants reproduces earlier racial assemblages of public threat, including "Arab, East Asian, African, African American, (mixed race) Latina/o, and even one White American" (Olguín 2010, 4).[45]

Less widely noted during this period was the federal strengthening of sex offender policing, registration, and detention done under the cover of whiteness. The risk-assessment protocols produced through SORN derived authority through their alleged scientific neutrality, in contrast to the historical forms of racial profiling aligned with criminological data collection (Muhammad 2010). Risk assessment promises to submit *all* populations to a face-neutral scientific evaluation, even as it produces new profiles organized around dynamic risk categories rather than fixed status categories. Describing this shift, Janus (2006, 104, 107) argues that "risk functions in much the same way that race did as a marker of degraded status," and in so doing "the move from guilt to risk entails increased (and qualitatively different) surveillance of citizens." Legislative reforms targeting sex offenders against children were part of a broader security revolution that supplemented the policing of enclosed spaces with the surveillance of open spaces, or publics and publicities. The Adam Walsh Child Protection and Safety Act of 2006, which included the Sex Offender Registration and Notification Act (SORNA), federalized mandated reporting and tied state police block grants to federal compliance. Jurisdictions not compliant with SORNA guidelines for these reporting structures may lose 10 percent of Edward R. Byrne Justice Assistance Grant funds. Yet as of July 2012, only fifteen states, two territories, and twenty-seven federally recognized Indian tribes were in substantial compliance, since compliance is more expensive than the loss of Byrne funding. At the same time, failure to comply has not resulted in the promised financial penalization, creating a system in which federal power is expressed as regulatory rules that are not necessarily enforced (or, perhaps, enforceable).

The cluster of practices often referred to as SORN focuses far more directly on the promise of management to solve the threat posed by child sex predators. In the new century, the call for increased data and profiling, even as data and profiling are proved ineffective, provided the logic for government initiatives aimed at effective management as the mode of predictive protection.[46] Management is not protection; nor is it prediction. It is simply, and overtly, a state of permanent crisis introduced as federal rationality. In the 2000s the capacity to profile, prevent and protect moves more definitively from federal identification and investigation to federal information management and dissemination to broader publics armed by information about dangerous sex predators.[47] These undertakings issue in even more research reports, more public databases, more online curricula allegedly providing crucial information for public safety from sex predators. Yet despite the increased focus on data and information, and the seeming aim for transparency in the presentation of readily available public information, the major data collection services since SORNA are still not correlated to one another in clear ways, leading to ongoing difficulty with gathering composite information relevant to sex offenses and sex offenders against children in particular. At this point, information related to sex offenses and sex offenders gathered by the federal government can be found online through a rather large array of resources, and none of this information is conclusive or even particularly informative.

The problem posed by data compilation for sex offenses against children has not been corrected in the years since the Greenfeld Report of 1997, despite multiple institutions and programs founded and funded to manage this task and multiple laws requiring increased data collection. Federal data gathering has increased significantly since the late 1980s: the National Child Abuse and Neglect Data System (NCANDS) in 1988; the National Incidence Studies of Missing, Abducted, Runaway, and Thrownaway Children (NISMART-1) in 1988, updated as NISMART-2 in 1999; the National Violence against Women Survey of 1995–96; the National College Women Sexual Victimization Study in fall 1996; the Developmental Victimization Survey in 2003; the National Survey of Children's Exposure to Violence (NatSCEV) 2007–2008; the National Intimate Partner and Sexual Violence Survey (NISVS); and the UCR, revised to include broader sexual assault categories in 2013.[48] But the data collected never consolidated a clear empirical picture of sex predators against children.

Efforts to disinter data about sex offenses against children age thirteen and younger have proved equally elusive. David Finkelhor, Heather Hammer, and Andrea J. Sedlak (2008, 2) concluded that "sexual assaults against children are among the most highly publicized serious crimes. However, accurate and complete national estimates of their incidence have not been readily available." Their efforts to reanalyze various federal reports yielded a range of findings that seem to validate claims for statistically significant rates of sexual assault against children, with a subfinding that the racial demographics of victims were roughly proportionate to the general population.[49] Yet these studies have done little to change the circulation of the white sexual offender against white children as the main predator behind the sex offender registries. And they have not rectified the dearth of widely available statistics about rates of sexual abuse. As of 2009, Whittier could still report, "It is impossible to obtain accurate information about the prevalence of child sexual abuse" and "exact figures on the gender of victims are difficult to come by" (Whittier 2009, 215–16).

While state-supported data collection appeared unable to come up with empirical approaches to the statistically announced threat of white sex offenders against children, state-affiliated profiling efforts were equally stymied. In 1986, Lanning's FBI manual *Child Molesters: A Behavioral Analysis* took only forty-three pages to explain the problem of child molestation as criminal behavior and psychological pathology. In 2010, the updated fifth edition of the manual totaled 195 pages without reaching more satisfying conclusions.[50] Pointing out the problem of pedophilia's signifying slide, Lanning (2010, 30) asks readers of his expanded *Child Molesters: A Behavioral Analysis* to face the impossibility of locating a pedophile among the cascading scenes of potential child predation:

> Is an individual with adolescent victims a pedophile? Is everyone using a computer to facilitate having sex with children or trafficking in child pornography a pedophile? Is an adult soliciting sex with adolescents (or law-enforcement officers pretending to be adolescents) that are met online a pedophile? Is a 19-year-old dating a 14-year-old online a pedophile? Is an individual who has both child and adult pornography in his possession or on his computer a pedophile? Is an adult who has sexually explicit images of pubescent 16 year olds a pedophile?

Many people—professional or otherwise—would be hard-pressed to answer these questions. The Center for Sex Offender Management (CSOM), also founded in 1997 through federal justice funding as a clearinghouse for information about sex offenders, includes in its online curriculum "Understanding Sex Offenders" a section on "The Myth of the Sex Offender Profile."[51] This section explains that, while there is no consensus about a sex offender profile, "for a variety of reasons . . . some professionals may believe that if there truly is a profile, we can identify persons who might be at risk of becoming a sex offender and therefore be able to prevent sex offenses from happening to begin with." In other words, predictive profiles continue to circulate as nonvalidated forensic-diagnostic black holes. No one agrees there is one, but no one can say for sure there is not.

Efforts to analyze this information have more recently turned to the registries, since those databases produce SORN data more coherently than other, diverse sources on arrest, charge, plea, conviction, and sentencing data. But it remains extremely difficult to parse the demographics of the registries, particularly as they correlate to registered offense, or even more remotely to rates of arrest, charge, and conviction. Studies of registry and notification data by Filler (2004), Alissa Ackerman and her colleagues (2011), and Trevor Hoppe (2016) emphasize how little is known about racial disparities in SORN, including the disproportionate punishment of African American men through community notification practices that claim to be race-neutral and transparent in their effects. Rueful portions of Filler's (2004, 159) study indicate the problem of turning to data as information about SORN: "I contacted the relevant government agencies of the fifty states and the District of Columbia to determine the number of people subject to notification, with a focus on racial group. This information proved fairly difficult to obtain." Even Ackerman and her colleagues' (2011) data set, produced by scraping the registries directly, do not disclose the full racial disparities introduced through SORN, since data on "Hispanic" or "Latino" demographics are not gathered across jurisdictions. This compounds confusion about black-white per capita comparisons, since Latinx registrants might be listed as white, black, or "other" in many jurisdictions. Categories of "Asian" or "Native" are also inconsistent in their application across jurisdictions, and registries in sovereign tribal reservations or U.S. territories such as Puerto Rico and Guam often are not clearly situated in relation to "national" statistics. And, of course, gender is always registered in a male-female binary, making differential impact on nonbinary or trans-identified people very difficult to assess.

In sum, the elaboration of federally mandated protocols and the use of federal resources to gather data does not lead to greater transparency in either data dissemination or regulatory coherence. Data insufficiency becomes a mode of state reason that centers the state as managerial force even as the state is disqualified from effective action. This leads to a federal discourse of vile sovereignty about its own role: one Office of Sex Offender Sentencing, Monitoring, Apprehending, Registering, and Tracking (SMART; 2012, 4) report on SORN case law states that "the federal government does not register sex offenders," while at the same time noting that it does register offenders through the Department of Defense for military operations personnel (including civilian), the Tribe and Territory Sex Offender Registry System, and the Federal Bureau of Prisons upon prisoner release. The Sex Offender Registration and Notification Act also makes the U.S. Marshals Service the lead investigator for cases of registry violation of federal law, which in turn creates the National Sex Offender Targeting Center. The federal government uses the goal of information management to enable policing powers from which it has formally disqualified itself. You know you are in trouble when the word "hybrid" is used in a government report: "This hybrid framework of state, territorial, tribal, local, and federal laws and policies is the context in which the case law regarding sex offender registration and notification has developed" (4). While the government's own research experts declare its data insufficient for government action, it continues to enact laws with farther-reaching effects. The 2015 SOMAPI Research Brief "Incidence and Prevalence of Sexual Offending (Part I)" (Wiseman 2015, 5) explains that "scientific evidence" is not fully available to ground "sex offender management," which means public and policy discourses should "be tempered" to reflect this limitation.[52] Yet in 2016 the U.S. Congress passed an International Megan's Law to Prevent Child Exploitation and Other Sexual Crimes through Advanced Notification of Traveling Sex Offenders, which includes a unique passport identifier presumably to enhance public security.

The post-2006 SORNA period completes our circuit through late twentieth- and early twenty-first-century transformations in the pedophilic function. The federal government is seemingly centralized in this circuit, developing information and investigative powers for federal authority over public sexual safety. But this authority has little expertise, yielding, paradoxically, power without limits. Between 1989 and 2016 we saw not the complete erasure of diagnostic and criminal distinctions but, once again, a shift in how such distinctions are made, by whom, and to what ends. This proliferation of opinion over expertise emerged alongside changes in the psychiatric and legal professions forged through the search for the predatory pedophile. Frequently, everyone and no one was in charge of making final distinctions, while players such as the APA, the FBI, and the U.S. Supreme Court were enlisted but failed to decisively diagnose and detain this new monster. Thus, we arrive once again at common sense. Common sense is my marker for the collocation of empirical and actuarial failure as incorporated into the promise of populist solutions. Like the racial prerequisite cases of the late nineteenth century, a popular common sense trumps legal or disciplinary criteria (López 1996). This is the way the long-standing racial and colonial state incorporates more recent modes of vile sovereignty: by inducing an animated populace aimed at finding the white pedophile as an ever-present, yet undetectable, presence hiding in the visible signs of statistically normalized whiteness.

THREE

INFORMATIONAL IMAGE AND PROCEDURAL TONE

The equipment-free aspect of reality here has become the
height of artifice; the sight of immediate reality has become
an orchid [*blau blaume*] in the land of technology.
—**WALTER BENJAMIN**, "The Work of Art in the Age of
Mechanical Reproduction"

By the 2010s, the term "pedophile" could be applied to a strikingly wide array
of scenarios. To provide just a few examples from my own experience: walking down a Budapest street in 2014, I see a street-crossing sign whose silhou-
ette of an adult figure holding the hand of a child has "PEDO" scrawled across
it (presumably making fun of securitizing panic, but just as possibly scrawled
in public warning). In a cab in central Pennsylvania in 2015, the driver warns
me that taking Uber is dangerous because its unvetted driver might be a pedophile (presumably referencing security issues of nonunionization, but seemingly directed at a middle-age woman traveling alone). Tuning in belatedly
to the high-brow television serial *Six Feet Under* in 2016, I hear a season one
(2001) Billy Chenowith turn down an offer to hang out with Claire Fisher by
saying, "Come on, Claire, you're what? Sixteen? What do you think I am, a
pedophile?" (since he previously instigated a make-out session, he presumably references pedophile panic ironically).[1] This deliberately random sample
is meant to refresh readers' own memories of the pedophilic signs all around
them, which have become so ubiquitous that they summon a rather stunning
repertoire of signifieds within and about a security-era common sense. By the

2010s, the breakout signs of the 1980s had been incorporated into the background noise of virtual pedophilia. The term "pedophile" could signify either sexual danger or sex panic, immoral sex or sexual moralism—literally, sound and fury, signifying just about anything. Pedophilia had become a perfect vehicle for vile sovereignty to enter the realm of cultural aesthetics.[2]

Across the 1990s and 2000s, members of the general public were increasingly warned to be on the lookout for predatory pedophiles. But clear and consistent information about how to spot them proved hard to find. One simple example can be found in an online search for information about pedophilia and sexual predation. Web sleuths interested in government-certified data might consult the Center for Sex Offender Management's "CSOM Fact Sheet: What You Need to Know about Sex Offenders" (2008). Or they might consult the U.S. Department of Justice's National Sex Offender Public Website, which, under the heading "Education & Prevention," includes pages titled "Facts and Statistics" and "Common Questions," or the Office of Justice Programs' Sexual Assault Response Team (SART) Toolkit (Office of Sex Offender Sentencing, Monitoring, Apprehending, Registering, and Tracking 2018a, 2018b). Each of these sites includes a breakdown of "sex offender" data—not only numerical and statistical, but also profile-based—and correctives to common misconceptions about people who seek sex with children. Key takeaways are that no clear consensus on the threat exists, but people identified as sexual offenders on the whole are not mentally ill, may have high levels of alcohol use, and are often white men. The National Center for Missing and Exploited Children (NCMEC 2014) explains, for example, that "contrary to popular belief, most online predators are not pedophiles. Pedophiles target pre-pubescent children, while online predators typically target adolescents who engage in risky online behavior."

Yet this pronouncement that pedophiles are not necessarily predators, and vice versa, is frequently followed by tips on how to spot this somewhat unspecified threat. This is particularly true of nongovernment websites. The Religion News Service warned in 2014, "Unfortunately, many Christians still believe that they can spot a child molester simply by appearance. We are most often on the lookout for the 'creepy looking' guy who hangs out at the park or outside of the school" (Tchividjain 2014). It then went on to list five "common behavioral characteristics of child sexual offenders." Dr. Phil weighed in on his website in 2005, offering "Sexual Predator Warning Signs" from Dr. Frank Lawlis that correlate deficient intimacy skills with a sexual turn to children.[3] His site also culminates in a section titled "Tips on Spotting a Sexual Predator." And in 2018, the Child Lures Prevention website offered "A Profile of the Child Molester," only to explain that the author "found child molesters and abductors to be a diverse group that possesses no tidy criminal profile and does not discriminate by race, gender, class or age" (Wooden 2018). This nonprofile is then followed by the question, "How many child molesters live in the United States?" Answer: "Approximately 400,000 convicted pedophiles currently reside in the United States, according to Department of Justice estimates."[4] There are, of course, no statistics on "convicted pedophiles," since "convicted" is a nonpsychological criminal category and "pedophile" is a noncriminalized psychological category. Further, even if they existed, such statistics would not tell us much about "child molesters" as a general, nonincarcerated group.

Across these sites, a common pattern emerges: (1) a sexual threat is not visually apparent, despite stereotypes about creepy men; (2) a sexual threat exists all around us and must be discerned for self-protection; and (3) the profile of this sexual threat clusters behavior and situations that could include virtually anyone. Almost nowhere on such sites does an image appear depicting an actual pedophile. The shadowy figures of J. Edgar Hoover's midcentury fire fanning are no clearer in their twenty-first-century profiles: a pant leg, a street sign, or clip art most often stand in for distinct or recognizable visages as visual signs. In the past two decades, the "pedophile" has signaled a sexual insecurity that could not be represented in familiar ways. Such a virtual threat could be made visible only by partnering emergent information technologies with residual modes of representation. Through this process, the virtual pedophile became part of a broader cultural logic of informational prophylaxis. Informational prophylaxis names the process whereby temporal diffusion and spatial indeterminacy are seemingly resolved by more and better information. Information can be used to target potential rather than probable dangers — dangers that are not easily imagined and therefore test the bounds of representation. This required the production of analog images that were always not quite the real thing: the image remains distinct from the predator portrayed, the pedophile on-screen only analogous to the monster still at large. Analog images could be produced through media such as television or film to conjure the pedophile on-screen through the superimposition of information and image. The pedophile appeared on-screen when information unveiled a virtual predator among the normal white men.

This chapter turns to television programming to explore how this interpretive black hole — where a proliferation of information meets a paucity of visual signs — popularized the virtual profile of the predatory pedophile.[5] I focus on Dick Wolf's *Law and Order: Special Victims Unit,* among other programs, to explore how serial television shows sought to make the pedophile visible as a white male predator on-screen. These shows produced the pedophile as a virtual predator whose unnaturally normal sexuality must be made to appear on-screen by mapping information onto the performances of a range of white men who may or may not be sexual predators. Individual shows thematized the limited capacity of police and psychological professionals on-screen while providing a pedagogy in the information identifying the predatory profile in unnaturally normal signs. Long-running television programs helped compose the white pedophile as a threshold of the visible world (Silverman 1995), a composition of static and dynamic signs that could actualize the otherwise always only potential child sex predator before a mass audience. The pedophile, in other words, became a sign in search of an audience.

While "pedophile" remained a term without consensus across scientific, forensic, and judicial protocols, the virtual pedophile took center stage in the 1990s–2010s as a primary villain in the court of popular opinion. The virtual pedophile performed a particular function in this cultural domain. First, it combined figure and mechanism to remediate predictive information as technological image. Second, it produced a procedural tone that transformed informational lacunae into visual aura. Predictive information promised to make the pedophile visible to attentive viewers. By matching information about pedophiles to the on-screen images of white men, viewers might learn to spot the pedophile in an otherwise "normal" lineup. But the predictive capacities of information are, as I have argued, astoundingly limited. They promise to make signs such as smiling or being friendly into behavioral clues and psychological symptoms, without clarifying how, precisely, cultural sign becomes forensic or diagnostic signified. The potential presence of the pedophile exists in the signs of successful normalcy, which required the audience to decipher what Walter Benjamin (1969, 221) theorized as the "aura" of authenticity that accrues to explicitly unnatural objects in the age of art's technological reproducibility. Only when audiences could properly read the pedophilic signs could clues and symptoms be differentiated from symbols and other aesthetic devices. Audience "apperception" (235), to develop Benjamin's term, was trained to exhume evidence from the aura produced through visible surfaces of reality's representation, or to see the virtual pedophile as an orchid in the land of technology. Through this process, the pedophilic function aestheticized information and taught audiences to secure increasingly virtual spaces and times through the exercise of forensic common sense.

The newly popular crime procedural of the 1990s and 2000s helped transform relations between representation and reality by making audience into auteur in unfamiliar ways. These programs featured transformations in forensic technologies, from mug shot and fingerprint identification to DNA profiling and searchable multijurisdictional criminal databases.[6] At the same time, they drew attention to and remediated existing visual technologies, from handheld video-recording devices and computer nonlinear video editing systems to new digital platforms. Frequently, declarations about new technologies announced expanded capacities to increase security and capture danger before it happened: in the virtual realm. In the search for pedophilic predators, in particular, the audience functioned as the fourth wall of forensic prediction. On-screen detectives and psychologists often bemoaned their inability to prevent or detect pedophilic threats. By watching expert efforts meet their limit, the audience was positioned to take up those experts' thematically disqualified role of interpreter capable of reading the signs of virtual danger. But the audience, too, needed training to see clue and symptom among normal signs. This required the production of a procedural tone in which the virtual pedophile's aura of unnatural nature could be detected in the surface signs of normalcy. Proper sleuthing required detectives trained in aesthetic interpretation: they needed to be able to engage a work of art to differentiate aesthetic effect from analogic threat.

We can return to 1989 once again to reenter this genealogy with the pedophile's televisual transformation from abnormal predator into virtual monster. The virtualization of the pedophile coincided with larger changes in the television industry and the rise of reality-based serial programming.[7] The year 1989 was the one in which the reality television series *Cops* began its now twenty-six-year run, a format that was first attributed to the writers' strike of 1988 but rapidly grew in popularity, as demonstrated by long-lasting reality-based crime serials such as *America's Most Wanted* (1988–2012) and *Cops* (1989–).[8] Even as the reality-TV circuit gained viewers and sponsors, the procedural *Law and Order*, produced by Dick Wolf, began its twenty-year run (1990–), to be followed by the spinoffs *Special Victims Unit* (*SVU* [1999–]), *Criminal Intent* (2001–11), *LA*, and *Trial by Jury*. The *Law and Order* spinoffs were followed by the Jerry Bruckheimer *CSI: Crime Scene Investigation* (2000–15) machine—*CSI: Miami*, *CSI: New York*, *Cold Case*, *Without a Trace*—

whose forensic procedurals took off in the new millennium alongside a growing number of programs about profilers psychological and psychic (*Criminal Minds*, *The Mentalist*, *Profiler*, *Medium*, and the list goes on). The boom in network TV program franchises spanning multiple decades (*ncis* could be added here) competed with new cable programming that pushed the envelope of reality and genre TV. Programs such as HBO's first television serial drama production, *Oz* (1997–2003), and its later critical success, *The Wire* (2002–2008), promised edgier, more naturalistic fare in more aestheticized and cinematographic formats than network TV had previously offered (Mittell 2015).

The crime procedural serials that came to dominate the early 2000s were definitionally genre television, even as they introduced new elements to the crime procedural through a focus on changing technologies.[9] In his study *Genre and Television* (2004), Jason Mittell defines television genres through the program text, as well as "across the cultural realms of media industries, audiences, policy, critics, and historical contexts" (ix), arguing that television genre studies must treat "specific industry and audience practices unique to television (such as scheduling decisions, commonplace serialization, habitual viewing, and channel segmentation)" (1).[10] The seeming ubiquity of the *Law and Order* franchise is linked to its subsidization by the New York State Film Tax Credit Program, started in the early 2000s and expanded in 2008 to its current level of $420 million, covering up to 30 percent of the production budget. *Law and Order: svu* has also drawn funding from the Gates Foundation to embed social messaging in shows that reach a wide and varied audience.[11] *Law and Order: svu* is, among the franchises, the program that offers the most consistent focus on pedophilic predators, as well as the most developed focus on vile sovereignty and its shift to popular detection. While *Law and Order* and *csi: Crime Scene Investigation* introduced child sex predators routinely enough, *Law and Order: svu* offers the most single-minded focus on sex crimes over its sixteen-year run from 1999 to the present (2020).

This chapter develops its argument by treating a small selection of program texts or episodes, departing from Mittell and other media scholars' call to treat "specific industry and audience practices," as well as textual analysis. These episodes are chosen to provide an introduction to the *svu* genre (episode 1.1, "Payback" [1999]); a cross-section of its most common tropes in depicting pedophilic suspects (1.11, "Bad Blood" [2000]; 4.6, "Angels" [2002]; 5.19, "Sick" [2004]; 6.11, "Contagious" [2005]; 7.7, "Name" [2005]; 7.21, "Web" [2006]; 11.5, "Hardwired" [2009]; and 13.2, "Personal Fouls" [2011]); an extended reading of an exemplary pedophile episode (10.2, "Confession" [2008]); and a closing gloss of the genre's recognition of its racial profiling (14.5, "Manhattan Vigil" [2012]).[12] Treating these episodes allows me to demonstrate the generic function of pedophilia across episodes and explore this function's effects in a close reading of a single show. My argument is that the procedural tone produced by the search for the virtual pedophile is itself an effect of *"television genre"* (Mittell 2004, 18). Through its mediation by television genre, virtual pedophilia becomes what Mittell calls "a cultural category, constituted by the generic discourses that posit definitions, interpretations, and evaluations" (18). The appearance of the pedophile on-screen relies on genre coding to train the audience in emerging modes of common sense. Watching the detectives on-screen trains audiences in detection of the screen, allowing them to recognize the pedophilic function as "the culturally specific interplay of texts, audiences, producers, and contexts" (Mittell 2004, 118). The key effect I study here is a procedural tone encoded within the program texts themselves. This procedural tone trains audiences to recognize and negotiate the relations between (1) psycho-forensic *definitions* and (2) aesthetic *interpretations*, to arrive at (3) affective *evaluations* of pedophilic performance from among its virtual avatars. That such performance is always itself only an analog, never the real thing, becomes a mechanism for serial reproduction associated with the longest-running program in the franchise.

The *Law and Order* franchise overall is known for its "ripped from the headlines" sourcing and production, as well as its overt genre coding. From its Dragnet-style opening voice-over to its sonic chapter breaks (bum-bum), each program in the franchise announces its formula and stays true to it. Each episode plays on a scale set to the same basic pitch and score. A *Law and Order* satire produced by Robot Chicken on *Adult Swim* captures this formula well, condensing a one-hour episode into four minutes and replacing all characters with animated chickens who modulate the same sound, "Bock Ba-Cock," to evoke various stock attitudes: accusation, menace, solicitation, cajoling, threat. The scenes move quickly from crime to street to station interviews to courtroom, conveying an entire episode's arc without words. While this parody reduces genre conventions to caricature, it also points out the centrality of caricature to *Law and Order*'s particular play on genre. The programs produce a series of recognizable and repeated attitudes as set pieces against which the particularities of detection will play out. Thereby, genre is encapsulated as repeated formal qualities, sequence, chapter, and arc, but also as performed attitudes or acted feelings.

Law and Order: svu follows the same generic format, although it relies less heavily on the courtroom sequence to enable a more extended focus on the difficulties of identifying sex predators. Its opening voice-over intones: "In the criminal justice system, sexually based offenses are considered especially heinous. In New York City, the dedicated detectives who investigate these vicious felonies are members of an elite squad known as the Special Victims Unit. These are their stories." *Special Victims Unit* in particular plays up its sensational formula and incorporates it routinely as irony in and of the show itself. As an *Entertainment Weekly* article in 2012 quipped about the three-hundredth episode of the series: "svu has ridiculosity running through its very veins, which may be the reason the series has survived so long" (Busis 2012). Critics have linked the show's success to its ability to exploit the seeming contraction between sincerity and sensationalism. As Ian Barnard (2017, 8) points out, "The show's narratives themselves seem to be richly aware of these contradictions, or at least to activate them."[13] In his essay "E Unibus Pluram" (1993), David Foster Wallace famously asserts that television of this period incorporates postmodern aesthetics as a production strategy. While postmodern aesthetics allegedly flatten the tonal politics of irony as a mode of interruption (parody) and render it indistinguishable from its deadpan analogs in direct utterance (pastiche), television programming, Foster Wallace argues, reaches its widest audiences by reproducing irony as an overt production strategy. Embedded irony at the level of production and programming induces positive audience evaluation; the audience is in on the joke of television's program era.

In the case of svu's specific mode of genre television, the episodes offer moments of performed irony about the show's genre even as irony is played straight within the program text. The very first episode of svu, "Payback," opens with a cigar joke: arriving on the scene of a white male victim, mid-thirties, dead of stab wounds, Detective Elliot Stabler (Christopher Meloni) asks why Special Victims has been called, since stabbing does not always specify sex. "Sometimes a cigar is just a cigar," Elliot jokes, to which the beat cop replies, "Well, someone sliced off his cigar, that specific enough for you?"[14] This establishing episode, where we first meet the central police detectives, continually alludes to various regimes of definition (forensics/diagnostics) and interpretation (aesthetics) associated with sexual signs. In the procedural realm, the signs indicate symptom (illness) or clue (crime). In the aesthetic realm, the signs signify sincerity (melodrama) or irony (satire). Thus, the episode introduces its signature mix of such signs by presenting some backstory on Detective Stabler through his testimony at the trial of a white flasher in his mid-thirties. The accused flasher's defense attorney accuses Stabler of being a prude, the "Kenneth Starr of the New York police force." Stabler retorts with angry sincerity that sex crimes are no joke, only to joke moments later about the defendant's "shortcomings" as a flasher. This provokes the alleged flasher to take out his penis to prove Stabler wrong, and finis! Trial over.

What *Entertainment Tonight* calls "ridiculosity" properly captures what Thomas Pynchon (1966, 124) calls "that high magic to low puns" as itself a kind of postmodern evidence. Only here what counts as evidence will play across the terrain of the referentially real and the ostensibly figurative: the actual penis, the verbal pun. Across the regimes of definition and interpretation featured on the show, svu draws together referents and signifieds from Freud to Starr to collapse the distance between symptoms and clues, melodrama and satire. This ridiculosity is part of the bizarre camp of the show, which manages to maintain its sensational realism by incorporating irony as distance between the detectives' on-screen performance of "real" (character persona) and "play-acted" (interrogation persona) sleuthing. In the first instance, actors such as Mariska Hargitay and Christopher Meloni play the characters Detective Olivia Benson and Detective Elliot Stabler as realistically as possible, where realism is defined by the generic repetition of signature personality traits. In the second instance, actors Hargitay and Meloni play Detectives Benson and Stabler putting aside their diegetically "real" on-screen personalities to playact an outsize "detective" role within the plot, most often to intimidate suspects. This includes on-screen performances of good cop/bad cop (or, more accurately, sad cop/mad cop) for a camera that defines crime procedural as surveillance.

Most episodes feature some combination of the main four detectives in their diegetically "real" on-screen personalities—Munch (Richard Belzer), the old-fashioned conspiracy theorist; Benson, the victim-detective; Stabler, the angry man of reason; Tutuola (Ice-T), the blunt truth teller—alongside their on-screen performances as detectives playing detectives for an audience of witnesses and suspects. The aestheticization of crime procedure is enabled by this acknowledged split between performed sincerity (diegetic personality) and performative irony (detective role play). The performance of seemingly "real" feelings that move the show forward (diegetic or thematized as part of the plot) are offered up as pleasing repetition of generic formulas distributed across detectives (their character traits). So, too, the performance of "play-acted" feelings that each detective offers when playing the on-screen role of stereotypical cop interrogating a suspect. Both of these performances, however, are differentiated from those suspect feelings performed by the rotating cast of white men portraying potential pedophiles. Watching the white men who play suspected pedophiles, audiences are unable to quickly discern whether their performed feelings are diegetically authentic or suspiciously performative. Defining their feelings as clues or symptoms requires interpreting their performance as sincere or ironic. Audiences are tasked with using the genre formula to learn how to spot the difference between acting like a normal white man (the actor playing a nonpedophile) and acting normal, as a white man (the actor playing a pedophile).

Learning to spot the difference between actors playing a nonpedophile versus a pedophile depends on the audience's ability to understand the difference between signs as signifiers (aesthetic interpretation) and signs as clues/symptoms (forensic/diagnostic definition). This pedagogy is delivered through the genre itself, where audiences are trained in serial format to recognize the difference between the ironic performativity thematized as dramatic sleuthing and the performance of acted feelings as if actual. The first level of audience response requires interpretation. The detective/actors are part of a work of art, however lowbrow, who take off the mask of cop performed for suspects to deliver information about pedophilia directly to the audience. The audience must learn how to read their often out-sized performance as cops in relation to their calm delivery of information about pedophilia. The second level of audience response requires evaluation: they must be able to evaluate guest actor performances in relation to the information delivered within the genre. This requires viewers to assess a suspect/actor's performance of feelings in relation to the aesthetic/information split produced by the main characters of the show. The audience, in other words, must be able to distinguish among an aesthetic sign (signifier), a forensic/diagnostic one (clue or symptom), and an informational one (code). Only when audiences can assign signifieds to signs across these domains can they translate an on-screen suspect into the analog of the show's pedophilic information.

This pedagogy could be distilled down into training on the differences among signs as image, analog, and affect. "Payback," for example, includes an early scene in which Captain Cragen (Dann Florek) looks at a cab driver's hack license through a magnifying glass to assess its authenticity (figure 3.1). The camera records his face through the looking glass, magnifying one eye grotesquely superimposed over its smaller doppelgänger. First, the eye amplifies the gaze of the camera through the look of the detective, creating an analog for audience attachment to the aesthetic distance enabled by the show. Then Stabler mockingly says, "Police work." Stabler's joke seemingly introduces an ironic distance on the aesthetics of the procedural. Stabler's humor

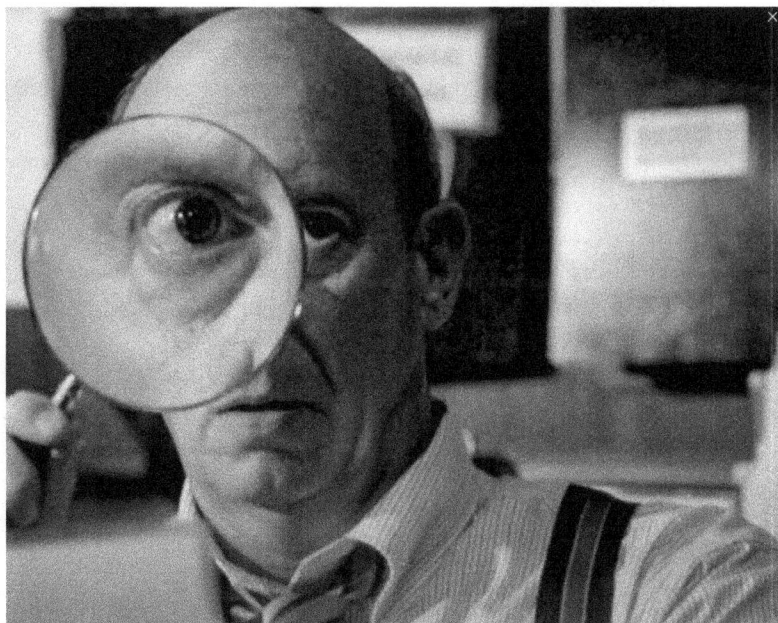

FIGURE 3.1 Captain Cragen through the spyglass, "Payback," *Law and Order: svu* (dir. Jean de Segonzac), September 20, 1999, Wolf Films Studios, nbc.

is immediately undercut, however, as the superintendent's old-fashioned technique reveals seams in the driver's license that are not discernible to the naked eye. It is a fake, we find, through ridiculous and ridiculed procedures. This is the informational reveal of the show's camp ridiculosity: even as aesthetic detection is subject to disqualification, its informational codes are confirmed as evidence of an extratextual truth. Some on-screen images have signifieds in the aesthetic realm (the pointedly dated magnifying glass as signifier of detective work). Some are meant to be analogs for off-screen realities (the "fact" of dangerous deception by criminals signaled by the forged license). The audience must learn to tell the difference.

This involves the audience in the pedagogy of the svu genre. Audiences must learn to recognize the show's signifiers of aestheticization: svu's knowing jokes about its own campiness. And they must be able to differentiate this aesthetic distance from the show's codes of proximity: svu's simultaneous seriousness regarding its subject matter. In other words, audiences must learn to interpret the signifiers of pedophilia's artwork in order to decode its correlated information about pedophilia's reality. This is an affective pedagogy through which audiences supplement the limited forensic technologies both within and of the show itself. "Payback" for example also dramatizes the overall low-tech apparatus featured in the show, as well as the difference between the mise-en-scène and the television camera. *Special Victims Unit* is remarkably low tech, featuring verbal reports from the medical examiner, an evidence board composed of photographs and handwritten notes, and video surveillance reviewed on a large-screen TV. The detectives are the technology—much like the magnified eye jokingly representing the human body as forensic prosthesis. The revelation enabled through ironic distance collapsed into proximate information is that, yes, humans are the best technology. In-person observation and gut feeling are the detectives' primary technologies, in particular in their encounters with potential pedophiles. The actors' on-screen performance of failed detection finds its analogs, figured here in the actual magnifying glass magnified across scenes as the failed effects of both aesthetics and information. This combination situates audience affect as the real analog to be amplified across scenes and episodes of the serial. The viewer takes up the affective charge of exercising that human technology—forensic common sense—produced by what I call the show's procedural tone.

Procedural Tone

Procedural tone names the aesthetic function of virtual pedophilia across television crime procedurals of this era.[15] Procedural tone is a subset of what Mittell (2015, 42, 44) calls the "operational aesthetic," developing the art historian Neil Harris's concept describing the pleasures of seeing how machines work to discuss television programs in which "we watch the process of narration as a machine rather than engaging in its diegesis." In what Mittell calls "Complex TV," exemplified in more recent serials such as *Lost*, *The Sopranos*, and *The Wire*, the operational aesthetic names the spectacle of technological reproducibility as a high production value.[16] One key example of this is what he calls the "*narrative special effect*," a "device" that creates "moments of spectacle push[ing] the operational aesthetic to the foreground" (43). Irony about television production and technological reproducibility becomes a key feature of the "complex" as high-value programming. *Special Victims Unit* does not achieve this kind of elite status. Quite the contrary, in fact. It operationalizes instead an aesthetic of unresolved contradiction: sincerity and sensationalism seem to compete without narrative pause for metareflection. In place of such metareflexive "complexity," svu offers common sense: audience affect closes the distance between contradictory poles by *feeling* the pedophile haunting screen and street.

The tonal affects and effects of programs presenting pedophilic predators hail audience common sense as a new mode of forensic prediction. Here I borrow from Sianne Ngai's (2005, 43) approach to tone as a "global and hyper-relational concept of *feeling* that encompasses attitude," where textual strategies meet audience reaction. Tone, in other words, is not merely a formal quality of texts but a "co-assembling" of visceral sensations, cognitive significations, and relational attachments constituted between text and audience (52).[17] The procedural tone I study here resembles what Homay King (2004, 109) calls "free indirect affect," a strategy allowing the cinematic text as a whole to take on the affective charge of specific analogs or images that belong seemingly to neither specific characters nor the cinematic apparatus. In King's example, the director Pier Paolo Pasolini creates "decentered structures of enunciation" (107) by splitting the camera's focus from the seeming source of a feeling. This creates a "crisis of attribution" for feelings generated by the cinematic text itself. The distance between visual shot and its alleged affective analog make the affect itself float, an effect of film's overt technological reproducibility (cutting referent from image) (109). The free indirect affect produced by svu's procedural tone is closer to what Ngai calls "virtual feeling," a feeling that no one within the text directly feels but on which the text seems to run. This tone exceeds free indirect affect, with its indirection quotation that is still part of, yet distinct from, filmic enunciation, to create a broader atmosphere that seems to exceed the text itself. Thus, in Ngai's (2005, 69, 76) words, the text "*runs on a feeling that no one actually feels*," creating "tone" as "a feeling which is perceived rather than felt and whose very *nonfeltness* is perceived."

Processed through the pedophilic function, such virtual feeling runs svu's procedural tone: audience members can *feel* the presence of the pedophile, even though they cannot easily locate him in a visual analog. This requires audiences to use their training in svu's own, ridiculous failures to learn how to decode the on-screen presence of white men for signs of potential pedophilia. On-screen images might be read as clue (criminology), symptom (diagnostics), or signifier (aesthetics). Only by learning how to match a specific code (information) to the on-screen image would the pedophile reveal himself as the potential lurking in the white norms of everyman. The seriality of pedophilic programming routes aesthetic signifiers through informational code in order to constantly reproduce virtual pedophilia as haunting white male presence on-screen. Each white actor introduces the specter of potential pedophilia; each scene amplifies specific analogs as clues or symptoms; and each episode magnifies the behavioral assemblage required to catch the predator in his acts. Yet every time an actual pedophile is revealed among the cast of white male actors at episode's end, we return immediately to the start. We are reminded that, because he is an actor, the white man on-screen is always only "acting" like a pedophile, performing signs for affective evaluation, thereby reintroducing the analogic limit to actual capture. And so the hunt for the virtual predator begins anew.

While the hunt for pedophilic predators is a routine feature of *Law and Order: svu*, the show repeatedly reminds viewers it has no clear view of its target. The show's own contradictions are captured in the *svu* online fan wiki, which, as of January 2019, lists sixty-six characters as "pedophiles" under a two-paragraph definition exemplifying the vile sovereignty studied in chapter 2.[18] The first paragraph provides a nearly verbatim Diagnostic and Statistical Manual of Mental Disorders (DSM) psychological diagnosis, including persistent sexual fantasies or desires for six months. The second includes a summary of all of the possible behaviors that constitute sex crime, including "characters who have committed child molestation, child rape, or [were] in possession of, produced, or distributed child pornography, etc." The parataxis of the DSM bullet points is replicated alongside the Federal Bureau of Investigation's similarly uncorrelated behavioral lists. A pedophile is someone with a desire or a behavior, as the show's detective characters routinely debate. Opportunities to test this definition come in various forms. Episodes of *svu* include international adult-child sex tourism; child sex trafficking and slavery; philanthropy-enabled child molestation; online child pornography; self-identified pedophile rings; stepfathers marrying to gain sexual access to children; advocacy groups for pedophiles; and more than one sexually abusive coach, alongside the occasional stranger abduction presumably for the purpose of child sexual abuse. Here I note key tropes as they appear in six sample episodes drawn from across the series.

Throughout *svu*, child sexual abuse is almost always presented as deliberate predation rather than opportunistic molestation. Even those who know their victims seem to have chosen intimacy as a volitional path toward child sexual abuse (women with young children living in shelters or in rehab are the "perfect family for a pedophile," we are told in "Hardwired").[19] All predators, potential and actual, are called pedophiles by characters within the show. The episode "Web" calls men who view a porn site run by a male teenager "his pedophile subscribers," while "Sick" jokes "pervert ahoy" about a billionaire's treasure room, before calling him at episode's end the "Teflon pedophile."[20] But despite the serial use of "pedophile" to define potential predators, the criteria for identifying a pedophile are debated over the course of many episodes through the investigating detectives' comments about specific suspects. These explanations are occasionally performed diegetically within scenes of detection (by detectives in their professional role). But they are more often provided in explicitly public service announcement-style information sessions in which the detectives gather at the station to debate nature or nurture across various contemporary psychobiological or genetic-sociological spectrums.

In these informational debate sessions, the detectives perform their diegetically real feelings as a blend of hard-line position taking and seeming confusion. They seem to agree that pedophiles are child molesters, but otherwise they are all over the map across episodes in terms of causation, cure, and prevention. In "Hardwired," we meet a coach with a child sexual abuse record who has not reoffended yet. Stabler comments, "Give him time," before Benson agrees that they must preventatively send him back to prison for failure to register before he abuses again. Yet in an episode treating false accusations and parental hysteria ("Contagious"), we are told that a "garden variety pedophile would never hurt a victim. This guy is a violent child molester."[21] Advocacy for normalization is a major theme across episodes, in which the lack of "medical or psychiatric research" ("Hardwired") is frequently raised in legal settings to disqualify advocates.[22] In "Hardwired," once again, the president of Our Special Love (a pedophile group associated implicitly with the North American Man/Boy Love Association) argues that pedophilia is a "genetically based sexual orientation." Dr. Huang (B. D. Wong) complains in the detectives' debriefing that "pseudoscience like this offends" his profession as a psychiatrist and his "humanity as a gay man." In contrast to the advocacy-science binary, the show consistently affirms the threat of online, or "virtual," pedophilia. In "Angels" we are told that "pedophiles operate their own netherworld" and "operate in cells like Al-Qaeda," while "Web" reminds viewers that "the web connects pedophiles to each other," and "Hardwired" reminds viewers that websites such as Our Special Love are the "perverts' pot of gold at the end of the digital rainbow" (figure 3.2).[23]

These public service announcements also include the presentation of forensic science as validated information, including references to databases run by Innocent Images, Interpol, NCMEC, and the National Crime Information Center. Detectives assert the importance of "knowing the recidivism rate for

FIGURE 3.2 High-tech pedophilia, "Possessed," *Law and Order: SVU* (dir. Constantine Makris), January 5, 2011, Universal Media Studios, NBC.

sexual predators" ("Bad Blood)" and allude to "cutting-edge" software from Homeland Security to track pedophiles ("Web").[24] The end result, however, is always the same: the predatory pedophile is killed, usually violently and in multiple instances including genital mutilation or anal rape. We never really get to explore the kill-or-cure educational question, given that the show often kills those it suspects and saves audiences the trouble. Standard ironies performed across episodes draw attention to the threat of prison rape as a punishment for sex crimes (sex offenders are the "bottom of the food chain in prison," where, suspects are told, "They're going to rip your cherry ass apart unless you tell us where you buried Laura Swift" ["Contagious"]) or the use of intrusive medical examinations to determine sexual violation that themselves enact sexual violation. These ironies are incorporated as part of the audience's training: clearly the experts veer dangerously close to the fantasies and behavior of the predator when they find their own expertise challenged by the virtuality of the pedophile. At times, this process of the pedophilic function—mapping information and images onto sequential behavior—is extended to lay detectives. In "Name" we find one parent of a missing child defending a suspect with the assertion, "He was always nice to the kids," while another rejoins, "That's what they do. That's how they get the kids to trust them."[25] This same paranoiac interpretation of signs backfires in other episodes, such as "Contagious," however, where a wave of hysteria following one nine-year-old white girl's accusation of her gym teacher (her "Uncle Mark") leads multiple parents to identify him as a pedophilic predator before, exonerated, Uncle Mark asks his long-term friends, "How could you believe I would do that?"

Most episodes begin with a case of suspected abuse, then the show dwells on which suspect is secretly hiding pedophilic urges. Across almost all episodes of *svu*, along with other crime procedurals of the era, the suspected pedophile is presented as a phenotypically white man.[26] Little information is presented about the legal race of the predator, although during profiling detectives will frequently say the word "white," and some light-skinned Latino or indistinctly ethnic men are occasionally routed through as secondary figures (part of a ring, in a group scene, as accomplices, and so on). Potential pedophiles are most often middle class, if not affluent, with some exceptions to fit specific plots (seemingly those with Latino victims). Their names are often northern European—Erik Weber, Jake Berlin, Frank Maddox, Clayton Mills, Richard Dwyer, Andrew Keener, Bob Clinton, Avery Huntington, Simon Fife, and so on (figures 3.3–3.10). Child victims are more diverse, although a pattern emerges here, as well. White children (male and female; there are no nonbinary or trans-identified children) are most often presented in individualized cases. A single white child is sexually abused or abducted, and this becomes the focus of the episode. Latino children (male) are most often presented in mass cases, in which multiple children have been targeted through sex trafficking and international tourism or have been left for decades as unsolved cases due to neglect ("Name"). Black children (male again) are taken up in only one episode of the show ("Personal Fouls"), a case in which a white victim accuses his white basketball coach of abuse many years after the event, and his black teammates are forced to admit that they were also sexually abused (racial difference is thematized when Tutuola explains that sexual abuse is still a "taboo," along with homosexuality, in black communities).

To discern the actual pedophiles among the performed suspects, detectives, psychiatrist, and audience alike are tasked with aligning confusing and contradictory information about pedophilia with the white men arranged before them. The *svu* episode "Angels" (2002) provides a clarifying case, although the tone I analyze here is consistently developed across the program. This episode features four suspects, all upper-middle-class white men, who may be involved in a "ring of pedophiles" and sex traffickers routing through Central America. Who is the pedophile among these four? Is it the "ladies' man" with the "terrible temper" and "strange sense of humor" (the corporate executive Brett Jansen)? Yes, early on we know this man has kept young

FIGURES 3.3–3.10 Pedophile headshots, "Pedophiles," Law and Order Wiki, accessed January 18, 2019, Lawandorder.fandom.wiki /Category:Pedophiles.

boys as sexual captives in his apartment. But is it also the "never been mar-ried" guy who has three adopted male children, the plastic surgeon Dr. Lynch (Patrick Cassidy)? Or is it the "single, no children" travel agent who facilitates men's international travel, Anthony Damon (Will Arnett)? What are the signs of pedophilia? Is the children's dentist Dr. Walt Massey (Michael Hayden) creepily cheery? Is the travel agent too well-groomed, too handsome? Is it more suspicious to be open and helpful with direct eye contact or to be casual and relaxed without eye contact? Which is supposed to be the performance, which is supposed to be "real" (figures 3.11–3.13)? (It doesn't help that the sus-pect Anthony Damon is played by the wonderful Will Arnett, who in squash whites seems like the parody of normalcy he has perfected across his career.) Later in this episode, Detective Stabler pretends to be on Damon's side: "I've busted my share of child abusers. I'm not getting that vibe from you."

"Angels" exemplifies the tone that produces the virtual pedophile across these episodes: it focuses on those scenes or situations in which a specific white male performance *may or may not* signify predatory pedophilia. This unresolved ambiguity becomes central to the virtual feeling that runs the show's procedural tone. I began this section by arguing that procedural tone is a subset of the operational aesthetic, which works by drawing attention to its own technological mediation. The knowing irony lubricating the sensa-tionalist sincerity of the genre becomes central to the audience's ability to identify the pedophile among the line-up of white male actors and characters. The actors playing suspects play their role but also disappear into its virtual shadow—the potential pedophilia in all white men. In order to evaluate the signs of actors playing suspects, audiences must learn to interpret the aesthetic levels of the show and situate suspect performance according to its signs.

Actualizing the pedophile from his virtual presence requires the audience to develop common sense, rather than metareflection, or in other words re-quires them to "feel" the presence of the pedophile when there are no clear or consistent signs for his identification. This is not a problem of interpreta-tion; it is a problem of feeling. The signs are not going to become symptoms or clues (versus signifiers) until the audience learns how to make feelings into evaluation. These feelings need not take one particular affective tone; it may include disgust, fear, excitement, bemusement, superiority, or laughter. *All* of these tones register the magnification of predictive information and affec-tive analogs into a broader televisual code of virtual threat. Reviling the show is part of the pleasure of watching it for some, even as the *is it him? or him?* creates a strange aura around potential pedophilia that is beyond this or any

FIGURES 3.11–3.13 Prime suspects: Dr. Walt Massey (Michael Hayden), Dr. Stewart Lynch (Patrick Cassidy), and Tony Damon (Will Arnett), "Angels," *Law and Order: SVU* (dir. Arthur W. Forney), November 1, 2002, Universal Television, NBC.

screen. Through this process, each episode, each series, each year can compose endless cycles of pedophilic narration, satirical and sincere, and regardless of its overt attitude of irony or sincerity accrue a tone that accretes as forensic common sense. For every ridiculous actualization of a pedophilic predator on-screen, for all of the vile sovereignty disqualifying each and every show as ridiculous sex panic or ridiculable genre, the tone of virtual pedophilia resonates more deeply.

Small-Screen Confessional

This tone is not necessarily registered consciously in the five senses but is felt as a kind of sixth sense, an intuitive feeling of "creepy" or "off" whose attitudinal stance becomes associated with the screen as well as the viewer. The static image assembles audience affect through a specific analog—the crumpled shirt, the pressed shirt; the furrowed brow, the bright smile—and then mobilizes that affect to magnify it through sequential events. Here the image serves as a peculiar kind of an affective analog, constituting a tone induced by relations among characters within the visual field (diegesis), the camerawork constituting the visual field (mimesis), and the audience relationship to those dynamics as coproducers of affective effects. The isolated image becomes connected to a sequence of scenes in which white masculinity is profiled for potential pedophilia and yet exonerated as a failing norm when it can be successfully distinguished from criminal deviance. Through images as affective relays, free indirect affect comes to permeate the show's overall tone beyond any specific episode. Audiences may be attuned to the irony of genre or enmeshed in its immediate pleasures, but either way they become the vehicle for virtual pedophilia's extension beyond the small screen. The aura of the virtual pedophile translates into an atmosphere that exceeds his capture.

Walter Benjamin's theory of the "aura" can be used to clarify the effects of virtual pedophilia in creating this broader atmosphere. Benjamin (1969, 221) argues that "aura" was once produced through the "authenticity" and "authority" of a singular artwork made by human hands. This allegedly older form of artistic aura was dissipated in the era of art's mechanical reproduction (or technological reproducibility), when authenticity and authority accrued not to the art object itself (as the singular event of human aesthetic and physical labor) but through its mass-produced images. The aura was redistributed through new technological mediations from objects to subjects of observation.[27] In this new technological landscape, film seemed to replace the authenticity and authority of specific human artwork with "the cult of the movie star" or the "spell of the personality" (231), whose magical "glow," as theorized by Richard Dyer, made "whiteness" into a highly valued commodity image.[28] Benjamin was obviously not predicting the advent of television when he wrote "The Work of Art in the Age of Mechanical Reproduction" in 1936, and his essay focuses primarily on the legacies of European perspectival painting in still photography and cinematic motion. But his account of aura can be mobilized to explain the way virtual pedophilia conjures its on-screen analog: "The equipment-free aspect of reality here has become the height of artifice; the sight of immediate reality has become an orchid [*blau blaume*] in the land of technology."

The predatory pedophile does not have a clear profile, an absence that is readily and repeatedly circulated as the unique problem it poses. Information is inconclusive, but it is still circulated as promise to compose likely signs of suspicious activity or latent desires. Meanwhile, the signs appearing on-screen cannot be interpreted exclusively as either symptom (psychology) or clue (policing); nor are they allowed to create open-ended meaning as signifier (semiotics) or open-system logic as code (informatics). Audiences must be trained to apperceive the technological reproduction of signs *as images* in order to interpret them correctly and assign the proper referent: innocent or guilty. This requires viewers to develop a forensic common sense capable of determining which images are analogs for information (symptoms or clues), which are signifiers of aesthetic distance (semiotics), and which are codes for technological reproducibility (informatics). Audiences must become, in other words, capable of reading what Mittell calls the operational aesthetic as *a key part of* the technological reproducibility of the virtual pedophile. The white pedophile becomes an orchid in one very specific land of technology, one in which forensic common sense becomes the only protection against the perpetual insecurity produced through vile sovereignty.[29]

Let me offer a more extended analysis of a single episode of svu to indicate how its procedural tone creates the aura of virtual pedophilia. This analysis will break down the three specific visual and sonic layers that structure an episode: the noisy background sounds of social realism; the silence of the interview confessional; and the musical soundtrack indicating scene significance. Audiences can use these three layers to focus their interpretation for each new episode, separating generic seriality from the unique problem posed by the virtual pedophile in this specific episode. Sonic choices help organize the relation among visual signs, helping the audience connect still shots or static images with dynamic scenes of character action. Through the sonic cut and suture of static images with dynamic scenes, svu organizes a televisual code for risk assessment whose instruments can be wielded by everyman as forensic common sense.[30] Coming near the start of season ten, the svu episode "Confession" enters the already well-worn groove of svu's episodes about pedophilia. The episode begins with the indistinct noise of angry men just preceding a medium shot of white men in face paint, alluding, perhaps, to a drunken fraternity party or sports fandom, before the shot narrows to Benson shoving one man into a cell as he leers, "I love cougars." This scene of normative male debauchery will rapidly be contrasted with first unacceptable (domestic violence) and then unimaginable (pedophilia) iterations of white male love. Immediately following this cold open, we watch Captain Cragen enter the squad room with the new assistant district attorney, Cragen's voice audible above the din: "September is hell. . . . Get abused at summer camp and nobody tells until they get back home; Greek Week plus alcohol equals rape in the first degree; and there's a spike in DV [domestic violence] calls because all the kids are back in school." His monotonous, sing-song tone is delivered with a slightly lifted voice to be heard in the teeming police room, a metamoment for viewers tuned in for just this self-consciously serial entertainment quality. Like his magnified eye in season one, Captain Cragen's speech establishes the gaze for an episode filled with metacommentary on the relation between ironic distance as aesthetics and aesthetic analog as code.

This opening segment establishes the first of svu's characteristic three layers of visual and sonic diegesis: the noisy background sounds of social realism. In the first layer of this code, as in during Cragen's cold open, the superimposition of professional dialogue over noisy background sounds signals social realism either in the station or on the street. Here the dynamic images are almost always horizontally situated within the scene, as if registering the point of view of a secondary scene participant, or else organized in standard shot-reverse-shot attributed to major players. In the next few minutes of confession, the main detectives Tutuola and Munch are seen playing tough with a man and a woman brought in for a domestic violence report. These scenes in the interview rooms establish the second level of visual and sonic diegesis: silence as close-up images of affect are coupled with movement between adversarial points of view (including the camera's point of view moving freely around the space). In interview room one, Tutuola threatens the white male suspect with prison rape if he does not confess to causing both his wife's physical beating and her vaginal tearing: "Sweet meat. That's what they're going to say before they reach for you in the dark." In room two, Munch also seems to threaten the white woman if she does not press charges, responding to her claim that "he didn't do it" with the probability that she will eventually be brought in in a body bag.

Across these two levels we are reminded of the serial quality of the show's mimesis—the shift from noisy reality of social space to silent retreat of enclosed interrogation/confessional—as well as its diegesis, the heteronormativity of sexual violence routinely requiring police intervention. This is the setup when we zoom in to the main storyline: a seventeen-year-old white male comes to Detective Olivia Benson seeking help for pedophilic desires he claims he has not yet acted on. Here we begin in the noisy social space and then enter the quiet confessional. In the first scene, the young man, Eric Beyers (Marshall Allman), is treated sympathetically as a possible victim. Benson is told he has possible sexual assault info, and his performance seems to signal the affect of fear (we watch him rub his sweaty palms on the legs of his jeans in close-up). Benson encourages him to talk, with all her Benson victim sympathy, but it is "hard to say," he murmurs. Then the scene turns as, eyes wet, he takes out a photo and says, "I love him, but I know it's wrong, and it's getting hard not to touch him." He holds out the photo, and the camera takes up Benson and the audience's gaze at a reproduced image of a small white boy in a cowboy outfit. Cue theme music, the first nondiegetic soundtrack reminding the audience that we are watching svu, and the show has only just begun.

We return, post-commercials, to the second interview scene, where Eric is treated hostilely as a probable predator in the interrogation room. Benson's opening question admitting his youth—should she call his parents?—leads to his disclaimer that he has not "done anything wrong," but is drinking a lot and blacking out to avoid his thoughts. "So what do you think about?" Benson asks, and we move into the third layer of visual and sonic diegesis: a musical soundtrack that overlays the scene in ways that aestheticize its presentation. Ominous string music begins as Eric says, "If I tell you, you'll hate me," then slowly swells as he follows up, "Everybody will." The sonic interruption of the realist diegesis introduces aesthetics as a televisual question. Is Eric performing for Benson? For the audience? For svu's serial camera? The young white man who turns himself in for feelings, not actions, befuddles the protocols of the separate interview spaces and introduces more complex questions of interpretation than did-he-or-didn't-he? In the interrogation room, Detective Benson tells the young confessor seeking access to treatment that rehab is for "people who struggle with addictions," clarifying that pedophilia is not an "addiction" meriting treatment. Yet she also goes on to explain, "It's my experience people like you can't control themselves," associating pedophilia with compulsive behavior. The ironic performance of policing in the interviews about domestic violence is juxtaposed with the performance of sincerity in delivering "information" about pedophilia to a possible perp who may also be a victim of his own desires.

The music follows Benson out of the interrogation room, suturing the aesthetic question introduced there to her follow-up discussion with Cragen. The problem pedophilia poses for standard police work is simultaneously an aesthetic question for the audience and a diegetic question for the detectives. How does one identify a pedophile, and is a pedophile always dangerous? Does confessing to "bad thoughts" equal a "crime"? Does potential abuse signified by pedophilia justify any means necessary to remove a pedophile (or possible pedophile) from the street? Can pedophilia be treated? "Programs don't work," we are told. "Neither does Depo-Provera, or surgical castration." Thus, in this episode we are told that possession of child pornography— associated with "bad thoughts" —must be used to incarcerate likely predators, whether or not they have committed other "crimes." Much of this episode, in keeping with the pedophile episodes in general, focuses on the alleged nature of pedophilia and its dangers, including how you can tell whether someone is (1) a pedophile and (2) guilty of committing sexual abuse. Detective Benson struggles to believe that Eric is in fact a pedophile, since his behavior both does not fit her experience ("I've never had a pedophile turn himself in before") and does ("I mean, the drinking, and the way he caressed that photo says he's a pedophile").

The majority of the episode focuses on the detectives' efforts to read the signs of pedophilia and sexual abuse. The music sutures Benson's interrogation of Eric with her collegial debate and then her knock at the door of the "Kelley Residence," where Eric lives with his mother, Dana (Teri Polo); stepfather, Sean (Josh Charles); and five-year-old brother, Cory (Aaron Mayer). The music fades back into the first layer of sonic and visual diegesis, the background noise of the scene itself here featuring a loud television program for children. The questions return to diegetic reason, without the overt aestheticization announcing a scene of audience interpretation. Has Cory been sexually abused? No: there is no physical evidence after a medical examination. Yes: he has played doctor with another boy (labeled "serious"). In future scenes this debate continues among lay and professional experts. "Only a twisted pervert would admit to abusing a child," Eric's stepfather asserts, while "oral or digital assault" does not leave marks for a medical examination. Semen is found on Cory's shirt. Is Eric guilty of sexual abuse? No: the semen on Cory's shirt is from his stepfather, who used Cory's dirty T-shirt to wipe clean his guilty bathroom masturbation. Yes: "He's a textbook loner"; he has child pornography on his computer.

The effort to turn signs into evidence introduces the debate about nature versus nurture familiar from earlier criminal sex figures. But here we find, as Andrew Vachss argues, the predatory pedophile as a naturally unnatural paradox of sick and evil. On one hand, the detectives offer a familiar narrative about slippery slope deviance: "It starts with the fantasies, which scared you at first, but then you started drinking, [and] so you started surfing the net to find people who would understand, people who were just like you." We do indeed soon meet Jake Berlin (Tom Noonan), a middle-age "white male" who runs a website called Pediphax that Eric consulted seeking help, where he was consoled that it was not his fault that he was "born this way," but he should refrain from touching children. Detective Benson seems to echo this information, telling Eric's mother, "You didn't make your son a pedophile. That's what he is." On the other hand, Detective Stabler responds to Berlin's "I was born this way" claim with, "No one is born a deviant." That a pedophile "is" ontologically, is not something caused by environment, yet is not born that way is one of the crucial repetitions of the show. The show repeatedly presents and dismisses arguments that pedophilia is a sexual abnormality rather than a criminal behavior, frequently by disqualifying as false asserted analogies to homosexuality's historical trajectory from perversion to abnormality to natural (genetic or biological) trait. In contrast, the pedophile is a species being without cause or justification. He is an utterly unique mode of sexuality always expressed as predator.

The generic repetition of the show makes the detectives' performance of acting a key feature of their police role; they shift between good cop/bad cop antics in the interview process while dropping the role to slip into their realist version of professional chatter. The cops put on and take off various roles during their investigation: "We believe he has been abusing Corey," Benson says with authority to Eric's mother and stepfather prior to any evidence gathering. "Did you trade photos of little boys, like baseball cards?" Stabler sneers at Cory during an interrogation. Audiences must discern the difference between the actors performing their characters' sincere personality as detectives versus their playing the role of detective in specific situations for suspects or witnesses. Thus, in "Confession" the avowed pedophile Jake Berlin explains to

Detectives Stabler and Benson that he provides a valuable service by creating safeguards against abuse for people who identify as pedophiles. Berlin's Pediphax code, "Look, but don't touch," includes permission to regard children at play or photographs of children in erotic ways and the safeguard of reporting activity on the site to maintain honor. The detectives tacitly support this separation between look and touch, aesthetics and actualization, in a separate conversation, admitting that the only way to get treatment for pedophilia is to be registered as a sex offender (to already have committed an act). Thus, "Look, but don't touch" describes the code of the professional detectives, as well: you cannot prevent a pedophile from sexually abusing children. The only thing you can do is watch and wait.

Against All Odds

This aestheticization cannot simply present the pedophile as "artwork," however, or it would risk opening the pedophilic sign to readings as a signifier rather than a symptom or clue. Aestheticization must instead create a code through which the pedophilic sign can be actualized as forensic information.[31] Thus, the sutures of the third musical soundtrack across scenes clarifies how aestheticization inheres in the aura of the virtual pedophile. The actor must perform an aesthetic function, acting like a potential predator who might also be a normal white man, to provide opportunities for the detectives and audience to compose aesthetic signs into information and information into clue and symptom. A range of abnormals are thereby introduced, evaluated, and affixed on a changing spectrum of normality, even as the monsters seized among them become merely human once again as their virtual aura withdraws. Actualized information dissipates aura, revealing each potential predator as merely one more abnormal failure hiding in normal human guise, the true monster still lurking in the aura around us.

Audiences are trained how to see the role-playing of the detectives in contrast to the fall into compulsive affect of the other characters: Eric's stepfather, who eventually rapes Eric with Cory's wooden baseball bat as punishment for his desire for Cory; Jake Berlin, the pedophile ringleader who eventually stabs Eric with multiple blunt knives for breaking the code by admitting on the website that he broke down and sexually abused a young boy. Ultimately in this episode Detective Stabler slips from his professional performance of aesthetic distance into affective collapse, yelling at Jake Berlin in detective mode,

"You're a steaming bag of crap I would love to shove down a hole," before becoming personally embroiled when Berlin posts a picture of Stabler's daughter and Stabler beats him severely (music soundtrack sutures Stabler's spiral to Berlin's self-justification).[32] The episode is resolved through another main theme of svu: neither therapeutics nor policing can finally stop a pedophile, and the audience is enveloped in this final punishment when we hear the phone recording of Eric yelling for help while he is repeatedly stabbed to death with blunt knives after being sodomized with a child's baseball bat.

This kind of violent resolution does not need to be repeated in every episode of every program for the procedural tone of virtual pedophilia to achieve hegemonic hold. Virtual pedophilia creates a linkage, or what Stuart Hall in 1973 named a televisual "code," across programs of very different modes, genres, and seeming tones (2001, 165). The communicative medium of television depends on the signs encoded through processes of production and decoded through reception, including dominant, oppositional, or mixed modes in both cases. This means that any code can have multiple levels of determination and signification. Direct eye contact or shifty squint, welcoming smile or reclusive scowl, angry flare or passive resignation—all can be signs of pedophilia. To become symptom or clue in televisual discourse, however, they must become code. Yet the affective charge of procedural tone is also coupled with the perception of effective paralysis: the televisual audience experiences itself as the only true witness to a sexual danger that it can never place under arrest. For each diegetic resolution, the mimetic effect amplifies the experience of virtual threat.

My implicit assumption is that these broader genre paradigms of production and scheduling organize the popularization of the pedophile as virtual predator, even as those production decisions are encoded *as ironic recognition* of the limitations of television as a medium for pedophilic detection. *Special Victims Unit* provides exemplary training in aesthetic and evidentiary discernment. Viewers are serially presented with choices in how to read signs as either aesthetic signifiers (part of the show's artwork) or forensic evidence (clue and symptom of pedophilic predation). In so doing, the show purports to draw realism into its orbit, no matter how campy or outsize some of its diegetic *méconnaissance*. In fact, the disqualification of the show as "artwork" enables its effectiveness as pedagogical procedural. On-screen experts struggle to define signs as evidence, from the physiological (e.g., "blood and fluids in his underwear" ["Angels"] or medical findings of anal assault or sexually transmitted infection ["Hardwired"]) to the behavioral (e.g., "classic signs of being molested" such as touching other children ["Sick"] or wrestling naked with another boy ["Hardwired"]). Viewers are presented with expert opinion ("Children often reenact abuse they experience in order to understand what happened to them"), as well as common sense ("Well, something happened to him. That's obvious" ["Personal Fouls"]). The possibility of consensual or positive experiences of adult-child sexuality is also presented, including a girl who describes her involvement with a thirty-year-old male while she was eleven to fourteen as "probably the most normal relationship I've been in," or one adolescent's dissent from the statement "It's obvious Teddy is the victim here," with, "No, I'm not."

The three-hundredth episode of svu dramatizes this ironic display of televisual code when it takes up the show's own participation in racialized distributions of detective focus. In earlier episodes. this distribution is occasionally noted by on-screen characters who ask whether Latino, and specifically Puerto Rican, boys are treated as disposable by mainstream media and police. In "Name," for example, the crime scene unit technician Millie Vizcarrondo (Paula Garcés) points out, "To most people, they were just four Puerto Rican thugs who just ran away," and asks, "Do you think if there were four white boys missing, the case would still be open?" Vizcarrondo has a four-episode arc in season seven to call out the closed case of a nameless Latino boy that obsessed her father. The three-hundredth episode of the series, "Manhattan Vigil," takes up this diegetic enunciation explicitly and turns it into a mimetic story arc. "Manhattan Vigil" tells the story of an Etan Patz–style case in which a single white child from a wealthy family (named Wyatt) is abducted from a rapidly gentrifying neighborhood associated with Morningside Heights, the same neighborhood where a single Latino boy (named Hector) went missing thirteen years before. While the missing white child is the diegetic subject of media and police attention for this episode, the episode reckons with the fact that the Latino boy received little media or police attention when he disappeared. This parallel unfolds through the perspective of Detective Benson, who allegedly worked Hector's case thirteen years earlier and finds herself confronted with his still angry mother as she attempts to find the more recently missing Wyatt.

This episode offers a metacommentary on the series by confronting its mimetic complicity—*its actual failure to produce any episodes such as the one retroactively referenced as Hector's case*—with this diegetic complaint of racial erasure through the pedophilic function. There was no previous episode in which Benson investigated Hector's case. "Manhattan Vigil" presents Detective Benson tracking Wyatt's killer in the present diegesis, which is intercut with actual footage from season one in which a clearly earlier version of Detective Benson (a younger and differently styled Mariska Hargitay) is presented *as if* in a previous episode's search for Hector. But the footage intercut to represent Benson's earlier case work is itself reproduced from unrelated episodes.[33] Because svu never produced an episode on Hector's case, the show reproduces images to refer to a virtual episode that marks the racial limits of its mimetic reproduction. This is the show at its most ironic. The three-hundredth episode diegetically performs a critique of police and media lack of interest in the sexual abuse and abduction of individual nonwhite children, even as its mimetic complicity with such lack of interest is made visible as the reproducibility of the television screen.

This balance of sincere concern and ironic distance create a televisual code for virtual pedophilia that proliferates its potential signs. If virtual pedophiles trend toward cool and "Teflon" on svu, televisual pedophiles depicted as actual predators trend nervous and "sweaty." One review of csi: *Cyber* episode 2.4 satirically reduces its plot to "a sweaty-faced pedo made the app to convince kids to come to his Rape Cabin" (Knibbs 2015). The nbc reality-entrapment show *To Catch a Predator* (2004–2007) features many sweaty-faced men caught after using an app or other online media platform to convince teenage girls they are crush-worthy Lotharios (the satire is already embedded). Hosted by Chris Hansen, *To Catch a Predator* is a component of nbc *Dateline*'s news programming. Each episode features a series of adult men, mostly but not always white, who enter a decoy house to meet an underage sexual hookup introduced online. If television critics of the 1980s lamented the rising tide of infotainment, by the 2000s the procedural tone of virtual pedophilia made a show such as *To Catch a Predator* possible. Transfiguring virtual pedophilia into televisual code saves the show from seeming to cross an important line between documentary and entertainment, news and melodrama. Or, more accurately, it legitimates the show's decision to redraw the line to secure television audiences against danger. The show began in coordination with the citizen watchdog group Perverted Justice, which enacts similar decoy-based efforts to solicit sexual interest in underage avatars online. Hansen is perhaps a leading voice in the cultural expansion of vile sovereignty when he sutures the documentary function of journalism to the spectacular entertainment function of true crime: "'People can say: Okay, it's not the old-fashioned traditional journalism that took place in the *Houston Chronicle* in 1975—it's different,' Hansen said. 'But that's also why newspapers are having a hard time staying relevant, you know? You have to reassess the way you do things and be creative and enterprising about it, and this is a perfect example of that'" (Woodman 2015).

The show's unusual collaboration among a television crew, the police, and an online group yielded real-world results that went beyond the official capture of predators by police.[34] Pushback on the show has frequently accused it of fomenting sex panic—or, at least, benefiting financially from it. But as Joseph Fischel (2016, 39) points out, the show features a kind of sad or failed masculinity more than its threatening predatory doppelgänger: "Racially diverse, they are more often than not overweight, frumpy, painfully unattractive (against any norm of American masculinity), and socially dysfunctional. Their fleshiness, sweatiness, and twitching comportments mark them as politically unfit and socially deadweight, but not imminently sexually dangerous." While Fischel argues this makes the show "less . . . a reflection and stimulant of moral panic and more . . . a hybrid genre of reality crime television and pornography" (37), I see this diversity of encoding as part of the emergent code of virtual pedophilia. The show enables multiple decoding strategies: dominant, mixed, and oppositional—or, in this case, panicked, confused, and ridiculous (Hall 2001). Some audiences could embrace shows such as *To Catch a Predator* as heroic attempts to break through the unnecessary legal restrictions hampering law-and-order procedures in real life. Other audiences could laugh out loud at its mock sincerity in a cynical bid for ratings and funding to revive lackluster careers and networks.

What Hansen describes as cultural entrepreneurship fits neatly into the mechanisms of vile sovereignty expanded through televisual code. The code can span high-drama monsters (murder, abduction, rape) to low-level molesters (creepy, loving, insistent in their affection) to just pathetic wannabes who wandered into the field by accident looking for a temporary Humbert moment of their own. But if *To Catch a Predator* already played as both sincere and farce, its subsequent spinoffs seem almost impossibly grotesque. In 2015, Hansen proposed a show titled *Hansen vs. Predator*, an independent spinoff not backed by the industry ("America's first-ever Kickstarter-funded sex sting"). This new show came out of a collaboration with Sheriff Grady Judd of Polk County, Florida, who was described in one article as "an evangelical Christian who routinely preaches in uniform" (Woodman 2015). Also, in 2014 an Australian reporter noted that "*The Paedophile Hunter* Stinson Hunter raised almost $30,000 five days after launching a Kickstarter campaign, after appearing in a UK documentary of the same name" (Reynolds 2014). At this point, it is hard to believe there has not been a mainstream hit called *The Pedo-Files.*

The procedural tone I study here has been central to creating a "code" for forensically legitimated representations of child sexual abuse, in contrast to its pornographic exploitation for illegitimate sexual and economic extraction. As I have argued, procedural tone creates an aesthetic system that encodes signs into specific signifieds as clue, symptom, or signifier. All representations of pedophilia are subject to a hermeneutics of suspicion; all encoders are possible predators purveying child pornography or legitimating the sexualization of children. This seems to help explain why child pornography haunts the screen and seeps into interpretations of both encoding and decoding processes whenever pedophilia is at stake. Take the example of Jace Alexander, the director of thirty-two episodes of *Law and Order* who was reported as an "alleged pedophile" before being convicted of charges related to child pornography (depicting minors younger than sixteen) in 2015 (Abrams 2015). Like the detectives in svu, producers of cultural materials about pedophilia must create representational distance—must flag their representations as aesthetic—to decrease proximity between their own real feelings and fictional representation. Yet aestheticization is also dangerous, since it runs the risk of making child sexual abuse pretty, appealing, or erotic—it runs the risk not of sensationalism (distant) but of sensation (proximate). Suggestions of latent pedophilia haunt many producers of "artwork" about pedophilia, resulting in the endless thematization of detection as the legitimate form of looking in svu and other crime procedurals and the insistent distantiation and displacement of bad forms of looking onto the pedophile himself.

This code enables audiences aware of their own hypersurveillance in the information age to invest in shows that suggest it remains hard to catch a predator (Zimmer 2015). Virtual pedophilia requires the technology of human apperception—gut feeling, the enlarged eye provided by the show's magnifying glass—to be remediated by information, as well as visual technologies. In the encounter with the virtual pedophile, a popular affectivity highly conditioned by extensive surveillance technologies is situated to experience analog shock. The low-tech policing, the gut feelings, the disqualified power of the officers, the extrainstitutional punishments—these all propose pedophilia as simultaneously virtual and real. Pedophilia is beyond the actual realized in sensational realism and its "ripped from the headlines" referents, even as watching its serial reproduction on television screens helps train audiences to defend against this predator in daily life. By the late 2000s the hunt for the virtual pedophile could be traced across programs well beyond the scope of the crime procedural. The virtual pedophile could be found creeping into serious, as well as campy, melodramas and even serving as a periodic punchline for half-hour comedies.[35] Across a range of potential predators, the pedophile would appear on-screen only to remind audiences that this is just television, a training technology for decoding images that must take place beyond its screens. They enlarged the atmosphere produced through the pedophile's aura and made everyday life into a procedural drama requiring forensic common sense.

This code lends itself to a broader atmosphere of suspicion and detection that extends beyond television genres, in which pedophilic analogs are sought for otherwise intangible or invisible threats. In his study of modernism's affective mapping, Jonathon Flatley (2008, 19) uses the concept of "atmosphere" to name the way a broader or shared affective relation is created through specific analogs. Christina Sharpe's (2016) study of cultural texts produced "in the wake" of slavery clarifies that atmosphere is itself always part of a racial ecology forged through antiblack racial hierarchies and white supremacy. Virtual pedophilia enters a broader atmosphere in which historical signs of blackness, brownness, indigeneity, and foreignness are treated as if analogs are real, rather than virtual, threats. The pedophile participates by making the *insecurity* of analogs into a sign of virtual threats. Virtual pedophilia enhances many viewers' experience of insecurity, in other words, *without actually making white masculinity analogous to sexual threat*. Routed through the aesthetic function, such analogs are disqualified from ever ultimately "being" the threat itself. White male actors on-screen are scare-quoted as always already potentially absurd or overdramatized (sensationalism), even as the reality behind their performance remains too scary to fully represent on-screen (sincerity). Through this process, efforts to capture the pedophile will continue to reproduce this atmosphere, even if his aura is dismantled and his actuality is drawn into question.

FOUR

CAPTURING THE PAST AND
THE VITALITY OF CRIME

> But, like, if they had an island just for baby rapers and
> chicken hawks? Just airlift food in a few times a week,
> fill the water with mines. No one gets off. First-time
> offenders, fuck you, you get life on the island.
> —DENNIS LEHANE, *Mystic River*

Films of the 1990s and 2000s took up the pedophile with almost as much fervor as television. In the 1990s, the pedophile appeared as the subject of films exploring the impact of adult-child sexuality. During this decade, *Sleepers* (1996) best captured the idea that children's experience of adult sexual violence created a delayed recognition that would shape the future of gendered adulthood. Todd Solonz's *Happiness* (1998), in contrast, focused on the impact of pathologizing pedophilia and routing it into secretive predation. These films generally treated pedophiles as people who disrupt gendered and generational normalization, most often focusing on masculinity in question if not in crisis (Davies 2007). The pedophile emerged as a consistent cinematic figure only in the 2000s, when a series of films presented pedophilia as a problem not of individual characters but of the overall logic of cinema itself. This shift from psychological to cinematic impact made pedophilia the subject of cinematography rather than merely the film's subject matter. Across several films of this period, the pedophile emerged as a specter of cinematic reproducibility, an image that could be mass-produced and popularly disseminated without tethering its virtual reach to a specific threat. Virtual pedophilia's expansive impact could exacerbate audiences' experience of threat in ways that precipitated real-life panic.

Several films of this period centered this cultural atmosphere to explore its visual production and cinema's unique role in its dissemination or interruption. The two films I treat in this chapter—one documentary, one narrative—explore how cinematic technology can be used to disseminate as well as interrupt virtual pedophilia's atmospheric effects. Both Andrew Jarecki's *Capturing the Friedmans* (2003) and Clint Eastwood's *Mystic River* (2003) explicitly meditate on the aestheticization of reality in the context of virtual pedophilia, focusing in particular on the histories of analog images that enable the contemporary visuality of the predatory pedophile. These films reveal the on-screen image of the pedophile being assembled from older modes of representation, even though this virtual predator is not fully visualizable through those outdated modes and can appear only as a flickering signifier of potential realities lost to history. In these films, the pedophile appears as an image both of and out of technological reproducibility. This makes the on-screen pedophile a kind of virtual memory (King 2015). He appears through an assemblage of technological effects that compose his absent presence haunting the on-screen actor as an aura, as in the case of procedural tone. Only in these cinematic translations, the aura is revealed as an effect of technological mediation. The pedophile becomes an object of screen memory rather than the subject of narrative resolution.

The first half of this chapter focuses on Jarecki's Oscar-nominated documentary *Capturing the Friedmans*, arguing that this documentary seeks to reveal the technological mediations through which the white pedophile appears as a virtual image of cinematic memory. Jarecki seeks to unpack the technological mediation of child sexual abuse from the 1970s through the 2000s to propose memory itself a technology of panic. The visual media used to represent the pedophile on-screen—televisual discourse in particular—is situated as precipitating panic about child sexual predation in white middle-class neighborhoods. *Capturing the Friedmans*, produced in 2001 and released in 2003, revisits this visual genealogy by incorporating a variety of technologically documented footage from the 1970s and 1980s in its search for the truth in one case of alleged predation. Jarecki's documentary incorporates changing technologies of home recording and television newscasting as he traces the Friedman family's interactions with the public and the police over accusations of sexual abuse. The resulting art-house documentary incorporates various media capturing seemingly private moments of family history as a newly available public memory. *Capturing the Friedmans* situates changing technologies of recording memory as key to the emergence of the white pedophile as a virtual predator, the search for which catches various men in ways the public should question as panic.

This activity of looking—thematized in the self-referentiality of *Capturing the Friedmans*—is absorbed back into the fourth wall of narrative films such Clint Eastwood's Oscar-winning *Mystic River*. In Eastwood's adaptation of Dennis Lehane's 2001 novel of the same name, the quest for the virtual pedophile takes the viewers into a noir world of naturalist forces seemingly beyond human control. What appears from among the shadows of Eastwood's updated noir is the atavistic return of the predator, the white pedophile's virtuality assembled on-screen as an unnatural monster in human clothing. The film's visual interrogation of virtual pedophilia works to revive a seemingly residual white working-class community as a barricade against the real threats of societal restructuring, rather than the virtual threats of sexual predation. As one character flickers on-screen as a potential pedophile, the other white men are able to regain their lost agency as formal and informal detectives seeking to protect their neighborhood from invisible threats: first from potential pedophilia, but ultimately from neoliberal disposability. In Eastwood's film the virtual pedophile creates a cinematic opportunity for nostalgic working-class resistance to Fordist modes of production and Keynesian modes of governance to reappear as the only boundary between mystic threats and actual survival.

Picking up on the procedural tone analyzed in the previous chapter, these films translate televisual code into cinematic discourse. In *Capturing the Friedmans*, this code is presented as precipitating sex panic, an amplified affect that the documentary remediates to reveal the aesthetic misdirection of virtual memory. In *Mystic River*, this code is presented as misdirecting sex panic where only routine criminality exists, a proper white working-class criminality that triumphs over pedophilia's mystic amplification and aesthetic misdirection. In these films, pedophilia refunctions residual images of perverse whiteness to present a sexual predator whose criminality can always only be technologically remembered. The virtual pedophile relies on residual imagery—specifically, in this instance, the cinematic history of art-house documentary and film noir—to become visible. Yet analog figures of cinematic memory that seek to portray the pedophile on-screen disqualify that screen from ever capturing the virtual truth. In truth, both films suggest, normal white men are being subjected to amplified and misdirected surveillance while real crimes continue off-screen. The truth lies always just beyond, before, and yet somehow also through the big-screen productions of this period, creating an account of history in which white men regain a form of agency that otherwise has been lost in the structural adjustment of sexual security.

Capturing History

When *Capturing the Friedmans* came out in 2003, reviews instantly dubbed it a runaway success.[1] Following on the recent crossover appeal of documentaries such as Michael Moore's *Bowling for Columbine* (2002) and Jeffrey Blitz's *Spellbound* (2002), *Capturing the Friedmans* was hailed as "a stirring examination of truth at odds with perception, the high price of privacy in the media era and the blinding veil of blood ties" (Foundas 2003). It was nominated for twenty-six awards, including an Oscar for Best Feature Documentary in 2004, and won the Grand Jury Prize for Documentary at Sundance, as well as Best Documentary from numerous film critics' societies. As Jami Bernard (2003) summarized the film's impact in the *New York Daily News*, "This extraordinary film refracts truth through the prism of memory, until what you get is a tragedy of Shakespearean dimensions, full of sacrifice and betrayal." *Capturing the Friedmans* picks up where television crime procedurals left off, examining the technologies and aesthetics that sought to detect child sexual predators in the 1980s and 1990s. In the atmosphere of virtual pedophilia, both documentary and critic suggest, technologies of popular "perception" took over the "prism of memory." Past becomes present, and both are overdetermined by the technological reproducibility of images. Through this process, "truth" itself becomes a technological effect of media. Once again, visual technologies must be used to map information onto image, but this time, documentary film will be used to interrupt virtualization and retrain perception to see memory as artifice, a site of technological reproducibility rather than an unfiltered link between past and present.

The story told by *Capturing the Friedmans* frequently has been linked to the story told about its production. After selling his founding shares in Moviefone, Andrew Jarecki set out to make his first documentary, about birthday clowns in New York. He focused in particular on the celebrity clown known as Silly Billy (David Friedman). Minimal sleuthing turned up the story that would become the basis for the documentary: between 1984 and 1987, David's father, the retired high school science teacher Arnold Friedman, was under surveillance for trafficking in child pornography. In late 1987, federal agents assisted

Postal Inspector John McDermott in a raid on Friedman's home in Great Neck, New York, where they found child pornography in his study. They also found the names of students who had been enrolled in after-school computer classes at the Friedman home, which they gave to Detective Sergeant Fran Galasso of the Nassau County Police Department. Detectives immediately began interviewing children previously enrolled in classes about possible sexual abuse, leading to the arrest of Arnold Friedman and his eighteen-year-old son Jesse, his classroom assistant. The two were arraigned on fifty-two counts of child sexual abuse against five children; both ultimately pled guilty and were sentenced for multiple counts child sexual abuse.[2] These facts were much reported in the mainstream press at the time. In fact, in the Friedman case television cameras and news photographers were allowed into a Nassau County courtroom for the first time, making the media active agents in the dissemination of images and information about the alleged sexual abuse.

While Arnold and Jesse Friedman had already been made famous in mass journalism as convicted pedophiles, *Capturing the Friedmans* transformed their infamy into celebrity by translating their 1980s trial by media into a highly aestheticized documentary about the mediations of memory and the making of virtual pedophilia. In the documentary, new characters are introduced: Arnold's wife, Elaine Friedman, who plays a leading role, as does their non-accused son David, the birthday clown; Arnold's brother Harold; and the silent middle son, Seth (who refused to participate in the 2001 interviews). The investigative and courtroom team is interviewed extensively, including talking head interviews with McDermott; the Sex Crime Unit detectives Frances Galasso, Anthony Sgeugloi, and Lloyd Doppman; Assistant District Attorney Joseph Onorato; Judge Abbey Boklan; Arnold's lawyer, Jerry Bernstein; and Jesse's attorney, Peter Panaro. Former computer students from Arnold's class are interviewed, as is a former student's parent, and Judd Maltin, Jesse's high school best friend. Debbie Nathan, an investigative journalist for the *Village Voice* and author, with Michael Snedeker, of *Satan's Silence: Ritual Abuse and the Making of a Modern American Witch Hunt* (2001), is interviewed as the single outside expert witness (although she makes it clear that she is also a friend of the Friedman family). Cutting across these various approaches to the truth, Jarecki's directorial hand composes the interface of *Capturing the Friedmans* itself, orchestrating reversals and surprises carefully edited by Richard Hankin and brought to life by the music of Andrea Morricone.

Through the juxtaposition of these 2000–2001 interviews with mainstream media coverage and family home videos shot over the course of the original investigation, the film re-creates and remediates the trial that never took place (although for a very different audience, as we shall see in the next section). Contradictory claims about the past build over the course of the film: Arnold sent Debbie Nathan a letter entitled "My Story," detailing a lifetime of pedophilic urges and sexual activity with two young boys outside Great Neck, as well as his brother Howard during their childhood. Howard rebuts the claim, stating that he has no memory of such activity and no latent hostility toward Arnold. Jesse claims that his lawyer, Peter Panaro, told him to lie and confess rather than face a jury trial in the media maelstrom, and to claim that he had been sexually abused by Arnold as a sympathy appeal (which he repeated in a phone interview conducted by Geraldo Rivera in 1989 while Jesse was in prison). Panaro insists that Jesse willingly told him that he was guilty of child sexual abuse and had also suffered such abuse at his father's hands. Detective Galasso recalls finding child pornography in plain sight around the Friedmans' house. Debbie Nathan points to police photos from 1987 that show an orderly house with pornography tucked in a pile behind the piano. Detective Doppman explains that children should never be interviewed with leading questions and that his team carefully followed this protocol. Detective Sgeugloi explains that children have to be told what to say to get them to admit the truth. Meanwhile, Elaine and David offer competing versions of what went wrong in the family, with Elaine blaming Arnold's secrecy and exclusiveness with his sons and David blaming Elaine's emotional instability and sexual frigidity.

The film's strategic use of remediation thus brings us to the central questions typically asked about the film: What position does the film take on the guilt or innocence of Jesse and Arnold Friedman? Were the Friedmans persecuted based on child sexual abuse hysteria of the 1980s, part of a "witch hunt" rounding up day-care providers and other professionals working with children outside the family home?[3] Or did they take advantage of children placed in their care, extending Arnold's admitted sexual interest in children to a contamination of kinship itself? *Capturing the Friedmans* deliberately avoids answering these questions, although the DVD does allude to Jarecki's support of Jesse. Almost all critics agree that the film refuses to take an overt position on the guilt or innocence of Arnold and Jesse Friedman. Where they differ is the meaning of such avoidance. For critics such as Doris Toumarkine (2003, 20), "Jarecki's disciplined journalistic balance and story-savvy organization" is a strategy for engaging the audiences, for getting them "passionately taking sides, if not taking to the barricades, for what they believe to be true in this wrenching real-life drama of family tragedy and alleged felonies." For other critics, however, Jarecki's strategies of remediation verge on unethical, exploiting the ambiguity of memory to enhance the film's market reach and aesthetic reception. For both sides, the film's cinematic ambiguity is linked to its ethical aims, its effort to create effects in the audience—or "affects," as Vikki Bell theorizes the film's main objective. Bell suggests that the seeming ethical dilemma in *Capturing the Friedmans* is in fact an affective demand, one that seeks to "deliver *compositions*, rather than truths, which operate through the *sensation* of vision" (Bell 2008, 94). The documentary does not engage its audience in a search for truth, in other words. Instead, it involves them in the affective experience of mediation. As the film critic Paul Arthur (2003, 7) summarizes this aspect of the film's reception, citing the film critic Elvis Mitchell's radio interview with Jarecki, "Thank you for not telling me what to think."

Jarecki's use of the Friedmans own home movies marks the ethical and affective center of the documentary for almost all of its critics. If Jarecki became a famous auteur for *Capturing the Friedmans*, the Friedmans themselves are frequently credited with doing their own capturing. As the film critic Rand Richards Cooper (2003, 23) comments, "In effect, the Friedmans themselves had done Jarecki's work for him." Obsessively filming almost every family incident, the Friedmans had long been the film stars of their own lives. Their home movies, shot first on 8 mm and Super-8 film and then finally on video, had been in production since before the children were born. There are the Friedman recordings from the dawn of their familial time, including a 1940s short of Arnold and Howard's little sister twirling in a tutu; Super-8 footage of Arnold and Elaine's early relationship; and home films and videos of David, Seth, and Jesse from early childhood through the 1970s and 1980s. Some of the videos capture the Friedman boys performing as a family, just "being themselves"; some aspire to be films in and of themselves, with credit sequences, musical accompaniment, acting roles, and narrative plots. In addition, David had purchased a new camera to take home movies after his father's arrest on child pornography charges. These tapes document the period of Arnold's house arrest as he prepares for his trial, the night before Arnold is to begin serving his sentence, and Jesse's last night and morning before going to jail. Jesse had also made audiotapes of the family during the weeks before Arnold proceeded to jail, including some of the most vituperative exchanges between the family members over their last Seder together. All told, Jarecki was given some twenty-five hours of video and twenty hours of audio from the family's private collection to use for his film.

Some critics have pointed out that Jarecki deliberately used the Friedmans' footage to maximize ambiguity, decontextualizing memory and aestheticizing its referents. In her exploration of the film's relationship with "institutional denial," Susan Bandes (2007, 295) suggests that the documentary's touchstone is Akira Kurosawa's *Rashomon* (1950) more than Errol Morris's *The Thin Blue Line* (1988) in that "audiences leave the theater shaken; uncertain of the moral of the filmic story, but jolted from complacent belief in the stock legal story of dispassionate justice." This technique echoes the seminal experiments of early silent films on "white slavery," such as George Loane Tucker's *The Traffic in Souls* (1913), and the first feature film representing a child sex predator, Fritz Lang's *M* (1931), each of which reveals the multifaceted and overlapping technologies of forensic and cinematic detection as they developed across the early twentieth century. But here Sigmund Freud's early twentieth-century model of memory as the "mystic writing pad" (1966) is transmogrified into what Linda Williams (1993) calls "mirrors without memories." In her study of contemporary documentary films (including *The Thin Blue Line*), Williams (1993, 13) argues that "it has become an axiom of the new documentary that films cannot reveal the truth of events, but only the ideologies and consciousness that construct competing truths—the fictional master narratives by which we make sense of events." But if the camera can no longer be considered a "mirror with a memory," we must understand that "this mirror nevertheless operates in complicated and indirect refractions" (Williams 1993, 12). The cinematic becomes part of a broader technological struggle over the making of the material world through mediated images, producing what Janet Walker (2005) calls "trauma cinema," or film participating in the meaning of memory itself.[4] *Capturing the Friedmans* is, in effect, an exploration of remediation, focused in particular on how technological transformations have been linked to transformations in popular consciousness.[5]

The home videos play a central role in constituting the ambiguity of the film, making explicit use of what Snowden Becker (2004, 148) calls "the dramatic trope of the play-within-a-play . . . long ago adapted to cinema as the film-within-a-film." The home movies do not resolve the problems of memory. Instead, they reveal the ways that changing technologies transform popular understandings of access to and construction of truth, including the uses and abuses of "memory" to construct verifiable pasts. Since lightweight cameras enabled cinéma vérité in the 1960s, the technological explosion from 16 mm and 8 mm safety film to Super-8, VHS, video cameras, camcorders, digital storage devices, and camera phones have transformed the accessibility of film production. These new technologies enable home footage to be shot informally as well as for professional use. *Capturing the Friedmans* makes use of more than one new technology for its cinematic depiction of memory. Incorporating shots of handwritten letters, typewritten pages, computer screens, still photos, VHS tape, and 8 mm, Super-8, and 16 mm film, "Jarecki's feature feels like watching technology evolve before our eyes" (Hayes 2003). Through the intercutting of different technologies of self-representation, the film stages a series of contradictions between competing narrative memories and the technological record of the past.

Virtual Memory

This technological remediation begins with the opening credits of the film. The HBO Documentaries and Magnolia Pictures logos in white font fade in and out against a black screen, followed by white text flashing out of focus then adjusted to reveal "A Film by Andrew Jarecki" in block handwriting. This flickers to the sound of a film projector, flickering out of focus again and disappearing as we hear a voice-over greeting us: "Hi, it's me, it's — Are we not ready yet? Hi, it's me. It's Jesse." The screen reveals a teenager talking to the camera against what might be a backyard backdrop, "Jesse Friedman" in subtitle. The soundtrack draws attention to the disjunct introduced by filmmaking, the sense of knowing performance that will mark a good portion of the Friedman home movies. Jesse introduces himself to an intimate audience, "It's me," only to interrupt the intimate address with a question about collective uncertainty, "Are we not ready yet?" Jarecki seems to use the Friedmans' own filmmaking as a metaphor for the film that will unfold. But this metaphor is actually the starting point for the virtual world of the film. This is the first interface with what will remain an ever-elusive scene of reality. Speaking into a microphone he holds, Jesse announces that he will conduct an interview with "Arnold Friedman, my father," whom he pulls into the spotlight, father and son smiling and hamming in front of the camera. As the two perform celebrity for their own home documentation, a new voice-over continues: "I still feel like I knew my father very well. I don't think that just because there were things in his life that were private and secret and shameful that that means that the father that I knew and the things I knew about him were in any way not real."

This opening sets up a template for the film that will follow. Across their home movies, the Friedmans' volition to perform and record performance will dominate the information conveyed, constituting scenes of consumption for the doubled and redoubled audience (the family member holding the camera; the family who will later watch the movie; the possible public who will someday view the movies; the actual public who currently consumes it). The viewer is positioned in multiply mediated positions as part of the movie's scenes of memory and subjectivity. The unnamed adult son whose voice floats, unattached, through this opening credit sequence offers to compose this past for us but will do no more than allude to information as the site of mediation: "I still feel like I know my father." The content of this knowing, past and continuous, is deferred; an empty signifier remains, the "real" that the son's voice marks and leaves without referents. What is "real," the film suggest, is the site of memory. But even more, it is the site of technological mediation, the site of filmmaking or even filmmaking as memory. As the credit sequence continues, the Buck Owens song "Act Naturally" plays over home videos flickering on and off the screen, each accompanied in a brief freeze-frame by a title printed to the side or below the image: "Capturing the Friedmans," "Arnold," "Elaine," "David," "Seth," "Jesse."

The opening sequence foregrounds the way in which various forms of memory are intercut in the film to create thematic centers and new contexts for the referents of memory, setting up a filmic technique that will ultimately focalize referents through performances of gender and race within changing scales of space. "They're gonna put me in the movies, they're gonna make a big star out of me" is intended to convey a presumed desire of the Friedmans, as we see in their flickering home movies. This performative desire is at first explicitly linked to the family's historical performance of Jewishness and their position in the middle-class Jewish community of Great Neck, on Long Island. The Friedmans are presented as a family engaged in historical forms of Jewish performativity; their mugging for the camera and irreverent sense of what Jarecki calls "Borsht Belt humor" is explicitly linked early in the film to young Arnold Friedman's performance as "Arnito Rey" when he attempts a career as a mambo musician in the Catskills (Dretzka 2003). But what the film presents as the Friedman family's efforts to "act naturally" will be realized only through their capture in the lens of this other camera, in the images that constitute the whiteness of the virtual pedophile. In other words, the documentary's audience is intended to see the Friedmans as natural, as a nice Jewish family captured in the media frenzy of pedophilia panic.

This requires the audience to see their "unnatural acts" as the unintended effect of their capture in different visual media: photographic child pornography and new media coverage of the pedophile. "Arnold liked pictures," Elaine explains in an early segment. That Arnold liked to look is uncontested in the film. What this looking means, what it signifies for viewers within and of the film, becomes the moral and aesthetic center of the documentary's many scenes. From its opening, the film begins to organize a dyad of performing to become an image and consuming images already made. "Act naturally" seems to promise the Friedmans a form of celebrity, one now realized in the mass distribution of *Capturing the Friedmans*. But appearing to act naturally in this context is tied to the unnatural acts of pedophilia, as an act of both consumption (viewing pornography) and being consumed (being in view for the policing cameras). What the opening sequence indexes is a mediated temporality of memory: a future-oriented performance beckons to memory's audiences, anticipating a gaze back that will recognize its gestures, its actions, as "natural." Recognition becomes tied to scenes of surveillance that denaturalize performance, only to "see" it through new and changing patterns of information.

Jarecki's film seems to strip more traditional ideas of historical context away in order to propose pedophilia as a problem of looking, of technological imaging itself. According to Katherine Hayles (1999, 29–30), "New technologies will instantiate new models of signification [that] affect the *codes* as well as the subjects of representation." Thus, what Jacques Lacan called "floating signifiers" become in the information age "flickering signifiers" (Hayles 1999, 30), modes of representation rendered virtual through transformations in technological media. *Capturing the Friedmans* articulates such flickering signifiers as a new mode of memory—memory for new times (Hall and Jacques 1990). In an interview in 2003 with Charlie Rose, Jarecki explicitly likens memory to a flawed reproductive technology: "I felt that . . . one of the things that had to come across about the film . . . was how hard it was to find the truth, how hard it is to find the truth, how our memories change over time to suit our needs. You know, we think we put our memories away in a box, and we can go check on them later, and they'll be the same. They're never the same. They're just these electrochemical bubbles that continue to bubble over time."[6] Through the remediation of the documentary, Jarecki turns these "electrochemical bubbl[ings]" into the "flickering signifiers" of the information age. Memory becomes a mode of virtualization, a way to make reality "flicker" as it is processed through the vile sovereignty recoding truth and knowledge.[7]

Jarecki capitalizes on changing visual technologies to virtualize pedophilia, making it into the vanishing point of history at century's end. The documentary is coded as an "interface" in which the images take priority, leading viewers to access reality as a series of images whose relation to history as information is unclear (Hight 2005, 9). *Capturing the Friedmans* therefore seems to modify Williams's (1993, 15) claim that postmodern documentaries "contributed not to new fictionalizations but to paradoxically new historicizations [that] are fascinated by an inaccessible, ever receding, yet newly important past which does not have depth." In place of "historicization," *Capturing the Friedmans* makes "virtualization" the horizon of possibility and meaning making. The film, in other words, does not avoid context; it makes virtuality its context (King 2015). The film's historical information is revealed piecemeal, in bits and pieces of data about Arnold's possession of child pornography (he liked pictures), his confessed interest in and even activity with boys, and, finally, his actual confession to the sexual abuse of all boys named in his indictment in a close-out statement made after his confession and sentencing. The sought-after image of the pedophile constitutes what appears as historical information within the film.

In its sequencing of image and sound, the documentary constitutes new historical and virtual regimes of looking within the filmic text. These new regimes of looking engage viewers in what José van Dijck (2008, 71–72) theorizes as "'cinematic hindsight': audiovisual retrospectives of remembered life as an aggregate of (actual or fictional) home videos and filmic (re)constructions." *Capturing the Friedmans* explores cinematic hindsight as both an exercise of its main subjects—the Friedmans' constant anticipatory filming of their own future memories—and a task for the audience for the film itself. The sequences present the body as a scene of technological interface, replacing models of gendered and racialized public and private space with regimes of looking at the images associated with pedophilia. One key example can be found in the early introduction of David Friedman's video journal from 1988. The entry from November 18 of that year is the second video within a film that we see, following an extended sequence of B-roll footage that emphasizes the larger spatial contours of the town, including a car driving toward us on tree-lined street, a slow pan up to a mid-aerial shot in which we can see sky in the upper frame, then a shot through the trees to a blue sky with clouds. The final image of the blue sky slowly fades into a technological representation of such empty space: a blue screen that resembles either a computer screen (where

Arnold allegedly stored pornographic games for children) or video monitor (where scenes of remembering will be displayed).

The piano and light string music accompanying the B-roll are replaced with static sound as the blue screen goes visually static, until we hear a throat clearing and see David Friedman sitting in a white T-shirt and boxer shorts, with the words "video diary" at the lower left and "11.18.88" at the lower right (figure 4.1). This transition emphasizes the social space of technology, so that when David waves to the camera and then sits slumped over, scratching his left ear and sighing, his physical isolation is encoded as technological visibility. Clarifying this point, David begins, "Well, this is private, so if you're not me, then you really shouldn't be watching this. This is between me and me, between me now and me in the future." The temporality of David's address—as a private memory to be made for himself in the future—is belied by the spatial contexts of the establishing sequence; there is no visible cut. As we will see in the later sequences treating Arnold's pedophilia, the use of public space to site the body on-screen will be central to the film's remediation of pedophilia. David points out this sense of a policing gaze, exclaiming, "If you're the fucking—If you're the fucking cops, go fuck yourselves, go fuck yourselves, 'cause you're full of shit." This sequence tracks the spatializing context given to a visual scene in which the suffering son speaks (privately) directly to the camera but in order to reprove an audience whose policing function is always already part of the scene itself.

The address to the police is an early interface with the policing surveillance of the investigative team, to whom we will soon be introduced, as well as the tacit surveillance of looking in or at this film at all. Meditating on the spatial organization of scenes of punishment, Eve Kosofsky Sedgwick (1993, 182) suggests that the spanking of a child creates "a small temporary visible and glamorizing theater around the immobilized and involuntarily displayed lower body of a child." This scene of David, in the theater of a body revealed, "involuntarily," to a desire gaze of spectators, echoes Sedgwick's formulations. In removing the visual scene from a broader spatial context, Sedgwick (1993, 183) argues that the isolation of the body in a visual frame combats "the entire visible mechanism of the gaze to which the child is exposed, the graphic multicharacter drama of infliction and onlooking, the visibly rendered plural possibilities of sadism, voyeurism, horror, *Schadenfreude*, disgust, or even compassion." David's video diary therefore exploits the domain of his own body, the visual isolation of his body from the context of the punishing gaze.

Yet the film returns this body to a broader spatial context, insisting on its

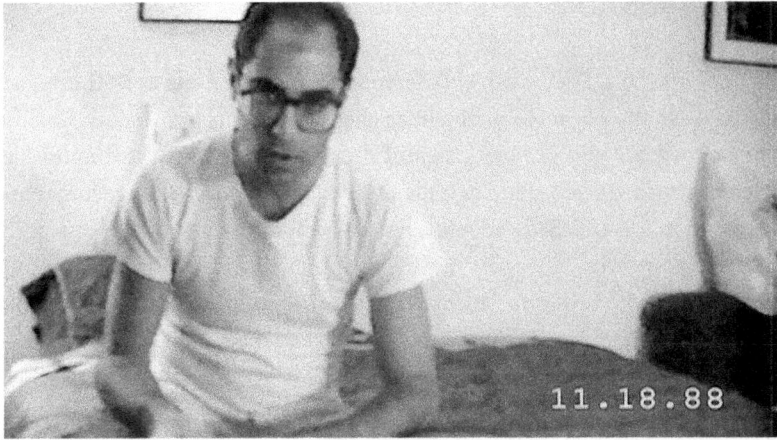

FIGURE 4.1 David before the camera, *Capturing the Friedmans* (dir. Andrew Jarecki), Magnolia Pictures, 2003.

location in scales of surveillance that become the hallmark of seeing pedophilia. This filmic sequence locates David's body as a space within the gaze of forensic common sense constructed by the pedophilic function. The deferred "real" of the son's voice in the opening sequence redounds across the image contexts of the film, constituting a body of information through which virtual reality is constituted. But here the body on-screen becomes information, such that the documentary "privilege[es] the body as an information-filtering agent" and situates "memory construction at the junction of body and technology" (van Dijck 2008, 72). The Friedmans themselves are virtualized through the film, constantly revealed in a private filming directed to a future audience who can see their films only through the retrospective gaze of the police, an audience looking for visual evidence of the pedophile. This is what Bell (2008, 95–96) describes as the documentary's "trajectories of affect," which seek to trace "the contagion of disgust and outrage" within the embedded filmic contexts and its implied and actual audiences. The documentary seeks to induce, diegetically and mimetically for its audiences, the technological sensations linked to the "virtuality of the real" (Bell 2008, 101). Thus, as Steven Bruhm and Natasha Hurley (2004, xxix) point out about pedophile narratives more generally, "There is a sense of trauma, but trauma as Freud describes it, where the meaning lies not in the experience but in the memory, that temporally displaced nexus of narratives that cannot help but pathologize the event."

Seeing Pedophilia

In *Capturing the Friedmans*, this temporally displaced nexus is the visual media itself, the impact of pedophilia's allegedly inevitable virtuality. David's body on the screen becomes a sign of pedophilia's virtuality, its impossible referents in an age of technologically reproducible media, an impact that inheres not in the so-called pedophile but in the bodily scenes of the "displaced nexus of narratives" that constitute the 2001 film interviews. Thus, David will later say, "Maybe I shot the videotape so that I wouldn't have to remember it myself. It's a possibility. Because I don't really remember it outside of the tape. Like when your parents take pictures of you, do you remember being there, or just the photograph hanging on the wall?" Here David's retroactive narrative memory will explain the failures of present memory formation, will reflect on the need to document the body as the scene of a cinematographic failure. Memory can only come afterward, in the screening of virtual images. This peculiar temporality is echoed in the closing sequence of the movie, titled, "It's the night before Jesse is to enter his guilty plea." Jesse says to the camera, "Today's the day before I went to jail." Laughing at his slip with David, Jesse admits that, yes, he thinks of this time as the past, since "at this point in time my life is as good as over." He also indicates that a future audience will exonerate him, making him anticipate that his case will be reopened in four-and-a-half years.

These sequences organize the interface of the movie to re-pose Carol-Ann Hooper and Ann Kaloski's (2006, 149) question about films treating child sexual abuse: "What might it mean to gaze at a paedophile?" Pursuing the same sequencing I have already analyzed, the film queries the informational core of reality by showing Arnold's emergence as a pedophile only through such image making. It is in the vortex of these gazes—self-directed, looking forward, looking back—that the historically situated Jewish community and family is transformed into the flickering whiteness of the virtual pedophile. The filmic sequences that follow David's 1988 video diary insist on relocating the body as a virtual space produced by the gaze of pedophilia's surveillance. The film introduces Arnold-as-pedophile through sequences similar to the one that introduces David's video journal, opening with a spatial montage of Great Neck that emphasizes images of class privilege and familial normalcy. The Friedmans, we are told by various interviewees in this sequence, are a good middle-class family in a good middle-class home, evidenced in happy home movies that play in background.

The images and narrative memory insist on the visibility of the normal, its spatial coordinates. The private home movies are contrasted with middle-class public space. Against this mode of historical referentiality, associated with the normalcy of middle-class Jewish Great Neck, the film will posit the hypermediation of the virtual pedophile. Through its sequencing of multiple remediations, the film interrogates the stereotyped image of the pedophile as having "a white, disheveled and loosely creepy appearance" (Hooper and Kaloski 2006, 149). The segments treating the interviews with former children from the computer classes are shot almost entirely in shadow; only one inter-view subject is named and lit; only one upholds the claim that there was sexual abuse. The film suggests that the children were given the image of the pedo-phile through hypnosis and the media, enabling fantasy and projection. The film participates in this visual discourse, leaving children's testimony clouded in shadow and their bodies illegible.

In these sequences, what has been coded as the public space of Great Neck and its middle-class formations begins to recede, with Arnold recoded into the virtual whiteness of pedophilia. The B-roll of the town is replaced by B-roll of courtrooms, prison fencing, and television coverage of the case. And this recoding occurs entirely through the recasting of the gaze as virtual memory, as the film makes clear. The gaze is signified in the film through the explicit mediations of technology, certainly, but also in the diegetic footage of remem-bered looking. In the middle of this sequence, Elaine discusses the first time the police showed her Arnold's child pornography (intercut as extreme close-up shots of naked white skin in an indecipherable tangle and what seem like blurry line drawings of naked boys [figure 4.2]). Elaine says she could not see what she was looking at: "My eyes were in the right direction, but my brain saw nothing, because when it was all over the lawyers showed me the maga-zine, and then I saw it for the first time. I really saw it." This temporal dy-namic of mediated recognition is linked to the first segment depicting Arnold Friedman under arrest, the Arnold Friedman not of home movies or family remembrance but captured on news footage as an alleged pedophile. Here the footage is familiar, overly familiar, almost stock footage of arrest and arraign-ment. We see Arnold walking in custody from his home at night, head down, and walking toward the courthouse, increasingly disheveled and blank, a spot-lighted lost figure held together by police hands and glaring crowds (figure 4.3). We see images of a prison, a chain-link fence, and hear the murmuring sound of crowds over a newscaster's solemn detailing of crimes.

This image of the pedophile is at the heart of the documentary's virtual

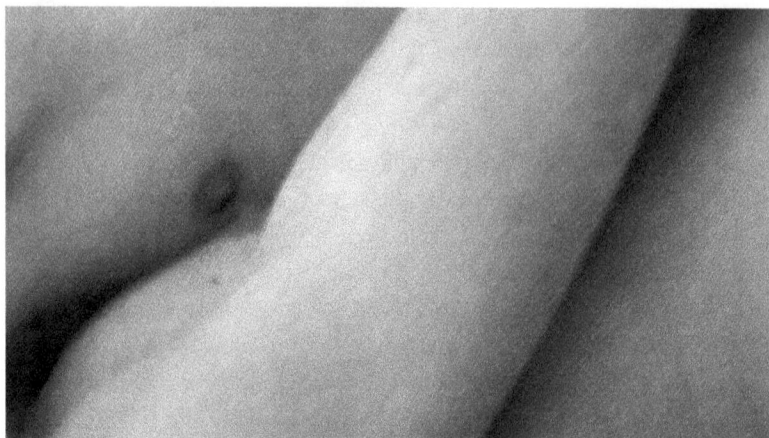

FIGURE 4.2 What Elaine cannot see, *Capturing the Friedmans* (dir. Andrew Jarecki), Magnolia Pictures, 2003.

FIGURE 4.3 Arnold on TV, *Capturing the Friedmans* (dir. Andrew Jarecki), Magnolia Pictures, 2003.

memory. Elaine cannot see what is literally in front of her eyes, very much, *Capturing the Friedmans* suggests, a parallel for the audience's relationship to Arnold. Like the images of child pornography, the image of Arnold as pedophile is impossible to really see. It is mediated for us in advance, making it impossible ever to recognize the image as present tense. The pedophile, *Capturing the Friedmans* suggests, is pure image. If Jarecki seems to enact a "refusal of the role of adjudicator" (Arthur 2003, 6), he does make pedophilia the historical nexus for the virtualization of memory. As part of an emerging visual code, virtual memory of the white pedophile provides a vehicle through which to translate older regimes of representation into new codes of figurative agency. In *Capturing the Friedmans*, the virtualization performed through pedophilia—as an emergent or dynamic visual repertoire coupled with an archaic series of static images—captures residual forms of gendered and racialized performance.[8] This residual iconography of failed performance is referenced and abstracted into new forms of performative failure: the cinematographic virtuality of the white pedophile. The Friedmans come to appear "natural" when their whiteness is seen through pedophilic acts of looking: looking as (and at) a pedophile. That this looking *is itself an act of failure* is precisely the point: remember Elaine's failure to see what is before her eyes, reproduced as the blurred referent for the cinematic viewer. The film transfers failure from the performance to the look, seemingly liberating performance for new technological relations of sexual security.

Pedophile Noir

Clint Eastwood's *Mystic River* also asks its audience to encounter the virtual mechanisms of pedophilic predation. In its manifest plot, *Mystic River* explores the relationship between the abduction and sexual abuse of a seven-year-old boy and the disappearance and murder of a nineteen-year-old girl within a gentrifying Boston neighborhood. The basic plot of the movie is lifted from the Lehane novel: three boys living in Buckingham, Massachusetts, a fictional setting in what is presumably East Boston, find their lives interrupted when one of the boys is abducted by two men pretending to be police officers. While Sean Devine (Kevin Bacon) and Jimmy Markum (Sean Penn) continue on their seemingly predetermined life trajectories (Sean as son of the upwardly mobile, respectable working class and Jimmy as entrenched working-class tough), Dave Boyle (Tim Robbins) finds his life permanently altered by his four-day captivity with two men who call themselves "Henry" and "George." Once Dave escapes and returns to the community, his development as "damaged goods" contrasts sharply with Sean's and Jimmy's seemingly uninterrupted maturation. Sean makes good by becoming a state cop who returns to the community as a vehicle of law and order; Jimmy, as ex-con-turned-family-man, holds the community together against encroaching change. But Dave is a haunted man, gentle and broken, seemingly lost to the time in which he lives.

When their lives are drawn together once more after the murder of Jimmy's teenage daughter Katie (Emmy Rossum), each character is forced to confront his shared past to solve the mystery of an uncertain present. Ultimately, the whodunit focuses on two major mysteries about the relation between past and present: Dave's mysterious activities the night of Katie's murder, which are linked to Dave's history of childhood sexual abuse; and the possible motives of Katie's boyfriend, Brendan Harris (Tom Guiry), which are linked to Jimmy's history of organized crime. The night Katie is murdered, Dave returns home later than usual, bloody and shaken. His story about a foiled mugging briefly convinces his wife, Celeste (Marcia Gay Harden), who later comes to doubt his story and puts her trust instead in Jimmy Markum's community authority. In this first plotline of tangled pasts and presents, the State Police, represented by Sean and his partner, Whitey Powers (Laurence Fishburne), pursue one investigation into Dave's activities the night of the murder while Jimmy and his old crew, the Savage brothers, conduct their own community-based inquiry. In the second plotline, Jimmy's full history of criminal violence slowly unfolds over the course of Sean's police investigation into Katie's boyfriend. Jimmy served time after his old partner in crime, "Just Ray" Harris, turned him in after a robbery; Just Ray disappeared once Jimmy was released (we learn at the film's denouement that Jimmy killed him), leaving a missing link in the cycle of retaliation that could explain who would want to kill Jimmy's daughter.

The relationship between past and present serves as the core mystery of *Mystic River*. Amid this historical tangle Dave's childhood sexual abuse is described by all three boys as pivotal to their subsequent lives yet mysterious in its actual effects. It serves as a primary reference point for many of their interactions in the aftermath of Katie's murder. When Sean and Jimmy sit down to talk to each other after Katie's murder, Jimmy asks: "What if you or I had gotten in the car instead of Dave Boyle?" And at film's end, Sean will say, "Sometimes I think—I think all three of us got in that car. And this is all just a dream. In reality, we're still eleven-year-old boys, locked in a cellar, imagining what our lives would be if we escaped." Dave, the only one who knows the event in its entirety, is himself erased as a self-knowing subject by the experience. "Dave's dead," he explains to his wife. "I don't know who came out of that cellar, but it sure as shit wasn't Dave." *Mystic River* presents these three men as the answer to a mystery unfolding within and against the transformations of Boston from the 1970s to the 1990s. While their Irish working-class community is slowly eroded by changes in the labor structure and modes of governance, each man symbolizes one trajectory through the historical tumult: Sean, the upwardly mobile working-class boy turned State Police officer; Jimmy, the tough, streetwise kid incarcerated at nineteen and then reformed as a neighborhood store owner; and Dave, the quiet local son kidnapped by pedophiles and returned as "damaged goods" to grow up into an introverted, stooped shadow of the men around him.

Lehane's novel positions Dave's childhood sexual abuse as a key to understanding the broader structural transformations of the era. Many of his popular detective novels include child sexual abuse, often situated within historically specific working-class enclaves defined by economic precarity and interpersonal violence. His first novel, *A Drink before the War* (1994), introduced what one interviewer calls Lehane's interest in "paedophilia, a subject that developed into one of his major obsessions as a writer" (Grant 2009). According to Lehane's comments in that interview, child sexual abuse stands out even in volatile contexts defined by scarcity, a defilement adding "one extra level of rage that the rest of us cannot even fathom." Lehane holds what his interviewer calls a "hardcore right-wing" belief that pedophilia is a "contagion" that infects those it touches, turning victims into potential predators. But he also links pedophilia to economic and social structures that curse victims with "marginalized lives with marginalized jobs."[9] *Mystic River*, the sixth of his fourteen novels and the one that is arguably the most focused on pedophilia, unfolds this complicated linkage between contagion and marginalization in the fictional town of "East Buckingham," which refers to Charlestown geographically but combines elements of South Boston and other traditionally Irish American locales, as well (Richards 2001).[10] The novel traces the experiences of Sean, Jimmy, and Dave as they grow up amid social and economic restructuring, depicting violent events (child rape and the murder of an adolescent) as one contagious effect of neoliberalism's war on the young and its logic of marginalization.

Dave's childhood abduction and sexual assault and Katie's murder are presented as part of the community's struggle amid specific historical forces—

particularly, the struggle of Irish American working-class men and women against their seemingly inevitable loss. In an introduction to his edited anthology *Boston Noir*, Lehane (2009, 13) situates his work overall within the genre of noir: "Noir is a genre of loss, of men and women unable to roll with the changing times, so the changing times instead roll over them." What is particular about neoliberal noir, however, is its focus on dispossession and the marketization of all human value: "What's lost has, in many cases, been taken; what's left is what people can't sell" (Lehane 2009, 13). If the structural adjustment associated with neoliberalism takes what it can of value and leaves behind what people cannot sell, the book proposes, violence against youth is one mode of this broader restructuring.[11] Some of East Buckingham's youth succumb to vulnerability (loss through predation); others, to disposability (economic and social devaluation). While child sexual abuse is presented as having particularly marginalizing effects, it is not necessarily situated outside the historical frame of the novel. Even though Lehane himself speaks of pedophilia in exceptionalist or mystical terms—contagion among them—the novel itself largely avoids resolving its mystery through such formulations. Instead, exceptionalist interpretations are attributed to specific characters rather than to the overall narrative. And those characters are clearly situated within shared historical conditions in ways that the reader (if not the author) can recognize, making some characters' marginalization key to others' survival.

In contrast to the novel, the film makes Dave's childhood sexual abuse into the cinematic vanishing point of history and a mystic phenomenon whose contagion must be contained by the manly efforts of Sean and Jimmy.[12] The film uses Dave to produce a realm of virtual pedophilia seemingly outside the historical conditions in which Sean and Jimmy struggle to regain human agency. Dave is not an actual pedophile—he does not have sex with children in the movie—but his potential pedophilia constitutes him as the object of both the camera's gaze and the policing look of other characters, as well as the audience. The film's treatment of Dave as a virtual pedophile picks up the threat of contagion, in other words, as self-generating and delinked from processes of social and economic marginalization that shape the broader conditions of all three main characters. In the film, Sean's partner, Whitey, explains that "baby rapers and chicken hawks" are a unique criminal type who must be permanently separated from the general population: "But, like, if they had an island just for baby rapers and chicken hawks? Just airlift food in a few times a week, fill the water with mines. No one gets off. First-time offenders? Fuck you. You get life on the island." Sex predators against children are of nature: first-time offenders are completely determined by their actions, and for human safety they must remain in nature—that is, they get "life on the island." Since it is naturally predatory, pedophilic life must be technologically circumscribed, bordered by technologies of life sustenance (airlifted food) and life destruction (mines).

Through this depiction of Dave, the film engages the pedophilic function to create an "orchid in the land of technology," or a virtual "island just for baby rapers and chicken hawks" in the land of restructured humanism.[13] The inhuman, virtual realm of pedophilia associated not only with Dave's assault, but also with his tainted humanity, across the remainder of the film provides the condition through which Sean and Jimmy regain their human agency. Through their capacity to see Dave as a potential pedophile, Sean and Jimmy emerge as the agents of more properly historical struggles in which survival is defined by the thin blue line of the carceral state: Sean joins the State Police; Jimmy has served time for armed robbery.[14] These seemingly more human forms of criminality and policing, associated with an earlier period of economic exploitation and political discipline, are a contrast to the inhuman or mystic criminality of pedophilia. The film therefore recasts the historical conditions of the book—its explicit treatment of structural adjustment as a war on the young—as a mystic story of inhuman violence (pedophilic predation) and human vengeance (the return of human agency amid the ruins of history).[15] This allows the film to "lose" Dave, but in so doing, to revalue the humanity of those who are "left": Jimmy and Sean. In Eastwood's adaptation, Jimmy and Sean "roll with the times" to reenter history as agents of their own destiny, even if that agency is no longer associated with productive labor or political action.

The Law of Montage

The film *Mystic River* opens with a scene of adult men, the fathers of the protagonist boys, sitting obscured on a second-story porch (at times behind the bars of the porch slats) while they listen to a Red Sox game on the radio (Ardolino 2007). The first utterance of the film, "What time is this going on?" leads to a barely audible exchange ending with, "Can you imagine a ninety-two-mile-an-hour fastball coming down at you? You don't have time to think." This short exchange contrasts with the rapid movement of two boys on the ground below, a young Sean (Connor Paolo) and Jimmy (Jason Kelly). The boys rush out to play stickball on the street while the men rock in their chairs, betting their labor on the outcome of the game ("If he gets on base twice tonight, I'll paint your porch"). The short opening sequence creates the sense of a community in stasis, represented by an older generation seemingly just out of the camera's full capture. Their relative immobility is coupled with their barely audible commentary on a faraway game. Resilience will require adapting to rapid change, creating forms of agency that the two men obscured by the porch bars seem to lack. The bars themselves indicate the alternative future available to those who "don't have time to think"—the criminalization of those men no longer able to participate in the labor markets coming at them.[16]

The potential disposability of the older generation, with its hierarchical shots from the second story, gives way in this sequence to the horizontal and mobile shots following young Jimmy, Sean, and Dave (Cameron Bowman, wearing a Red Sox cap) playing stickball in the street. Here the camera follows Jimmy and Sean in the flight of the game, emphasizing their rapid movement through space from the perspective of lateral motion while Dave remains relatively still as catcher, his one moment of action leading to the loss of their ball in a storm drain. The boys then begin to carve their first names into a patch of newly poured cement. Jimmy and Sean finish, but as Dave begins to carve the letters "DA" a man calling himself a police officer accosts them for violating municipal property. Dave, the only boy to admit he does not live nearby, is taken in the car by the "police officer" and a second man wearing a ring with a cross. Dave is reluctant to get in at first, so the first man slams his hand on the hood of his car, and we see a close-up of his angry face as he says, "Get in." The last thing we see is Dave looking out the back window, growing smaller and smaller as the car drives away from the position Sean and Jimmy share with the camera, intercut with shots of Sean and Jimmy receding from Dave's view.[17]

The past recedes along with the connection among the three boys, leaving us with the images of their still faces staring at one another across an ever-increasing distance. Here the necessity of staying in motion is supplemented by the dangers of not seeing "what is coming down at you." What can be seen—by the boys and by the audience—will be contrasted with what can be understood and reacted to. Following the images of the boys watching one another's faces recede, the film breaks into two distinct temporalities and two distinct relations between face and place. The first follows Sean and Jimmy, who return to Jimmy's home and report that Dave has gotten into a car with two men they do not know. This plot is shot in sequences that unfold in the movie's realist time articulated through the logic of cause and effect and its juxtaposition of face and place; the "motion" of the fastball sets the pace of the two boys and the men they will become. The second follows Dave, who appears in a recursive temporality that continually returns him to the scene of the captivity. From the moment of his abduction, Dave seems outside the time of the film's plot. While Sean and Jimmy return to the tenement porch to seek help, Dave disappears into a sequence situating his captivity and assault in shadows that will come to fully identify him.

For the remainder of the movie, all three will be shot in shadowy close-ups, and all three will be situated in relation to establishing shots of the river, but the significance of their affect and its capacity to move them into community will be shown as intrinsically different. The majority of the plot unfolds in urban landscapes, featuring gray cement, police station interiors, and housing in a muted palette of urban decline.[18] In contrast, Dave's childhood assault and Katie's murder take place in lush green parks, seemingly isolated from urban time and space. The film begins to dramatize this tension between urban history and eternal nature through two visual motifs: the repeated shots of the Mystic River and the emotionally charged close-ups of characters' faces. Breaks in the segments of the filmic plot are signified by an establishing shot of the Mystic River, emphasizing the river's permanence in relation to changing man-made landscapes.[19] Close-ups of Sean and Jimmy establish them as part of a changing landscape, their affective potential linking them to family and community within what would otherwise appear as static urban space (Aitkin 2006). Dave's affective close-ups locate him instead in a realm of virtuality, an atavistic animal caught in his own compulsive potentiality until he is brought into historical reality through the informational profile of the pedophile.

Across four major shot sequences Dave assembles an image of virtuality through what Walter Benjamin (1969, 234) calls the "law of montage," in which the cameraman's unique task is to create "multiple fragments which are assembled under a new law." This "law of montage" operates through techniques such as the close-up and slow motion such that "the camera introduces us to unconscious optics as does psychoanalysis to unconscious impulses" (Benjamin 1969, 237). The law that emerges in *Mystic River* regulates which optics will become conscious and which unconscious through the montage of the flashback (Turim 1989). In the film, we apprehend the pedophile primarily through Dave's cinematic flashbacks of childhood abduction and sexual assault. But what appear as flashbacks are in fact the camera's montage of previously seen and new elements, carefully assembled so that

Dave's face becomes both the object of the camera's gaze and the seeming subject of involuntary memory. First, Dave's face on-screen disappears into the realm of virtuality, seemingly dissolved through the camera's insertion of involuntary memory. Then, out of these flashbacks Dave's face reappears as itself an assemblage of images associated with the virtual object of his memory—the man who kidnapped him. Through the montage that assembles Dave on-screen, the film creates Dave first as a site of virtuality, then as an emerging unnatural monster whose potentiality can be realized only as pedophilia. These sequences draw attention to their own technological mediation as they locate as "Dave" the aura otherwise lost to the film's historical time (the main detective plot).

The first Dave sequence comes in the opening segment of the film and is ostensibly the real-time action of his abduction and captivity. The main shot sequence shifts between the point of view attributed to Dave, looking slightly upward at two backlit shadowy male figures as they come through a doorway into a dark room, and that of the two men, looking downward at Dave lying in the dark on a dirty mattress, the doorway light casting Dave's shadow ominously against the brick wall behind him. The seeming antagonism of these opposing perspectives (predator and prey) is then resolved into a single chiaroscuro effect in which Dave's body and shadow are covered by the shadow of the approaching men. As this happens, Dave's shadow on the dark wall looks eerily like a pose of seduction, in contrast to his pained face in the light and his repeated, "Please, no more" (figure 4.4). The sequence ends when their shadows blend into a full fade-out while animal noises seem to drown out Dave's final whispered, "Please." The next shot fades in to Dave's well-lit face staring directly into the camera before he turns away to run through a forest of very green foliage, pursued by animal sounds that resolve into something akin to wolves howling. It seems that Dave has escaped from the shadows, yet the animal sounds following him into the woods signal an ominous potentiality linking Dave's dissolution into the predator's shadow and his flight into "nature."

This first sequence establishes a pattern of light and shadow in which predator and prey become one object of the camera's gaze, their antagonistic roles blended into a confusing potentiality. Even though Dave escapes, it is unclear whether his return to the light redeems this shadowy experience (or whether nature can restore him to the urban community left behind). The film registers Dave's ominous potentiality in its split between what is said by characters within the film and the knowing assemblage of the camera. Dave's "no" within the scene of predation is coupled with the image of his shadow

FIGURE 4.4 Dave says, "Please, no more," *Mystic River* (dir. Clint Eastwood), Village Roadside Pictures, Malpaso Production, 2003.

seemingly seducing the predator, ultimately becoming one with him. This dynamic between shadow and light, sight and speech will continue across the next three Dave sequences, in which he experiences "flashbacks" of his abduction and begins to fade into the realm of virtuality. We will find that Dave's verbal articulation slowly situates him more deeply in the atavistic nature of the predator, blending agency and passivity in a form of compulsion, even as his ominous potentiality will be repeatedly associated with a return to "nature" against the more technologically "real" human urban world.

We next fade into the brightly lit urban world of the present day. The static world of the early 1970s, where white working-class men see what is barreling down upon them but cannot react to it, has been replaced by a world fully enmeshed in the changes of the neoliberal era. It is thirty years on, and we begin with a shot of Dave (now wearing a black Red Sox cap) walking down the street with his own young son, the Tobin Bridge spanning the Mystic River in the background. As Dave crosses over to the shadowed side of the street, the camera starts to swirl slowly around him and then cuts to their childhood names scrawled in the cement. The shot of the names at first seems to replicate Dave's point of view, but then we slowly travel up Dave's body to see his face looking into the camera. Dave's half-finished name is linked to Dave's blank face (partially obscured by the shadow of his hat). The camera seems to look for the completion of Dave's name in his face, extending Dave's blank look from the cement to his own face and ultimately "through" his face into the past. Dave's face fades into a quick image of his kidnapper and then back

FIGURE 4.5 Dave blends with the predator, *Mystic River* (dir. Clint Eastwood), Village Roadside Pictures, Malpaso Production, 2003.

again, the two men's faces briefly superimposed in one image (figure 4.5). The face of the pedophile emerges as the object of involuntary memory, that which interrupts the film's historical time and crystallizes memory as the site of a new assemblage. Dave becomes the site of this assemblage, his face both subject of involuntary memory and object of technological reproducibility, a composite image through which the pedophile begins to emerge in a virtual realm.

This strategy is repeated and amplified across the next two sequences depicting Dave's slow dissolution into the realm of virtuality created by the film. Dave's atavistic nature first enters into his speech (separated from the montage of his flashbacks), and then takes over his presence entirely within the diegetic time of the film. The third Dave sequence comes further into the plot when he tells his son a bedtime story about "the boy who escaped from wolves." This sequence echoes and blends the prior two. We open in a dark room reminiscent of Dave's captivity, only here it is a grown-up Dave who appears in the shadowy foreground (the position of the predator) while his young son lies before him in a shaft of light from the window. The shot-reverse-shot sequence echoes Dave's captivity sequence, the camera moving between Dave's view of his son and omniscient side shots of Dave barely lit against the dark space. We find Dave in mid-story, whispering, "Because sometimes the man wasn't a man at all. He was the boy." Ominous string music rises as Dave's face slowly shifts to the left side of a mostly dark screen, leaving the right side of his face half-illuminated, his son shadowy in the shot before him as he continues: "The boy who escaped from wolves, an animal of the dusk, invisible, silent, living in a world the others never saw, a world of fireflies, unseen except as a flair in the corner of your eye, vanished by the time you turn your head toward it." As Dave slowly moves from man to boy to animal, his isolated face shifts entirely off the dark screen and we are returned to the montage of Dave's running escape through the green woods, wolves howling.

Dave becomes both boy and wolf through this montage, which moves from cuts to fades to superimposition to the slow blend of Dave with the negative space of the frame. This practice of montage matches what Mark Seltzer (1998, 49) describes as the visual representation of serial killers: "a minimalist distinction between the subject and dark space—the minimalist representation of the killer that defines, for instance, the cinematographic formula, and the terrible and deadly places, of the film noir." In this noir, the negative space that "others can't see" becomes the realm of virtuality, the space of Dave's involuntary memory. But here it is not, in fact, Dave's memory we are seeing at all. It is the cinematic reproducibility of the image. Dave becomes the site of virtuality as what Brian Massumi (2002, 30) calls "a realm of *potential* . . . where futurity combines, unmediated, with pastness, where outsides are infolded."

Dave appears as a screen or seemingly flat surface whose "outsides are infolded": he appears through the "infolding" of pastness (depicted as involuntary memories of child sexual abuse) and futurity (his potentiality as a sex predator). This cinematic treatment of Dave updates the naturalist aesthetics of atavism for a new technological age. In her study of racial science in U.S. modernity, Dana Seitler (2008, 6) argues that in the early twentieth century "atavism functioned as a way to make visible, to exteriorize on the surface of the body, characteristics that might otherwise conceal themselves in the more undetectable realms of the body's interior spaces." Here atavism becomes virtual, articulated not on the surface of the body but in the body's disappearance into the surface of the image. As Seltzer (1998, 49) characterizes this style, "This is, in brief, the assimilation of the subject to dark spaces: a chameleon-like melting or fading into place that is experienced at once as the lure of anonymity (disguise or impersonation) and as the threat of anonymity (impersonation as impersonality: the serial killer as 'nonperson')."

Across the Dave sequences, the virtual pedophile takes on the characteristics of the noir killer but updates them to incorporate the atavistic compulsion of the inhuman sexual predator. The fourth Dave sequence becomes even more explicit in its citation of the building montage, now moving from the blended faces and shot coding to a more complete identification of Dave with the virtual pedophile as a technologically reproducible image. His presence in the diegetic scene becomes ghostly and flickering, while the distinction between flashback and present is slowly erased. During this sequence Dave's wife comes home to find him watching a vampire movie, his body half-illuminated by the flickering television in a dark room. In place of the external light coming in through door and window (as in the previous scenes), here the light comes from the source of technological reproducibility itself—the television set. Dave's shadowy presence has gone from prey (captured boy) to potential predator (father hovering over his own sleeping son) to technologically revealed monster (vampire reflected by the television screen). Across these sequences Dave has remained caught in the shadows of the men who captured him: this shadow falls across him first from his Red Sox hat (the shadow of childhood he has never left), then from the window of the bedroom where he is confronted by the vulnerability of his sleeping son, and finally from the television's flickering images of vampires. It is only in this final scene that Dave emerges from these shadows into the visual image of inhumanity.

Reproduction among the Ruins

Dave's own revelation in this scene weds articulation to image. As Celeste tries to voice her suspicions about his involvement in Katie's murder, Dave offers a seemingly detached monologue on vampires and werewolves: "They're undead, but I think maybe there's something beautiful about it. Maybe one day you wake up and you forget what it's like to be human. Maybe then it's OK." Throughout much of this conversation Dave is shot in side profile, looking away from Celeste and the camera into an unavailable distance, similar to his position in the scene with his son. After he accuses Celeste of thinking he killed Katie, Dave ultimately ends up sitting across the room beside a bright light, his head in his hands, muttering, "Henry and George, they were wolves, and Dave was the boy who escaped from wolves." But here the boy, Dave, and the wolves are all narrated in the past tense. What emerges from these shadows is the vampire. We see Dave's face once again in side profile in the lamplight, but this time the shadow cast over it comes from his own hand raised to his forehead.

"Dave" has emerged as the virtual pedophile, the object made legible through the conjunction of articulation (inhuman vampire) and image (a human shadow cast across what is revealed now as his inhuman form). While in the previous sequence Dave was both boy and wolf, by the end of this sequence Dave has broken away from Celeste's one effort to touch him. He says, "Dave is dead. I don't know who came out of that cellar, but it sure as shit wasn't Dave." As he finally narrates the information that explains his revealed image—"You see, honey, it's like vampires. Once it's in you, it stays"—Dave has become an assemblage of chiaroscuro effects linked to the virtual realm of pedophilia, a realm that, in turn, collapses distinctions between perpetrator and victim into a single form of inhumanity. If the wolf refers to fairy tale as mythic embodiment and naturalism as organic embodiment, the vampire refers to scientifically mediated imaginaries of the inhuman. By making Dave into the explicit site of technological reproducibility, Sean and Jimmy are freed to pursue the information that will distance them from vulnerability, coded now as penetrability by technology, and disposability, coded as irrelevance to a new political economic order. They will emerge as the human agents who can protect the community from both inhuman predation and human irrelevance: traditional working-class men with a new role to play in protecting their community from generational destruction. All that remains is for the new police—state and community—to catch up to the audience, documenting the information that makes Dave into a potential predator.

Mystic River leaves a level of ambiguity in its resolution of the Dave plotline in relation to the resolution of Katie's murder. As the film draws to a close, the police ultimately discover that Brendan Harris's younger brother killed Katie in a random act, using a gun from the long-ago robbery joining Brendan's father and Jimmy. In the meantime, Jimmy has killed Dave for his suspected role in Katie's murder, using Dave's own logic of poisoned inhumanity to justify the belief that he was turned into a killer by his sexual abuse. And the audience is told by Dave, via a final flashback sequence, that he in fact did kill someone: a man he found having sex with an underage male prostitute in a parked car.[20] Through this process, *Mystic River* participates in what Eva Cherniavsky (2006) describes as the split between filmic diegesis and cinematic apparatus that characterizes film noir, in which the femme fatale suffers diegetic punishment even as her aura survives as the exalted effect of the cinematic technology. This noir split works to the opposite effect in *Mystic River*, however, in which the filmic plot exonerates Dave for Katie's murder even as the cinematic apparatus leaves his aura of compulsive inhumanity intact. Thus, even as the film itself posits Dave's act as a justified homicide and Jimmy's as an act of false revenge, the cinematography maintains Dave's radical isolation from the human plot as vampire/inhuman predator. He is left as the virtual antidote to the structural adjustment of safety and sexuality imposed on the film's white working-class community.

The virtualization of Dave makes possible new relations between face and space for the other two men, whose still images of affective condensation are revitalized and reconnected to the human community in contrast to Dave's virtual pedophilia. During Sean and Whitey's investigation of Katie's murder, both Jimmy and Dave are considered possible contributors to her death. In both cases, their potential criminality is evaluated through the amassing of information deemed relevant by Whitey, the non–community-affiliated police officer and the only main black character within the film's plot, whose role in the investigation seems to signify the success of other minorities within a system that continues to profile criminals through visual etiologies of violence. When Jimmy is interviewed by the police immediately after Katie's death, he tells Sean and Whitey that when he got out of jail, Katie had given him a look like she would never see him again; she looked at him again that way the night she disappeared. When Whitey seizes upon this anecdote, Jimmy protests, "It's just a look." But according to Whitey, "It's information. We collect it, put it together, see what fits. Little things, like, you say you were in prison?" Here Whitey insists on translating the "look" into "information," linked instantly to the criminal profiling of Jimmy as an ex-con. Similarly, Whitey does not like the "look" of Dave, translating his face into an informational sequence: "Boyle fits the profile to a fucking T. Mid-thirties, white, marginally employed, sexually abused as a kid. Are you serious? On paper, this guy should be in jail already."

But Whitey's focus on etiological information breaks down in the film's cinematic differentiation among criminal types, affiliating the potential of the "look" to restore human connection to Jimmy while Dave remains merely the static object of the technological gaze.[21] The criminality of the two men is contrasted explicitly through the role of gender and family to connect them to community. Jimmy's experience with violence will be coded as part of a traditional working-class past, in which his crime—robbery, murder as community policing—will become an important resource for his reconnection to community in a changed present. While Jimmy remembers feeling isolated when he was first released from jail, saying of his daughter Katie, "It's like we were the last two people on earth. You know—forgotten, unwanted," he goes on to meet what his current wife's father calls his "domestic responsibilities." Jimmy is told he will always "come through, 'cause you're a man . . . a real old-

FIGURE 4.6 Sean shoots with his hand, *Mystic River* (dir. Clint Eastwood), Village Roadside Pictures, Malpaso Production, 2003.

school man." Jimmy's experience with violence reconnects him to both family and community as the sovereign agent of self-determination: after Jimmy has killed Dave, his wife tells him that she knows he "would do do anything for those he loved, and that can never be wrong," explaining that their children know "their daddy's a king, and a king knows what to do and does it." In contrast, Dave's experience of violence isolates him from all forms of human collectivity. When he comes home bloody after killing the john in the car, he explains to his wife: "Makes you feel alone, you know, hurting somebody. . . . Makes you feel like an alien."

The film uses the cinematic apparatus to differentiate Jimmy's normalized criminality from Dave's irreversible atavism. It contrasts the use of information as forensic evidence (the gun ballistics on the computer screen, the 911 tape) versus the visual as forensic evidence (the look within the film, the cinematographic gaze itself).[22] The famous parade scene at the movie's end becomes in this reading far less enigmatic than some critics have suggested. Ultimately, Sean and Jimmy are each shown reunited with their wives and daughters watching a parade. As Jimmy and Sean exchange a long look, Sean raises his hand in the sign of a gun and points it at Jimmy (figure 4.6). Jimmy has become the hero of residual modes of collective resilience in the face of external political economic exploitation and police surveillance, with Sean as the ameliorating new police able to recognize the failures of white ethnic community in the face of neoliberalism. Yet this seeming humanized battle between community and state (with the hand as gun) ultimately dissolves into a new shared terrain of social reproduction, grounded now in the refigured "nature" of human reproduction and the bonds of family.[23] Sean and Jimmy become men able to rebuild community, not through productive labor or political action, but through their capacity to make families. Through the technological prosthesis of the pedophile, a new human family emerges as the bulwark against extinction.

Both *Capturing the Friedmans* and *Mystic River* trace how virtual pedophilia's turn to a security logic of the potential rather than the probable legitimates expansions of predictive policing, forensic speculation, and statistical aberration as hyper-threat while exonerating normative whiteness from the worst criminalization. Here the virtual pedophile transfigures potentiality into risk and assembles a seemingly more horizontal and even empowering mode of sexual countersurveillance that promises survival. This temporalized biopolitics—what Elizabeth Freeman (2007, 4) calls chronobiopolitics—connects the management of bodies to populations through "a larger temporal schema" in which subjects "experience belonging itself as natural." This naturalized experience of belonging has, of course, always required its abject or object others, as scholars of queer inhumanism and insurgent genres of the human such as Mel Chen and Dana Luciano (2015), Zakiyyah Iman Jackson (2013), Jasbir Puar (2017), and Jordy Rosenberg (2014) remind. But in the era of virtual pedophilia, this naturalized experience has itself been subjected to insecuritization. New conditionals on nature routed through criminality and sexuality required securitization in order to protect against an eruption of the unnatural nature.[24] To adapt to this newly denatured experience, both "normal life" (Spade 2015) and its "sexual dissidents" (Freeman 2007, 7) are transfigured to create Sex Offender Registration and Notification–era subjectivities routed through virtual pedophilia. This shift depended not only on the heterocentric narrative of family and reproduction, but also on the absorption and redirection of queer experiences to render pedophilia the horizon of sexual futures.

FIVE

CAPTURING THE FUTURE AND THE SEXUALITY OF RISK

To know it was happening was one thing.
To see it was another.
—**SCOTT HEIM**, *Mysterious Skin*

This chapter explores what happens when viewers know they are supposed to be looking at a pedophile on-screen. In several narrative films of the 2000s, the pedophile appears as an identifiable character rather than a virtual image. Films such as *L.I.E.* (dir. Michael Cuesta [2001]) and *Hard Candy* (dir. David Slade [2005]) present an on-screen pedophile or youth-oriented adult in order to query the queer possibilities and heterosexist inequities of intergenerational sexuality, while films such as *Little Children* (dir. Todd Field [2006]) and *The Lovely Bones* (dir. Peter Jackson [2009]) present the on-screen pedophile as a stereotypically creepy white man stalking innocent youth. The two films I treat in this chapter—Gregg Araki's 2004 adaptation of Scott Heim's novel *Mysterious Skin* (1995) and Nicole Kassell's 2004 adaptation of Steven Fechter's play *The Woodsman* (first produced in 2000, published with Samuel French in 2009), present the on-screen pedophile as a way to interrogate the origins of its virtual image. Within these two films, the virtual pedophile is returned to its scenes of production. The aura of the virtual pedophile is tracked as a product of 1980s discourses of trauma and risk that are ultimately translated into the 2000s prioritization of risk in Sex Offender Registration and Notification (SORN). While the last chapter clarified how virtual pedophilia becomes a kind of visual trauma, this chapter focuses on how virtual pedophilia becomes a source of risk.

The films in this chapter track the pre-emergence (in the 1980s) and dominance (in the 2000s) of the virtual pedophile as a figure requiring new and ever-expanding technologies of security that delimit the possibilities of queer life. Here "queer" marks that which is outside racialized and territorialized repro/heteronormativities, itself a kind of surplus, as well as specific figures of sexual subjectivity associated with this surplus.[1] Many critics have queried the relation between the sex offender and queer figures, asking how the normalization of homosexual desires and practices dovetailed with the criminal pathologization of the sex offender. As the pedophile shifted in association from homosexual to sex offender, scholars such as Joseph Fischel (2016, 17) point out that the sex offender has become the new "exhaustive figure of sexual amorality and dangerousness." The sex offender is less homosexual replacement than supplement, Fischel explains, a sexual minority that absorbs what remains as "queer" once adult homosexuality is allegedly normalized through "age of consent." Araki's *Mysterious Skin* and Kassell's *The Woodsman* explore what sexual subjectivities were produced by the emergence of the pedophile as a sex offender in the SORN era. In these films the presence of the pedophile on-screen visualizes the juncture at which Michel Foucault's (1988b, 281) account of sexuality as "roaming danger" begins to take hold of information and images to enclose sexuality in figures of trauma and risk.

By representing the pedophile on-screen from the start, his accrued aura of virtuality is transferred onto a series of images freighted with the sensation of enigmatic potentiality. In her study *The Witch's Flight: The Cinematic, the Black Femme, and the Image of Common Sense*, Kara Keeling (2007, 6) uses cinematic "surplus" to name "an affective register that simultaneously exceeds and yearns toward" something not yet knowable by sight.[2] Even as this surplus "evad[es] currently accessible common senses," it "still can be felt—like an intuition or premonition, something unseen, but nonetheless present(ly) (im)-possible." These two films register as cinematic surplus that which exceeds the proper figures of sexual subjectivity organized through SORN. This surplus appears in images that do not coordinate knowledge and sight, but instead present a cognitive and visual contradiction or misalignment that registers in the senses as enigmatic. Each film produces this surplus without providing an interpretive or evaluative code, leaving viewers to determine how *cinematic* surplus does or does not register a *queer* surplus produced by this era's common sense. These films position viewers to experience the affective charge of queer experience as it might have been used both to fuel the emergence of SORN and to figure the sexual subjectivities it produced.

The first section of this chapter reads Araki's *Mysterious Skin* as depicting modes of experience that were rechanneled into sexual figures of trauma and risk over the course of the 1980s and 1990s. The story traces two Kansas boys' experience following sexual encounters with an adult Little League coach in 1981, when they are eight years old. One boy seems to experience the encounter as it happens and recalls it with an ambivalent pleasure that organizes his subsequent sexual experiences throughout his teens. All sexual sensation and mobilizing desire that precedes or follows this experience is represented in its terms. The other boy does not seem to experience the encounter as it happens. He "lost five hours," he repeatedly intones, not only unable to remember those hours but seemingly determined to repeat them endlessly in his losing battle to create nonsexual experiences (such as alien abduction) to give such loss meaning. The two boys' stories unfold in parallel projections and retrospections, echoing each other as passing images flash up and forge an assemblage across their separate stories. This assemblage figures a sensory surplus—including fragments of fleshly encounter with sticky surfaces and interiors—that exceeds the historical conditions in which the two boys struggle to make narrative sense of their experiences. Through this process the film reveals the "mysterious skin" cloaking sexual subjectivities produced through encounters with virtual pedophilia.

The second section of the chapter turns to Kassel's *The Woodsman*, which picks up long after the installation of SORN to follow one man's release from prison after serving twelve years for sexually abusing a twelve-year-old girl. The opening sequence of the film offers a short primer in informational aesthetics as his registration and reentry are filmed through freeze frames and movement images that disassemble the pedophilic profile as a sequence of static and dynamic risk factors. Following this opening sequence, the main character is shown navigating repeated run-ins with the police, his mandated therapist, family members, and coworkers who experience his mysterious skin as a threatening enigma. As he struggles to adapt to the codes of acceptable sexual subjectivities around him, a sensory surplus starts to be projected outside the main time of the film. As in *Mysterious Skin*, passing images flash up and slowly create an assemblage that appears outside narrative time. Here, however, sensory surplus is presented in flash-forward rather than flashback, creating temporally disjointed frames articulated to the aftermath of SORN and its figurative enclosure of potentiality as knowable surplus: a rolling red ball (citing Fritz Lang's 1931 film *M*), a ghostly white girl (citing Lewis Carroll's 1865 *Alice's Adventures in Wonderland*), and a red-cloaked birdwatcher in the woods (citing the European fairy tale *Little Red Riding Hood*).

This chapter reads *Mysterious Skin* and *The Woodsman* together to track their historical narrative about sexual subjectivities forged through the era of the pedophilic function, from the 1980s through the 2000s. *Mysterious Skin* proposes that sexual experience of the 1980s becomes sexual subjectivity of the 1990s by adapting affect to fit logics of trauma and risk. In this narrative, the two boys' flat affect becomes a sign of unintegrated surplus, figured on-screen as floating sensational images. *Mysterious Skin* could be read as resolving when each boy transforms flat affect and floating images into socially acceptable "feelings" founding sexual subjectivites: traumatized risk-taking and traumatized risk aversion become mature gay and straight subjectivities. *The Woodsman* proposes that sexual subjectivities of the 1990s and 2000s have, indeed, adapted to enclose surplus into acceptable subjectivities articulated to SORN. *The Woodsman* could similarly be read as resolving when its main character's flat affect transforms into socially acceptable subjectivities and leaves unacceptable images floating: pedophilic desires become abnormal but acceptable adult heterosexual practices. Yet both films end precisely at the moment their characters' adaptation truly begins. Futurity is left up for grabs, with images of sensational surplus remaining for audience members to assemble through their own experience of knowing and seeing pedophilia.

Mysteries of Skin

Mysterious Skin contemplates one decade in the lives of two boys becoming young men between 1981 and 1991. The author and critic Connie May Fowler calls Heim's source novel "a devastating portrait of a new lost generation," linking this decade to the one immediately following World War I.[3] This "new lost generation" faces not the immediate aftermath of a world war but the conditions of Cold War and détente, conditions in which life in Hutchinson, Kansas, seems doubly removed from what might once have been recognizable sources of conflict or agency. The novel's dedication—"For Tamyra Heim / and for Jamie Reisch / *before, during, after*"—captures the spirit of the film, as well. In both the novel and its film adaptation, this "before, during, and after" is articulated to the temporal rifts created by the events of summer 1981. On one hand, Neil McCormick (played as a child by Chase Ellison and as a teenager by Joseph Gordon-Levitt) narrates life in forward motion, as if it is unfolding on-screen as it happens and filtered through his active interpretation of events. On the other hand, Brian Lackey (played as a child by George Webster and as a teenager by Brady Corbet) narrates his life as retroactive even as it unfolds, constantly questioning the relation between reality and its interpretive frameworks. Neil signifies his sexual relationship with his Little League baseball coach (Bill Sage) as love; Brian, as alien abduction.

The novel experiments with point-of-view narration as a form of restricted realism, a Midwestern realism that differs in almost every respect from Lehane's hard-boiled style in *Mystic River*. Scott Heim's debut novel, like Lehane's, returns to his hometown origins (both authors are to some degree regional realists).[4] But Heim's Hutchinson is riddled with boredom and stasis rather than the masculine violence and marginalization that preoccupies Lehane. The interplay of his characters' points of view situates readers within the remaindered subjectivities made surplus through the very same processes that revitalize Lehane's noir masculinities. In the novel, both Brian and Neil (as well as the interwoven narration by their friends and family) are shown stuck in their first-person perspectives of life with few paths forward. Sexual subjectivities that do not fit existing discourses and practices become surplus to life itself, leaving both boys to narrate their futures within trajectories of possibility assembled in the 1980s: trauma and risk.

The film adaptation uses these interwoven accounts to reimagine 1980s struggles to interpret adult-child sex as a problem of visuality and knowledge. The color titles of the novel's sections—"Blue: 1981, 1983, 1987"; "Gray: Summer 1991"; "White: Autumn–Winter 1991"—become titular breaks in the segments of the film, while the colors themselves provide palettes for particular temporal moods. Araki's film adaptation calls the status of memory into question as the camera plays with each boy's ability to imagine his childhood sexual experience through the lens of various media. Like *Capturing the Friedmans* before it, *Mysterious Skin* allegedly "offers no resolutions and refuses to moralise, wrestling instead with subjective experience" (Said 2005, 32). "Subjective experience" is produced through the screen as the capacity to experience sensation as it happens and to store that sensation as a memory image. Events that happen to both boys become on-screen images only for Neil. Brian instead is left with a black screen. Both boys are haunted by their subjective experience. But while Neil struggles to incorporate these memory images into his normal life (leading to a logic of risk), Brian struggles to find images that will signify his missing past (leading to a logic of trauma).

The film's narrative also produces repeated images of sensational surplus routed through the materialism of the body, its bloody cavities, discordant sensations, sugary surfaces, and sticky flesh. Araki's films are known for their use of sensational surplus, part of his signature style as an auteur of 1990s New Queer Cinema. From his earliest offerings with the low-budget *Three Bewildered People in the Night* (1987) and his alternative breakthrough, *The Living End* (1992), Araki has been associated with an avant-garde style and ideology reminiscent of the latter film's slogan, "Fuck Everything." His films are critically acclaimed and have received multiple awards and nominations, despite mixed reception of the Teen Apocalypse trilogy *Totally F***ed Up* (1993), *The Doom Generation* (1995), and *Nowhere* (1997). Araki describes his trilogy as "a rag-tag story of the fag-and-dyke teen underground," continuing the antinormative and outsider queer sensibility definitive of what that film critic B. Ruby Rich dubbed New Queer Cinema in 1992.[5] This earlier work is known for its strategies of punk bricolage, surprise-angle close-ups, and "extreme images of sex and violence meant to test the viewer's gag reflexes" (Hart 2003, 32).

Araki's later movies, beginning with *Mysterious Skin*, have been associated with a more mainstream style and content. As Lisa Selin Davis (2005) points out, *Mysterious Skin* "leaves behind much of the irony, sarcasm, and gore that categorized his previous work and trades in the comic book look of earlier works for something more stylized, ethereal, and dream-like that, like a spoonful of sugar, helps us ingest the difficult subject matter of the movie." *Mysterious Skin* is Araki's first adaptation of someone else's text, an adaptation that translates many of his earlier themes into a surplus sweeter than visceral violence. In an interview in 2015, Araki explained his cinematic shift by stating "each movie is a snapshot of a certain time" (Jenkins 2015). *Mysterious Skin* is a snapshot of the mainstreaming of sexual potentiality in the early 2000s through SORN. Araki's film translates the novel's boring realism into boredom vérité, revealing what Lauren Berlant (2015) calls "structures of unfeeling" as a mode of queer experience in which affective blanks contribute to a kind of atonal or mute sociality. Berlant interprets the film's flat affect as "recessive," creating an on-screen space for affective disidentification with cultural demands for emotional belonging.

Araki's *Mysterious Skin* captures 2000s nostalgia for a queerer time, when gay abnormalization and sexual respectability had not yet appropriated queer experience into what Berlant (2011) calls "cruel optimism." Adult-child sexuality once again provides the scene for this appropriation, as well as its filmic

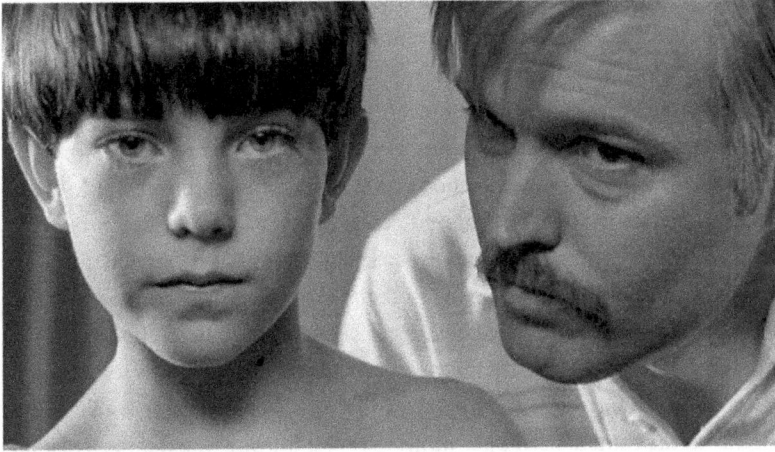

FIGURE 5.1 Coach and Neil in contrast, *Mysterious Skin* (dir. Gregg Araki), Tartan Films, 2004.

disruption. This is nowhere more apparent than in Araki's choice to translate the novel's representation of the coach into a series of scenes riddled with what Laura Marks (2000, 22) calls "haptic visuality, or a visuality that functions like the sense of touch." Haptic visuality is created through the filmic presentation of "auratic, embodied, and mimetic" (Marks 2000, xiii) images that insistently draw attention to their cinematic production as images, as well as the life of objects beyond the screen.[6] Although he appears on-screen for only a total of six minutes, Coach provides the affective relay through which page becomes screen. He has the loose good looks of an early 1980s porn star, complete with bushy mustache, blond locks, and blue eyes. In the film his presence is rather shocking: wide-angle shots of his pornstachioed appeal are matched with uncomfortable close-ups of his eager eyes, the view of his out-size lips coming toward the camera juxtaposed with the uncanny reveal of him sitting next to the oh-so-much-smaller child-actor playing eight-year-old Neil (figure 5.1). While the novel begins with Brian's lost five hours, on-screen this loss is replaced with a disembodied voice-over: "Are you ready? Here we go." In the novel, the refrain "Here we go" (Heim 1995, 35) is attributed to Coach, a stock line he uses to begin sexual encounters with children. Here the added question—"Are you ready?"—primes the audience for its entrance into ambiguous sex along with the children on-screen.

The "spoonful of sugar" that helps this medicine go down is presented as itself cruel optimism about childhood sexuality. The movie opens with a scene of adult-child sex, only the audience does not know what it is seeing immediately. The credit sequence unfolds over a muted white screen with red blurry circles descending slowly at first, then more quickly as the credits end. The falling red images, increasing in number and speed, become "visible" or identifiable only when a small white boy's head rises from the bottom of the screen and the images resolve into colored cereal pieces as they strike his brunette hair and slightly upturned face. Eyes closed, smiling, the boy lets the Fruit Loops bounce off his skin, leaving in their wake a sugary coating to a soundtrack by Slowdive.[7] The movement itself is emphasized here, the descending orbs of color sharpened into image only as the boy's face moves into the shot from below. The enigmatic signifier of the round colored blur is released to signify as the camera itself pans down to reveal the boy who has been just off-camera the entire time, revealed as still-life-in-motion when his eyelids tense each time the cereal hits him. The purpose is not to eat the candy but to make it visible; to allow visuality to whet the response of the other senses. Thus, the boy's closed eyes ripple with reaction each time a candied sphere strikes his skin, the reaction a microsphere of haptic touch as the visual signifiers rain down.

This mysterious opening is indeed Araki's film's skin, whose delayed signification will become the diegetic narrative of the movie, as well as its mimetic force: "Only later will we realize that this ravishing shot is the beginning of a scene of sexual abuse" (Said 2005, 32). The signs delivered here, to the audience as to the small boys at its center, will remain both overly visible and enigmatic throughout the camera's movements and the still-frame capture of each boy's blank face. After the film establishes the brunette boy as its primary visual object, the screen goes black, and we have our first voice-over: "The summer I was eight years old, five hours disappeared from my life." The screen presents the title "Brian Lackey Summer 1981" while the voice continues, "Five hours, lost, gone without a trace," and a different small white boy's head rises from the bottom of the screen (through the same pan-down movement)— this time, a blond boy wearing large glasses and a baseball cap. The cinematography identifies them while making them photo negatives: white screen, black screen; pleasure, terror. The cinematic is linked to the affective; his face appears, as if he is the lost five hours embodied on-screen. This second boy is in a small, dark space looking directly forward, yet not into the camera, his blank stare aimed nowhere as blood drips from his nose and we hear, "Last thing I remember I was sitting on the bench during my Little League game,

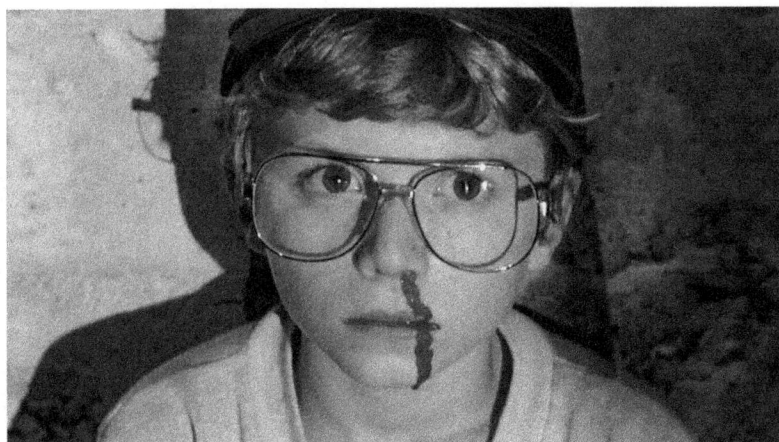

FIGURE 5.2 The Brian shot, *Mysterious Skin* (dir. Gregg Araki), Tartan Films, 2004.

and it started to rain. What happened after that remains a pitch-black void" (figure 5.2). We follow the voice-over to see the boy on the bench, looking up at the sky for rain in a scene of anticipation, in contrast to the first boy, who lets the future rain down with eyes closed in pleasure, and then returns to a pitch-black screen on cue.

Brian's face appears where the "void" might be. The presence of his face on-screen confirms temporal absence, the void where events will become slowly enfleshed. In the scenes that follow, we watch Brian's blank nonregistration of nosebleeds and family ministrations. We see a flash of Brian in his baseball uniform, lying, eyes open, upside down in the frame, head pointed to the bottom of the screen, bathed in blue light, before we cut to his point of view looking up into a bright bluish light slowly blocked by a large, shadowy figure. Brian's voiceover intones, "This is when the nightmares began. And the nosebleeds." We see in quick succession Brian looking into the camera with a nosebleed, his parents gesticulating with his wet sheets ("I wet the bed several times"), and Brian staring blankly into the camera before fainting ("and then there were the blackouts"). Brian's face directly before the camera maintains its blank surface (the Brian shot) while his voiceover drones details to fill in the narrative constituted by this short montage. Yet Brian's elisions become cinematically mimetic. When Brian says "blackouts," the screen goes black. When Brian tries to find an image to fill this blank, we see a blue blurry image through Brian's eyes that looks like a movie image of a UFO. This blue image— part movie, part memory—first appears on-screen when Brian and his family interrupt their TV watching to spot a possible UFO; the on-screen small screen goes *Poltergeist* staticky, causing the family to troop to the window looking for answers to their family's technological interruption.[8] The sequence ends with Brian and his family seated on their roof, looking to the sky in a shot that will repeat across the film to assemble a future presenting itself for a camera's eye in the sky.

Sexual Futures

The future is the film's main subject, one might say—not really as Lee Edelman's (2004) "no future" but as another queer sign for a historical itinerary that, in José Muñoz's (2009) account, has not yet happened.[9] Araki's film confronts viewers with the sugar-coated schema of childhood experience interrupted by visceral sensations of pleasure and confusion. This is more akin to Kathryn Bond Stockton's concept of "growing sideways." Stockton (2009, 3, 5) theorizes all childhood as "queer" in that the demand for sexual "delay" structures a developmental temporality that cannot but go sideways.[10] Thus, even as Neil is presented as "proto-gay" and Brian as without sexuality, both boys experience sexual futurity the same way: affective blankness at the site of temporal recursivity (Sedgwick 1991). Brian's narrative blackouts in the novel become the black film screen itself, with cut or fade to black marking Brian's experiential pause as cinematic break. Meanwhile, Neil's future orientation becomes the film's main temporal assumption. Neil's protogay subjectivity is tracked in forward motion as a vehicle for narrative development, as well as a symptom (risk-taking) of surplus experience. Neil's insistent narration of sexual risk appears to require Brian's paused supplement (slowly encoded as trauma) to cocreate an emerging historical narrative of mature sexuality and healthy affect.

Neil's story unfolds through a split between his narrated experience of emerging gay sexuality and a haptic surplus registered by the camera. Viewers begin Neil's story in "Summer 1981," watching eight-year-old Neil masturbate to climax for the first time while watching his mother (Elisabeth Shue) give her boyfriend, Alfred (David Lee Smith), head on Neil's swing set. As Alfred comes, a close-up of his face flashes to a face we do not yet know, another mustached man with head thrust back in ecstasy, which, in turn, makes Neil's face scrunch into what must presumably be an orgasm, followed by the return of the second man's face relaxing into a smile, and then Neil's, and then

Alfred's. Neil's voice-over intrudes, "Maybe I should start at the beginning," and we do, indeed, begin again with Neil's mother taking him to his first Little League practice. Coach turns to the camera and removes his Tom Selleck sunglasses with an iconic early '80s smile. Neil recognizes immediately the gay iconography he has only recently encountered: "Desire sledgehammered me. He looked like the lifeguards, cowboys, and firemen I'd seen in *Playgirl* that my mom stashed under her bed." Signifiers for his sensation bypass words to align with images that flash on-screen as he names them, six rapid shots of men's faces.

His mother's joke about him being shy when he meets strangers reminds viewers that we are looking at a child, the object of a gaze that rarely reveals interiority. This split between looking at Neil and hearing his thoughts continues in the first sex scene between Neil and Coach. When Neil visits Coach's house, his voice-over deems it "awesome," and he proceeds to list Coach's 1980s videogames before we watch Neil become the object of such period technologies: a cassette recording of Neil belching, a Polaroid of Neil putting Coach's thumb in his mouth. In the film, the camera translates what the novelistic Neil calls "images shuffled in my head" (Heim 1995, 35) into images of Neil's reactions on-screen. In the novel, the concept of "image" is part of an impossible mode of articulation in which signs do not yet cohere to the visceral field of response: "Occasionally I'd open my eyes, catch a random image, then snap them back shut. The images shuffled in my head: his fingers, loosening his circle-and-horse-head belt buckle; teardrops of green glass on the chandelier; his shirt's pouncing, drooling panther; silver fillings in the recess of his mouth" (Heim 1995, 35–36). These images are translated on-screen into close-ups of Neil's affectively blank face.

Neil's interior monologue from the novel revealing ambivalence — "Half of me realized it wasn't right. The other half of me wanted it to happen" (Heim 1995, 35) — is omitted, and viewers are left trying to decipher Neil's reactions to increasing sexual contact. In the kitchen, as the sugar-cereal scene begins and Coach's face slowly becomes serious and romantic, Neil looks away, and we see the broken candy on the cracked linoleum floor to the sound of crickets. The scene that unfolds offers a realist translation of the film's opening Fruit Loops sequence. Shot-reverse-shot camerawork translates the opening's pleasing blur into creepy sensation, while perspective tracking forces us to look up at Coach and down at Neil, making realistic scale surreal or, at least, uncanny. "Here we go," creepy Coach says, his face slowing coming lower and closer on-screen, while we cut to Neil's face looking blank, then again back to Coach's

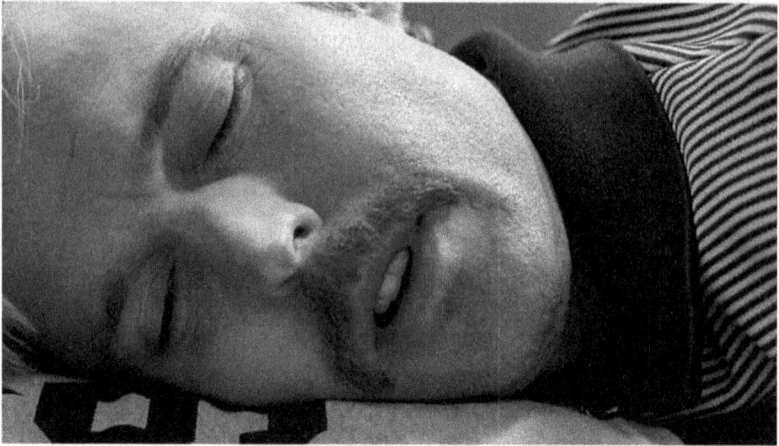

FIGURE 5.3 Mannequin Neil on the kitchen floor, *Mysterious Skin* (dir. Gregg Araki), Tartan Films, 2004.

face even closer, lips parted to say, "I like you, Neil. I like you so much." Cut to Neil being laid down on the candy-covered floor, a shot of his face against the floor in close-up, then a shot of Coach rubbing the side of his face on the boy's stomach (figure 5.3).

This shot ventures further into the uncanny valley, since what appears as the most intimate reveal of disturbing scale is in reality the actor playing Coach rubbing his face on a small mannequin. Child actors cannot participate in some sequences to avoid re-creating child sexual abuse. Each shot-reverse-shot becomes more unsettling. Neil looks distinctly concerned and confused, slightly whimpering before Coach first kisses him. This visual grammar communicates something far more enigmatic than the interior monologue of the novel: "I focused on a vein in his bicep"; "My body tensed, canting against the support of his other arm, nearly nine years of anticipation clamping in each tendon and muscle. I couldn't hold it. I moaned again to let him know, and then he shuddered"; and "I saw the full size of his dick, candy pink and unreal, as it arched over my chest" (Heim 1995, 36). On-screen, a blackout finally relieves the viewer of watching a child experience sex with an adult, while the voice-over regains control: "It happened. That's what I told myself. It just happened." The lights come on, and we see the linoleum covered with broken cereal and two spoons as Neil's voiceover continues: "And after it was over, I looked down at the mess on the floor. It was like a kaleidoscope had shattered."

The shattered kaleidoscope is slowly pieced into more acceptable images of reality across the boys' teenage years in 1983, 1987, and 1991. Kansas provides the flat backdrop as the two boys navigate childhood and adolescence without discernible lines of flight away from a terminal middle.[11] In the sequential narrative, the film appears to move toward a resolution in which the two boys provide the missing answers to the mysteries of each other's experience. Neil and Brian are intercut first slowly, in full, separated sequences, then more rapidly, within single sequences that include both of their stories. While the diegetic plot of the film suggests that the two boys move from flat to full affect, Berlant's reading allows us to see their recessive affect being forcibly filled in by the structural adjustments of cruel optimism. The demand for healthy affect, or what Sarah Ahmed (2010) calls "the promise of happiness," is here situated as a narrative demand that creates an affective surplus to the 1980s–90s plot. This is registered on film as cinematic surplus, sensational encounters that do not entirely mesh with the narrative's development.

Neil's teenage tricks take him to green spaces of the town park and end up repeating key figures of his childhood sex, including the presence of candy and fragments of Coach's patter. When Neil spots his first john (Richard Riehele) rolling up in a car, his muttered "Here we go" launches a scene in which he navigates sex for pay and the possible dangers of stranger intimacy. (They go to a hotel to avoid police in public space.) The john, Charlie, is a candy sales rep with boxes of sugary treats in his back seat who praises Neil repeatedly for his youthful good looks and ultimately brings him to orgasm only when Neil flashes on Coach's face; then we see Neil's childhood face smiling as the colored cereal falls on him. When he is not turning tricks, Neil hangs out with his childhood friend Wendy (Michelle Trachtenberg) and gay fellow teenager Eric (Jeffrey Licon). We watch the trio in classic ride-around doing nothing but looking punk and declaring, "Can't wait to get out of this fucking nowhere town!" envying Neil his imminent move to New York City.[12]

The contrast to Brian's teenage development could not be more pronounced, nor could the direction to which they look: New York; the stratosphere. As Neil and his rebel friends experiment with risk, Brian seeks answers in trauma. After seeing a young white woman named Avalyn (Mary Lynn Rajskub) on a *Ripley's Believe It or Not*–style television program about UFO abductions, Brian seeks her out, and she tells him, "Every single thing we do stems from our abduction."[13] Avalyn shows him a close-up of her leg where "the scar can't be seen" from a tracking device aliens inserted; Brian offers in turn his dream in which another boy in a Panthers uniform watches an alien with big black eyes touch his face. Across these scenes mysterious skin appears as a clue for something not legible and yet inscribed on the surface (of the skin, of the film). In Avalyn's words, the audience, too, is encouraged to "think of yourself as a detective, following clues." Over the course of the developmental narrative, both boys become clues for something beyond the film itself. Diegetically, this is resolved as the boys find their way toward each other as the missing piece of a mystery they purportedly need to solve to become adult men.

Neil's association with risk and Brian's with trauma escalates across the final two sections of the film. As Neil departs for the big city, his narrative becomes more and more associated with risk. Neil's mother's parting request to "be careful" is coupled with Eric's "be safe" when he realizes Neil has contracted crabs. Neil struggles to earn money safely turning tricks in New York's uptown bars.[14] After turning to allegedly more legitimate low-wage work at Subz, Neil is raped by a final anonymous john (Pete Kasper) in a scene reminiscent of Coach. "Are you ready? Here it comes," echoes Coach's "Here we go," but this time we watch Neil's face leaking blood against the white porcelain after he is beaten with a shampoo bottle and called a "slut." When he returns to his apartment, we see him curl up and begin to shake until he cries for the first time in the film. Meanwhile Brian's narrative becomes more and more associated with trauma. Brian appears at Neil's door just after Neil has left for New York, dressed like an "incognito Boy Scout," as Eric notes (or possible "FBI"). Brian's undercover agency searching for the "N. McCormick" inscribed on the back of his Panthers photograph is presented as a childlike effort to create social connection by contacting every McCormick in the phone book. Brian enrolls in community college and seeks answers in Kansas, where his "asexual vibe" seems ill-suited to his strange drawings of hybrid alien men featuring manly legs and baseball cleats below an alien head and torso.

All Over the Rainbow

Two exemplary sequences depict mysterious signifiers that yield both narrative closure and cinematic surplus. In the first sequence, the boys each produce their own versions of "clues" about the mystery of their own skin. Before Neil has left for New York, Eric returns to Neil's house one evening and discovers a Polaroid of child Neil with an adult's finger touching his tongue and a cassette labeled "Neil M.—8" recording an adult man's voice saying, "You like that?" before we hear child Neil's "It tickles a little." We watch Eric's face as he looks at Neil's childhood Panthers picture again, then slowly zoom in to Neil's eight-year-old face as we hear child Neil say, "Can we put the blankets over our heads like we did last time?" and Coach's reply: "Here we go." For Brian, the search for evidence of his own skin's mystery takes him to the green spaces of farm fields and animal nature, looking outside the town's cultivated conditions for evidence of lost time. Brian has found the same Panthers photo of their childhood baseball team in the town library and realizes that Neil's image is the one from his dreams. At the farm, Avalyn immediately breaks the frame's glass so a close-up finger can trace the words "N. McCormick" on the photograph's reverse side. Her suggestion that the photographed face confirms the mystery ("Look at his face. It's almost like you can tell he knows something") only affirms the importance of visceral evidence when she states, "Meanwhile, I have to show you something only you will understand."

As we watch Brian's face looking at Neil's childhood image, *Brian's face fades directly into Neil's*. Brian's skin turns into Neil's sitting in Hutchinson's gay bar with Eric, complaining he has fucked everyone there already. This failed bar pickup scene then cuts back to Brian and Avalyn walking in the dark with her dog, Patches, to where we see a calf lying dead on its side. Avalyn expresses excitement that a "mutilated" cow has been found again; apparently, this is a serial phenomenon her father explains as the work of "Satan worshippers" but Avalyn experiences as proof of UFO abduction. She pushes Brian's hand into the cow's open side, and we watch his hand go into a bloody red cavity for a split second before returning to her face: "Feel that? The sex organs. They're gone." We watch Brian's face in close-up intercut with shots of his hand sliding farther into the cavity. Suddenly, Brian's nineteen-year-old face cuts to the upside-down image of eight-year-old Brian lying on the blue floor, and we enter a sequence filling in the gap of Brian's lost time.

Rather than traumatic repetition or intrusion of memory images reproduced from prior scenes, as in the previous chapter, here repeated images are themselves transfigurations, assemblages of sensation that refer to a surplus beyond the filmic diegesis. Avalyn's command—"Look at his face. It's almost like you can tell he knows something"—spurs a visual sequence culled from visceral surplus. The following images appear in rapid sequence: Brian's current nineteen-year-old face; Brian as a child on the blue floor; Brian's current face, his hand going deeper inside the cow; child Brian on the blue floor with alien fingers touching his face; Brian's current face beginning to shake as Avalyn's voice calls "Brian?"; his hand deep inside the cow ("Oh my god, Brian!");

child Brian on the blue floor with human fingers touching his face; Brian's current face shaking as his nose starts to bleed ("Brian!"); child Brian on the floor with an adult human hand caressing the side of his face; current Brian with nosebleed; child Brian on a blue floor, with an adult human hand turning his face to the side, where we next see child Neil lying against the same floor, saying, "Here we go." The final two shots show current Brian from the side with his nose dripping blood, then child Brian with child Neil leaning into the shot, whispering, "Tell him you like it," while an adult human hand covers much of Brian's face. To close the sequence, Brian pulls his hand from the cow and falls onto his back while an aerial shot pulls slowly back from where Avalyn ministers to him on the ground.

The second sequence begins on "Christmas Eve 1991," when Neil returns to Kansas for a long deferred face-to-face with Brian. As they drive to Coach's old house, Neil asks Brian, "This starting to look familiar?" Coach's blue-lit house seems to provide a manifest referent to the affective surfaces of the film, the signified filling in alien figuration and risky desire as an atmospheric tone. Neil says, "You ready?" and walks toward the door, while Brian hangs back in the blue light and says, "Blue." The sequence that follows sutures Brian's flickering images into a historical narrative: Coach used Neil to pick up Brian and take him home, leading to a series of sexual acts that included fellatio and anal fisting in exchange for money. As Neil narrates the story of the past, point-of-view shots through child Brian's eyes, images of Brian's child face, and shots of current Brian interweave with the developing narrative.

This sequence seems to suture not only Brian's but also Neil's surplus back into a narrative of sexual exploitation and abuse. Neil explains that they played "the $5 game," in which money is awarded for increasingly difficult sexual acts. The screen fills with a shot of Coach's naked, sweaty back; he is looking over his shoulder and saying, "It's OK, Neil," before writhing in pleasure. Only after this shot do we hear Neil say, "He made us fist him. Do you know what that is?" We return to the shot of Coach's face while Neil says, "I'll never forget how that felt. Like his whole body was trying to suck me in, devour me." Brian says, "And then I did it, too," and Neil breathes in, eyelids fluttering, and sighs while he nods. Neil eyes get a little harder as his voice finishes the story, saying that they drove Brian back and left him in his driveway: "The end."

This extended sequence replays every mysterious signifier over the course of the film, from those that passed as overt (Neil's discourse of desirous agency) to those presented as covert (Brian's blue alien abduction). Suddenly, all referents are consolidated into a single scene of adult-child sex, one now narrated as coercive and exploitative for both boys. When Brian asks how his nose ended up bleeding, he lays his head in Neil's lap while grasping a teddy bear borrowed from under the tree. Neil shakes his head, his narrative full of pauses: "After, your face looked like you'd been erased." The familiar shot of child Brian looking directly into the camera now appears framed by Coach's large torso to the right and Neil's small body to the left. Temporal potentiality is sutured to historical memory, their flat affect a sign that skin is a mystery that can be resolved by remembering a specific historical event. Neil's adult voice continues, "Like you were just empty inside. And you just fell, face first," as we watch child Brian fall forward, into the gap now filled with explanatory movement as Neil and Coach lift child Brian from the carpet and we see his bleeding nose. In case this literalization of referents remains unclear, the camera cuts to current Brian saying, "Like this?" as he shoves his fingers into his bleeding nose, starting to freak out and shouting with rage: "Like this?" while Neil holds him tight, repeating, "Shhh," somewhere between comfort and control, Brian's body shaking in his arms.

The movie ends by re-creating scenes of beginning. It cuts to two small children looking through the blue glass of the door from outside who begin to sing "Silent Night." Brian continues to shake as Neil slowly looks up, still running his fingers through Brian's hair, and quiet piano begins. The two boys have become physically one, seemingly made whole by the affective touch that eluded them until this narrative release. Neil's voice-over returns to close the film, still past tense, as if from nowhere: "And as we sat there listening to the carolers, I wanted to tell Brian that it was over now and everything would be OK. But that was a lie, plus, I couldn't speak anyway." The shot then suddenly looks down at Neil and Brian sitting on the couch from above, bathed in clear light on the yellow couch, a pieta held while Neil's voiceover continues: "I wish there was some way for us to go back and undo the past." The camera slowly pans out, back, higher as their image recedes into its small circle of light: "But there wasn't. There was nothing we could do. So I just stayed silent trying to telepathically communicate how sorry I was about what had happened. And I thought about all the grief and sadness and fucked-up suffering in the world . . . and it made me want to escape. I wished with all my heart that we could just leave this world behind. Rise like two angels in the night and magically . . . disappear." Throughout, the two boys grow smaller and smaller, until their image is finally an isolated blue light and couch in darkness before the image fades to black.

But beyond the narrative resolution of the boys as aspirational "angels," the cinematic surplus produced across earlier scenes remains. In this final sequence, the two boys seem to close the gap between risk and trauma as mysterious agencies originating in childhood sexual experience. Yet this seeming diegetic and mimetic resolution leaves a cinematic residue whose blue light registers the sensational surplus of emerging sexual logics. While trauma and risk become the figures for sexual experience in a developmental narrative begun in the 1980s and continuing to the 2000s, a sensational vitality—the colored orbs becoming candy, the animal wound becoming anus—remains present as the screen objectifying "skin." On one hand, this surplus materialism could be seen as the remaindered debris of trauma and risk that must be left behind for proper sexual subjectivity. On the other, it might be read as a kind of queer excess excised from narratives of developmental sexuality of the 1980s and '90s. In either instance, this surplus resonates with a vitality that lends the film and its characters the aura of life, an atmospheric "blue" that, as the next film suggests, became fuel for SORN as emerging regime of life management.

Out of the Woods

Kassel's *The Woodsman* explores the visual regime organized by SORN's risk-management protocols as they unfold more than a decade later. The film's plot follows a forty-something white man named Walter (Kevin Bacon), who returns to Philadelphia after serving twelve years in prison for sexually abusing a twelve-year-old girl. He must navigate postrelease relationships with a therapist (Michael Shannon), a cop (Mos Def), various coworkers (David Alan Grier, Eve), his brother-in-law (Benjamin Bratt), and his new girlfriend, Vicki (Kyra Sedgwick), as a registered sex offender. Walter emerges from the blue light of *Mysterious Skin* as Coach caught, a man convicted of child sexual abuse in the 1980s and registered as a sex offender in the 2000s. *The Woodsman* picks up where *Mysterious Skin* leaves off, questioning how the interpretive protocols of trauma and risk—or the reading of flat affect as untreated damage—naturalizes security in the era of normality's dismantling. The boys in *Mysterious Skin* imagine a future leaving "this world behind" but have no figures for such an allegedly posthuman future beyond angels (and their requisite demons). *The Woodsman*, in turn, asks how imagining alternative futures has itself become a sign of risk in the era of SORN, such that fantasy and desire outside the range of normal affect can be considered criminal acts. Walter appears caught between the normalizing demand to display proper positive and negative affects, or to show himself adjusting to the promise of happiness as cruel optimism, and the demonizing threat that his affect will always read as more than merely abnormal, always one tic away from revealing the pedophile's compulsive criminality.

The Woodsman uses the cinematic tactic of cliché to induce audience recognition of the image regime organized by the virtual pedophilia. Keeling (2007, 14) describes Gilles Deleuze's approach to the cliché as a visual code suturing images without requiring their full elaboration in sequential movement: "Clichés provide a way of continuing movement because, in the face of a present perception that affects the sensory elements, they re-establish a relation between the sensory and the motor elements of the sensory-motor schema, allowing for recognition to occur and present movements to continue." The cliché enables cinematic shorthand to convey quickly what the work of montage was required to do in the phase of auratic reproduction. *The Woodsman* explores what happens when that visual labor—where technological reproduction becomes the means of sensory production—no longer needs to belabor its points. *The Woodsman* picks up where auratic reproduction leaves off: where forensic common sense has become cliché, to the point where sex panic and institutional denial can operate as shorthand for conditions of cultural (re)production now perhaps available for interruption and redistribution once again.

The Woodsman began as a stage play by Steven Fechter. After seeing the play in its initial four-week run in 2000, Kassell decided to adapt it as her first post–masters of fine arts film project. Fechter and Kassell worked together to create the screenplay, retaining most of the original dialogue scenes while situating them in more cinematic settings. "Making it visual was the primary concern, and also grounding the film in realism," Kassell says in the voice-over extras in the DVD release of the film. Added were several scenes shot in cars or at the workplace, including dialogue framed by movement and more realistic mise-en-scène and background wide-angle shots. Also added was the job-site character Mary-Kay, who provides an embodiment of the citizen-surveillant cliché also shown in its conditions of production.[15] After the script won the Slamdance Screenplay Competition in 2001, Kassell interested Lee Daniels in it (he had just completed *Monster's Ball*), but he initially had trouble raising funds for a project that did not fit expectations about his production of "urban" films. In an interview for the DVD, Daniels argues that he pursued the project to "make a point as a filmmaker of color" by focusing on how to "tell the truth in film."[16] The script found its way into Bacon's hands, who expressed interest in playing the lead role (Walter) opposite real-life wife Sedgwick (playing his on-screen girlfriend, Vicki). The hip-hop entrepreneur Damon Dash agreed to coproduce the film with Brook and Dawn Lenfest, and then they brought in the actors Benjamin Bratt (as Walter's brother-in-law Carlos), Mos Def (Detective Lucas), Eve (workmate Mary-Kay), and David Alan Grier (his boss). The seemingly accidental or providential story of the film's journey from color-blind or de facto white casting into a racially diverse cast makes overt the often-covert racial formations of SORN: it reveals virtual pedophilia as legitimating cliché of a security society built on long-term anti-black, brown, indigenous, and noncitizen policing and punishment.

The Woodsman has a distinct visual style. Carol-Ann Hooper and Ann Kaloski (2006, 151) describe it as "a slow, claustrophobic film with lots of shots of railings, window curtains and blinds, isolated figures walking, thinking, eating, working. The predominant images that remain with us are of a grey, grainy, grimy environment, shot through with occasional images of a red ball rolling along the ground which, rather obviously, represents those aspects of Walter's desire that are for children and therefore dangerous." The first half of this description aligns the film with Mystic River: barrier railings, shadowy window curtains, and solitary close-ups help create the gray environment of urban life. The film re-creates in part the cinematic realism of noir, with pedophilia appearing on-screen as the threat of a denatured nature or mystic animality against which the solitary protagonists must fight. The second half of this description brings us closer however to Mysterious Skin: the rolling red ball announces symbolism's eruption within the realist frame along the lines of blue-lit atmospheres and cleated aliens. The key difference between this film and the other narrative films I have discussed thus far lies in its focalization through the adult, rather than the child, in the experience of adult-child sex. It is our first film not to look at a pedophile but through the eyes of one.

The film seeks to disinter cinematic realism (as background) from reality coded as myth or symbol (Walter's foreground).[17] Kassell argues that, while "ultimately the film is a character study, of Walter," it seeks to differentiate seeing from Walter's point of view (which is sometimes distorted) and seeing through the lens of the realist camera: "When is reality in real time, and when is it kind of distorted by his perception of it?" Walter's alleged distortions, however, are not always clearly attributed to Walter. They often float, detached from his point of view, as analog images for affect perhaps generated by Walter's presence on-screen but not inevitably attributed to his look. The "images of a red ball rolling along the ground" noted by Hooper and Kaloski do seem to "represent those aspects of Walter's desire that are for children and therefore dangerous." But it is not clear whose imaginary they represent: Walter's, the film's, or the viewer's. The images certainly refer to the Fritz Lang classic *M* of 1931, with its iconic scene of a little girl bouncing her ball against a wanted poster describing child abduction and murder overshadowed by Peter Lorre's M.[18] And the red-coated figure of a little girl trailed through the woods by Walter is no doubt an allusion to the fairy-tale original.[19] Even the cover of the 1947 issue of *American Magazine* featuring J. Edgar Hoover's "How Safe Is Your Daughter?" registers the cliché of red orbs and erotic children. The red ball, however—particularly in its recurrent rolling or overt signification of unfinished movement—seems to invoke and create something more complex than its referent in Walter's distortion or modernist fantasy.

The Woodsman can be read as using this cinematic surplus of adult-child sexuality to interrupt the SORN-inspired production of "Walter" as visual image and virtual object. Three main aesthetic modes organize the film: (1) an informational aesthetic that composes "Walter" on-screen; (2) realist sequences that center racial capitalist (re)production and its incorporation of heterogeneity as difference; and (3) the fairy-tale surplus, whose potential "queerness" is associated with modernist fantasy or a return of naturalist vitality. Through these modes, informational aesthetics become a cliché interrogated by the filmic mimesis and its relation to diegesis itself. The informational aesthetic is made haptic as a scene of reproduction, the "aura" of the virtual pedophile slowed down into its means and modes of forensic and cultural production. The main narrative then experiments with Walter's actualization in "real time" or entrance into the film's diegetic realism, in which we track Walter's on-screen composition as visual object in relation to the reality making of cinematic narrative. Here his alleged "point of view" seems to serve as the structuring lens of "fantasy" or distortion in the film (allegedly isolated to him, not the work of the camera itself). By slowing down the presentation of informational aesthetics and intercutting the sexual realism of the SORN era with a potentially queer surplus—the fantasy images of modernist adult-child sexuality—*The Woodsman* situates the cliché of forensic common sense within scenes of cinematic (re)production.

The film opens with a sequence slowing down informational aesthetics into a scene of virtual production and cinematic reproduction. The four-minute credit/title sequence tries to convey "as much information in as little time" as possible, in Kassell's words, inspired by the opening credits of Sam Peckinpah's

The Getaway. Each cut is clearly marked by a musical shift until the credits appear over the moving landscape. The music builds on itself across the cuts, a synthetic-sounding beat as rhythm introduced when the actor Kevin Bacon's face appears from a side view before the rolling green, on the viewer's side of the bus window.[20] For a brief moment the screen cuts to a shot of the exterior view from the bus. This shot may mimic Walter's point of view by suturing the camera to Walter, turning Bacon into the focalized character from whose perspective we will view the world even when we need to look at him looking to do so. Or it may leap from the scene to depict the world seen "outside" the film, reminding viewers of the camera's agency in focalizing Walter in its free indirect affect. In either case, the camera produces the effect of motion against stasis — the outside world in motion, both nature and culture, organic green and concrete gray, is available to Walter only through the artifice of the camera. He is on one side of the bus window; we, as viewers, are on both. We see him from behind where he sits (the gaze of forensic information) and from outside of his window (the gaze of cinematographic viewing).

This dynamic continues across the opening sequence, where freeze-frames interrupt the momentum translating information into narrative. We see Walter inside a police station being fingerprinted and registered, bits and pieces of his body shot in close-up (thumb rolling in ink) alongside information presented as typing on a computer screen. This procedure is intercut with shots of Walter sitting on the bus with his hands in his lap, their inaction a sign of his danger. A gentle black fade blurs into a side shot of Walter looking out the window on the bus again. We watch Walter being registered on an out-of-date desktop computer, seeing typing appear on-screen while a voice-over delivers requirements for registry. The voice says, "You must check in with your P.O. [parole officer] once a week. The P.O. is entitled to visit at any time." Hands type, "WALTER," "BRO," "BLU," "45." Voice-over: "You cannot come within three hundred feet of where —" and fades out before an audible "you must register." We next see Walter in street clothes facing the camera against an unnatural blue background, his deadpan face prepared for the single photographic flash of the mug shot it slowly becomes (figure 5.4). In contrast to his frozen forensic image, Walter the film character exits the bus and enters the realist city. He stands beside a woman unlocking an apartment door. The screen goes dark until we realize we are suddenly looking through the peephole from inside as Walter closes the apartment door. This seemingly deliberate citation of cinematic voyeurism situates the profile shot of Walter closing the door as a comment on his

FIGURE 5.4 Mugshot Walter, *The Woodsman* (dir. Nicole Kassell), Dash Films, Lee Daniels Entertainment, 2004.

entrance into a potentially point-of-view realism, shot from behind him as he surveys his apartment. The frame freezes: Walter's new life begins.

Hetero-realisms

The film's dominant realistic sequence begins here, two minutes and thirty-three seconds into the movie and still only halfway through the credit sequence. I use the term "hetero-realism" to describe the film's main cinematic narrative, in which heterogeneity is transfigured into benign or threatening difference and redistributed among subjectivities organized through intersecting workplace and domestic relations.[21] Hetero-realism takes up residual valorizations of labor and norms of sexuality and transfigures them into modified forms of gender, sexual, class, and racial difference capable of incorporation into newly proper or proprietary subjectivities. When Walter first steps off the train he appears *as visual information*, marked and shot through with information's enigmatic time, composed through static and dynamic sequences as pedophilic potential and human survivor. A shift occurs in sound, color palette, and speed of motion as he enters hetero-realism: yellow and red equipment breaks the color palette thus far; a truck drives more quickly across screen than its tracking shot (both camera and objects are in motion now), and sound is suddenly simultaneous with action (the truck goes, "vroom"). The workplace scene opens with the camera looking at the labor and trucks from behind wood stacks, as if through slats, before cutting to Walter looking at the same yard through slats in the window blinds. This aligns the camera again with Walter's point of view, even though we are actually looking at Walter looking out the blinds. We see him from behind in the shot—making his watching into the object of the camera's gaze—aligning him with his profile. This time, however, Walter moves into the realist scene among other characters, meeting his boss, Ben, with the office worker Mary-Kay watching in the background, Walter's presence ominously marked by Ben saying he does not want any trouble on the job.

In the final sequence of this informational opening, we see Walter traverse the hetero-realisms suturing work and domestic space. Walter unpacks his clothes and makes the bed, the cool blue tones of his domestic scene frozen for an instant as he disappears behind blue sheets. This freeze frame startles, cutting into the rhythm of cinematic realism with a freighted significance that cannot signify anything to the audience yet. The sheets return to motion, and two small birds appear through a transparent blue, accompanied by the sound of Walter opening the blinds and looking out the sheer blue curtains. This enigmatic freeze, so different from the blue freeze of Walter in his mug shot or the data collected on the blue computer screen, is the first flash to fantasy, the birds/children to which Walter's perspective will soon turn. The two birds cheep and hop, one moving from behind the muted blue to clear glass, and we cut to Walter behind wet glass in the blue-toned shower. Whether he is bird or prey in this movie is subject to multiple messages: there is the sad music, his vulnerability naked in the shower, his positioning as the bird visible through the slats. But then dressed again, Walter looks between the slats of his own window and we see him looking (watching him watch from behind) at a children's playground, seemingly empty but the sound of play haunting the image (ominous music cues audience concern here).

Walter is assembled on-screen as a virtual pedophile through the opening sequence, only to enter cinematic hetero-realism as an informational enigma. He appears on public streets, in domestic space, and at the workplace bearing with him an aura of opacity that marks him as different from the other characters (Birchall 2011). The realist segments of the film thus show various characters trying to decode Walter's awkward white masculinity—his blue shirts buttoned nearly to the chin, his blank face a study in affective neu-

FIGURE 5.5 Social Walter, *The Woodsman* (dir. Nicole Kassell), Dash Films, Lee Daniels Entertainment, 2004.

trality, his eyes downcast, his hands pocketed—into familiar signifieds. Is he a queer? A creep? A convict? "What did he do?" Mary-Kay asks Ben in the workplace. "Drugs, armed robbery, manslaughter?" "Something happened to you," Vicki says to Walter in his apartment before asking about his "deep, dark secret." Walter is subject to a range of surveillant and sousveillant techniques deployed across a multiracial cast evaluating his fit into regimes of difference (figure 5.5).[22] As the familiar agents of vile sovereignty—the psychiatrist and the police—are disqualified in the filmic diegesis, these diffuse and inharmonious networks of watching produce new forms of social agency codified through refigured relations of production and reproduction.[23] From these networks a mode of realism is assembled that seeks to incorporate difference—as respectability rather than normalcy—while still, in this case, leaving a fairy-tale surplus marking the outside of security society.

Scenes at work focus on the attention drawn by Walter's flat affect and his noticeable difference from normal difference. From its opening scenes, life on the woodlot is multivalent. The job site is presented as a space of heterogeneity carefully organized into segments of population. On one hand, labor is presented as a relatively harmonious union of nature and culture: human and machine (forklifts, saws) work together to transform trees into wood as use and exchange value. On the other hand, labor is presented as a site of social antagonisms, especially as it shapes "culture" as relations among race, gender, class, and sexuality on and off the job site. Walter's awkward inhabitation of labor draws attention to the conflicts within and contradictions among these modes, making him into a cipher of difference that does not immediately have a name. His effort to eat lunch alone draws attention from Mary-Kay, who strikes up conversation about the value of homemade food (she repeatedly asks him to try her lunch, which he refuses) before he apologizes and says, "I gotta get back to work." The frame freezes on Mary-Kay looking suspiciously after Walter, a suspension of the look in time as the sign of watching. She looks for the camera, its extension, but is also shot in profile—she is profiled by the camera as an agent of surveillance, an agent of forensic identification who will watch Walter for signs. Walter is not yet part of the arrangements of heterogeneity that can be absorbed into class or race formations at work or gender and sexual relations at home, or the crossover between them enacted by Mary-Kay, who reminds the audience that domestic and work realisms are naturalized in the interstices of flirtation and nutrition.

Walter is seemingly unfit for either labor or domesticity. More artisanal woodsman than wage laborer (we later learn that he made a cherry wood table as a family wedding present), more bird lover than simple beast of prey (he later follows Robin [Hannah Pilkes], the girl of his fantasies, into the woods, only to share their mutual love of ornithology), he is in the realist scenes but not entirely of them. He, like the reality he regards, is always behind the "slats" imposed by both the camera and forensic common sense. The film shows Walter navigating these scenes of work and domestic space, always being looked at by other social agents (diegetic) and by the camera (cinematic). This is true at the job site, where Walter meets Vicki, the white, working-class feminist rebel, and in domestic space, where he navigates cross-racial masculinity with his brother-in-law Carlos. Vicki inspects him as part of patriarchal heteronormativity, looking suspiciously at him when he holds the door for her before she flips off male coworkers with a "Fuck you, asshole" and "Kiss my ass." Meanwhile, Carlos hails him as outside white supremacist versions of the same, saying Walter was the only family member who talked to him when his sister "married the brown-skinned boy from down the street."

The relation among these characters' signs of difference becomes central to the film. Each character interprets Walter through their own position among seemingly horizontal relations of power. Professional help is disqualified early in the film, with Walter repeatedly shown in a low-level government-style office revealed as court-mandated therapy. His therapist, Rosen, seems incapable of helping or healing Walter, proposing, for example, that he keep a journal—which, Walter points out, could just be used as "evidence." In the wake of such vile sovereignty, coworkers and social companions take up the mandate of diagnosing and detecting Walter's enigmatic affect. This is made explicit through staggered depth shots emphasizing embedded scenes of surveillance. "Have you met any friends there?" Rosen asks, and we are suddenly looking at Walter's back at the lunch table once again, Walter's voice-over stating, "I'm not running for Mr. Popularity," as we watch Mary-Kay watching Vicki watching Walter. Meanwhile, domestic scenes with Carlos show his seeming friendliness mediated by unspoken distrust. Walter points out that Carlos is the only family member who will talk to him and that transitioning from prison is difficult, to which Carlos evades direct responses. The conversation ends after Walter asks about Carla, Carlos and Annette's daughter, whose twelfth birthday party will not include Walter. Across these scenes Walter minds what information he exposes and how he performs himself for others, including his affect. Since Walter is always available to decoding by others, he cultivates flat affect to reveal nothing, which, in effect, signifies anything.

It is in this context that the developing relationship between Walter and Vicki presents an emergent counterrealism that possibly incorporates registered sex offenders into benign abnormality. Once again, the workplace scene begins with lumber in close-up, moved by forklift, but now Vicki is driving and watching Walter unload. She offers him a ride after work and says, as they drive, "Something is wrong with this picture. There's this nice, hardworking guy, suddenly appears out of the blue, takes the bus to and from work. I mean, who takes the bus anymore?" In response to her labeling it "weird," he says, "Not as weird as a sharp, young, good-looking woman working in a lumberyard." Their shared weirdness unfolds as a critique of norms, a position they inhabit for different reasons. His effort to decode her difference suggests a knowable counternorm: "I thought you were a dyke." She declines to disclose, instead flirting with his difference, skirting it, saying she thought he was shy at first but now thinks "something happened to you." She performs a nonjudgmental audience whose interest is driven by her own, possibly nonnormative desire. She is not easily shocked, she says, asking about his "deep, dark secret" as flirtation: "Don't you think you should tell me before we have sex?" He declines to disclose, and once again this does not arrest their sexual momentum, although it does seem to disrupt its order. The sex scene that follows is presented without progressive sequence, intercut between them together on the couch, him alone in the bathroom, and them naked in the bed.

Kassell has described this scene as shot partially in "flash-forward," with

Walter looking at his reflection in the mirror "suddenly past tense." While Kassell suggests that this technique represents Walter's psychological reality, more relevant here are how his psychological reality requires cinematic mediation and what this approach does to the forensic profile of looking at watching. After the sex, the scene restarts in forward motion with Walter coming out of bathroom to bed, saying, "So you're not a dyke," as Vicki exhales smoke, smiling, and says, "Not tonight." They can perhaps both have dynamic, rather than static, sexuality and desires, as well as ways of forging connection and relationship. We end with Walter looking in the mirror establishing himself as his own object, the scene closing with him pulling open the slats of his window to watch Vicki going to her car. The promised self-reflection of the journal seems to have been achieved through consensual, adult, heterosexual sex, as per the guidelines of risk-assessment instruments. Yet this new mode of reflection/aperture is countered with the ominous music drawing his attention back to the open bedroom door, where a reverse shot seemingly from the floor of the bedroom looking back at him creates an enigmatic surplus actualized only in a later scene, when the aforementioned red ball rolls out his bedroom door.

Fairy-Tale Surplus

The "deep, dark secret" is here linked to temporal disjunction, whose enigmatic surplus will slowly be signified through elements of fairy tale. From this moment onward, Walter's point of view preoccupies the film. A repeated scene shows Walter sitting in profile at his handmade table by the window, writing in pencil in a lined paper journal, creating a "reflection" of a life in wood. During these scenes of seemingly organic self-production, Walter records his surveillance of a handsome young white man he calls "Candy" (Kevin Reyes) who hovers by the playground engaging its young boys. Walter's becoming-nature, rather than normal, is contrasted with Candy's sugary surface. When Walter similarly flirts with Vicki by making childlike puppets out of paper napkins, his face flashes sorrow as he looks questioningly into hers before the scene cuts to green tree tops against a blue sky: our first foray into the woods. This enigmatic sequence—fantasy? memory? future?—brings us to the film's a priori, trees before the cut, before lumber mills or tables or pencils, even as it presents that a priori as itself a fantasy or/of fairy tale. We watch two pairs of feet crunch through leaves on the forest floor, childish sneakers and adult men's loafers, each walker shot separately and presented without order, leaving

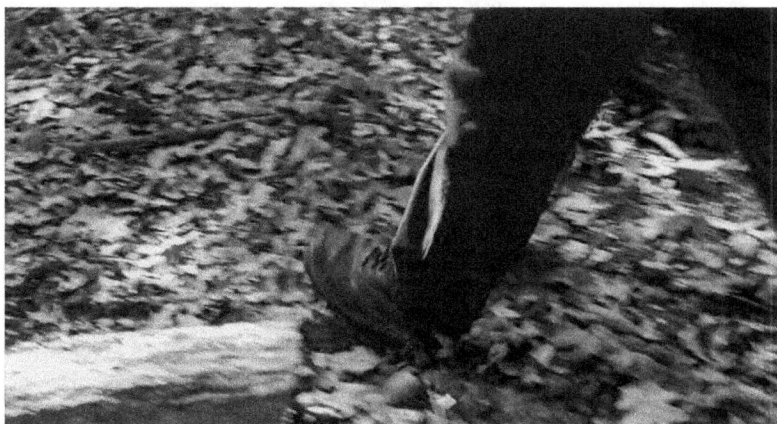

FIGURE 5.6 Into the woods, *The Woodsman* (dir. Nicole Kassell), Dash Films, Lee Daniels Entertainment, 2004.

unclear whether we are witnessing strolling or stalking (figure 5.6).[24] Shots of small birds on the ground and sounds of quickened breathing (with treetops reminiscent of *Mystic River*) are interrupted by Walter jerking in his sleep next to Vicki. When Vicki awakens him, she asks him more seriously: "Walter, what did you do? What happened to you?"

It is a repeat—perhaps a mirror—of their first exchange before sex, before the future opened up within the diegesis of the film. He discloses his history of sexually abusing girls: "Between ten and twelve. Well, once a nine-year-old told me she was eleven; once a fourteen-year-old told me she was twelve. I always asked how old they were."[25] Their conversation is intercut with the same enigmatic forward/memory shots of a man and girl walking in the woods. Through his relationship with Vicki, Walter slowly begins to become more able to adapt to his environment. Vicki and Walter's new relationship is a contrast to the film's seeming critique of the norms associated with respectable heterosexuality that transect work and domestic space. Mary-Kay isolates Vicki in the women's bathroom and warns her to stay away from Walter, an interaction of mirrored indirection in which Mary-Kay's propriety (putting on makeup in the mirror, refusing to say precisely what she means by "damaged goods") is juxtaposed with Vicki's seeming gender rebellion (barely checking the mirror, identification with the sexual damage implied by Mary-Kay). When Walter asks his brother-in-law Carlos whether he worries that his surveillance of his twelve-year-old daughter might have a sexual tone, Carlos warns him angrily that he doesn't "have your disease." But the film aligns Carlos's looking at his daughter with his looking at pretty waitresses: normal entitlement protected by the veneer of sexual respectability ("Hey, I see a pretty lady, I look").

Across these scenes the film tracks the emergence of subjectivities proper to SORN. While we find most obviously the pedophile as registered sex offender (RSO), we see also the respectable citizen protecting the world from sexual predators (Mary-Kay), the tolerant outsider who seeks to understand whether sexual abusers are human after all (Vicki), and the hybrid characters navigating these poles (Carlos, Ben). These forms are presented as hegemonic in some cases (the respectable black woman whose unexplored experiences are presented on-screen only as opposition to white sexual predators) and counterhegemonic in other cases (the tough white woman whose ambiguous gender and sexual experiences include surviving childhood incest *and* dating an RSO).[26] These subjectivities are contrasted with the cinematic surplus produced through Walter's subjection as pedophile. In response to an early therapeutic demand that he keep a journal, Walter exhales audibly and says, "Evidence."

His heavy sigh transforms into the shwoosh of bird seed pouring as we cut to a close-up of Walter's hands filling a glass feeder. We hear the sound of children playing, although a shot from his point of view reveals an empty playground, and cut to Walter counting his footsteps to the closed playground gate. "Three hundred twenty feet," he announces and touches the padlock. "How about that." The unreal quality of coincidence that his lodging would exactly fit the residential restriction for RSOs here introduces the first cut to the rolling red ball. Three tympani strikes distinguish the moment from any audio or visual conditions thus far, as a profile shot of Walter looking into the playground cuts to a large red rubber ball rolling toward the chain-link fence in the foreground, hitting the wall, and bouncing out the now open gate into Walter's hands. The first low horizontal shot tracks the ball upward as Walter raises it to his chest and looks into the yard, down at the ball, then back to the yard. We then cut to Walter standing before the closed chain-link gate, no ball in sight.

In the scenes that follow, Walter seems to enter more and more into the cinematic surplus that was once reserved for isolated sounds or images. The more he is surveilled, the more he enters the world of the red ball. At home, Walter begins to get visits from Sergeant Lucas, a police officer who insists he is watching Walter all the time.[27] At work we see Mary-Kay looking at the Central Pennsylvania Identification Database for Sex Offenders; Walter soon finds a flyer for childhood asthma taped inside his locker with "We're Watching You" written on it. After Lucas tells him he is disposable waste, Walter leaves his apartment and sees Candy talking to a boy at his car. (It is unclear whether Candy, like the red ball, is a fantasy image.) Walter gets on the bus, walks through the mall, and follows young girls whom he watches through the fronds of plants dotting the mall's walkways—a journey into the half-woods. After a scene in which Rosen tries to make Walter's childhood memories into pedophilic clues, Walter begins to follow a white girl wearing a red coat on the public bus, eventually tracking her into a wooded park, leaves crunching underfoot, small birds hopping on the ground, and we realize we have seen this before: it is the enigmatic scene presented as if it is a dream sequence that provoked Walter to tell Vicki about the molestation. Now the scene unfolds on-screen, as if in real time, but also in an impossible speculative time that has and has not already occurred.

As the cinematic surplus takes over the screen, Walter becomes the camera, and movie viewers become the evaluative audience now missing in-scene. Watching Candy make his move on a boy across the street, Walter seems to become a voice mimicking a sportscaster at a prize fight.[28] The following surreal montage includes close-ups of Walter's eyes, Walter riding the bus at night, window lights running across the screen, an image of a different little girl rolling the red ball toward the viewer, red circular stoplights blurrily reflected across Walter's face on the bus, Walter sitting on a stoop in front of a red front door, Walter behind the watery shower door, Walter's hand writing "The boy gets in the car" over and over in his journal (music cues suture the sequence together). Another run-in with Sargent Lucas in his apartment includes the exposition of Walter's fairy tale: the story of the Woodsman. After a prelude about a man who kidnapped a seven-year-old girl from her home before her body was found ten days later, Lucas recites the fairy tale of the Woodsman, which Walter correctively titles Little Red Riding Hood. But unlike the fairy tale, in which the girl is saved, Lucas's story tells of a little girl "sodomized in half": "There ain't no fucking woodsmen in this world. I don't know why they keep letting freaks like you out on the street. It just means that we gotta catch you all over again." After Lucas leaves, Walter's deadpan exterior finally erupts into horror as he destroys his journal, looking up, wet-eyed, to see the red ball placed in his bedroom doorway, a girl's figure disappearing into the bedroom behind it. Placing his hands over his ears, Walter shakes and cries before laying his head down among the papered debris on the floor, and a sustained long shot blurs over his image in the near distance.

Seemingly pushed by his surveillance at home and outing at work, we find Walter alone in the park again with the red-coated girl, seducing his own Cherub (Robin, age eleven) by flattering her for being different from other girls (she's an "uncommon beauty"). She seems also to identify with him at first, sharing the experience of solitude (she, too, writes in a journal) and love of watching other creatures (certain kinds of birds, the both of them). He says he has few friends because he was sent away, and she tries to soothe him by saying that it "sounds like you were banished" and offering as a solution the friendship of birds, "'cause they like being watched, if they know you won't hurt them." Walter seems to take this as an invitation to ask her whether she would like to sit on his lap. As she reflects, he suggests they go somewhere quieter to hear new birds. She looks at him and says, as if in response, "My daddy asks me to sit on his lap." He asks whether she likes it when her father asks, and she says no, becoming increasingly upset as Walter asks whether they are alone when this happens and whether her father says "strange things" and "move[s] his legs in funny ways." Robin cries and Walter nods to himself in seeming grief. She turns to him and seems to prioritize his feelings over hers: "Walter . . . do you still want me to sit on your lap? I will. I don't mind." He tells her to go home (a dubious salvation), and she hugs him before leaving.

This sequence proposes that Walter can find a new subjectivity as Woodsman, not wolf. Robin walks away, red coat in hand. (The wolf is really at home, waiting for her as in the fairy tale.) Walter walks home, only to come upon Candy letting the boy back out of his car. Walter lunges forward and attacks Candy, holding him down and punching him repeatedly in a face that is sometimes Candy's and sometimes Walter's (a cliché from *Mystic River*). After this seeming redemption—letting the girl return to her father, beating the child lover out of himself—Walter reunites with Vicki and is only caught doing laundry (not just unfolding stiff new shirts) when he responds to a knock on the door with, "Come on in. It's open." Sargent Lucas has come to ask Walter about a man wanted for child rape who was beaten outside his apartment; Walter explains his scratches as evidence of a "passionate girlfriend" with whom he is moving in. And so the movie draws to its happyish ending. Vicki and Walter pack her truck and drive away; Walter meets his sister by a river in the woods, and in a final voice-over we hear Rosen saying, "Change is going to take time, Walter. How do you feel about that?" and Walter replying "I feel . . . OK." Walter's suture to a possible counter-realism here remains ambiguous, as the final shot trails birds flying while Patti LaBelle sings "His Eyes Were on the Sparrow."

My engagement with *Mysterious Skin* and *The Woodsman* asks what is queer about the creation of SORN and its aftermath. As I suggested at the outset, queer studies scholars have pondered how SORN fits into longer histories of sexual policing and pathologization. In summarizing this scholarship, Fischel (2016, 20) has suggested that "sex offenders are the new queers" to the degree that they enable "demonizing projection" while disentangling the sex offender from historical homophobia. But is all demonizing projection a mode of queering? How are demonizing systems related to the subjectivities they target? Kadji Amin (2017, 5) has observed that queer studies as a field tends "to *extract theoretical and political value* from the most transgressive objects of study" from its own historical vantage point originating in the United States of the 1990s. Cathy Cohen's (1997, 437) exploration of "the radical potential of queer politics" remains relevant: presumptions about relations among gender, sexuality, race, and territory delimit what appears "transgressive" and how value is valorized across theory and politics. At stake is what kinds of sensational surplus are appropriated by emerging figurations of "queer." The films I have studied here remind us that demonization and valorization are closely entwined, and discerning the queer among the heteronormalizations may require new theoretical and political frameworks. To move beyond these films' proposed figures of respectability, abnormality, and queerness, we may need to turn to the alternative movement-based paradigms that move beyond SORN-era cultural mediation and its critical apparatus I treat in the conclusion.

CONCLUSION   EXCEPTIONAL PEDOPHILIA AND THE EVERYDAY CASE

> Common sense creates the folklore of the future, a relatively
> rigidified phase of popular knowledge in a given time
> and place.
>
> —**ANTONIO GRAMSCI**, *Selections from Cultural Writings*

My conclusion steps back from the archive assembled in the main chapters of the book to ask what might be on the horizon following this peculiar formation of virtual threats and vile sovereignties. The five chapters of this book read across governmental and cultural media to center sexuality within racial and territorial assemblages of policing and to add the pedophile to emerging arguments that security, in its uneven neoliberal and biopolitical modes, takes sexuality as a central tactic. These chapters situate the rise of the predatory pedophile as part of a broader shift not just toward expanding policing for a carceral state, but also into the interpretive paradigms of a security society. Virtual pedophilia served as one function for a security society enlisting everyone into its biopolitics of permanent insecurity and total surveillance. This occurred not merely by strengthening and expanding state power through mass containment and branding but also by disqualifying the state and other traditional agents of public safety from executing their familiar function. Virtual pedophilia plays an important role in this period precisely because it provides a function—combining figure and mechanism—through which existing modes of expertise are disqualified and supplemented by new modes of citizen surveillance. Older agents of surveillance proved inadequate to protect the public from this virtual predator, requiring as assistance new subjects of security trained in the protocols of forensic common sense.

The procedural tone developed through the virtual pedophile, routed through technologically reproducible screen images, precipitates a more general unease when adult white men and children appear together on-screen (enveloping even the mumbly rom-com icon Hugh Grant in *About a Boy* [2002]). This unease might be articulated emotionally as disgust, a response to the mimetic shock of spotting a sex predator in action, or as thrill, a response to the mimetic shock of spotting a sex panic in action. But whether encoded or decoded as serious or ridiculous, the atmosphere associated with virtual pedophilia breathes life into affective effects. This absorption of panic and denial in the cultural repertoire of virtual pedophilia participates in the broader atmosphere of racial and territorial terror in which white people as a population could still identify (and be identified) as target rather than threat, in the imaginative guise of endangered white children. But a far broader range of viewers, across demographic categories, has experienced the allure of pedophilic cultural media. (The number of acquaintances who enjoy *Law and Order: svu* continues to surprise me.) The categorical populism of those mobilized to stop this particular predator includes anyone willing to speak up for children and spot a pedophile before he strikes. This mode hails in complex ways those who understand white male predation against structurally, institutionally, and interpersonally vulnerable populations as a legitimate, if historically underaddressed, threat.

By the 2010s, virtual pedophilia had produced a mode of common sense dependent on information technologies and yet independent of their institutional sites of production and expertise. What emerged from this conjunction of insecure representation and governmental disqualification was an expansion of vile sovereignty into the realm of cultural reproduction. Thus, the proliferation of the pedophilic function in journalism, television, and film over the course of this period is not a reflection or documentation of a process occurring elsewhere. It is a central part of the process through which representation itself becomes part of security culture. In closing, I pose the question of how this argument should be taken up in relation to two main problems: first, what assumptions are mobilized in efforts to dismantle Sex Offender Registration and Notification (sorn); and second, what atmosphere might remain in its aftermath. The first problem focuses on recent efforts to critique sorn and evaluate its systems of harm, including an investigation of subjectivities emerging as figures for sexual liberation. The second focuses on the after-effects of virtual pedophilia as an atmosphere that exists beyond any specific figure or subjectivity.

Efforts to dismantle SORN tend to center its alleged white male profile and once again figure the pedophile as the real threat behind a regime that has overreached. The most common critique of SORN is that its net has been spread too wide in efforts to secure the population against this particularly vile but statistically less significant predator. As "Branding Sex Offenders," a law firm's blog post, summarizes: "Convicted sex offenders may be the most demonized group in our country. And here's the problem: when I say 'convicted sex offenders' most people immediately think violent rapist or pedophile, and then they stop caring about the fairness of the laws" (Loevy 2016). While "violent rapist" makes the list here, most commonly the pedophile alone stands for violent predation uniquely requiring SORN-style intervention. As I have argued, the pedophile also uniquely enables a white frame narrative that isolates the sexual threat to children from broader approaches to racialized and territorialized threats in this era. Thus, the pedophile enables a critique of SORN that often bypasses its relationship to a broader criminal legal system and movements for prison abolition. By encoding pedophilia as an exceptional reach or breach of law and order, both those in favor of expanding the reach of law and those critical of its alleged breach can describe those processed through SORN as the "most demonized" group marking the limit of judicial "fairness." Even in organizing against the legal arm of the security apparatus, the pedophilic function frames the issue in a way that prevents broader forms of oppression from registering as related, or perhaps even real.

Several advocacy groups now work to oppose SORN and its impact not only on the individuals registered, but also on their families, friends, and wider communities. Groups such as the National Center for Reason and Justice (NCRJ), founded in 2002; National Association for Rational Sex Offense Laws (NARSOL), founded in 2007; Center for Sexual Justice (CSJ), founded 2014; and Center on Youth Registration Reform (CYRR), founded 2016, struggle to rebrand SORN as a criminal justice issue. This rebranding is perhaps best exemplified by NARSOL, which changed its name from Reform Sex Offender Laws (RSOL) in 2017 to remove the words "sex offender" from the title.[1] These organizations include a wide spectrum of stakeholders and aims, from the NCRF's focus on wrongful convictions for child sexual abuse and NARSOL's focus on registered individuals and their affected families to CSJ's focus on queer communities and targeted sexual minorities and CYRR's focus on registered juveniles. The American Civil Liberties Union (ACLU) has joined the growing chorus of SORN critics, using pedophiles once again to draw a bright line between justice and panic. "There are few crimes more heinous than child molestation" explains the article "Why Sex Offender Laws Do More Harm than Good," by Deborah Jacobs (n.d.), the executive director of ACLU New Jersey. If SORN is supposed to stop child molestation, it commits three wrongs: wrong target (actual offenders are mostly known or in the home); wrong scope (overly broad inclusion of acts); and wrong tactic (increased penalty and spatial restrictions actually increase risk).

Reporting on cases of people unfairly registered as offenders has been on the rise in recent years. Popular media has started to question the need for broad-based sex offender registration and community notification, mostly focusing on Romeo and Juliet cases, juvenile registration, and nonviolent/nonsexual offenses. Journalists now open with questions such as, "How can someone who had consensual sex with a person who misrepresented her age end up on the sex offender registry for life?" (Bostick 2015). Those punished by this system—the wrong targets—are presented primarily as white men caught up in its overly inclusive sweep. One *New York Times* article begins, "ELKHART, Ind.—Until one day in December, Zachery Anderson was a typical 19-year-old in a small Midwestern city" (Bosman 2015). His typicality rests on the published photo of his parents (seemingly white), his educational status (enrolled in community college), description of his home (replete with boat and family photos), and his dating style (online). Anderson's prototypical Romeo and Juliet case, in which he had sex with a fourteen-year-old girl who claimed she was seventeen, stands in for those "people found guilty of lesser offenses that run the gamut from urinating publicly to swapping lewd texts." This group is then contrasted to SORN's legitimate targets: pedophiles. As the former Michigan Judge William Buhl is quoted in the article, "I think it's utterly ridiculous to take teenage sex and make it a felony. This guy is obviously not a pedophile."

Efforts to draw attention to SORN's wrong scope and tactics have included reporting on "outlier offences," "expanded duration of registration," and "collateral consequences" (Mellema et al. 2014). These conditions are addressed in a *Slate* magazine series that used data from "Human Rights Watch, the American Bar Association, and the Government Accountability Office" (Mellema et al. 2014) to create maps showing which jurisdictions register teenage sex below the age of consent, urinating in public, and prostitution/solicitation (Sethi 2014b). These articles also include an interactive multiple-choice quiz about jobs that prohibit registered sex offenders by state—for example, hearing aid dealer (Alaska) and plumber (Delaware) (Mellema 2014). Even

Business Insider has run articles clarifying the harms inflicted by overly broad registration, listing, in addition to the registration offenses mapped earlier: minors taking nude photos of themselves, women flashing their breasts, having sex with a sibling, and children hugging each other (Fuchs 2013). *Men's Health* adds to this list of registrable offenses: having a live Internet connection on an open laptop near children (porn pop-ups), parents who let teenage children have sex, and accidental indecent exposure; the article lists "You are naked inside the garage and your wife opens the door" as both probable and spoof (Levitan and Bettmann/Corbis 2015).

The image repertoire associated with sex offenders is changing along with this growing popular resistance to SORN. The *Men's Health* article opens with the image of a uniformed police officer handing a citation to a naked child, but since the child faces directly into the adult officer's crotch, this could just as easily be a scene of sexual predation (figure Conc.1). Here the police are the ones preying on children, even as the image allows the magazine's readers to make what they will of the child's naked buttocks. Documentaries have also begun to explore sex offenders as human beings impacted by the SORN regime. The *New York Times* documentary "Sex Offender Village," for example, introduces viewers to "a small community in Florida known as Miracle Village": this settlement of more than one hundred registered sex offenders, "surrounded by sugar cane fields, . . . has become a rare refuge for them as they try to rebuild their lives."[2] The documentaries pick up a strategy familiar from earlier phases of SORN, such as the 1990s *Frontline* series "Innocence Lost" and "Divided Memories" on child sexual abuse accusations that were written, directed, and produced by Ofra Bikel. Both of the *Frontline* programs sought to deconstruct the aura of virtual pedophilia installed as forensic common sense, blending talking-head interviews; B-roll footage of white, middle-class families and communities; and embedded footage from mainstream news media to make the visual argument that social and technological mediations of memory have come to produce a contaminated approach to truth. More recent documentaries also seeking to dismantle the aura of virtual pedophilia work to reveal its banal human face behind alleged evil (Levine and Meiners 2016a).

This recent media coverage draws much-needed attention to the excesses of SORN. But on the whole, this coverage tends to assume that pedophiles are its appropriate target. As a corollary to that assumption, mainstream media tends to center otherwise respectable white men as the group most harmed by this system. As Judith Levine and Erica Meiners (2016c) point out, "In

FIGURE CONC.1 Untitled digital image, in Corey Levitan and Bettmann/Corbis, "You Might Be a Sex Offender and Not Even Know It!" *Men's Health*, May 19, 2015.

stark contrast to earlier iterations . . . these 'new' sex offenders are humanized: attractive, promising, law-abiding heterosexual sons and fathers who made some youthful mistakes and deserve a second chance." They are also, in contrast to the allegedly more appropriate targets of juvenile and criminal justice systems, frequently presented in "journalism, activism, and popular culture [as] white." There are certainly exceptions to these trends, including articles that draw attention to how SORN disproportionately affects people by race, gender, sexuality, region, and ability by Levine and Meiners, Mariame Kaba and Kelly Hayes (2018), Victoria Law (2017), Andrea Ritchie (2012–13), and Mia Mingus (2017). These activists and intellectuals insist on framing sex offenses as part of a larger system of criminalization and punishment that distributes harm disproportionately to those most affected by racism, capitalism, hetero-cis-sexism, ableism, and colonial nationalism—*for both victims and offenders*. But mainstream media uptake continues to frame SORN as white-focused or color-blind, an exception to legitimate law and order that unfairly targets men who have sex with younger peers, look at porn, pee in public, or hug their children.

Across an emerging liberal discourse that SORN is a flawed system, reason and fairness are once again opposed to hysteria and persecution. The series on SORN overreach in *Slate*, for example, declares that we are finally starting to replace "flawed stereotypes" with "solid evidence" that might make SORN "actually grounded in science" (Sethi 2014a). The science of evidence is, however, one part of the problem I have tried to analyze in this book. Ongoing efforts to generate any data on the disappearance, sexual assault, and murder of LGBTQ, black, brown, indigenous, and noncitizen people draw attention to the glaring disparities reproduced through statistical logics, whether those of panic or denial. Appalled at the lack of statistics about missing and murdered indigenous women in North America, for example, the activist Audrey Huntley and others formed the community-run database *No More Silence* (Huntley 2014), while Annita Lucchesi created a doctoral project tracking these harms as data (Hegyi 2018).[3] Reports written by Kimberlé Crenshaw, with Priscilla Ocen and Jyoti Nanda (2015), and by Crenshaw and Andrea Ritchie, with Rachel Anspach, Rachel Gilmer, and Luke Harris (2015), track the impact of these systems on black girls and women, in particular, while Malika Saada Saar and her colleagues (2015, 15) note disproportionate criminalization of "traumatized" girls of color who have *experienced* sexual harm (Pember 2015). Alison Parker and Nicole Pittman (2013) analyze harm to juveniles inflicted by SORN, which has been taken up more broadly in mainstream media as part of a growing consensus that children should not be branded sex offenders by the regime created to protect them (Stillman 2016).

Despite the growing number of academic and movement-based efforts to draw attention to gendered and racial disparities in the actual distribution of sexual harm, however, popular arguments about reforming SORN have continued to promote statistical reason as a correction to irrational fears. This most recent return-to-reason argument is likely to deny or minimize the actual realities of sexual harm that organize both systemic and subjective experience. By focusing on the alleged wrongs of this system *as it has been defined in reference to pedophilia*, the subjects "most harmed" by SORN will appear to be white men. Despite the fact that white men are more or less proportionately incarcerated and registered as sex offenders in relation to their numbers in the general population, this proportionality is figured as a breach of fairness and justice, an outlier to U.S. criminal justice (Levine and Meiners 2016b). Are white men impacted by SORN and its focus on the pedophile? Yes, absolutely. White men are directly impacted by mass incarceration, although often in highly class-differentiated ways. And they are directly impacted by SORN, seemingly in less class-differentiated ways, although still in proportion to their numbers in the overall population. White men's seeming suitability for jobs in childcare, teaching, and related arenas has also been affected by SORN-enhanced profiling, which tends to reinforce gendered and racialized divisions of caring labor and provides cover for the continuing policing of gender and sexual normativity askew to the traditions of "homophobia."

The problem comes when the system becomes the *only* focus of the story and the system's own framing discourse of white pedophilia is incorporated into the critique. Sex Offender Registration and Notification inflicts harm. But it inflicts harm on a far wider range of people targeted for sexual and gendered nonnormative practices, often disproportionately impacting people of color, as is the case across a wider range of past and current criminalization and pathologization regimes. And the harm inflicted by SORN cannot be the only focus in efforts to reduce and redress sexual harm and enable and expand sexual pleasure. At least some of the subjects caught up in SORN, and certainly many of those who elude its grasp, do inflict sexual harm on other people. Quite a few people sexually harm children, as well as adults. Efforts to dismantle SORN must include approaches that create accountability and transformation for those who actually inflict sexual harm. Centering white men in efforts to reform SORN occludes not only the actual distributions of systemic harm but also that of subjective harm (including intragroup sexual harm) unevenly articulated to that system. One major consequence is the ongoing minimization, if not normalization, of sexual harm not perpetrated by exceptional white predators, including harm inflicted by people across various axes of race, class, and region, and harm that targets children outside high-status or protected demographics. In other words, it occludes while exacerbating harm to those outside the scope of white male exceptionalism (either as threat or as victim).

Let me be clear on this point, or else risk minimizing the impact of this system: most childhood sexual harm across demographics occurs in domestic, familiar, or institutionally intimate settings and is "situational," or committed by people who may not otherwise experience a persistent child-oriented desire. The criminal or psychological systems organized through SORN do little to address the interpersonal, institutional, and structural distribution of opportunities for sexual abuse, particular when those younger than thirteen are targeted. There is little evidence that SORN addresses disparities in the proportionality of sexual harm distributed across and within diverse communities. "Sexual offenses" are policed and prosecuted along familiar axes of social entitlements to privacy and privilege, with lower levels of intervention and prosecution in the home or community for those protected by the shield of privacy and higher levels for those already subject to increased policing and regulation across space and time. In contrast, serial sexual offenders, the proverbial pedophiles driven by criminal psychopathology, are policed and prosecuted for harming other people's children—in particular, high-status or white children. This may reflect distributions of public sexual entitlement and the devaluation of children identified as racialized, colorized, working/poor, or disabled more than an individualized profile.

Given this interpersonal, institutional, and structural context, the numbers of white men impacted by SORN may in fact continue to reflect white male entitlement to protection from sexual charges. This has been at least part of the focus of the #MeToo movement, which in its more popularized incarnation since Alyssa Milano sent out her tweet in 2017 has drawn attention to the sexual harm inflicted by highly privileged or powerful men enabled by interpersonal, institutional, and structural systems. This focus on high-status, mostly white men has, however, tended to sideline Tarana Burke's 2006 coinage centering black girls and women in a broader critique of interpersonal harm that is shaped by institutional and structural distributions of power. Thus, even as the mainstream #MeToo movement has called attention to the systemic privileging of upper-class white men that the powerful women speaking most often encounter, it has tended to be mediated as a problem of individual predators rather than those everyday systems of inequity that minimize diverse people's experience of sexual harm. It also has not yet shifted the distribution of intra-white entitlement that enables Brett Kavanaugh to sit on the U.S. Supreme Court while Kevin Spacey is labeled a pedophile, or the racialized hierarchy of victims that have until recently minimized attention to allegations against R. Kelly.

The overreliance of SORN on pedophilia as its zero-sum predator spectacularizes the problem of stranger danger as individual criminal pathology requiring exceptional efforts toward prevention and protection. This is a common conclusion drawn by critics and scholars who study this system, and this is what makes "sex panic" an important piece of a larger puzzle. But when that spectacle is framed solely or primarily as sex panic, its seeming solutions threaten to reproduce the processes of amplification as misdirection that virtualized this white profile in the first place. What most concerns me is that virtual pedophilia has produced an atmosphere that fundamentally appropriates and redirects actual experiences of sexual harm. It appropriates the historical experiences of sexual harm distributed through age, gender, race, ability, and territory and redirects them through the vile sovereignty of virtual pedophilia. At its most damaging, virtual pedophilia works to appropriate what Neferti Tadiar (2009, 4, 15) calls the "living labor" of "dispossessed historical experience." In *Things Fall Away*, Tadiar (2009, 5, 10) argues that "valorized forms of political subjectivity," including sexual subjectivity, are built on "supplementary modes of experience" such as "cognitive, semiotic, affective, visceral, and social practices of relating to the world." Processed through SORN, virtual pedophilia creates valorized forms of subjectivity built on dispossessed historical experiences of actual sexual harm. It appropriates actual historical experiences of sexual harm and turns them into a living labor that animates those valorized subjectivities adapted to the structural adjustments of sexual security.

How does the hunt for white pedophiles (1) appropriate the experience of the most likely historical and contemporary targets of white sexual violence and (2) redirect those experiences to secure systems that, in fact, make sexual violence seem white-targeted or race-neutral? Let me offer one brief example as it unfolds across the SORN period, which is also, not coincidentally, the period of official queer studies in the U.S. academy: the concept of "everyday pedophilia" developed in James Kincaid's *Erotic Innocence* (1998) and Richard D. Mohr's "The Pedophilia of Everyday Life" (2004), among other titles. Queer studies has been among the rare places where inquiry into the social construction of pedophilia is possible. In an essay originally drafted in 1995, Mohr (2004, 20–21) argues that "the pedophile must exist, but in an immature, if germinal, phantom, if fearsome, form," because he allows people to feel normal in contrast. Branding a "certain type of *mind*" as "perverted," Mohr avows, "allows everyone else to view sexy children innocently." This is the projection hypothesis at the heart of sex panic analyses of the folk devil or monster of the predatory pedophile: "We fear him because he is us" (Levine 2002, 26). As Judith Levine (2002, 27) explains, "We project that eroticized desire outward, creating a monster to hate, hunt down, and punish."

In this reading, the pedophile becomes the locus of uniquely problematic looking, an approach that frees up all other erotic surveillance to become a normalized condition of heteropatriarchy (Adler 2001). Yet this reading also centers white looks normalized and pathologized through pedophilia as if they exist in a color-blind frame. For whom does looking at children as an exceptional object become sexual or innocent? For whom, and in what contexts, does this become a threshold question for normalization as a project of colonial modernity? As visual cultural studies scholars across fields such as Nicholas Mirzoeff (2011), Nicole Fleetwood (2011), Laura Wexler (2000), Simone Browne (2015), Zahid Chaudhary (2012), Jacqueline Goldsby (2006),

and Jasbir Puar (2007) have demonstrated, the racialization and territorialization of looking is central to formations of national, colonial, racial, gendered,
and sexual power. In the U.S. context, looking while black has been a moral
and, at times, criminal offense, regardless of age, as in the infamous cases of
the Scottsboro boys (1931) and Emmett Till (1955). Less infamous but equally
deleterious conditions of black, brown, indigenous, and noncitizen looking
define the conditions in which white looks become the terrain of normality, as
well as perversion. The account of race-neutral intergenerational looking attributed to the isolation and demonization of the pedophile makes sense only
if it is organized in the broader framework of racial and territorial formations
of age-differentiated, gendered sexuality I have tried to trace in this book.

The binary of exceptional versus everyday pedophilia (or the racialized
politics of looking at "children") is, in other words, part of the atmosphere
of virtual pedophilia. Efforts to expose this false binary propose that normalizing erotic children depends on demonizing sexual scapegoats. This is true
enough. But they too rarely situate this process of normalization/demoniza-
tion within broader conditions of racialization and territorialization that center white male sexuality as the locus of vile sovereignty's expansive power.
This appropriation of dispossessed historical experiences provides the living
labor of SORN's legitimacy. The subjectivities assembled through the pedophile
draw energy from dispossessed historical experience produced through the
migratory and violent rearrangement of lifeworlds around the globe (Lowe
2015), appropriating the racialized and territorialized domains of legitimate
and dangerous looks for an atmosphere that seems to make white men and
children their target. In this logic, adult-child sexuality produces a spectacle
through which white male sexuality as gaze and act appears to be a central
problem, and thus the center of the solution.

This has the corollary effect of erasing or minimizing the relevance of sexual
liberty for those beyond this assigned demographic. It erases the sexual liberty
sought by a far wider variety of people, including the liberty claims of those
who *directly experience sexual harm*. This includes not only those typically assigned the role of victim but also those whose sexuality may track them into
punitive systems. As those working with people directly impacted by sexual
harm but marginalized or targeted by existing systems point out, the values
of a carceral state and prison nation tend not only to impose interpersonal,
institutional, and structural hierarchies *on* marginalized communities but also
reinforce such hierarchies *within* them. This means that victims of harm are
often treated as offenders when they appear in the crosshairs of racist, colonial

and cis-heteronormative policing. This appropriation by misdirection tethers sexual liberation to the sexual liberty of an already dominant group, making sexual pleasure an evaluative principle for only a select few. It risks, as well, centering queer studies on a narrowly construed domain of pleasure and danger, as Kadji Amin (2017) has argued in relation to queer studies' disturbing attachments in the 1990s to pederasty and pedophilia as bad objects.

This overview clarifies the stakes of those cultural materials in my archive that seem to displace exclusively white entitlement to act as detective, decoder, and interpreter of racialized sexual threat. The archive of virtual pedophilia assembles a multiracial and cross-class mode of agency often focalized through historically minoritized characters revitalized by their capacity to capture a predator that neither the state nor the clinic can tame. At times, this agency can even include a critique of the racist myopia of state actors and ineffective arrogance of psychological professionals (as in *The Woodsman*), although it more frequently remains color-blind in its treatment of the pedophile's seemingly white-on-white action. This cultural archive seems to acknowledge the problem of white male sexual predation, including unevenly in communities of color or against marginalized subjects, but it rarely addresses sexual harm or sexual liberty as an interpersonal, institutional, and structural condition. The misdirection of actual harm to virtual targets enables an atmosphere that reproduces racial and territorial hierarchies by seeming to target white men while actually recentering them as victims of unfair systems. This might be described as securitization through selective cultural entitlement, routed through an optics of respectability. Across this archive, the antipedophilic look is no longer tethered to normative whiteness. In fact, the capacity to toggle between evaluations—sympathetic, demonic—is routed through white male subjection to racialized and gendered looks. In the cultural archive of virtual pedophilia, the tactic of looking devolves from state or disciplinary surveillance to what often appears to be sousveillance, a looking horizontally or among similarly situated actors (Browne 2015).

If my hypothesis about the broader atmosphere produced by virtual pedophilia is correct, then its effects are unlikely to diminish if and when SORN's formal governmental regime ends. The worst elements of SORN's management regimes could be removed. New subjectivities emergent from SORN could be mobilized in unexpected ways. Alternative and perhaps even liberatory formations might be—in fact, certainly are—already in formation, even as this system remains strong (among the only carceral index still increasing as other rates decline). But even if the system is dismantled, some fairly unwelcome effects are also likely to inhere in its afterlife. One specific threat posed by continuing to center pedophilia in efforts to reform SORN is its capacity to capture potentiality in its net and control the figures used to analogize it. Such SORN figures as the predatory pedophile, the child lover, the child victim, and the child agent reproduce some of the racial and territorial hierarchies forged through earlier regimes of adult-child sexuality, while SORN-era bystander figures are generated and offered up for adaptation through seemingly more horizontal relations, including the disqualified state and disciplinary professional. This supposedly preemptive capture severely reduces emancipatory imaginations by seeking to prefigure and direct its possibility rather than merely its reality. This reduction is how virtual pedophilia appropriates the potentiality of living labor and transfigures it into either a capacity for survival or a destination for disposability. Subjects must adapt their living labor to figure recognizable subjectivities in this world order or else risk becoming part of the appropriated surplus that enables it.

The atmosphere produced through virtual pedophilia makes insecuritization into an expanding regime whose subjects must succumb to structural adjustments of safety and sexuality in order to survive. This atmosphere frames sexual liberation as a resistance to *systems*, agnostic in relation to the subjectivities such systems appropriate or occlude. Certainly, SORN inflicts sexual harm on its targets, but what about the sexual harm perpetuated by at least some proportion of those people caught up in SORN's nets? How might we develop a queer approach to sexual harm that is both anchored in prison abolitionism and responsive to widespread gendered, racialized, and territorialized distributions? Legal scholars continue to demonstrate that SORN is costly, ineffective, and harmful and to develop alternative approaches founded in broadened principles of autonomy and interdependence and narrowed definitions of dangerousness and risk. We must also move away from binary models of sexual power (including panic-denial, as well as victim-offender) and toward movements that challenge the broader atmosphere. Nancy Whittier (2009, 12) points out that declarations of sex panic often target the "outcome of social movements" that have struggled to make sexual harm relevant. While mainstream mediations of social movements' demands may be presented as sex panic, social movements have, in fact, continued to produce alternative and transformative justice approaches to sex panic easily accessed online at the Audre Lorde Project (including TransJustice), Creative Interventions, Critical Resistance, Community United against Violence, INCITE!, Southerners on New Ground, and Survived and Punished.[4] Alternative and transformative approaches to child sexual abuse in particular can be found at Generation Five, the Living Bridges Project at Just Beginnings Collaborative, and Stop It Now![5] Many of these efforts began at the very start of modern SORN laws and have offered alternatives the entire time; they should be centered in efforts to transform the atmosphere virtual pedophilia has wrought.

My suggestion is that, even if the figures change or if SORN is dismantled and alternative regimes take its place, we must work collectively to challenge its atmospheric aftermath or else risk reproducing the genres of adults and children that are most troubling here. To make what seems like an obvious point, there is not a currently existing standard of sexual freedom to be protected against paranoid claims about harm. When we are forced to tabulate accountability through violent systems, even the best of us might waver on whether inflicting more harm through punishment is an acceptable response. If calling everyone who sexually assaults a young person a pedophile would *actually stop harm*, I might be willing to accept it. But nothing in my own life experience, the wide-ranging discussions I have had with others, or the work I have done in this book suggests this is true. Rather, everything suggests that we must work together to reframe the problem of age and sexuality in relation to broader dynamics of gendered, racial, and territorial power central to the era of SORN and its likely aftermath. At issue is liberty for some, versus liberation for all.

NOTES

Introduction

1 Special Agent Greg Wing, cyber squad, FBI Chicago Field Office, quoted in Federal Bureau of Investigation 2011; Lanning 2010, 20.

2 Andrew Vachss coined "predatory pedophile" in "How We Can Fight Child Abuse" (1989). The article also called for national registries and enhanced penalties. A note on language: There are no value-neutral terms for my subject matter. This book shifts between referring to acts and epistemes as harmful (abuse, violence, coercion, exploitation) and as neutral (adult-child sexuality, adults who seek out or have sex with children, intergenerational sexuality). I run the risk of using value-neutral language when audiences might expect, or rightly want, evaluation of the acts under discussion (abuse, harm, violence) in the service of clarifying how language changes in relation to the systems I study. I adhere to people-first language when discussing the human beings impacted by these systems ("people convicted of sex offenses," "people who have been harmed by sexual abuse") but retain the objectifying language produced by these systems when I am analyzing mediation or figuration ("sex offender," "sex offending," "victim").

3 Studies connecting longer-standing and more recent policing as part of geopolitical warfare include Puar 2007; Cacho 2012; Nguyen 2012; Lloyd et al. 2012.

4 The term "population" names group differentiation through biopolitical governmentality (Foucault 1990).

5 Some argue that this population's safeguards are diminished by the #MeToo movement of the 2010s, but such shifts seem uneven, at best (see the conclusion).

6 Studies evaluating racial disparities include Ackerman et al. 2011; Filler 2004; Hoppe 2016. Gender and sexual disparities are difficult to track since incarcera-

tion and registration data use a male-female binary and omit sexuality; see for overviews Mogul et al. 2011; Stanley and Smith 2011.

7 The acronym for the Sex Offender Registration and Notification Act is SORNA. I use SORN as shorthand for the broader sex offender management regime, which built on earlier state registration systems (see De Orio 2017; Leon 2011).

8 This is treated in Harkins 2009, chap. 1.

9 Greenfeld (1997, 18) notes that between 1980 and 1994, "Other Sexual Assault" demonstrated "a more rapid rate of change than for any other category of violent crime," increasing an average of 16 percent per year. This rate is second to "Drug Offenses," at 18 percent per year during this period.

10 Most statistics related to sex offenses and sex offenders gathered by the federal government can be found through the Office of Justice Programs in the U.S. Department of Justice, including the Bureau of Justice Statistics, National Institute of Justice, Office for Victims of Crime, Office of Juvenile Justice and Delinquency Prevention, and Office of Sex Offender Sentencing, Monitoring, Apprehending, Registering, and Tracking (SMART).

11 Adams 2002, cited in Parker and Pittman 2013, 32.

12 The NCMEC gathers registry data from fifty states; Washington, DC; and the U.S. territories Puerto Rico, U.S. Virgin Islands, Guam, American Samoa, and Commonwealth of the Northern Mariana Islands. Separate registries are kept by U.S. states and the U.S. territories U.S. Virgin Islands, St. Thomas, and St. Croix. Registries for Indian Country and military bases have been maintained by the federal government. The Native American Sex Offender Management Project is piloting registries and reentry programs in four tribal jurisdictions.

13 William Dobbs, "The Dobbs Wire," listserv, June 8, 2018. Dobbs reports NCMEC will no longer update its charts (personal communication, October 2019).

14 Studies finding disproportionate rates of African American registration include as per note 10 Ackerman et al. 2011; Filler 2004; Hoppe 2016. Studies of juvenile impacts include Finkelhor et al. 2008; Parker and Pittman 2013; Snyder 2000.

15 For summary overviews of SORN in relation to broader carceral shifts, see Gottschalk 2014; Wacquant 2009.

16 Monographs focused on SORN include Corrigan 2013; Ewing 2011; Fischel 2016; Horowitz 2015; Lancaster 2011; Leon 2011; Meiners 2016; Rickard 2016,

17 Extensive scholarship on these systems include Alexander 2010; Diaz-Cotto 2006; Hernández 2017; James 2002; Kunzel 2008; Law 2009; Mogul et al. 2011; Murakawa 2014; Olguín 2010; Ritchie 2017; Ross 1998; Simon 2007; Sudbury 2004.

18 On political counterinsurgency in particular, see James 1996; Davis 2005; Rodríquez 2006; Berger, 2014.

19 For early twentieth century studies of racialization and criminalization, see Gross 2006; Muhammad 2010; Hicks 2010. On racialized figures in this period, see Lubiano 1992, 2008.

20 Monographs on the actuarial turn in policing include Ferguson 2017; Harcourt 2007, 2012.

21 For broad overviews of U.S. neoliberalism, see Brown 2015; Duggan 2003; Harvey 2005.

22 On related carceral geographies, see Gilmore 2007 and Lloyd et al. 2012. On long-standing practices of coerced subjection through colonizing capitalist property relations, see Byrd, Goldstein, Melamed, and Reddy 2018. For retheorizations of disposability and debility decentering U.S. exceptionalism, see Hong 2015; Povinelli 2011; Puar 2017; Tadiar 2009.

23 Studies of childhood as human capital include Foucault 2008; Postman 1994; Prout and James 1997; Zelizer 1994.

24 Security regimes of this period connect environmental-militarized "green security" (Ybarra 2017, 5) and extractive-financialized "debt securitization" (McClanahan 2016, 26) with state-territorialized population targets. The broader turn to security is treated in Amar 2013; Katzenstein 1996; Barry et al. 1996; Birchall 2011, 2014; Bratish 2008; Clough and Willse 2011; Doyle 2015; Melley 2012; Puri 2016; Ybarra 2017.

25 On this biopiolitics of childhood, see in particular Edelman 2004; Sheldon 2016; Meiners 2016.

26 The Jacob Wetterling Crimes against Children and Sexually Violent Offender Registration Act, part of the Violent Crime Control and Law Enforcement Act of 1994, was the first federal law to require state-by-state offender registration. Megan's Law, passed in New Jersey in 1994, was the first state law to require community notification. It was federally enacted as an amendment to the Jacob Wetterling Act in 1996 to require state-by-state public disclosure of data via internet registries by 2003 and was extended internationally through the International Megan's Law to Prevent Child Exploitation and Other Sexual Crimes through Advanced Notification of Traveling Sex Offenders in 2016, which includes a unique passport identifier. The AMBER Alert originated in Texas in 1996, then spread state by state, nationally, and internationally to alert the public about missing and abducted children. The Adam Walsh Child Protection and Safety Act created the federal SORNA in 2006, which includes a national registry and mandates for uniform state registry and notification systems, as well as SMART and the Sexual Offender Management Assistance (SOMA) Program. For legislative details, see Couture 1995; Office of Sex Offender Sentencing, Monitoring, Apprehending, Registering, and Tracking 2012; Petrucelli 1995; Wright 2009.

27 Overviews of these impacts are in American Bar Association 2017; Wright 2009. On broader uses of incapacitation, see Wilson 2013. On banishment, see Beckett and Herbert 2009.

28 On uneven criminalization of sexting, for example, see Forbes 2011; Hasinoff 2015.

29 *Kansas v. Hendricks*, 521 U.S. 346 (1997).

30   Recent sex panics include proclamations about racialized and noncitizen sexual predators and dangers posed by HIV status, commercial sex, and gender identity. Anthologies treating these issues include Bhattacharjee and Silliman 2002; Dangerous Bedfellows 1996; Halperin and Hoppe 2017; Lamb 1999.

31   Some blame feminism as social movement and ideology (see, for example, Angelides 2004). For a related review, see McCreery 2004.

32   In contrast to this sex panic approach, see Jyoti Puri (2016, 33, 29), who reads "statistics and statistical accounts on crimes against women" in relation to India's antisodomy law Section 377 to demonstrate that "rationality is not opposed to affect but is in fact another form of it."

33   Structural exposure to sexual abuse is exacerbated, however, by the disruption of social fabrics perpetrated through state, institutional and interpersonal violence. Sarah Deer (Muscogee (Creek)) (2006) for example points out that U.S. legislation restricting tribal sovereignty over sexual assault committed on reservations by non-enrolled people promotes high rates of assault against indigenous women; see her reading of the 1885 Major Crimes Act [MCA]; 1953 Public Law 280 [PL 280]; and U.S. Supreme Court case *Oliphant v Squamish Indian Tribe* [1978]). See also Amnesty International Report 2007; Ross 2016; EchoHawk 2001–2002.

34   See, for one example, claims about white women's vulnerability to rape by black men, which, as the activist intellectuals Ida B. Wells (1895) and Angela Davis (1983) point out, stand in marked contrast to the actual vulnerability of people of color in general and black women and children in particular to white predators (as well as white women's and children's more likely vulnerability to sexual harm by white men); see Feimster 2011; Freedman 2013.

35   On the making of genders through these processes, see Snorton 2017; Stryker and Aizura 2013; Driskill et al. 2011.

36   John Oliver, "Prison," *Last Week Tonight with John Oliver*, HBO, July 20, 2014.

37   Generation Five, accessed September 18, 2018, http://www.generationfive.org.

38   Glossing Michael Warner's *Fear of a Queer Planet* (1993), this phrase links Hoover's antihomosexuality campaigns with anticommunist red-baiting and antiblack race-baiting connecting the Cold War and the color line (Borstelman 2003).

39   On racialization across vitality and virtuality, see Jones 2010; Nakamura 2007.

40   Film theorist Kara Keeling (2007, 3–5) builds on Gilles Deleuze (1986, 1989) to clarify how specific cultural and social frameworks are composed as the "cinematic image of common sense." My study explores the virtual image of common sense produced through pedophilia.

41   "How to Identify a Pedophile," WikiHow, accessed January 2, 2018, http://www.wikihow.com/Identify-a-Pedophile. The page has since been updated with new images but similar text (accessed January 18, 2019).

42   See the argument on the solicited recursivity of pedophilic threat in Fischel 2016.

43   On dominant logics of what Simone Browne powerfully theorizes as "racializing

surveillance" and resistant modes of "dark sousveillance," see Browne 2015, 12. See also Fleetwood 2011; Mirzoeff 2011.

Chapter One. Monstrous Sexuality and Vile Sovereignty

1 For a Eurocentric history of childhood, see Aries 1962. For U.S. overviews, see Bernstein 2011; Brewer 2005; Brown 2001; Duane 2010; Sánchez-Eppler 2005; Stephens 1995. On age as a racialized category in the United States, see Feld and Syrrett 2015; Meiners 2016, 31–57. For a powerful investigation of the child produced transnationally, see Castaña 2002. On the child as an ecological category, see Shelton (2016). See also the argument that transforming social, economic, and political meanings of "age" have been a constitutive part of the black racial formation from the modern era onward (Ibrahim 2016).

2 Sample studies of colonial impositions of gender and sexuality include Byrd 2011; McClintock 1995; Povinelli 2006; Rifkin 2011; Stoler 2002; Thomas 2007. Related anthologies include Cruz-Malave and Manalansan 2002; Driskill et al. 2011.

3 On European psychiatry and sexology, see Bland and Doan 1998; Tobin 2015.

4 On debates about pederasty and/as homosexuality in ancient Greece, see Halperin 1989; Ormand 2008.

5 For overviews of white slavery in England in particular, see Kincaid 1992; Walkowitz 1992.

6 On the whiteness of sexual protection laws, see Freedman 2013; Haag 1999; Jenkins 1998.

7 On *Plessy v. Ferguson* (1896), see Best 2004; Harris 1993. On the territorializing effects of racial terror, see Goldsby 2006; McKittrick 2006; McKittrick and Woods 2007.

8 The historical production of whiteness is treated in Delgado and Stephanic 1997; Lipsitz 1998; Jacobson 1998; Roediger 1994, 1999; Wiegman 1999, 2002.

9 On racial prerequisite cases and "commonsense" versus "scientific" racial categories, see López 1996. On the Dawes Act of 1887 and Dawes Rolls of the 1890s, see Fletcher 2011, Tallbear 2013. On the 1885 Major Crimes Act (MCA) that abrogated treaty rights to sovereign legal proceedings for native nations in order to allow federal prosecution of Native defendants in specific felony cases, including rape, see Deer 2015.

10 On civilizational discourse and late nineteenth-century empire, see Bederman 1995; Kaplan 2002; McCartney 2006; Wexler 2000; Churchill 2004; Lye 2005.

11 On juvenile courts, see Feld 2017; McGillivray 1997; Odem 1995; Ward 2012.

12 On European pre- and early modern shifts from ecclesiastical to state law prohibiting "unnatural" sexual acts as crimes, such as the English Buggery Act of 1533 that included as crimes against nature buggery, bestiality, and sodomy (defined de facto as acts between men), see Crompton 2003; Eskridge 2008.

13 The Oxford English Dictionary (OED) dates the English-language use of "paedo-philia," which it defines quite simply as "sexual desire directed toward children," to Ellis 1906. The English term is the more recent "paederasty," dated in the OED to 1603, which offers more restrictive parameters of both gender, age, and act: "Homosexual relations between a man and a boy; homosexual anal intercourse, usually with a boy or younger man as the passive partner." The term "pedophilia" was used across the twentieth-century United States but not as the dominant term it became in the late twentieth century (Jenkins 1998, 99).

14 On the arrest in 1912 of the African American boxer Jack Johnson through the Mann Act, see Diffee 2005; Pascoe 2009. Estelle Freedman (1987) argues that an earlier focus on women's purity turned to men's potential violence after the 1920s.

15 See also Hartman 2017; Hicks 2010. On Southern systems, see Haley 2016.

16 See for one example Shah 2005a and 2005b on sodomy cases involving "Hindoo" migrants and white juveniles in the Pacific Northwest.

17 The 1911 Massachusetts Briggs Act, for example, targeted habitual offenders and sexual offenders in particular as "defectives" subject to psychiatric examination and commitment to special institutions (Jenkins 1998, 40).

18 On sexual minorities defining their own role in this period, see Chauncey 1995; Hartman 2017; Mumford 1997; Somerville 2000; Terry 1999.

19 Stockton's terms resonates with Sylvia Wynter's (2001, 2003) treatment of the "genre of the human" overdetermined by the concept "Man"; see McKittrick 2015.

20 Treatments of these mid-century cases can be found in Denno 1998; Lancaster 2011; Lave 2009; Leon 2011.

21 Alfred Fish was originally named Hamilton Fish but took a dead brother's name. On this and related cases, see Jenkins 1998, 49–50; Robertson 2005.

22 Leon (2011) points out that civil commitment was part of a "three-track system" that differentiated among patients to be treated, culprits to be punished, and incur-ables to be incapacitated; see also Miller 2002.

23 As Freedman (1987, 97–98) summarizes, "In short, white men who committed sexual crimes had to be mentally ill; black men who committed sexual crimes were believed to be guilty of willful violence." See also Kunzel 2017.

24 For one sample ethnography, see Davis and Kennedy 1994.

25 On African American women's activism in this period, see McGuire 2011; Gore 2011.

26 Pedophilic practices were routinely projected outside Europe and the United States, in particular in Southeast Asia, North Africa, and East Asia; see Afry 2009; Al-Kassim 2008; Amin 2017; Boellstorff 2005; Boone 2014; Lim 2014; Massad 2007; Ramberg 2014. On 1950s–70s white migration to Morocco and Tangiers, see Mullins 2002; Shepard 2018.

27 For a broader history of respectability politics, see Higgenbotham 1994. On the "White Pervert" and African American respectability, see Schmidt 2013, 136–78.

28 More sexology in this period treated in D'Emilio 1983; Kinsey et al. 1953; Terry 1999. On sexuality within the family in this period, see Devlin 2005.

29 Muhammad (2010) remarks on the changing protocols of criminal data collection in this period, pointing, along with other scholars, to the rise of sociological expertise more broadly in relation to immigration; see Luibheid 2002; Ngai 2004. On the use of "moral turpitude" to disqualify immigration, see McGarry 2014.

30 Numerous jurisdictions funded studies to determine the facts behind the hype (New York City in 1939; New Jersey in 1949; California specifically on "Sex Crimes against Children" in 1949), yet the findings were inconclusive (see Lave 2009, 559–61; Leon 2011, 13–17).

31 Nearly identical language appears in the 1955 article, including calls for "aroused public opinion" as "common sense" (Hoover 1955, 101).

32 Hoover recommends new laws (the sexual psychopath laws) that withdraw offenders' consent from the procedures of "extreme" cure, rendering "specialized treatment" an "official secret" seemingly beyond law or medicine (Hoover 1955, 103).

33 Hoover contrasts the absence of solid data with stories citizens can access on the "front page of the daily newspapers"; his article provides nine short case narratives that include victims who range in age from seven to seventeen and offenders from seventeen to "elderly," in locations that cross the country from "Southern state" and "Midwestern town" to "Eastern city" and "New England" (Hoover 1955, 32–33, 102).

34 Between 1953 and 1969, for example, federal Termination and Relocation policies continued to carve indigenous sovereignty into smaller units while the 1953 Public Law 280 (PL 280) unevenly shifted federal jurisdiction over major crimes, including rape, on reservation lands to states; see Smith 2011–2012, Deer 2015, 2016.

35 The Free Joanne Little campaign of 1974, Inez García of 1974, and Yvonne Swan of 1972 brought together antirape, antiracist, and antistate activism and analysis (see Davis 1975; Thuma 2014). See also Thuma (2019) as a revision of the pure cooptation narrative in Bumiller 2008.

36 On the emergence of culture as a terrain of insurgent and counterinsurgent struggles over hegemony and domination, see Denning 2004; Ferguson 2004; Gordon and Newfield 2008; Yudice 2003.

37 On relations among institutionalizations, see Ben-Moshe 2013; Ben-Moshe et al. 2014.

38 Some form of sexual orientation disorder continues to be listed in the DSM covering "ego-dystonic" experiences related to sexuality (Drescher 2015; Puar 2015).

39 On Foucault's Eurocentrism, see James 1996; Stoler 1995; Thomas 2007; Weheliye 2014.

40 This period was also associated with an increased focus on child pornography, which Jenkins argues did increase through imports largely from the Netherlands and Scandinavia (Jenkins 1998, 121–24).

41 For popular histories of NAMBLA, see Andriette 1994; Califia 2000; Denizet-Lewis 2006; Levine 2017.

42 See North American Man/Boy Love Association 1986; Sandfort et al. 1991; Tsang 1981.

43 Organizations and serial publications include the Paedophile Information Exchange, a U.K. group founded in 1974 and ended in 1984; *Paidika: The Journal of Paedophilia*, published from 1987 to 1995; and the René Guyon Society. The Roman Polanski case (1977–78) also drew attention.

44 On use of children in global sex industries, see Davidson (2005, 127), which includes incisive chapters on the mythology of pedophilia as well as the reality of "Western men who travel as tourists, or take up permanent residence in poor and developing countries, in order to gain sexual access to children."

45 For critiques of Foucault's activism focused on gender, see Alcoff 1996; Bell 1993. On his elision of U.S.-based antiracist and race-radical struggles, see Heiner 2007; Thomas 2007.

Chapter Two. Profiling Virtuality and Pedophilic Data

1 Foucault (2003a, 12) describes "vile sovereignty" as a mode of political power that operates through its own odious disqualification (see chapter 1 in this volume).

2 On the milk carton campaigns, see Berlant 1997; Ivy 1993; Kitzinger 2004.

3 On the emergence of child sexual abuse, see Ashenden 2003; Conte 2002; Reavey and Warner 2003.

4 In contrast, see structural and institutional analyses in EchoHawk 2001–2002; Hesford 2011; INCITE! Women of Color against Violence 2016; Million 2013; Patterson and Gossett 2016; Smith 2005.

5 Kimberlé Williams Crenshaw (1995) theorized "intersectionality" to name the limits of using single-axis legal categories such as race and gender to describe black women's lives.

6 Recent efforts to displace this paradigm include ethnographies and qualitative research such as Cox 2015; Crenshaw et al. 2015; Epstein et al. 2017; Vaught 2017.

7 President Ronald Reagan only acknowledged HIV/AIDS in 1985, after White's case drew publicity, despite long-running efforts to raise official and public awareness of HIV/AIDS since its first cases in 1981 and the formation of activist institutions such as Gay Men's Health Crisis in 1982 (Patton 1990).

8 On NY Stock Exchange action, see Handelman 1990. On letting die and necropolitics more generally, see Foucault 1990; Mbembe 2003; Haritaworn et al. 2012.

9 On the criminalization of HIV status and transmission, see Strub 2017; Tomso 2017.

10 On the Central Park jogger case, see Burns 2011; Byfield 2014; and Ava DuVernay's Netflix series *When They See Us* (2019).

11 Overviews of HIV/AIDS in this period found in Cohen 1999; Patton 2002.

12 Yvonne Wanrow's case (1972) drew attention to white male predation on indigene-

ous children, for example, as a feminist self-defense issue rather than an exceptional issue of child endangerment.

13 Later revised in Rubin 2011. On the 1980s sex wars, see also Duggan and Hunter 1995.

14 Early three-strikes laws responded to the Westley Allan Dodd case in Washington State in 1989, focused on the rape and murder of eleven-year-old Cole Near, ten-year-old William Near, and four-year-old Lee Iseli by a previously convicted and repeatedly arrested sex offender. Washington passed Initiative 593 in 1993. The Richard Allen Davis case in California in 1993 focused on the kidnapping and murder of twelve-year-old Polly Klaas by a previously convicted and repeatedly arrested sex offender, California passed Proposition 184 in 1994.

15 Manuel fought to have a Sherrice Iverson Good Samaritan Law passed in Los Angeles in 1997, making it a crime to witness an act against someone younger than fourteen without notifying police (Terry 1998).

16 See n. 26 in the introduction to this volume. "Ashley's Laws," begun in Texas in 1995, describes a cluster of laws enhancing penalties, registration, and notification requirements at the state level, replicated across states. Florida's Jessica Lunsford Act of 2005 sets a first-time sex offense against a child younger than twelve as a capital felony, with a minimum twenty-five-year sentence and lifetime electronic monitoring. It was introduced federally without a vote in 2005 by being added as an amendment to the Jacob Wetterling Act. See Knox (2003) on President Bill Clinton's radio address on the Wetterling Act in 1996.

17 On these legal rulings, see *Kansas v. Hendricks* (1997); *Stogner v. California* (2003); *Connecticut Department of Public Safety v. Doe* (2003); *Smith v. Doe* (2003). Cases related to interstate and international travel are outliers: *Carr v. United States* (2010); *United States v. Lunsford* (2013); *Nichols v. United States* 2016. Two of these cases involve men registered in Kansas moving to the Philippines.

18 The use of electronic monitors and GPS tracking began here and has been expanded into nonsexual criminal case management; see Kilgore 2018.

19 Pedophilia was listed alongside paraphilias, or sexual psychopathologies, including exhibitionistic disorder, fetishistic disorder, frotteuristic disorder, pedophilic disorder, sexual masochism disorder, sexual sadism disorder, transvestic disorder, and voyeuristic disorder.

20 The DSM-5 defines paraphilia as "any intense and persistent sexual interest other than sexual interest in genital stimulation or preparatory fondling with phenotypically normal, physically mature, consenting human partners." Paraphilias are divided into: (1) anomalous activity preferences, including courtship disorders and algolagnic disorders; and (2) anomalous target preferences, either human directed or otherwise.

21 The American Psychological Association distanced itself from the American Psychiatric Association publication with its own press release clarifying that pedo-

philia is always a disorder and its accompanying behaviors criminal; see "State-ment of the American Psychological Association Regarding Pedophilia and the Diagnostic and Statistical Manual of Mental Disorders (DSM-5)," American Psychological Association, October 31, 2013, accessed July 10, 2019, https://www.apa.org/news/press/releases/2013/10/pedophilia-mental.

22 Blanchard (2010, 309) acknowledges that "not all child molesters are pedophiles" and suggests setting a threshold for "the absolute number of sexual encounters with children" as three, a number disputed by others who say one event is evidence of a disorder (O'Donohue 2010). This behavioral focus is meant to create diagnos-tic clarity for those who deny that they have persistent desires, urges, or fantasies involving children, but who have committed documented sexual acts with chil-dren. Berlin (2014, 404) complains the DSM-V may be "contributing inadvertently to the misconception" that child molesting and pedophilia are "the same."

23 On the preclusion of DSM categories, including pedophilia, from the Americans with Disabilities Act (ADA), see Puar 2015.

24 This volume was among a growing number of publications by the federal govern-ment aimed at merging "various Department of Justice initiatives for proactive marketing in order to expand the practical effect of all our efforts" to clarify the "link between missing and sexually exploited children" (Lanning 1986, v).

25 Coric et al. (2005, 27) argue that, in terms of "forensic evaluation," "the only 'objec-tive' means of assessing pedophilic sexual interest is by directly measuring penile erections in response to visual, auditory, or emotional cues."

26 Okami and Goldberg (1992, 302) argue there is cause to use "heuristic" pedophilia as "a sexual preference for children," while Finkelhor and Araji (1986) argue that there are no valid criteria for pedophilia as a sexual preference but only as conduct.

27 Discussion of moral panic frameworks include Burgett 2009; Cohen 1972; Downes et al. 2007; Feeley and Simon 2007; McLuhan 1964.

28 Coded as the racialized use of excessive violence not necessary to complete an eco-nomic theft, "mugging" sought to signify postcolonial and racialized insurgency as a threat to society rather than the state; this would allow the state to intervene legitimately and shore up its police function even as it dismantled its safety net. On corollary "broken windows" policing, see Camp and Heatherton 2016; Kelling and Wilson 1982.

29 On these effects, see Agan 2011; Carpenter and Beverlin 2012; Hall 2004; Hoppe 2016; Sharpe 2014; Simon 2000; U.S. Department of Justice 2008.

30 On the use of expertise in such cases, see Melton et al. 2007. On this case, see King 1999; Rollman 1998.

31 The original state appeal combined the cases of Leroy Hendricks and Tim Quinn, both of whom were convicted of multiple accounts of child sexual abuse.

32 The dissent disagreed over whether legislative authority to determine psychologi-cal danger was in criminal or civil jurisdiction and therefore how the legislature

and the courts were allowed to "punish"—rather than merely "protect"—people for and from abnormal mental states.

33 On the *Comstock* case and the DOJ's civil commitment unit in Butner, North Carolina, see Aviv 2013; Bourke and Hernandez 2009.

34 For a reading of the Hendricks case, paraphilia Not Otherwise Specified (NOS), and vile sovereignty, see Lukes 2016.

35 Other instruments include the Rapid Risk Assessment for Sexual Offense Recidivism and the Minnesota Sex Offender Screening Tool-Revised (see Hanson and Morton-Bourgon 2005, 2009).

36 For updates, see "Static-99," *Static-99 Clearinghouse*, accessed July 15, 2018, http://www.static99.org.

37 These phrases quoted in Wong et al. 2013; on these instruments see also Zgoba et al. 2012.

38 For example, dangerousness is linked to compulsivity in SVP rulings, but there is no corresponding diagnostic term, with the personality category of impulsivity in sex offenders construed as both an "impulse-aggressive trait (e.g., unplanned with no consideration for consequences)" and "a compulsive-aggressive trait (planned with the intention of relieving internal pressures or urges)" (Hall and Hall 2009, 528).

39 Jyoti Puri's (2016, 32–33) related study of Section 377 in Indian law points out the "subjective differences between numbers and statistics": "while state agencies and units might enumerate all kinds of things, only some things are endowed with the gravity of statistics."

40 The FBI's Uniform Crime Report (UCR) historically defined attempted or forcible rape as "carnal knowledge of a female against her will." In 2013, the UCR expanded the definition of rape to "penetration, no matter how slight, of the vagina or anus with any body part or object, or oral penetration by a sex organ of another person, without the consent of the victim" (on changing definitions, see Federal Bureau of Investigation 2014). The NIBRS supplemented local crime-reporting data gathered by municipal police departments and reported federally through the UCR and expanded "forcible rape" to cover threat, attempt, and completed acts including force or nonconsent based on incapacity (age, temporary or permanent mental or physical impairment), with, however, separate categories for statutory rape, forcible sodomy, sexual assault with an object, forcible fondling, and incest. The NCVS is a phone survey that interviews more than 42,000 national households annually about reported and unreported assaults, with all members older than twelve responding. In the late 1980s, the NCVS was modified to include more expansive categories of sexual assault beyond rape and attempted rape across genders, run for the first time with the full sample in 1993.

41 Office of Justice Programs, "Sexual Assault Response Team (SART) Toolkit: Resources for Sexual Assault Response Teams," accessed January 15, 2017, https://

www.ncjrs.gov/ovc_archives/sartkit, referencing Greenfeld 1997. The SART Toolkit has subsequently been revised, and this citation has been removed.

42 The foreword was written by Jan S. Chaiken, director, Bureau of Justice Statistics, and Laurie Robinson, assistant attorney-general, Office of Justice Programs.

43 Francis X. Diebold, quoted in Lohr 2013.

44 On the broader cultural shift to "statistical panic," see Woodward 2009.

45 Studies treating related profiling phenomena include Cashin 2010; Diaz-Cotto 2006; Haritaworn 2016; Olguín 2010; Puar 2007; Reddy 2011.

46 As early as 1997, collected data were linked to governmental management, as the foreword to the Greenfeld Report explains: "This report was prepared as background information for the Assistant Attorney General's 1996 National Summit Promoting Public Safety Through the Effective Management of Sex Offenders in the Community" (iii).

47 The purpose of the Center for Sex Offender Management (CSOM) (1997–2008), for example, was to gather identification and prediction studies and disseminate information about profiles, actuarial instruments, and risk assessment through its website. The Office of Sex Offender Sentencing, Monitoring, Apprehending, Registering, and Tracking (SMART) was established through the 2006 Adam Walsh Act to implement "the entire spectrum of sex offender management activities needed to ensure public safety." In 2011, the SMART office created the Sex Offender Management Assessment and Planning Initiative (SOMAPI). This includes mandatory state reporting to the (Dru Sjodin) National Sex Offender Public Website (NSOPW) created by the DOJ in 2005 and administered by SMART; the National Crime Information Center (NCIC) database managed by the Federal Bureau of Investigation Criminal Justice Information Services (CJIS) division; the Integrated Automated Fingerprint Identification System (IAFIS); the National Palm Print System (NPPS): and the Combined DNA Index System (CODIS).

48 NCANDS began to collect child protective services data from fifty states, Washington, DC, and Puerto Rico annually in 1988 as part of the Child Abuse Prevention and Treatment Act and began issuing an annual report in 1992. NISMART is a collaboration between the National Institute of Justice (Office of Justice Programs, U.S. Department of Justice) and the Centers for Disease Control and Prevention, which collected a onetime national sample via telephone from November 1995 through May 1996 (reported in November 2000). NatSCEV, a project funded by the DOJ and run out of the University of New Hampshire, undertook a onetime national telephone survey of women at two- and four-year colleges; it focused on children's experience in the previous year and total life; was conducted in Spanish and English; and covered a range of conduct. The NISVS, a project of the Centers for Disease Control and Prevention, was started in 2010 to run an annual, national telephone (cell and landline) survey.

49 According to Finkelhor et al. (2008, 1), "A reanalysis of the FBI's NIBRS data from 12

states for 1991–96 indicates that in one-third of all sexual assaults reported to law enforcement, the victim was younger than age 12."

50 In 1986, the manual's proposed audience was "law enforcement professionals."; in 2010, the manual's proposed audience included an expanded list of "Professionals Investigating the Sexual Exploitation Film of Children" whom it could not authorize as sovereign agents, stating that the manual was being "provided for informational purposes only and does not constitute legal advice or professional opinion on specific facts."

51 Center for Sex Offender Management (CSOM), "Understanding Sex Offenders: An Introductory Curriculum," accessed December 15, 2015, http://www.csom.org/train/etiology/3/3_1.htm.

52 Part II of the SOMAPI Research Brief "Incidence and Prevalence of Sexual Offending" focuses on "special populations" and related topics, including stalking, sexual offending, colleges, Indian Country, developmental disabilities, and the military.

Chapter Three. Informational Image and Procedural Tone

1 *Six Feet Under*, season 1, episode 6.

2 Michel Foucault (2003a, 12) describes "vile sovereignty" as a mode of political power that operates through its own odious disqualification (see chapter 1 in this volume).

3 Frank Lawlis, "Sexual Predator Warning Signs," Dr. Phil website, accessed January 2, 2018, https://www.drphil.com/advice/sexual-predator-warning-signs.

4 The Department of Justice source cited is Snyder 2000. This website (accessed January 18, 2019) has since been updated, and the information has been removed.

5 See the discussion of James B. Waldram's (2012, 75) use of the term "forensic black hole" in his study of sex offender rehabilitation units (chapter 1 of this volume).

6 On visual forensics, see Finn 2009; Tagg 1988, 66–102. On TV depictions of forensic evidence, see Rhineberger-Dunn et al. 2017.

7 For broader TV history, see Hilms 2003; McCarthy 2001; Thomson 2016.

8 On reality television, see Kraidy and Sender 2011; Murray and Oulette 2008; Skeggs and Wood 2012.

9 On crime procedural television, see Magestro 2015; Rapping 2003; Ruble 2009; Snauffer 2006; Turnbull 2014.

10 For an overview of methodologies within television studies, see Gray and Lotz 2012.

11 *Law and Order: SVU* announced a move from production headquarters in New Jersey to New York when New Jersey cut its 20 percent production subsidies in 2010 (Andreva 2010; "New York State Film Tax Credit Program [Production]" 2018). On economic impact, see Bellafante 2011. *Law and Order: SVU* has also received Gates Foundation dollars (Arango and Stelter 2009).

12 Episodes will be cited by season number, episode number within that season, episode title, and date aired.

13 This contrasts with the flat tone of *Law and Order*, about which Susanna Lee (2003, 83) argues, "The true spectacle in this series, the principal story told, is not the characters' dramatic response to crime, but the absence of response—the absence of psychic commotion or unrest."

14 "Payback" focuses on the case of a man stabbed to death in a taxi, leading to Stabler's evaluation of a gay man in prison and a Serbian war crimes predator for gender and sexual signs: "This still reads gay to me"; it "could be a he/she" (with laughter); etc. For a sharp literary remediation of *svu* beginning with this episode, see Machado 2013.

15 Citing Jan Mukařovský (1970), Michael Bérubé (2004, 12) points out that an "aesthetic function" is "only one among many functions that can be assigned to objects," an assignation that changes historically and culturally.

16 For a compelling revision of the operational aesthetic for surveillance in serial television, see Zimmer 2018.

17 Ngai (2005, 52) relates tone to the psychologist Silvan Tomkins's (1963) concept of affect: "A mechanism that magnifies awareness and intensifies the effects of operations associated with other biological subsystems (drive, cognitive, motor, perceptual, homeostatic) by 'co-assemblage' with these other vital mechanisms." On Tomkins and affect, see Gregg and Seigworth 2010; Sedgwick and Adam 1995.

18 "Pedophiles," *Law and Order* wiki, accessed January 18, 2019, https://lawandorder .fandom.com/wiki/Category:Pedophiles.

19 "Hardwired" treats a Latino boy who was molested by his white stepfather.

20 "Web" treats a white teen who was molested by his father as a child and now runs his own porn site called "Teddy's Treehouse." "Sick" treats two accusations of child molestation against a white thirty-five-year-old billionaire who keeps a children's play world in his home as part of his charitable work for children.

21 "Contagious" treats parental hysteria leading to false accusations that ruin an innocent man's life; the true culprit is the preppy white male high school Lacrosse captain (Zach Gilford, best known as Matt Saracen in *Saturday Night Lights*).

22 In "Hardwired" the defendant's argument that "minor-adult relationships are normal, safe and healthy" meets with the prosecutor's question, "Do you have any medical or psychiatric research?"

23 "Angels" treats nine- to ten-year-old boys from Guatemala smuggled into the United States by a pedophile ring. Detectives discuss "bulletins from the North American Man/Boy Love Association" as "a how-to guide for pedophiles."

24 "Bad Blood" treats the nature-or-nurture problem of sexual abnormality versus monstrosity, or whether some people are "just born bad." In "Web," Detective Benson claims that that new technologies developed by the Department of Homeland Security "will change the way sexual predators are hunted online. . . . [T]races that used to take an entire day now take 24 hours."

25 "Name" treats the 1978 case of four missing Puerto Rican boys age twelve to four-teen, which is reopened when a child's bones are found with a *Battlestar Galactica* lunchbox.

26 Exceptions to the white pedophile can be found in the csi episode "Harvest," in which a black pedophile appears as a decoy in a story arc about mixed-race ge-netics, and season 4 of *The Wire*, treating a stepfather abuser of a main character within an African American household.

27 On Benjamin's concept of aura, see Davis 1995; Hansen 1987; Weinbaum 2007.

28 On cinematic whiteness, see also Bernardi 2001; Best 2004; Cherniavsky 2006.

29 On surveillance in television and film versus the turn to security, see Dubrofsky and Magnet 2015; Levin and Weibel 2002; Lotz 2014; Lyon 2006; Zimmer 2015.

30 This televisual strategy loosely correlates to the movement-image and the time-image theorized by the philosopher Gilles Deleuze in *Cinema 1* (1986) and *Cinema 2* (1989). The movement-image creates connection among images through the mo-bility of the camera, often combining perception images (point of view), affection images (emotion), and action images (cause and effect) in classic narrative cinema. In contrast, the time-image isolates an image from this type of narrative movement so that it signifies its own status as sign, a kind of image of virtuality or potentiali-ties that exceed a presented actuality. On broader treatments of temporality on television, see Ames 2012.

31 This is consistently thematized in svu as the problem of pornography. In "Hard-wired," the stepfather defends his photographs of a different Cory as "beautiful, artistic snapshots"; this defense is then linked to the claim, "What Cory and I have is special; it's more than love."

32 This is a stock behavior for Stabler, who in "Name" says, "I get a little clumsy around scumbag pedophiles."

33 "Manhattan Vigil" features shots of Benson saying, "Wow, this neighborhood's changed," which cuts to a "Bad Blood" scene presented as "flashback" of the neigh-borhood, and so on.

34 In 2006, an assistant district attorney named Louis Conradt killed himself during the production of the show when he faced exposure by a swat team and Hansen's film crew.

35 Not to mention endless repetitions in even smaller-screen productions. See, for example, *Marcel the Shell with Shoes On: Two*, in which Marcel mentions that his missing sister has a law named after her, but "we don't like to talk about it."

Chapter Four. Capturing the Past and the Vitality of Crime

Earlier versions of this chapter were originally published as "Documenting the Pedophile: Virtual White Men in the Era of Recovered Memory," *New Formations* 70 (2010): 23–40 (reproduced with permission of Lawrence and Wishart Limited through PLSclear), and "Virtual Predators: Neoliberal Loss and Human Futures in *Mystic River*," *Social Text* 31.2 115 (Summer 2013): 123–43.

1 After initial screenings at the Sundance Film Festival and Tribeca Film Festival, *Capturing the Friedmans* had a limited U.S. theatrical run through Magnolia Pictures before being released by HBO Home Video on DVD in 2004.

2 For a case chronology, see Jesse Friedman, "Exonerating Jesse Friedman," FreeJesse .net, accessed September 12, 2018, http://www.freejesse.net.

3 Related public cases of the 1980s include the Fells Acres Day School case in Malden, Massachusetts (1986); the McMartin preschool case in Manhattan Beach, California (1987); the Wee Care Nursery School case in Maplewood, New Jersey (1988); and the Little Rascals day-care case in Edenton, North Carolina (1989). Two major PBS *Frontline* documentaries by Ofra Bikel took up the status of memory as a forensic category in this context: the three-part, eight-hour series "Innocence Lost" (1991, 1993, and 1997) and the four-hour "Divided Memories" (1995).

4 On trauma in cinema during this period, see Saltzman and Rosenberg 2006; Santner 1990; Walker 2005.

5 On technology and documentary more broadly, see Gaines and Renov 1999; Moran 2002; Rabinowitz 1994; Renov 2004. For a history of 1930s debates about satire and documentary aesthetics, see Retman 2011.

6 Interviewer Charlie Rose has since been accused of serial sexual harassment and dismissed from CBS News (2017).

7 Michel Foucault (2003a, 12) describes "vile sovereignty" as a mode of political power that operates through its own odious disqualification (see chapter 1 in this volume).

8 The documentary makes visual references to histories of anti-Semitism and Jewish assimilation as problems of performance (echoing its opening sequence of the family's efforts to "Act Naturally"), and the DVD reveals racist threats left on the Friedmans' answering machine during the media frenzy.

9 Richard Grant (2009) writes, "Lehane, who describes himself as 'left of Canada' on most social and political issues, is hardcore right-wing when it comes to paedophilia." Lehane claims of victims that "these kids, their lives are over at 12," and if they do go on to survive their "marginalized lives with marginalized jobs," they are very likely to become pedophiles themselves: "Paedophilia is a contagion. It gets passed on and it spreads and people who say it can be fixed have no knowledge of it."

10 In the novel, "East Buckingham" originally housed the families of inmates and jailers (likely the Charlestown State Prison [1805–1955]), then agricultural and industrial laborers, and eventually people surplus to new financial and service industries and subject to off-site incarceration in prisons providing jobs to the nonurban working class (Lehane 2001, 397). Sean's and Jimmy's fathers both work at

the Coleman Candy plant, although Sean's father is a foreman and Jimmy's father loads trucks. (Dave's father is absent.)

11 On neoliberal youth more generally, see Katz 2008; Strickland 2002.

12 "Jimmy Marcus" is changed to "Jimmy Markum" in the film; "Whitey" is white in the book and African American in the film. Later film adaptations of Lehane's novels include *Gone Baby Gone* (2007), directed by Ben Affleck, which also treats child sexual abuse in Boston; *Shutter Island* (2010), directed by Martin Scorsese; and *Live by Night* (2016), also directed by Affleck. Lehane has also written for television, including *The Wire*, and in 2009 appeared on the show *Castle* as himself among a group of poker-playing crime novelists.

13 On "orchid in the land of technology," see discussion of Benjamin (chapter 2 in this volume).

14 On the film's masculinist agency, see Berkowitz and Cornell 2009; Redmon 2004; Watkins 2008. On its treatment of violence, see Tibbets 1993.

15 In the film, neoliberal structural adjustment is referenced only in passing, as neighborhood gentrification (condominiums and coffee prices). For a comparison of the book and the film, see Rowe 2008.

16 The bar motif is echoed in two shots later in the film: first, as Sean shows Jimmy out of the morgue, and second, when Jimmy sits alone on his porch wondering aloud, "I know in my soul I contributed to your death. I just don't know how."

17 This shot is echoed later when Dave is driven away in the Savage brothers' vehicle to the riverside location, where he will ultimately be killed.

18 This urban cinematography cites what Foster Hirsch (1981, 51) describes as film noir's naturalist tropes, "combining the objectivity and harshness of naturalism with the tough, stylized realism of the hard-boiled crime school." Classic film noir emerged in the 1940s as what Mike Davis (1990, 18) describes as "a fantastic convergence of American 'tough-guy' realism, Weimar expressionism, and existentialized Marxism." For a history of film noir criticism, see Silver and Ursini 1996.

19 Shots of the Mystic River occur ten times, opening and closing the film and creating eight distinct segments of narrative plot and cinematographic style. These shots emphasize the river's permanence in relation to changing man-made landscapes.

20 In this final "flashback" we see Dave separated from his atavistic image, beating the alleged pedophile on the ground while yelling, "Run, Dave, run." Jimmy does not believe him, because "most people don't care if a child molester dies. Why didn't you just tell [Celeste] the truth?" Dave helpfully replies, "I guess maybe I thought I was turning into him."

21 The discourse of the "look" dominates the final paired sequences of the detective plot. While begging for his life, Dave says, "Look at me, Jimmy," and Jimmy replies, "I'm looking at you. Why did you do it?" Meanwhile, Brendan yells at his brother, "Don't look at him. Look at me," to demand a declaration of false familial love.

After Dave has been killed, Sean confronts Jimmy about his death, saying, "Look at me. Look at me, Jimmy."

22 The police procedural juxtaposes what people see with "information" (ballistics, the 911 tape). While one witness complains about the limited use of visual evidence ("go tell a grin to a jury"), the police view the ballistic report details on an IBM computer screen (the subject of its own full-screen shot).

23 On changing reproductive and kinship politics, see Eng 2010; Nelson 2016; Roberts 1997, 2011; Tallbear 2013; Weinbaum 2004, 2019. On the enclosure and commoning of social reproduction in this period, see Federici 2018.

24 Sample scholarship on denaturalized ontologies and materialisms includes Bennet 2010; Blackman 2012; Chen 2012; Haraway 1991; Jones 2010; Coole and Frost 2010.

Chapter Five. Capturing the Future and the Sexuality of Risk

1 On uses of the term queer, see Berlant and Warner 1998; Cohen 1997; Haritaworn 2016; Stryker and Aizura 2013. On translations of trauma into sexual subjectivities, see Berlant 1997; Cvetkovich 2003; Million 2013.

2 I borrow Keeling's (2007) account of cinematic surplus, produced through her reading of the black femme in cinema, to think through the very different figuration of white male deviance as "pedophilia" and the surplus it produces.

3 Connie May Fowler, quoted in "Fiction Writer Scott Heim to Read for Writer Program Series Dec. 1," *The Source*, November 23, 2005, accessed February 3, 2018, https://source.wustl.edu/2005/11/fiction-writer-scott-heim-to-read-for-writer-program-reading-series-dec-1.

4 Lehane's and Heim's regional realisms during structural adjustment could be put into conversation with Cleary et al. 2012.

5 On new queer cinema, see Aaron 2004; Morrison 2006; Rich 2013; Villarejo 2001.

6 Marks (2000, xi) uses this phrase to describe how "film signifies through its materiality, through a contact between perceiver and object represented." Marks's (2000) account of haptic visuality is drawn explicitly from what she calls "intercultural cinema," which uses this strategy to re-create memories of place for diasporic subjects. This strategy was eventually appropriated in more Hollywood-style films. See also Barker 2009.

7 On erotic pleasures aligned with eating as "*queer alimentarity*," see Tompkins 2012, 5. Sugar and childhood have a complex history (see Merleaux 2015).

8 This incorporation of a *Poltergeist* reference looking *away* from the TV and into the world mimics the work attributed to Araki's mainstreaming of New Queer Cinema to Hollywood style, the demonology haunting technologies of domestic life now projected outside of the home.

9 On theories of queer temporality more broadly, see Nealon 2001; Halberstam 2005; Love 2009; Freeman 2010; Richardson 2016.

10 On queer childhood more broadly, see essays in Bruhm and Hurley 2004.

11 In 1983, Neil and his childhood friend Wendy (played by Riley McGuire) cross paths with Brian and his sister Deborah on Halloween night. That night, Neil and Wendy assault a young boy at Neil's instigation while Brian has another run in with an "alien," or blurred blue-lit figure, who causes him to awaken with a bloody nose.

12 This scene introduced by Araki (it is not in the book) is a nod to his earlier work, teen rebellion now isolated as nostalgic scene within the SORN frame.

13 Nostalgia figures in Brian's visual story, as well, this teen scene routed through a dawning culture of fear with on-screen footage of the television show *World of Mystery* and vintage 1980s voice-over, "Is it mass hysteria, or something ALL TOO REAL?" (with the final three words drawn out).

14 This is another ironic nod: "We're not in Kansas anymore," Wendy says. "Neil, you have got to be so careful." Neil's sex work in New York, however, is presented as an entrance into a safer world; during his first trick, the john says, "Fuck me up the ass with your hot teenage cock." He then exclaims, "Wait! What the fuck are you doing?" and hands Neil a condom. After giving a back rub to a john whose sarcomas visibly surprise Neil, his flat, self-contained affect breaks down, and he talks with Wendy about his relationship with Coach.

15 The script published by Samuel French includes six actors for seven characters: Walter, Girl/Robin, Rosen, Carlos, Nikki, and Lucas. Previous productions of *The Woodsman* indicate that casting is not based on race and ethnicity.

16 Daniels also reports negative responses to the film, including receiving a dead rat in a box delivered to his home.

17 Some reviews evaluate the film's medical or carceral realism (see, e.g., Bennett 2006; Sen 2005).

18 M appears only in shadow here, leaning down in front of the wanted poster to say, "You have a very beautiful ball. What's your name?" On M, see McGilligan 2013; Stewart 2016.

19 On the cultural work of the fairytale Little Red Riding Hood, see Orenstein 2002.

20 Here, the joke "Six Degrees of Kevin Bacon" helps explain how the actor establishes an aura of cinematic authenticity as well as real-life distance that secures audience members from experiencing themselves truly "gazing at a pedophile."

21 Strategically differentiated from Foucault's heterotopia (1984), heterorealism here is incorporative rather than diffracting (see Cherniavsky 2006; Melamed 2011).

22 Simone Browne (2015, 12, 19, 21) outlines the dominant uses of "racializing surveillance" and theorizes "dark sousveillance" as an "active inversion of the power relations that surveillance entails" that "chart the possibilities and coordinate modes of responding to, challenging, and confronting a surveillance that was almost all-encompassing."

23 Foucault (2003a, 12) describes "vile sovereignty" as a mode of political power that operates through its own odious disqualification (see chapter 1 in this volume).

24 Like the candy at the start of *Mysterious Skin*, the park scenes are deliberately shot

to be "beautiful," Kassell explains in her voiceover for the DVD. She reports asking the cinematographer Xavier Pérez Grobet to "come up with a different look of footage, to signify that we're in a different time and place."

25 Vicki later discloses her own experience of sexual abuse by her three brothers, countering his assumption that she must "hate them" by asserting the complexity of culpability and injury, stating that she "loves them," even as their self-identity as "good men" ("They're strong, gentle men with families of their own") means they would deny what they did.

26 On the differential politics of respectability and African American women's agency, see Higgenbotham 1994; Thompson 2012. On the white pervert in African American respectability politics after World War II, see Schmidt 2013.

27 From their greeting at the door—"Walter." "Cop."—a new dynamic is introduced of mutual but antagonistic recognition and direct address. ("Mind if I come in?" "You are in." "Yeah, I am." "Mind if I look around?" "Yeah, I do." "Why, you got something to hide?" "Doesn't everybody?")

28 A bag of gummy bears is used to seduce the "Cherub" in echoes of *Mysterious Skin* as well as *Hedwig and the Angry Inch*.

Conclusion

1 National Association for Rational Sex Offense Laws, "History," accessed September 3, 2018, https://narsol.org/about-us/history. The Center for Sexual Justice is no longer active.

2 Op-Docs, "Sex Offender Village," *New York Times*, May 22, 2013, accessed January 17, 2019, https://documentaries.io/film/sex-offender-village-op-docs-the-new-york-times.

3 No More Silence, accessed September 6, 2018, http://itstartswithus-mmiw.com.

4 Audre Lorde Project, accessed September 18, 2018, https://alp.org; Creative Interventions, accessed September 18, 2018, http://www.creative-interventions.org; "Addressing Harm, Accountability, and Healing," CriticalResistance.org, accessed September 16, 2018, http://criticalresistance.org/resources/addressing-harm-accountability-and-healing; Community United against Violence, accessed September 18, 2018, http://www.cuav.org; INCITE!, accessed September 18, 2018, https://incite-national.org; Southerners on New Ground, accessed September 18, 2018, http://southernersonnewground.org; "Survived and Punished: End the Criminalization of Survivors of Domestic and Sexual Violence," accessed September 18, 2018, http://www.survivedandpunished.org.

5 Generation Five, accessed September 18, 2018, http://www.generationfive.org; Living Bridges Project, Just Beginnings Collaborative, accessed September 18, 2018, http://justbeginnings.org/about-us; Stop It Now!, accessed September 18, 2018, https://www.stopitnow.org.

REFERENCES

Aaron, Michele, ed. 2004. *New Queer Cinema: A Critical Reader.* New Brunswick, NJ: Rutgers University Press.

Abrams, Loney. 2015. "These Are the *Law and Order* Episodes Directed by Alleged Pedophile Jace Alexander." Hopes&Fears.com. Accessed January 2, 2018. http://www.hopesandfears.com/hopes/culture/television/215829-jace-alexander-child-pornography-directed-these-episodes-of-law-order.

Ackerman, Alissa, Andrew Harris, Jill Levenson, and Kristen Zgoba. 2011. "Who Are the People in Your Neighborhood? A Descriptive Analysis of Individuals on Public Sex Offender Registries." *International Journal of Law and Psychiatry* 34: 149–59.

Adams, Devon. 2002. "Summary of State Sex Offender Registries, 2001." Bureau of Justice Statistics, March 1. Accessed April 19, 2013. http://bjs.gov/content/pub/pdf/ssso01.pdf.

Adler, Amy. 2001. "The Perverse Law of Child Pornography." *Columbia Law Review* 10, no. 2 (March): 209–73.

Afry, Janet. 2009. *Sexual Politics in Modern Iran.* New York: Cambridge University Press.

Agan, Amanda. 2011. "Sex Offender Registration: Fear without Function?" *Journal of Law and Economics* 54 (February): 207–39.

Ahmed, Sarah. 2010. *The Promise of Happiness.* Durham, NC: Duke University Press.

Aitkin, Stuart C. 2006. "Leading Men to Violence and Creating Spaces for Their Emotions." *Gender, Place and Culture* 13, no. 5: 491–507.

Al-Kassim, Dina. 2008. "Epilogue: Sexual Epistemologies, East in West." In *Islamicate Sexualities: Translations Across Temporal Geographies of Desire,* edited by Kathryn Babayan and Afsaneh Najmabadi, 297–340. Cambridge, MA: Harvard University Press.

Alcoff, Linda Martin. 1996. "Dangerous Pleasures: Foucault and the Politics of Pedophilia." In *Feminist Interpretations of Michel Foucault*, edited by Susan Hekman, 99–136. College Park: Penn State University Press.

Alexander, Jacqui M. 1997. "Erotic Autonomy as a Politics of Decolonization: An Anatomy of Feminist and State Practices in the Bahamas Tourist Economy." In *Feminist Genealogies, Colonial Legacies, Democratic Futures*, edited by M. Jacqui Alexander and Chandra Talpade Mohanty, 63–100. New York: Routledge.

Alexander, Michelle. 2010. *The New Jim Crow: Mass Incarceration in the Age of Colorblindness*. New York: New Press.

Amar, Paul. 2013. *The Security Archipelago: Human-Security States, Sexuality Politics, and the End of Neoliberalism*. Durham, NC: Duke University Press.

American Bar Association. 2015. *National Inventory of the Collateral Consequences of Conviction*. Accessed December 12, 2017. http://ww.abacolateralconsequences.org.

American Psychiatric Association. 1999. *Dangerous Sex Offenders: A Task Force Report of the American Psychiatric Association*. Washington, DC: American Psychiatric Publishing.

American Psychiatric Association. (1952). *Diagnostic and Statistical Manual of Mental Disorders*. Washington, DC: American Psychiatric Association.

American Psychiatric Association. (1980). *Diagnostic and Statistical Manual of Mental Disorders* (3rd edition) Washington, DC: American Psychiatric Association.

American Psychiatric Association. (1987). *Diagnostic and Statistical Manual of Mental Disorders* (3rd edition, text revision). Washington, DC: American Psychiatric Association.

American Psychiatric Association (2000). *Diagnostic and Statistical Manual of Mental Disorders* (4th edition, text revision). Washington, DC: American Psychiatric Association.

American Psychiatric Association. (2013). *Diagnostic and Statistical Manual of Mental Disorders* (5th edition). Washington, DC: American Psychiatric Association.

American Psychiatric Association. (2013). "Pedophilia." In *Diagnostic and statistical manual of mental disorders* (5th ed.): https://doi.org/10.1176/appi.books.9780890425596.dsm05.

Ames, Melissa, ed. 2012. *Time in Television Narrative: Exploring Temporality in Twenty-First Century Programming*. Jackson: University of Mississippi Press.

Amin, Kadji. 2017. *Disturbing Attachments: Genet, Modern Pederasty, and Queer History*. Durham, NC: Duke University Press.

Amnesty International Report. 2007. "Maze of Injustice: The Failure to Protect Indigeneous Women from Sexual Violence in the USA." New York: Amnesty International.

Andreva, Nellie. 2010. "'Law and Order: svu' Leaves New Jersey over Nixed Tax Credit." *Deadline Hollywood*, June 25. Accessed July 31, 2018. https://deadline

.com/2010/06/law-order-svu-leaves-new-jersey-over-nixed-tax-credit-may
-move-into-lo-set-49433.

Andriette, Bill. 1994. "Queerest Queers: Man/Boy Love Faces Violence out of Control." *Steam* 2, no. 2: 165–67.

Angelides, Steven. 2004. "Feminism, Child Sexual Abuse, and the Erasure of Child
Sexuality." GLQ 10, no. 2: 141–77.

Arango, Tim, and Brian Stelter. 2009. "Messages with a Mission, Embedded in TV
Shows." *New York Times*, April 1. Accessed July 26, 2018. https://www.nytimes
.com/2009/04/02/arts/television/02gates.html.

Ardolino, Frank. 2007. "From the Curse to Its Reverse: Red Sox Nation in Films,
1992–2000." *nine: A Journal of Baseball History and Culture* 16, no. 1 (Fall):
108–28.

Aries, Philippe. 1962. *Centuries of Childhood: A Social History of Family Life*, translated by Robert Baldick. New York: Knopf.

Arthur, Paul. 2003. "True Confessions, Sort Of: Capturing the Friedmans and the
Dilemma of Theatrical Documentary." *Cineaste* (Fall): 4–7.

Ashenden, Sam. 2003. *Governing Child Sexual Abuse*. London: Routledge.

Aviv, Rachel. 2013. "The Science of Sex Abuse." *New Yorker*, January 14. Accessed September 8, 2018. https://www.newyorker.com/magazine/2013/01/14/the-science
-of-sex-abuse.

Baldwin, James. 1985. *The Evidence of Things Not Seen*. New York: Henry Holt.

Bambara, Toni Cade. 1999. *Those Bones Are Not My Child*. New York: Pantheon.

Bandes, Susan. 2007. "The Lessons of Capturing the Friedmans: Moral Panic, Institutional Denial, and Due Process." *Law, Culture, and the Humanities* 3, no. 2:
293–319.

Barker, Jennifer. 2009. *The Tactile Eye: Touch and the Cinematic Experience*. Berkeley:
University of California Press.

Barnard, Ian. 2017. "Rhetorical Commonsense and Child Molester Panic—A Queer
Intervention." *Rhetoric Society Quarterly* 47, no. 1: 3–25.

Barry, Andrew, Thomas Osborne, and Nikolas Rose, eds. 1996. *Foucault and Political Reason: Liberalism, Neoliberalism and Rationalities of Government*. Chicago:
University of Chicago Press.

Becker, Snowden. 2004. "Capturing the Friedmans (Review)." *Moving Image* 4, no. 1
(Spring): 145–48.

Beckett, Katherine, and Steven Herbert. 2009. *Banished: The New Social Control in
Urban America*. New York: Oxford University Press.

Bederman, Gail. 1995. *Manliness and Civilization: A Cultural History of Gender and
Race in the United States, 1880–1917*. Chicago: University of Chicago Press.

Bell, Vikki. 1993. *Interrogating Incest: Foucault, Feminism and the Law*. London: Routledge.

Bell, Vikki. 2008. "The Burden of Sensation and the Ethics of Form: Watching *Capturing the Friedmans*." *Theory, Culture and Society* 25, no. 3: 93–105.

Bellafante, Ginia. 2011. "As Schools Sacrifice, TV Shows Flourish." *New York Times*, November 11. Accessed July 26, 2018. https://www.nytimes.com/2011/11/13 /nyregion/big-city-while-filmmakers-flourish-schools-sacrifice.html.

Benjamin, Walter. 1969. "The Work of Art in the Age of Mechanical Reproduction" (1936). In *Illuminations*, edited by Hannah Arendt, translated by Harry Zohn, 217–26. New York: Schocken.

Ben-Moshe, Liat. 2013. "Disabling Incarceration: Connecting Disability to Divergent Confinements in the USA." *Critical Sociology* 39, no. 3: 385–403.

Ben-Moshe, Liat, Chris Chapman, and Allison C. Carey, eds. 2014. *Disability Incarcerated: Imprisonment and Disability in the United States and Canada*. New York: Palgrave Macmillan.

Bennett, Jamie. 2006. "The Woodsman: Saying the Unsayable." *Jump Cut: A Review of Contemporary Media* 48 (Winter). Accessed September 10, 2018. https://www .ejumpcut.org/archive/jc48.2006/Woodsman/text.html.

Bennet, Jane. 2010. *Vibrant Matter: A Political Economy of Things*. Durham, NC: Duke University Press.

Berger, Dan. 2014. *Captive Nation: Black Prison Organizing in the Civil Rights Era*. Chapel Hill: University of North Carolina Press.

Bergson, Henri. 1912. *Matter and Memory*, translated by Nancy Margaret Paul and William Scott Palmer. New York: Macmillan.

Berkowitz, Roger, and Drucilla Cornell. 2009. "Parables of Revenge and Masculinity in Mystic River." In *Clint Eastwood and Issues of American Masculinity*, edited by Drucilla Cornell, 121–38. New York: Fordham University Press.

Berlant, Lauren. 1997. *The Queen of America Goes to Washington City: Essays on Sex and Citizenship*. Durham, NC: Duke University Press.

Berlant, Lauren. 2011. *Cruel Optimism*. Durham, NC: Duke University Press.

Berlant, Lauren. 2015. "Structures of Unfeeling: Mysterious Skin." *International Journal of Politics, Culture, and Society* 28, no. 3: 191–213.

Berlant, Lauren, and Michael Warner. 1998. "Sex in Public." *Critical Inquiry* 24, no. 2 (Winter): 547–66.

Berlin, Fred S. 2014. "Pedophilia and DSM-5: The Importance of Clearly Defining the Nature of a Pedophilic Disorder." *Journal of the American Academy of Psychiatry and the Law* 42, no. 4: 404–7.

Bernard, Jami. 2003. "Sex, L.I.E.S, and Videotapes." *New York Daily News*, May 30, 44.

Bernardi, Daniel, ed. 2001. *Classic Hollywood, Classic Whiteness*. Minneapolis: University of Minnesota Press.

Bernstein, Elizabeth. 2010. "Militarized Humanitarianism meets Carceral Feminism: The Politics of Sex, Rights, and Freedom in Contemporary Antitrafficking Campaigns." *Signs* 36, no. 1: 45–72.

Bernstein, Elizabeth. 2012. "Carceral Politics as Gender Justice? The 'Traffic in Women' and Neoliberal Circuits of Crime, Sex and Rights." *Theory and Society* 41, no. 3: 233–59.

Bernstein, Robin. 2011. *Racial Innocence: Performing American Childhood from Slavery to Civil Rights*. New York: New York University Press.

Bérubé, Michael. 2004. *The Aesthetics of Cultural Studies*. New York: Wiley-Blackwell.

Best, Stephen. 2004. *The Fugitive's Properties: Law and the Poetics of Possession*. Chicago: University of Chicago Press.

Bhabha, Homi K. 1994. "Of Mimicry and Man: The Ambivalence of Colonial Discourse." In *The Location of Culture*, by Homi K. Bhabha, 85–92. New York: Routledge.

Bhattacharjee, Annanya, and Jael Silliman, eds. 2002. *Policing the National Body: Sex, Race and Criminalization*. Boston: South End.

Birchall, Clare. 2011. "The Politics of Opacity and Openness: Introduction to 'Transparency.'" *Theory, Culture and Society* 28: 1–19.

Birchall, Clare. 2014. "Radical Transparency?" *Cultural Studies, Critical Methodologies* 14, no. 1 (February): 77–88.

Blackman, Lisa. 2012. *Immaterial Bodies: Affect, Embodiment, Mediation*. London: Sage.

Blanchard, Ray. 2010. "The DSM Diagnostic Criteria for Pedophilia." *Archives of Sexual Behavior* 39: 304–16.

Bland, Lucy, and Laura Doan, eds. 1998. *Sexology in Culture: Labelling Bodies and Desires*. London: Polity.

Boellstorff, Tom. 2005. *The Gay Archipelago: Sexuality and Nation in Indonesia*. Princeton, NJ: Princeton University Press.

Boone, Joseph Allen. 2014. *The Homoerotics of Orientalism*. New York: Columbia University Press.

Borstelman, Thomas. 2003. *The Cold War and the Color Line: American Race Relations in the Global Arena*. Cambridge, MA: Harvard University Press.

Bosman, Julie. 2015. "Teenager's Jailing Brings a Call to Fix Sex Offender Registries." *New York Times*, July 5. Accessed September 10, 2018. https://www.nytimes.com/2015/07/05/us/teenagers-jailing-brings-a-call-to-fix-sex-offender-registries.html.

Bostick, Dani. 2015. "Think All Pedophiles Need to Register as Sex Offenders? You're Wrong." *Huffington Post*, July 7. Accessed May 10, 2018. http://www.huffingtonpost.com/dani-bostick/think-all-pedophiles-need-to-register-as-sex-offenders-youre-wrong_b_7730280.html.

Bourke, Michael, and Andres Hernandez. 2009. "'The Butner Study' Redux: A Report of the Incidence of Hands-On Child Victimization by Child Pornography Offenders." *Journal of Family Violence* 24: 183–91.

Bratish, Zach. 2008. *Conspiracy Panics: Political Rationality and Popular Culture*. Albany: State University of New York Press.

Brewer, Holly. 2005. *Birth or Consent: Children, Law, and the Anglo-American Revolution in Authority*. Chapel Hill: University of North Carolina Press.

Brooks, Kim. 2018. "Motherhood in the Age of Fear." *New York Times*, July 27. Accessed August 25, 2018. https://www.nytimes.com/2018/07/27/opinion /sunday/motherhood-in-the-age-of-fear.html.

Brown, Gillian. 2001. *The Consent of the Governed: The Lockean Legacy in Early American Culture*. Cambridge, MA: Harvard University Press.

Brown, Wendy. 1995. *States of Injury: Power and Freedom in Late Modernity*. Princeton, NJ: Princeton University Press.

Brown, Wendy. 2015. *Undoing the Demos: Neoliberalism's Stealth Revolution*. New York: Zone.

Browne, Simone. 2015. *Dark Matters: On the Surveillance of Blackness*. Durham, NC: Duke University Press.

Bruhm, Steven, and Natasha Hurley, eds. 2004. *Curiouser: On the Queerness of Children*. Minneapolis: University of Minnesota Press.

Bryant, Anita. 1977. *The Anita Bryant Story: The Survival of Our Nation's Families and the Threat of Militant Homosexuality*. Ada, MI: Revell.

Bumiller, Kristin. 2008. *In an Abusive State: How Neoliberalism Appropriated the Movement against Sexual Violence*. Durham, NC: Duke University Press.

Burgett, Bruce. 2009. "Sex, Panic, Nation." *American Literary History* 21, no. 1: 67–86.

Burns, Sarah. 2011. *The Central Park Five: The Untold Story behind One of New York's Most Infamous Crimes*. New York: Knopf.

Busis, Hilary. 2012. "Law and Order: svu: The Five Craziest Episodes." *Entertainment Weekly*, October 24. Accessed January 2, 2018. http://www.ew.com/article/2012 /10/24/law-and-order-svu-300th-episode.

Byfield, Natalie P. 2014. *Savage Portrayals: Race, Media and the Central Park Jogger Story*. Philadelphia: Temple University Press.

Byrd, Jodi. 2011. *The Transit of Empire: Indigenous Critiques of Colonialism*. Minneapolis: University of Minnesota Press.

Byrd, Jodi, Alyosha Goldstein, Jodi Melamed, and Chandan Reddy. 2018. "Predatory Value: Economies of Dispossession and Disturbed Relationalities." *Social Text* 2, no. 135: 1–18.

Cacho, Lisa. 2012. *Social Death: Racialized Rightlessness and the Criminalization of the Underprotected*. New York: New York University Press.

Califia, Patrick. 2000. "No Minor Issues: Age of Consent, Child Pornography, and Cross-generational Relationships." In *Public Sex: The Culture of Radical Sex*, 2d ed., by Patrick Califia, 54–93. San Francisco: Cleis.

Camp, Jordan T., and Christina Heatherton, eds. 2016. *Policing the Planet: Why the Policing Crisis Led to Black Lives Matter*. New York: Verso.

Capshaw, Katharine. 2014. *Civil Rights Childhood: Picturing Liberation in African American Photobooks*. Minneapolis: University of Minnesota Press.

Carpenter, Catherine, and A. Beverlin. 2012. "The Evolution of Unconstitutionality in Sex Offender Registration Laws." *Hastings Law Review Journal* 63: 1071–133.

Cashin, Sheryll. 2010. "To Be Muslim or 'Muslim-Looking' in America: A Comparative Exploration of Racial and Religious Prejudice in the 21st Century." *Duke Forum for Law and Social Change* 2.1 (2010): 125–39.

Castañeda, Claudia. 2002. *Figurations: Child, Bodies, Worlds*. Durham, NC: Duke University Press.

Center for Sex Offender Management (CSOM). 2008. "Fact Sheet: What You Need to Know about Sex Offenders." Accessed December 15, 2015. http://www.csom.org /pubs/needtoknow_fs.pdf.

Chaudhary, Zahid R. 2012. *Afterimage of Empire: Photography in Nineteenth Century India*. Minneapolis: University of Minnesota Press.

Chauncey, George. 1995. *Gay New York: Gender, Urban Culture, and the Making of the Gay Male World, 1890–1940*. New York: Basic.

Chen, Mel Y. 2012. *Animacies: Biopolitics, Racial Mattering, and Queer Affect*. Durham, NC: Duke University Press.

Cherniavsky, Eva. 2006. *Incorporations: Race, Nation, and the Body Politics of Capital*. Minneapolis: University of Minnesota Press.

Churchill, Ward. 2004. *Kill the Indian, Save the Man: The Genocidal Impact of American Indian Residential Schools*. San Francisco: City Lights.

Cleary, Joe, Jed Esty, and Colleen Lye, eds. 2012. "Peripheral Realisms" (special issue). *Modern Language Quarterly* 73, no. 3.

Clough, Patricia Ticineto, and Craig Willse, eds. 2011. *Beyond Biopolitics: Essays on the Governance of Life and Death*. Durham, NC: Duke University Press.

Cohen, Cathy. 1997. "Punks, Bulldaggers and Welfare Queens: The Radical Potential of Queer Politics?" GLQ 3, no. 4: 437–65.

Cohen, Cathy. 1999. *The Boundaries of Blackness: aids and the Breakdown of Black Politics*. Chicago: University of Chicago Press.

Cohen, Stanley. 1972. *Folk Devils and Moral Panics: The Creation of Mods and Rockers*. London: MacGibbon and Kee.

Combahee River Collective. 1977. "Combahee River Collective Statement." Accessed September 10, 2018. https://combaheerivercollective.weebly.com/the-combahee -river-collective-statement.html.

Conte, Jon R., ed. 2002. *Critical Issues in Child Sexual Abuse: Historical, Legal, and Psychological Perspectives*. Thousand Oaks, CA: Sage.

Coole, Diana and Samantha Frost, eds. 2010. *New Materialisms: Ontology, Agency, and Politics*. Durham, NC: Duke University Press.

Cooper, Rand Richards. 2003. "Sex, Lies (?), and Videotape: 'Capturing the Friedmans.'" *Commonweal*, July 18. Accessed January 27, 2019. https://www.common wealmagazine.org/capturing-friedmans.

Coric, Vladimir, Seth Feuerstein, Frank Fortunati, Steven Southwick, Humberto Temporini, and Charles A Morgan. 2005. "Assessing Sex Offenders." *Psychiatry* (November): 26–29.

Corrigan, Rose. 2006. "Making Meaning of Megan's Law." *Law and Social Inquiry* 31, no. 2: 267–13.

Corrigan, Rose. 2013. *Up against a Wall: Rape Reform and the Failure of Success*. New York: New York University Press.

Couture, Jennifer L. 1995. "Constitutional Law—An Ex Post Facto Analysis of Sex Offender Registration: Branding Criminals with a Scarlet Letter." *Suffolk University Law Review* 29, no. 4: 1199–207.

Cox, Aimee. 2015. *Shapeshifters: Black Girls and the Choreography of Citizenship*. Durham, NC: Duke University Press.

Crenshaw, Kimberlé Williams. 1995. "Mapping the Margins: Intersectionality, Identity Politics, and Violence against Women of Color." In *Critical Race Theory: The Key Writings That Formed the Movement*, edited by Kimberlé Williams Crenshaw, Neil Gotanda, Gary Peller, and Kendall Thomas, 3573–83. New York: New Press.

Crenshaw, Kimberlé Williams, with Priscilla Ocen and Jyoti Nanda. 2015. *Black Girls Matter: Pushed Out, Overpoliced, and Underprotected*. New York: African American Policy Forum. Accessed September 5, 2018. www.atlanticphilanthropies.org/sites/default/files/uploads/BlackGirlsMatter_Report.pdf.

Crenshaw, Kimberlé Williams, and Andrea Ritchie, with Rachel Anspach, Rachel Gilmer, and Luke Harris. 2015. *Say Her Name: Policing Police Brutality against Black Women*. New York: African American Policy Forum. Accessed September 13, 2018. http://static1.squarespace.com/static/53f20d90e4b0b80451158d8c/t/55a810d7e4b058f342f55873/1437077719984/AAPF_SMN_Brief_full_singles.compressed.pdf.

Crompton, Louis. 2003. *Homosexuality and Civilization*. Cambridge, MA: Harvard University Press.

Cruz-Malave, Arnaldo, and Martin F. Manalansan IV, eds. 2002. *Queer Globalizations: Citizenship and the Afterlife of Colonialism*. New York: New York University Press.

Cvetkovich, Ann. 2003. *An Archive of Feelings: Trauma, Sexuality, and Lesbian Public Cultures*. Durham, NC: Duke University Press.

Dangerous Bedfellows, eds. 1996. *Policing Public Sex: Queer Politics and the Future of aids Activism*. Boston: South End.

Davidson, Julia O'Connell. 2005. *Children in the Global Sex Trade*. Cambridge, UK: Polity Press.

Davies, Jon. 2007. "Imagining Intergenerationality: Representation and Rhetoric in the Pedophile Movie." GLQ 13, no. 23: 369–85.

Davis, Angela. 1975. *Joan Little: The Dialectics of Rape*. New York: Lang.

Davis, Angela. 1983. *Women, Race and Class*. New York: Vintage.

Davis, Angela. 2005. *Abolition Democracy: Beyond Prisons, Torture, and Empire*. New York: Seven Stories.

Davis, Douglas. 1995. "The Work of Art in the Age of Digital Reproduction." *Third Annual New York Digital Salon* 28, no. 5: 381–86.

Davis, Lisa Selin. 2005. "Gregg Araki Gets Mysterious." *The Independent*, May 1.

Accessed December 15, 2015. http://independent-magazine.org/2005/05/gregg
-araki-gets-mysterious.

Davis, Madeline D., and Elizabeth Kapovsky Kennedy. 1994. *Boots of Leather, Slippers of Gold: The History of a Lesbian Community*. New York: Penguin.

Davis, Mike. 1990. *City of Quartz: Excavating the Future in Los Angeles*. New York: Verso.

Deer, Sarah. 2015. *The Beginning and End of Rape: Confronting Sexual Violence in Native America*. Minneapolis: University of Minnesota Press.

Deer, Sarah. 2016. "Federal Indian Law and Violent Crime: Native Women and Children at the Mercy of the State" in *The Color of Violence: The INCITE! Anthology*, edited by INCITE! Women of Color Against Violence, 32–41. Durham, NC: Duke University Press.

Deleuze, Gilles. (1966) 1991. *Bergsonism*, translated by Hugh Tomlinson and Barbara Habberjam. New York: Zone.

Deleuze, Gilles. 1986. *Cinema 1: The Movement-Image*, translated by Hugh Tomlinson and Barbara Habberjam. Minneapolis: University of Minnesota Press.

Deleuze, Gilles. 1989. *Cinema 2: The Time-Image*, translated by Hugh Tomlinson and Robert Galeta. Minneapolis: University of Minnesota Press.

Deleuze, Gilles. 2002. "The Actual and the Virtual." In *Dialogues II*, by Gilles Deleuze, translated by Eliot Ross Albert, 148–52. New York: Columbia University Press.

Delgado, Richard and Jean Stephanic, eds. 1997. *Critical White Studies: Looking behind the Mirror*. Philadelphia: Temple University Press.

D'Emilio, John. 1983. *Sexual Politics, Sexual Communities: The Making of a Homosexual Minority in the United States, 1940–1970*. Chicago: University of Chicago Press.

Denizet-Lewis, Benoit. 2006. "Boy Crazy." *Boston Magazine*, May 15. Accessed September 10, 2018. https://www.bostonmagazine.com/2006/05/15/boy-crazy.

Denning, Michael. 2004. *Culture in the Age of Three Worlds*. New York: Verso.

Denno, Deborah W. 1998. "Life before the Modern Sex Offender Statutes." *Northwestern University Law Review* 92, no. 4: 1317–413.

De Orio, Scott. 2017. "The Creation of the Modern Sex Offender." In *The War on Sex*, edited by David M. Halperin and Trevor Hoppe, 247–67. Durham, NC: Duke University Press.

Devlin, Rachel. 2005. *Relative Intimacy: Fathers, Adolescent Daughters, and Postwar American Culture*. Chapel Hill: University of North Carolina Press.

Diaz-Cotto, Juanita. 2006. *Chicana Lives and Criminal Justice: Voices from El Barrio*. Austin: University of Texas Press.

Diffee, Christopher. 2005. "Sex and the City: The White Slavery Scare and Social Governance in the Progressive Era." *American Quarterly* 57, no. 2: 411–37.

Downes, David, Paul Rock, Christine Chinkin, and Conor Gearty, eds. 2007. *Crime, Social Control and Human Rights: From Moral Panics to States of Denial*. New York: Willan.

Doyle, Jennifer. 2015. *Campus Sex, Campus Security*. Cambridge, MA: MIT Press.

Drescher, Jack. 2015. "Out of DSM: Depathologizing Homosexuality." *Behavioral Sciences* 5, no. 4 (December): 565–75.

Dretzka, Gary. 2003. "An Interview with Andrew Jarecki." *Movie City News*, June 10. Accessed January 27, 2019. http://archive.li/xwBfF.

Driskill, Qwo-Li, Chris Finley, Brian Joseph Gilley, and Scott Lauria Morgensen, eds. 2011. *Queer Indigenous Studies: Critical Interventions in Theory, Politics and Literature*. Tucson: University of Arizona Press.

Duane, Anna Mae. 2010. *Suffering Childhood in Early America: Violence, Race and the Making of the Child Victim*. Athens: University of Georgia Press.

Dubrofsky, Rachel E., and Shoshana Amielle Magnet, eds. 2015. *Feminist Surveillance Studies*. Durham, NC: Duke University Press.

Duggan, Lisa. 2003. *The Twilight of Equality: Neoliberalism, Cultural Politics, and the Attack on Democracy*. Boston: Beacon.

Duggan, Lisa, and Nan Hunter, eds. 1995. *Sex Wars: Sexual Dissent and Political Culture*. New York: Routledge.

Dyer, Richard. 1997. *White: Essays on Race and Culture*. New York: Routledge.

EchoHawk, Larry. 2001–2002. "Child Sexual Abuse in Indian Country: Is the Guardian Keeping in Mind the Seventh Generation?" *New York University Journal of Legislation and Public Policy* 5, no. 83: 83–128.

Edelman, Lee. 2004. *No Future: Queer Theory and the Death Drive*. Durham, NC: Duke University Press.

Edholm, Charlton. 1893. *Traffic in Girls and Florence Crittenton Missions*. Chicago: Women's Temperance Publishing Association.

Edholm, Charlton. 1899. *Traffic in Girls and Work of Rescue Missions*. Self-Published.

Ellis, Havelock. (1906) 1937. *Studies in the Psychology of Sex*, vol. 4. New York: Random House.

Eng, David. 2010. *The Feeling of Kinship: Queer Liberalism and the Racialization of Intimacy*. Durham, NC: Duke University Press.

Epstein, Rebecca, Jamilia J. Blake, and Thalia González. 2017. *Girlhood Interrupted: The Erasure of Black Girls' Childhood*. Washington, DC: Georgetown Law Center on Poverty and Inequality.

Escobedo, Elizabeth R. 2007. "The Pachuca Panic: Sexual and Cultural Battlegrounds in World War II Los Angeles." *Western Historical Quarterly* 38, no. 2 (Summer): 133–56.

Eskridge, William N. 2008. *Dishonorable Passions: Sodomy Laws in America, 1861–2003*. New York: Viking.

Ewing, Patrick. 2011. *Justice Perverted: Sex Offense Law, Psychology, and Public Policy*. New York: Oxford University Press.

Fechter, Steven. 2009. *The Woodsman*. New York: Samuel French.

Federal Bureau of Investigation. 2011. *Child Predators: The Online Threat Continues to Grow*. Washington, DC: U.S. Department of Justice. Accessed December 15, 2015. https://www.fbi.gov/news/stories/child-predators.

Federal Bureau of Investigation. 2014. "Frequently Asked Questions about the Change in the UCR Definition of Rape," December 11. Accessed July 9, 2019. https://ucr.fbi.gov/recent-program-updates/new-rape-definition-frequently -asked-questions.

Federici, Silvia. 2018. *Re-Enchanting the World: Feminism and the Politics of the Commons*. Oakland, CA: PM Press.

Feeley, Malcolm M., and Jonathon Simon. 2007. "Folk Devils and Moral Panics: An Appreciation from North America." In *Crime, Social Control and Human Rights: From Moral Panics to States of Denial*, edited by David Downes, Paul Rock, Christine Chinkin, and Conor Gearty, 39–52. New York: Willan.

Feimster, Crystal N. 2011. *Southern Horrors: Women and the Politics of Rape and Lynching*. Cambridge, MA: Harvard University Press.

Feld, Barry C. 2017. *The Evolution of the Juvenile Court: Race, Politics and the Criminalizing of Juvenile Justice*. New York: New York University Press.

Feld, Corinne T., and Nichola L. Syrrett. 2015. *Age in America: The Colonial Era to the Present*. New York: New York University Press.

Ferguson, Andrew Guthrie. 2017. *The Rise of Big Data Policing: Surveillance, Race and the Future of Law Enforcement*. New York: New York University Press.

Ferguson, Roderick A. 2004. *Aberrations in Black: Toward a Queer of Color Critique*. Minneapolis: University of Minnesota Press.

Ferguson, Roderick. 2012. *The Reorder of Things: The University and Its Pedagogies of Minority Difference*. Minneapolis: University of Minnesota Press.

Filler, Daniel M. 2004. "Silence and the Racial Dimension of Megan's Law." *Iowa Law Review* 89, no. 5: 1535–594.

Finkelhor, David, and Sharon Araji. 1986. "Explanations of Pedophilia: A Four Factor Model." *Journal of Sex Research* 22, no. 2 (May): 145–61.

Finkelhor, David, Heather Hammer, and Andrea J. Sedlak. 2008. "Sexually Assaulted Children: National Estimates and Characteristics." U.S. Department of Justice, Office of Justice Programs, Office of Juvenile Justice and Delinquency Programs. Accessed December 15, 2015. https://www.ncjrs.gov/pdffiles1/ojjdp/214383.pdf.

Finkelhor, David, Richard Ormrod, and Mark Chaffin. 2009. "Juveniles Who Commit Sex Offenses against Minors." U.S. Department of Justice, Office of Justice Programs, Office of Juvenile Justice and Delinquency Prevention. Accessed July 9, 2019. https://www.ncjrs.gov/pdffiles1/ojjdp/227763.pdf.

Finn, Jonathan. 2009. *Capturing the Criminal Image: From Mug Shot to Surveillance Society*. Minneapolis: University of Minnesota Press.

Fischel, Joseph J. 2013. "Against Nature, Against Consent: A Sexual Politics of Debility." *Differences* 24, no. 1: 55–103.

Fischel, Joseph J. 2016. *Sex and Harm in the Age of Consent*. Minneapolis: University of Minnesota Press.

Flatley, Jonathon. 2008. *Affective Mapping: Melancholia and the Politics of Modernism.* Cambridge, MA: Harvard University Press.

Fleetwood, Nicole. 2011. *Troubling Vision: Performance, Visuality and Blackness.* Chicago: University of Chicago Press.

Fletcher, Matthew L. M. 2011. *American Indian Tribal Law.* Aspen, CO: Aspen.

Forbes, Stephanie Gaylord. 2011. "Sex, Cells, and SORNA: Applying Sex Offender Registration Laws to Sexting Cases." *William and Mary Law Review* 52, no. 5 (April): 1717–46.

Foster Wallace, David. 1993. "E Unibus Pluram: Television and U.S. Fiction." *Review of Contemporary Fiction* 13, no. 2 (Summer): 151–94.

Foucault, Michel. 1984. (1967). "Of Other Spaces: Utopias and Heterotopias." Translated by Jay Miskow from *Architecture, Mouvement, Continuité* no. 5 (October): 46–49. Accessed July 18, 2019. http://web.mit.edu/allanmc/www/foucault1.pdf.

Foucault, Michel. 1988a. "Power and Sex," translated by David J. Parent. In *Politics, Philosophy Culture: Interviews and Other Writings, 1977-1984*, edited by Lawrence D. Kritzman, translated by Alan Sheridan, 110–24. New York: Routledge.

Foucault, Michel. 1988b. "Sexual Morality and the Law." In *Politics, Philosophy, Culture: Interviews and Other Writings, 1977-1984*, edited by Lawrence D. Kritzman, translated by Alan Sheridan, 271–85. New York: Routledge.

Foucault, Michel. 1990. *The History of Sexuality, Volume I: An Introduction*, translated by Robert Hurley. New York: Vintage.

Foucault, Michel. 2003a. *Abnormal: Lectures at the Collège de France (1974-1975)*, translated by Graham Burchell. London: Verso.

Foucault, Michel. 2003b. *Society Must Be Defended: Lectures at the Collège de France (1975-1976)*, translated by David Macey. New York: Picador.

Foucault, Michel. 2008. *The Birth of Biopolitics: Lectures at the Collège de France (1978-1979)*, translated by Graham Burchell. Basingstoke, U.K.: Palgrave Macmillan.

Foundas, Scott. 2003. "Capturing the Friedmans." Variety.com, January 26. Accessed January 2, 2018. http://www.variety.com.

Freedman, Estelle B. 1987. "'Uncontrolled Desires': The Response to the Sexual Psychopath, 1920–1960." *Journal of American History* 74, no. 1: 83–106.

Freedman, Estelle B. 2013. *Redefining Rape: Sexual Violence in the Era of Suffrage and Segregation.* Cambridge, MA: Harvard University Press.

Freeman, Elizabeth, ed. 2007. "Queer Temporalities." GLQ 13, nos. 2–3 (May): 159–421.

Freeman, Elizabeth. 2010. *Time Binds: Queer Temporalities, Queer Histories.* Durham, NC: Duke University Press.

Freud, Sigmund. (1925) 1966. "A Note upon the 'Mystic Writing Pad.'" In *The Standard Edition of the Complete Psychological Works of Sigmund Freud, Volume 19 (1923-1925)*, edited and translated by James Trachey, 225–32. London, Hogarth.

Fuchs, Erin. 2013. "Seven Surprising Things That Could Make You a Sex Offender."

Business Insider, October 9. Accessed September 3, 2018. http://www.business insider.com/surprising-things-that-could-make-you-a-sex-offender-2013-10.

Gaines, Jane M., and Michael Renov, eds. 1999. *Collecting Visible Evidence*. Minneapolis: University of Minnesota Press.

Gilmore, Ruth Wilson. 2007. *Golden Gulag: Prisons, Surplus, Crisis and Opposition in Globalizing California*. Berkeley: University of California Press.

Gilna, Derek. 2012. "Federal Sex Offender Civil Commitment Process under Fire." *Prison Legal News*, August 15. Accessed January 27, 2019. https://www.prison legalnews.org/news/2012/aug/15/federal-sex-offender-civil-commitment -process-under-fire.

Gladwell, Malcolm. 2012. "In Plain View: How Child Molesters Get Away with It." *New Yorker*, September 24. Accessed December 15, 2015. http://www.newyorker .com/magazine/2012/09/24/in-plain-view.

Goldsby, Jacqueline. 2006. *A Spectacular Secret: Lynching in American Life and Literature*. Chicago: University of Chicago Press.

Gordon, Avery, and Christopher Newfield, eds. 2008. *Mapping Multiculturalism*. Minneapolis: University of Minnesota Press.

Gore, Dayo. 2011. *Radicalism at the Crossroads: African American Women Activists in the Cold War*. New York: New York University Press.

Gottschalk, Marie. 2014. *Caught: The Prison State and the Lockdown of American Politics*. Princeton, NJ: Princeton University Press.

Gramsci, Antonio. 1985. *Selections from Cultural Writings*, edited and translated by David Forgacs and Geoffrey Nowell-Smith. London: Lawrence and Wishart.

Grant, Richard. 2009. "Dennis Lehane's *The Given Day*." *The Telegraph*, January 20. Accessed August 10, 2018. https://www.telegraph.co.uk/culture/books/4223368 /Dennis-Lehanes-The-Given-Day.html.

Gray, Jonathan, and Amanda D. Lotz. 2012. *Television Studies*. Cambridge: Polity.

Greenfeld, Lawrence A. 1997. *Sex Offenses and Offenders: An Analysis of Data on Rape and Sexual Assault*. Bureau of Justice Statistics Special Report NCJ-163392. National Criminal Justice Reference Service, Washington, DC.

Gregg, Melissa and Gregory J. Seigworth, eds. 2010. *The Affect Theory Reader*. Durham, NC: Duke University Press.

Gross, Kali N. 2006. *Colored Amazons: Crime, Violence, and Black Women in the City of Brotherly Love, 1880–1910*. Durham, NC: Duke University Press.

Haag, Pamela. 1999. *Consent: Sexual Rights and the Transformation of American Liberalism*. Ithaca, NY: Cornell University Press.

Halberstam, Jack. 2005. *In a Queer Time and Place: Transgender Bodies, Subcultural Lives*. New York: New York University Press.

Haley, Sarah. 2016. *No Mercy Here: Gender, Punishment, and the Making of Jim Crow Modernity*. Chapel Hill: University of North Carolina Press.

Hall, Rachel. 2004. "'It Can Happen to You': Rape Prevention in the Era of Risk Management." *Hypatia* 19, no. 3 (Summer): 1–19.

Hall, Ryan C. W., and Richard Hall. 2009. "A Profile of Pedophilia: Definition, Characteristics of Offenders, Recidivism, Treatment Outcomes, and Forensic Issues." *Focus: The Journal of Lifelong Learning in Psychiatry* 7, no. 4 (Fall): 522–37.

Hall, Stuart. (1973) 2001. "Encoding/Decoding." In *Media and Cultural Studies: KeyWorks, Revised Edition*, edited by Meenakshi Gigi Durham and Douglas M. Kellner, 163–74. Malden, MA: Blackwell.

Hall, Stuart, Chas Critcher, Tony Jefferson, John Clarke, and Brian Roberts. 1978. *Policing the Crisis: Mugging, the State, and Law and Order*. New York: Holmes and Meier.

Hall, Stuart, and Martin Jacques, eds. 1990. *New Times: The Changing Face of Politics in the 1990s*. New York: Verso.

Halperin, David. 1989. *One Hundred Years of Homosexuality: And Other Essays on Greek Love*. New York: Routledge.

Halperin, David M., and Trevor Hoppe, eds. 2017. *The War on Sex*. Durham, NC: Duke University Press.

Handelman, David. 1990. "Act Up in Anger." *Rolling Stone*, March 8. Accessed January 27, 2019. https://www.rollingstone.com/culture/culture-news/act-up-in -anger-241225.

Hanhardt, Christina. 2013. *Safe Space: Gay Neighborhood History and the Politics of Violence*. Durham, NC: Duke University Press.

Hansen, Miriam. 1987. "Benjamin, Cinema, and Experience: 'The Blue Flower in the Land of Technology.'" *New German Critique* 40 (Winter): 179–224.

Hanson, R. Karl, and Kelly E. Morton-Bourgon. 2005. "The Characteristics of Persistent Sex Offenders: A Meta-Analysis of Recidivism Studies." *Journal of Consulting and Clinical Psychology* 73, no. 6: 1154–63.

Hanson, R. Karl, and Kelly E. Morton-Bourgon. 2009. "The Accuracy of Recidivism Risk Assessment for Sex Offenders: A Meta-Analysis of 118 Prediction Studies." *Psychological Assessment* 21, no. 1: 1–21.

Haraway, Donna. 1991. *Simians, Cyborgs, and Women: The Reinvention of Nature*. New York: Routledge.

Harcourt, Bernard. 2007. *Against Prediction: Profiling, Policing and Punishing in an Actuarial Age*. Chicago: University of Chicago Press.

Harcourt, Bernard. 2012. *The Illusion of Free Markets: Punishment and the Myth of Natural Order*. Cambridge, MA: Harvard University Press.

Hargreaves, Allison. 2017. *Violence against Indigenous Women: Literature/Activism/ Resistance*. Waterloo, ON: Wilfrid Laurier University Press.

Haritaworn, Jin. 2016. "Hateful Travels: Queering Ethnic Studies in a Context of Criminalization, Pathologization, and Globalization." In *Critical Ethnic Studies: A Reader*, edited by Critical Ethnic Studies Editorial Collective, 106–31. Durham, NC: Duke University Press.

Haritaworn, Jin, Adi Kuntsman, and Silvia Posocco, eds. 2012. *Queer Necropolitics*. London: Routledge.

Harkins, Gillian. 2009. *Everybody's Family Romance: Reading Incest in Neoliberal America*. Minneapolis: University of Minnesota Press.

Harkins, Gillian. 2012. "Foucault, the Family and the Cold Monster of Neoliberalism." In *Foucault, the Family and Politics*, edited by Robbie Duschinsky and Leon Antonio Rocha, 82–120. New York: Palgrave Macmillan.

Harkins, Gillian. 2013. "Sex Offenses and the Imaginaries of Punitive Reason." *Political and Legal Anthropology Review* 36, no. 2 (November): 410–14.

Harris, Andrew, Amy Phenix, R. Karl Hanson, and David Thornton. 2003. *Static-99 Coding Rules: Revised—2003*. West Ottawa, ON: Corrections Directorate, Solicitor General Canada.

Harris, Cheryl. 1993. "Whiteness as Property." *Harvard Law Review* 106, no. 8: 1707–91.

Harris, Neil. 1981. *Humbug: The Art of P. T. Barnum*. Chicago: University of Chicago Press.

Hart, Kylo-Patrick R. 2003. "Auteur/Bricoleur/Provocateur: Gregg Araki and Postpunk Style in *The Doom Generation*." *Journal of Film and Video* 55, no. 1 (Spring): 30–38.

Hartman, Saidiya. 2017. "The Terrible Beauty of the Slum." *Brick* 99 (Summer 2017): 39–43.

Harvey, David. 2005. *A Brief History of Neoliberalism*. New York: Oxford University Press.

Hasinoff, Amy Adele. 2015. *Sexting Panic: Rethinking Criminalization, Privacy and Consent*. Champagne-Urbana: University of Illinois Press.

Hayes, Jarrod. 2000. *Queer Nations: Marginal Sexuality in the Maghreb*. Chicago: University of Chicago Press.

Hayes, Matthew. 2003. "Family Viewing." *Montreal Mirror* 19, no. 8 (August): 7–13.

Hayles, Katherine. 1999. *How We Became Posthuman: Virtual Bodies in Cybernetics, Literature, and Informatics*. Chicago: University of Chicago Press.

Hegyi, Nate. 2018. "Doctoral Student Compiles Database of Indigenous Women Who've Gone Missing." National Public Radio, July 21. Accessed September 3, 2018. https://www.npr.org/2018/07/21/627567789/doctoral-student-compiles-database-of-indigenous-women-who-ve-gone-missing.

Heim, Scott. 1995. *Mysterious Skin*. New York: HarperCollins.

Heiner, Bradley. 2007. "Foucault and the Black Panthers." *City: Analysis of Urban Trends, Culture, Theory, Policy, Action* 11, no. 3 (December): 313–56.

Hernández, Kelly Lytle. 2017. *City of Inmates: Conquest, Rebellion, and the Rise of Human Caging in Los Angeles, 1771–1965*. Chapel Hill: University of North Carolina Press.

Hesford, Wendy S. 2011. *Spectacular Rhetorics: Human Rights Visions, Recognitions, Feminisms*. Durham, NC: Duke University Press.

Hicks, Cheryl D. 2010. *Talk with You Like a Woman: African American Women, Jus-*

tice and Reform in New York, 1890–1935. Chapel Hill: University of North Carolina Press.

Higgenbotham, Evelyn Brooks. 1994. *Righteous Discontent: The Women's Movement in the Black Baptist Church, 1880–1920*. Cambridge, MA: Harvard University Press.

Hight, Craig. 2005. "Making-of Documentaries on DVD: *The Lord of the Rings* Trilogy and Special Editions." *Velvet Light Trap* 56, no. 1: 4–17.

Hilms, Michelle, ed. 2003. *The Television History Book*. London: British Film Institute.

Hinderliter, A. C. 2011. "Defining Paraphilia in DSM-5: Do Not Disregard Grammar." *Journal of Sex and Marital Therapy* 37, no. 1: 17–31.

Hirsch, Foster. 1981. *The Dark Side of the Screen: Film Noir*. San Diego: A. S. Barnes.

Hong, Grace. 2015. *Death beyond Disavowal: The Impossible Politics of Difference*. Minneapolis: University of Minnesota Press.

Hooper, Carol-Ann, and Ann Kaloski. 2006. "Rewriting the 'Paedophile': A Feminist Reading of *The Woodsman*." *Feminist Review* 83: 149–55.

Hoover, J. Edgar. 1937. "War on the Sex Criminal." *New York Herald Tribune*, September 26.

Hoover, J. Edgar. 1947. "How Safe Is Your Daughter?" *American Magazine*, July, 32–33, 102–4.

Hoover, J. Edgar. 1955. "How Safe Is Your Youngster?" *American Magazine*, March, 19, 99–103.

Hoppe, Trevor. 2016. "Punishing Sex: Sex Offenders and the Missing Punitive Turn in Sexuality Studies." *Law and Social Inquiry* 41, no. 3: 573–94.

Horowitz, Emily. 2015. *Protecting Our Kids? How Sex Offender Laws Are Failing Us*. Santa Barbara, CA: Praeger.

Huntley, Audrey. 2014. "On Grassroots Resistance to Violence against Indigenous Women." *Everyday Abolition*, January 21. Accessed September 5, 2018. https:// everydayabolition.com/2014/01/21/on-grassroots-resistance-to-violence-against -indigenous-women-independent-murder-investigations-atomic-bombs-and -burnout-an-interview-with-indigenous-feminist-revolutionary-audrey-huntley.

Ibrahim, Habiba. 2016. "Any Other Age: Vampires and Oceanic Lifespans." *African American Review* 49, no. 4 (Winter): 313–27.

Ibrahim, Habiba. Work-in-progress. *Oceanic Lifespans: Black Age and the Making of Historical Time*.

INCITE! Women of Color against Violence, eds. 2016. *The Color of Violence: The INCITE! Anthology*. Durham, NC: Duke University Press.

INCITE! Women of Color against Violence, with Critical Resistance. 2001. "Statement on Gender Violence and the Prison Industrial Complex." Accessed September 10, 2018. https://incite-national.org/incite-critical-resistance-statement.

Irwin, Mary Ann. 1996. "'White Slavery' as Metaphor: Anatomy of a Moral Panic." *Ex Post Facto* 5. Accessed December 15, 2015. http://www.walnet.org/csis/papers /irwin-wslavery.html.

Ivy, Marilyn. 1993. "Have You Seen Me? Recovering the Inner Child in Late Twentieth Century America." *Social Text* 37: 227–52.

Jackson, Zakiyyah Iman. 2013. "Animal: New Directions in the Theorization of Race and Posthumanism." *Feminist Studies* 39, no. 3: 669–85.

Jacobs, Deborah. n.d. "Why Sex Offender Laws Do More Harm than Good." ACLU New Jersey. Accessed September 3, 2018. https://www.aclu-nj.org/theissues /criminaljustice/whysexoffenderlawsdomoreha.

Jacobs, Harriet. 2000. *Incidents in the Life of a Slave Girl*, edited by Nell Irvin Painter. New York: Penguin Classics.

Jacobson, Matthew Frye. 1998. *Whiteness of a Different Color: European Immigrants and the Alchemy of Race*. Cambridge, MA: Harvard University Press.

James, Joy. 1996. *Resisting State Violence: Radicalism, Gender, and Race in U.S. Culture*. Minneapolis: University of Minnesota Press.

James, Joy, ed. 2002. *States of Confinement: Policing, Detention and Prisons*. New York: Palgrave.

Janus, Eric S. 2006. *Failure to Protect: America's Sexual Predator Laws and the Rise of the Preventative State*. Ithaca, NY: Cornell University Press.

Jenkins, David. 2015. "Interview with Gregg Araki." *Little White Lies*, March 6. Accessed August 10, 2018. http://lwlies.com/interviews/gregg-araki-white-bird -in-a-blizzard.

Jenkins, Philip. 1998. *Moral Panic: Changing Concepts of the Child Molester in Modern America*. New Haven, CT: Yale University Press.

Jones, Donna V. 2010. *The Racial Discourses of Life Philosophy: Negritude, Vitalism and Modernity*. New York: Columbia University Press.

Kaba, Mariame, and Kelly Hayes. 2018. "The Sentencing of Larry Nassar Was Not 'Transformative Justice.' Here's Why," February 5. Accessed September 10, 2018. https://theappeal.org/the-sentencing-of-larry-nassar-was-not-transformative -justice-here-s-why-a2ea323a6645.

Kaplan, Amy. 2002. *The Anarchy of Empire in the Making of U.S. Culture*. Cambridge, MA: Harvard University Press.

Karpman, Benjamin. 1954. *The Sexual Offender and His Offenses: Etiology, Pathology, Psychodynamics*. New York: Julian.

Katz, Cindi. 2008. "Childhood as Spectacle: Relays of Anxiety and the Reconfiguration of the Child." *Cultural Geographies* 15, no. 1: 5–17.

Katzenstein, Peter J., ed. 1996. *The Culture of National Security*. New York: Columbia University Press.

Kazanjian, David. 2003. *The Colonizing Trick: National Culture and Imperial Citizenship in Early America*. Minneapolis: University of Minnesota Press.

Keeling, Kara. 2007. *The Witch's Flight: The Cinematic, the Black Femme, and the Image of Common Sense*. Durham, NC: Duke University Press.

Keire, Mara L. 2010. *For Business and Pleasure: Red-Light Districts and the Regula-*

tion of Vice in the United States, 1890–1933. Baltimore: Johns Hopkins University Press.

Kelling, George L., and James Q. Wilson. 1982. "Broken Windows." *Atlantic Monthly*, March. Accessed January 27, 2019. https://www.theatlantic.com/magazine /archive/1982/03/broken-windows/304465.

Kilgore, James. 2015. "Electronic Monitoring Is Not the Answer: Critical Reflections on a Flawed Alternative." Center for Media Justice (October). Accessed September 20, 2018. https://centerformediajustice.org/electronic-monitoring-is-not-the -answer.

Kincaid, James. 1992. *Child-Loving: The Erotic Child and Victorian Culture*. New York: Routledge.

Kincaid, James. 1998. *Erotic Innocence: The Culture of Child Molesting*. Durham, NC: Duke University Press.

King, Cynthia A. 1999. "Fighting the Devil We Don't Know: *Kansas v. Hendricks*, a Case Study Exploring the Civilization of Criminal Punishment and Its Ineffectiveness in Preventing Child Sexual Abuse." *William and Mary Law Review* 40, no. 1427. Accessed January 27, 2019. http://scholarship.law.wm.edu/wmlr/vol40 /iss4/7.

King, Homay. 2004. "Free Indirect Affect in Cassavetes' Opening Night and Faces." *Camera Obscura* 19, no. 2/56: 105–39.

King, Homay. 2015. *Virtual Memory: Time-Based Art and the Dream of Digitality*. Durham, NC: Duke University Press.

Kinsey, Alfred, Wardell B. Pomeroy, and Clyde E. Martin. 1948. *Sexual Behavior in the Human Male*. Philadelphia: W. B. Saunders.

Kinsey, Alfred, Wardell B. Pomeroy, Clyde E. Martin, and Paul H. Gebhard. 1953. *Sexual Behavior in the Human Female*. Philadelphia: W. B. Saunders.

Kitzinger, Jenny. 2004. *Framing Abuse: Media Influence and Public Understanding of Sexual Violence against Children*. London: Pluto.

Knibbs, Kate. 2015. "Fake Slenderman and Pedophiles Haunted Last Night's *CSI: Cyber*," October 26. Accessed January 2, 2018. http://gizmodo.com/slenderman -haunts-csi-cyber-along-with-the-chilling-sp-1738691989.

Knox, Sara L. 2003. "Crime, Law and Symbolic Order: the Rhetoric of Transparency." *Theory and Event* 7, no. 1, Accessed January 27, 2019. http://muse.jhu.edu/article /48662.

Krafft-Ebing, Richard von. (1886) 1965. *Psychopathia Sexualis, with Especial Reference to the Antipathic Sexual Instinct, a Medico-Forensic Study*, translated by Franklin S. Klaf. New York: Arcade.

Kraidy, Marwan M., and Katherine Sender, eds. 2011. *The Politics of Reality Television: Global Perspectives*. New York: Routledge.

Kunzel, Regina. 2008. *Criminal Intimacy: Prison and the Uneven History of Modern American Sexuality*. Chicago: University of Chicago Press.

Kunzel, Regina. 2017. "Sex Panic, Psychiatry, and the Expansion of the Carceral State."

In *The War on Sex*, edited by David M. Halperin and Trevor Hoppe, 229–46. Durham, NC: Duke University Press.

Lamb, Sharon, ed. 1999. *New Versions of Victims: Feminists Struggle with the Concept.* New York: New York University Press.

Lancaster, Roger N. 2011. *Sex Panic and the Punitive State.* Berkeley: University of California Press.

Lanning, Kenneth V. 1986. *Child Molesters: A Behavioral Analysis.* Washington, DC: U.S. Department of Justice, Office of Justice Programs, Office of Juvenile Justice and Delinquency Prevention.

Lanning, Kenneth V. 2010. *Child Molesters: A Behavioral Analysis*, 5th ed. Washington, DC: U.S. Department of Justice, Office of Justice Programs, Office of Juvenile Justice and Delinquency Prevention.

Lave, Tamara Rice. 2009. "Only Yesterday: The Rise and Fall of Twentieth Century Sexual Psychopath Laws." *Louisiana Law Review* 69, no. 3: 549–91.

Law, Victoria. 2009. *Resistance behind Bars: The Struggles of Incarcerated Women.* Oakland, CA: PM Press.

Law, Victoria. 2017. "How $40 Can Land You in Prison for Seven Years and on the Sex Offender Registry for Life." *Truthout*, October 8. Accessed September 10, 2018. https://truthout.org/articles/how-40-can-land-you-in-prison-for-seven-years -and-on-the-sex-offender-registry-for-life.

Lee, Susanna. 2003. "'These Are Our Stories': Trauma, Form, and the Screen Phenomenon of 'Law and Order.'" *Discourse* 25, nos. 1–2 (Winter–Spring): 81–97.

Lehane, Dennis. 1994. *A Drink before the War.* New York: Harcourt.

Lehane, Dennis. 1998. *Gone, Baby, Gone.* New York: William Morrow and Company.

Lehane, Dennis. 2001. *Mystic River.* New York: HarperCollins.

Lehane, Dennis, ed. 2009. *Boston Noir.* New York: Akashic.

Lehane, Dennis. 2012. *Live by Night.* New York: William Morrow and Company.

Leon, Chysanthi. 2011. *Sex Fiends, Perverts and Pedophiles: Understanding Sex Crime Policy in America.* New York: New York University Press.

Levin, Ursula Frohne, and Peter Weibel, eds. 2002. *ctrl[space]: Rhetorics of Surveillance from Bentham to Big Brother.* Cambridge, MA: MIT Press.

Levine, Judith. 2002. *Harmful to Minors: The Perils of Protecting Children from Sex.* Minneapolis: University of Minnesota Press.

Levine, Judith. 2017. "Sympathy for the Devil: Why Progressives Haven't Helped the Sex Offender, Why They Should, and How They Can." In *The War on Sex*, edited by David M. Halperin and Trevor Hoppe, 126–73. Durham, NC: Duke University Press.

Levine, Judith, and Erica Meiners. 2016a. "Are Sex Offenders Human? New Documentaries Can't Get Past the Question." *The Baffler*, November 15. Accessed September 6, 2018. https://thebaffler.com/latest/sex-offenders-human-levine -meiners.

Levine, Judith, and Erica Meiners. 2016b. "Are Sex Offenders White?" *Counterpunch,*

April 11. Accessed January 17, 2019. https://www.counterpunch.org/2016/04/11/are-sex-offenders-white.

Levine, Judith and Erica Meiners. 2016c. "Don't Get Kids Off the Registries. Abolish It." *Counterpunch*, April 8. Accessed September 3, 2018. https://www.counterpunch.org/2016/04/08/dont-just-get-kids-off-the-sex-offender-registry-abolish-it.

Levitan, Corey, and Bettmann/Corbis. 2015. "You Might Be a Sex Offender and Not Even Know It!" *Men's Health*, May 19. Accessed September 3, 2018. http://www.menshealth.com/guy-wisdom/you-might-be-sex-offender-and-not-know-it.

Lim, Eng-Beng. 2014. *Brown Boys and Rice Queens: Spellbinding Performance in the Asias*. New York: New York University Press.

Lipsitz, George. 1998. *The Possessive Investment in Whiteness: How White People Profit from Identity Politics*. Philadelphia: Temple University Press.

Lloyd, Jenna, Matt Mitchelson and Andrew Burridge, eds. 2012. *Beyond Walls and Cages: Prisons, Borders, and Global Crisis*. Athens, GA: University of Georgia Press.

Loevy, Debra. 2016. "Branding Sex Offenders." Loevy and Loevy (blog), April 5. Accessed September 3, 2018. http://www.loevy.com/blog/brandingsexoffenders.

Lohr, Steve. 2013. "The Origins of Big Data: An Etymological Detective Story." *New York Times*, February 1. Accessed July 19, 2018. https://bits.blogs.nytimes.com/2013/02/01/the-origins-of-big-data-an-etymological-detective-story.

López, Ian Haney. 1996. *White by Law: The Legal Construction of Race*. New York: New York University Press.

Lorde, Audre. (1984) 2007. "Uses of the Erotic: The Erotic as Power." In *Sister Outsider: Essays and Speeches*, by Audre Lorde, 53–59. Berkeley, CA: Crossing.

Lotz, Amanda. 2014. *The Television Will Be Revolutionized*, 2d ed. New York: New York University Press.

Love, Heather. 2009. *Feeling Backward: Loss and the Politics of Queer History*. Cambridge, MA: Harvard University Press.

Lowe, Lisa. 2015. *The Intimacies of Four Continents*. Durham, NC: Duke University Press.

Lubiano, Wahneema. 1992. "Black Ladies, Welfare Queens, and State Minstrels: Ideological War by Narrative Means." In *Race-ing Justice, En-gendering Power: Essays on Anita Hill, Clarence Thomas, and the Construction of Social Reality*, edited by Toni Morrison and Leon Higginbotham, 323–63. New York: Pantheon.

Lubiano, Wahneema. 2008. "Like Being Mugged by a Metaphor: Multiculturalism and State Narratives." In *Mapping Multiculturalism*, edited by Avery Gordon and Christopher Newfield, 64–75. Minneapolis: University of Minnesota Press.

Luciano, Dana, and Mel Chen. 2015a. "Has the Queer Ever Been Human?" GLQ 21, nos. 2–3: 183–207.

Luibhéid, Eithne. 2002. *Entry Denied: A History of U.S. Immigration Control*. Minneapolis: University of Minnesota Press.

Lukes, Heather N. 2016. "Perversion, Terminable and Interminable: Foucault, Lacan, and DSM-5." *Discourse* 38, no. 3 (Fall): 327–55.

Lye, Colleen. 2005. *America's Asia: Racial Form and American Literature, 1893–1945.* Princeton, NJ: Princeton University Press.

Lyon, David. 2006. *Theorizing Surveillance: The Panopticon and Beyond.* Devon, U.K.: Willan.

Machado, Carmen Maria. 2013. "Especially Heinous: 272 Views of *Law & Order SVU.*" *American Reader*, May. Accessed September 12, 2018. http://theamericanreader .com/especially-heinous-272-views-of-law-order-svu.

Magestro, Molly Ann. 2015. *Assault on the Small Screen: Representations of Sexual Violence on Prime-Time Television Dramas.* New York: Rowman and Littlefield.

Marks, Laura U. 2000. *The Skin of the Film: Intercultural Cinema, Embodiment, and the Senses.* Durham, NC: Duke University Press.

Martinson, Robert. 1974. "What Works?" *Public Interest* 35: 22–54.

Massad, Joseph. 2007. *Desiring Arabs.* Chicago: University of Chicago Press.

Massumi, Brian. 2002. *Parables for the Virtual: Movement, Affect, Sensation.* Durham, NC: Duke University Press.

Mbembe, Achille. 2003. "Necropolitics." *Public Culture* 15, no. 1: 11–40.

McCarthy, Anna. 2001. *Ambient Television: Visual Culture and Public Space.* Durham, NC: Duke University Press.

McCartney, Paul T. 2006. *Power and Progress: American National Identity, the War of 1898, and the Rise of American Imperialism.* Baton Rouge: Louisiana State University Press.

McClanahan, Annie. 2016. *Dead Pledges: Debt, Crisis, and 21st Century Culture.* Palo Alto: Stanford University Press.

McClintock, Anne. 1995. *Imperial Leather: Race, Gender and Sexuality in the Colonial Contest.* New York: Routledge.

McCreery, Patrick. 2004. "Innocent Pleasures? Children and Sexual Politics." *GLQ* 10, no. 4: 617–30.

McGarry, Molly. 2014. "Base, Vile and Depraved: Blasphemy and Other Moral Genealogies." *Qui Parle* 22, no. 2 (Spring–Summer): 31–56.

McGilligan, Patrick. 2013. *Fritz Lang: The Nature of the Beast.* Minneapolis: University of Minnesota Press.

McGillivray, Anne, ed. 1997. *Governing Childhood.* Dartmouth, NH: Dartmouth Publishing.

McGuire, Danielle L. 2011. *At the Dark End of the Street: Black Women, Rape, and Resistance—A New History of the Civil Rights Movement from Rosa Parks to the Rise of Black Power.* New York: Vintage.

McKittrick, Katherine. 2006. *Demonic Grounds: Black Women and the Cartographies of Struggle.* Minneapolis: University of Minnesota Press.

McKittrick, Katherine, ed. 2015. *Sylvia Wynter: On Being Human as Praxis.* Durham, NC: Duke University Press.

McKittrick, Katherine, and Clyde Woods, eds. 2007. *Black Geographies and the Politics of Place*. Toronto: Between the Lines.

McLuhan, Marshall. 1964. *Understanding Media: The Extensions of Man*. New York: McGraw-Hill.

Meiners, Erica R. 2016. *For the Children? Protecting Innocence in a Carceral State*. Minneapolis: University of Minnesota Press.

Melamed, Jodi. 2011. *Represent and Destroy: Rationalizing Violence in the New Racial Capitalism*. Minneapolis: University of Minnesota Press.

Mellema, Matt. 2014. "Not Wanted: Sex Offenders." Slate.com, August 14. Accessed September 3, 2018. http://www.slate.com/articles/news_and_politics/juris prudence/2014/08/several_states_ban_people_in_the_sex_offender_registry _from_a_bizarre_list.html.

Mellema, Matt, Chankaya Sethi, and Jane Shim. 2014. "Sex Offender Laws Have Gone Too Far: Our Draconian Policies about Sex Offenses Reflect Our Ignorance of Them." Slate.com, August 11. Accessed September 3, 2018. http://www.slate.com /articles/news_and_politics/jurisprudence/2014/08/sex_offender_registry_laws _have_our_policies_gone_too_far.html.

Melley, Timothy. 2012. *The Covert Sphere: Secrecy, Fiction, and the National Security State*. Ithaca, NY: Cornell University Press.

Melton, Gary B., John Petrila, Norman G. Poythress, and Christopher Slobogin. 2007. *Psychological Evaluation for the Courts, Third Edition: A Handbook for Mental Health Professionals and Lawyers*. New York: Guilford.

Merleaux, April. 2015. *Sugar and Civilization: American Empire and the Cultural Politics of Sweetness*. Chapel Hill: University of North Carolina Press.

Miller, Neil. 2002. *Sex-Crime Panic: A Journey to the Paranoid Heart of the 1950s*. Los Angeles: Alyson.

Million, Dian. 2013. *Therapeutic Nations: Healing in an Age of Indigenous Human Rights*. Tucson: University of Arizona Press.

Mingus, Mia. 2017. "What Would It Take to Actually End Intimate Violence?" *Color-lines*, November 28. Accessed September 10, 2018. https://www.colorlines.com /articles/what-would-it-take-actually-end-intimate-violence.

Mirzoeff, Nicholas. 2011. *The Right to Look: A Counter-History of Visuality*. Durham, NC: Duke University Press.

Mittell, Jason. 2004. *Genre and Television: From Cop Shows to Cartoons in American Culture*. New York: Routledge.

Mittell, Jason. 2015. *Complex tv: The Poetics of Contemporary Television Storytelling*. New York: New York University Press.

Mogul, Joey L., Andrea J. Ritchie, and Kay Whitlock. 2011. *Queer (In)Justice: The Criminalization of lgbt People in the United States*. Boston: Beacon.

Mohr, Richard D. 2004. "The Pedophilia of Everyday Life." In *Curiouser: On the Queerness of Children*, edited by Steven Bruhm and Natasha Hurley, 17–30. Minneapolis: University of Minnesota Press.

Moraga, Cherríe, and Gloria Anzaldúa, eds. 1981. *This Bridge Called My Back: Writings by Radical Women of Color*. Watertown, MA: Persephone.

Moran, James M. 2002. *There's No Place Like Home Video*. Minneapolis: University of Minnesota Press.

Morrison, James. 2006. "Still New, Still Queer, Still Cinema?" GLQ 12, no. 1: 135–46.

Muhammad, Khalil Gibran. 2010. *The Condemnation of Blackness: Race, Crime and the Making of Modern Urban America*. Cambridge, MA: Harvard University Press.

Mukařovský, Jan. 1970. *Aesthetic Function, Norm and Value as Social Facts*. Ann Arbor: University of Michigan Press.

Mullins, Greg. 2002. *Colonial Affairs: Bowles, Burroughs and Chester Write Tangier*. Madison: University of Wisconsin Press.

Mumford, Kevin. 1997. *Interzones: Black/White Sex Districts in Chicago and New York in the Early Twentieth Century*. New York: Columbia University Press.

Muñoz, José. 2009. *Cruising Utopia: The Then and There of Queer Futurity*. New York: New York University Press.

Murakawa, Naomi. 2014. *The First Civil Right: How Liberals Built Prison America*. Oxford: Oxford University Press.

Murray, Susan, and Laurie Oulette, eds. 2008. *Reality tv: Remaking Television Culture*. New York: New York University Press.

Nakamura, Lisa. 2007. *Digitizing Race: Visual Cultures and the Internet*. Minneapolis: University of Minnesota Press.

Nathan, Debbie, and Michael Snedeker. 2001. *Satan's Silence: Ritual Abuse and the Making of a Modern American Witch Hunt*. New York: Basic.

National Center for Missing and Exploited Children (NCMEC). 2012. "Number of Registered Sex Offender in the U.S. Nears Three-Quarters of a Million," January 23. Accessed August 10, 2018. https://www.prnewswire.com/news-releases/number-of-registered-sex-offenders-in-the-us-nears-three-quarters-of-a-million-137880068.html.

National Center for Missing and Exploited Children. 2014. "Predators," June 13. Accessed December 15, 2015. http://www.netsmartz.org/Predators.

Nealon, Christopher. 2001. *Foundlings: Lesbian and Gay Historical Emotion before Stonewall*. Durham, NC: Duke University Press.

Nelson, Alondra. 2016. *The Social Life of dna: Race, Reparations, and Reconciliation after the Genome*. Boston: Beacon.

"New York State Film Tax Credit Program (Production)." 2018. New York State website. https://esd.ny.gov/new-york-state-film-tax-credit-program-production. Accessed September 27, 2018.

Ngai, Mae. 2004. *Impossible Subjects: Illegal Aliens and the Making of Modern America*. Princeton, NJ: Princeton University Press.

Ngai, Sianne. 2005. *Ugly Feelings*. Cambridge, MA: Harvard University Press.

Nguyen, Mimi. 2012. *The Gift of Freedom: The War, Debt and Other Refugee Passages.* Durham, NC: Duke University Press.

North American Man/Boy Love Association. 1986. *Boys Speak Out on Man/Boy Love.* New York: North American Man/Boy Love Association.

Odem, Mary E. 1995. *Delinquent Daughters: Protecting and Policing Adolescent Female Sexuality in the United States, 1885–1920.* Chapel Hill: University of North Carolina Press.

O'Donohue, William. 2010. "A Critique of the Proposed DSM-V Diagnosis of Pedophilia." *Archives of Sexual Behavior* 39 (March 5): 587–590.

Office of Sex Offender Sentencing, Monitoring, Apprehending, Registering, and Tracking (SMART). 2012. "Sex Offender Registration and Notification in the United States: Current Case Law and Issues," July. Accessed December 15, 2015. https://smart.gov/caselaw/handbook_july2012.pdf.

Office of Sex Offender Sentencing, Monitoring, Apprehending, Registering, and Tracking (SMART). 2018a. "Common Questions." U.S. Department of Justice, National Sex Offender Public Website. Accessed January 2, 2018. https://www .nsopw.gov/en/Education/CommonQuestions.

Office of Sex Offender Sentencing, Monitoring, Apprehending, Registering, and Tracking (SMART). 2018b. "Raising Awareness about Sexual Abuse: Facts and Statistics." U.S. Department of Justice, National Sex Offender Public Website. Accessed January 2, 2018. https://www.smart.gov/legislation.htm.

Ohi, Kevin. 2005. *Innocence and Rapture: The Erotic Child in Pater, Wilde, James, and Nabokov.* New York: Palgrave Macmillan.

Okami, Paul, and Amy Goldberg. 1992. "Personality Correlates of Pedophilia: Are They Reliable Indicators?" *Journal of Sex Research* 29, no. 3: 297–328.

Olguín, Ben V. 2010. *La Pinta: Chicana/o Prisoner Literature, Culture, and Politics.* Austin: University of Texas Press.

Orenstein, Catherine. 2002. *Little Red Riding Hood Uncloaked: Sex, Morality, and the Evolution of a Fairy Tale.* New York: Basic.

Ormand, Kirk. 2008. *Controlling Desires: Sexuality in Ancient Greece and Rome.* Westport, CT: Praeger.

Parker, Alison, and Nicole Pittman. 2013. *Raised on the Registry: The Irreparable Harm of Placing Children on the Sex Offender Registries in the U.S.* New York: Human Rights Watch.

Pascoe, Peggy. 2009. *What Comes Naturally: Miscegenation Law and the Making of Race in America.* New York: Oxford University Press.

Patterson, Jennifer, and Reina Gossett, eds. 2016. *Queering Sexual Violence: Radical Voices from within the Anti-Violence Movement.* Riverdale, NY: Magnus Imprint.

Patton, Cindy. 1990. *Inventing aids.* New York: Routledge.

Patton, Cindy. 2002. *Globalizing aids.* Minneapolis: University of Minnesota Press.

Pember, Mary Annette. 2015. "Sexual Abuse to Prison Pipeline Report: A Native Perspective." *Indian Country Today* (August 10). Accessed June 7, 2019. https://

newsmaven.io/indiancountrytoday/archive/sexual-abuse-to-prison-pipeline
-report-a-native-perspective-_BLlFvjiLUqB_QvsL_LYVg/.

Perrotta, Tom. 2005. *Little Children*. New York: St. Martin's.

Petrucelli, Patricia L. 1995. "Megan's Law: Branding the Sex Offender or Benefitting the Community?" *Seton Hall Constitutional Law Journal* 5, no. 3: 1127–69.

"Police and Neighbors Join in a SoHo Search for Missing Schoolboy." 1979. *New York Times*, May 27, 31. Accessed December 15, 2015. https://timesmachine.nytimes .com/timesmachine/1979/05/27/120970566.html?pageNumber=31.

Postman, Neil. 1994. *The Disappearance of Childhood*. New York: Vintage.

Povinelli, Elizabeth. 2002. *The Cunning of Recognition: Indigenous Alterities and the Making of Australian Multiculturalism*. Durham, NC: Duke University Press.

Povinelli, Elizabeth. 2006. *The Empire of Love: Toward a Theory of Intimacy, Genealogy, and Carnality*. Durham, NC: Duke University Press.

Povinelli, Elizabeth. 2011. *Economies of Abandonment: Social Belonging and Endurance in Late Liberalism*. Durham, NC: Duke University Press.

Prout, Alan, and Allison James, eds. 1997. *Constructing and Reconstructing Childhood: Contemporary Issues in the Sociological Study of Childhood*. Washington, DC: Falmer.

Puar, Jasbir. 2007. *Terrorist Assemblages: Homonationalism in Queer Times*. Durham, NC: Duke University Press.

Puar, Jasbir. 2015. "Bodies with New Organs: Becoming Trans, Becoming Disabled." *Social Text* 33, no. 3 124 (September): 45–73.

Puar, Jasbir. 2017. *The Right to Maim: Debility, Capacity, Disability*. Durham, NC: Duke University Press.

Puri, Jyoti. 2016. *Sexual States: Governance and the Struggle Against the Antisodomy Law in India's Present*. Durham: Duke University Press.

Pynchon, Thomas. 1966. *The Crying of Lot 49*. New York: J. P. Lippincott.

Rabinowitz, Paula. 1994. *They Must Be Represented: The Politics of Documentary*. London: Verso.

Ramberg, Lucinda. 2014. *Given to the Goddess: South Indian Devadasis and the Sexuality of Religion*. Durham, NC: Duke University Press.

Rapping, Elayne. 2003. *Law and Justice as Seen on tv*. New York: New York University Press.

Reavey, Paula, and Sam Warner, eds. 2003. *New Feminist Stories of Child Sexual Abuse: Sexual Scripts and Dangerous Dialogues*. New York: Routledge.

Reddy, Chandan. 2011. *Freedom with Violence: Race, Sexuality and the U.S. State*. Durham, NC: Duke University Press.

Redmon, Allen. 2004. "Mechanisms of Violence in Clint Eastwood's *Unforgiven* and *Mystic River*." *Journal of American Culture* 27, no. 3 (September): 315–28.

Reinhardt, James M., and Edward C. Fisher. 1949. "The Sexual Psychopath and the Law." *Journal of Criminal Law and Criminology* 39, no. 6: 734–42.

Renov, Michael. 2004. *The Subject of Documentary*. Minneapolis: University of Minnesota Press.

Retman, Sonnet. 2011. *Real Folks: Race and Genre in the Great Depression*. Durham, NC: Duke University Press.

Reynolds, Emma. 2014. "'Paedophile Hunter' Stinson Hunter Catches Internet Predators with Real-Life Stings." News.com.au, October 7. Accessed January 2, 2018. http://www.news.com.au/technology/online/paedophile-hunter-stinson-hunter-catches-internet-predators-with-reallife-stings/news-story/3b09377b8ba036262 7461b420b3a0b0 f.

Rhineberger-Dunn, Gayle, Steven J. Briggs, and Nicole E. Rader. 2017. "The CSI Effect, DNA Discourse, and Popular Crime Dramas." *Social Science Quarterly* 98, no. 2 (June): 532–47.

Rich, B. Ruby. 2013. *New Queer Cinema: The Director's Cut*. Durham, NC: Duke University Press.

Richards, Linda. 2001. "Interview with Dennis Lehane." *January Magazine*, March. Accessed January 27, 2019. http://januarymagazine.com/profiles/lehane.html.

Richardson, Matt. 2016. *The Queer Limit of Black Memory: Black Lesbian Literature and Irresolution*. Columbus: Ohio State University Press.

Richie, Beth E. 2012. *Arrested Justice: Black Women, Violence and America's Prison Nation*. New York: New York University Press.

Rickard, Diana. 2016. *Sex Offenders, Stigma, and Social Control*. Newark, NJ: Rutgers University Press.

Rifkin, Mark. 2011. *When Did Indians Become Straight? Kinship, the History of Sexuality, and Native Sovereignty*. New York: Oxford University Press.

Ritchie, Andrea J. 2012–13. "Crimes against Nature: Challenging Criminalization of Queerness and Black Women's Sexuality." *Loyola Journal of Public Interest Law* 14: 355–517.

Ritchie, Andrea J. 2017. *Invisible No More: Police Violence against Black Women and Women of Color*. Boston: Beacon.

Roberts, Dorothy. 1997. *Killing the Black Body: Race, Reproduction, and the Meaning of Liberty*. New York: Pantheon.

Roberts, Dorothy. 2011. *Fatal Invention: How Science, Politics, and Big Business Re-create Race in the Twenty-First Century*. New York: New Press.

Robertson, Stephen. 2005. *Crimes against Children: Sexual Violence and Legal Culture in New York City, 1880–1960*. Chapel Hill: University of North Carolina Press.

Rodríguez, Dylan. 2006. *Forced Passages: Imprisoned Intellectuals and the U.S. Prison Regime*. Minneapolis: University of Minnesota Press.

Roediger, David R. 1994. *Toward the Abolition of Whiteness: Essays on Race, Politics, and Working Class History*. New York: Verso.

Roediger, David R. 1999. *Wages of Whiteness: Race and the Making of the American Working Class*. New York: Verso.

Rollman, Eli M. 1998. "Mental Illness: A Sexually Violent Predator Is Punished Twice for One Crime." *Journal of Criminal Law and Criminology* 88, no. 3 (Spring). Accessed January 27, 2019. http://scholarlycommons.law.northwestern.edu/cgi /viewcontent.cgi?article=6966&context=jclc.

Rosenberg, Jordy. 2014. "The Molecularization of Sexuality: On Some Primitivisms of the Present." *Theory and Event* 17, no. 2. Accessed January 27, 2019. https://muse .jhu.edu.

Ross, Luana. 1998. *Inventing the Savage: The Social Construction of Native American Criminality*. Austin: University of Texas Press.

Ross, Luana. 2016. "Introduction: Settler Colonialism and the Legislating of Criminality" *American Indian Culture and Research Journal* 40, no. 1: 1–18.

Rowe, Nicolette. 2008. "Centrifugal Bostons and Competing Imaginaries in *Mystic River*." *Journal for Cultural Research* 12, no. 1 (January): 81–97.

Rubin, Gayle. 1984. "Thinking Sex: Notes for a Radical Theory of the Politics of Sexuality." In *Pleasure and Danger: Exploring Female Sexuality*, edited by Carole S. Vance, 267–319. Boston: Routledge and Kegan Paul.

Rubin, Gayle. 2011. "Blood under the Bridge: Reflections on 'Thinking Sex.'" GLQ 17, no. 1: 15–48.

Ruble, Raymond. 2009. *Round Up the Usual Suspects: Criminal Investigation in Law and Order, Cold Case, and csi*. Westport, CT: Praeger.

Saar, Malika Saada, Rebecca Epstein, Lindsay Rosenthal, and Yasmin Vafa. 2015. *The Sexual Abuse to Prison Pipeline: The Girls' Story*. Washington, DC: Georgetown Law Center on Poverty and Inequality.

Said, S. F. 2005. "Close Encounters." *Sight and Sound* 15, no. 6 (June): 32–34.

Saltzman, Lisa, and Eric Rosenberg, eds. 2006. *Trauma and Visuality in Modernity*. Hanover, NH: University Press of New England.

Sánchez-Eppler, Karen. 2005. *Dependent States: The Child's Part in Nineteenth-Century American Culture*. Chicago: University of Chicago Press.

Sandfort, Theo, Edward Brongersman, and Alex Van Naerssen, eds. 1991. *Male Intergenerational Intimacy: Historical, Socio-psychological, and Legal Perspectives*. New York: Haworth.

Santner, Eric L. 1990. *Stranded Objects: Mourning, Memory, and Film in Postwar Germany*. Ithaca, NY: Cornell University Press.

Schmidt, Tyler T. 2013. *Desegregating Desire: Race and Sexuality in Cold War American Literature*. Jackson: University Press of Mississippi.

Sedgwick, Eve Kosofsky. 1991. "How to Bring Your Kids Up Gay." *Social Text* 19: 18–27.

Segwick, Eve Kosofsky. 1993. "A Poem Is Being Written." In *Tendencies*, 177–214. Durham, NC: Duke University Press.

Sedgwick, Eve Kosofsky, and Frank Adam, eds. 1995. *Shame and Its Sisters: A Silvan Tompkins Reader*. Durham, NC: Duke University Press.

Seitler, Dana. 2008. *Atavistic Tendencies: The Culture of Science in American Modernity*. Minneapolis: University of Minnesota Press.

Seltzer, Mark. 1998. *Serial Killers: Death and Life in America's Wound Culture*. New York: Routledge.

Sen, Piyal. 2005. "Review: The Woodsman." *British Medical Journal* 330 (March 12): 605.

Sentencing Project. N.d. "Racial Disparity." Accessed June 23, 2018. https://www.sentencingproject.org/issues/racial-disparity/.

Sethi, Chanakya. 2014a. "Reforming the Registry." Salon.com, August 12. Accessed September 3, 2018. http://www.slate.com/articles/news_and_politics/jurisprudence/2014/08/sex_offender_registries_the_best_ideas_for_reforming_the_law.html.

Sethi, Chanakya. 2014b. "The Ridiculous Laws that Put People on the Sex Offender List." Salon.com, August 12. Accessed September 3, 2018. http://www.slate.com/articles/news_and_politics/jurisprudence/2014/08/mapped_sex_offender_registry_laws_on_statutory_rape_public_urination_and.html.

Shah, Nayan. 2001. *Contagious Divides: Epidemics and Race in San Francisco's Chinatown*. Berkeley: University of California Press.

Shah, Nayan. 2005a. "Between 'Oriental Depravity' and 'Natural Degenerates': Spatial Borderlands and the Making of Ordinary Americans." *American Quarterly* 57, no. 3: 703–25.

Shah, Nayan. 2005b. "Policing Privacy, Migrants, and the Limits of Freedom." *Social Text* 84–85 (Fall–Winter): 275–84.

Sharpe, Alex. 2014. "Criminalising Sexual Intimacy: Transgender Defendants and the Legal Construction of Non-Consent." *Criminal Law Review*, no. 3: 207–23.

Sharpe, Christina. 2016. *In the Wake: On Blackness and Being*. Durham, NC: Duke University Press.

Sheldon, Rebekah. 2016. *The Child to Come: Life after the Human Catastrophe*. Minneapolis: University of Minnesota Press.

Shepard, Todd. 2018. *Sex, France, and Arab Men, 1962–1979*. Chicago: University of Chicago Press.

Silver, Alain, and James Ursini, eds. 1996. *Film Noir: A Reader*. New York: Limelight.

Silverman, Kaja. 1995. *The Threshold of the Visible World*. New York: Routledge.

Simon, Jonathon. 2000. "Megan's Law: Crime and Democracy in Late Modern America." *Law and Social Inquiry* 25: 111–50.

Simon, Jonathon. 2007. *Governing through Crime: How the War on Crime Transformed American Democracy and Created a Culture of Fear*. New York: Oxford University Press.

Skeggs, Beverly, and Helen Wood, eds. 2012. *Reacting to Reality Television: Performance, Audience and Value*. New York: Routledge.

Smith, Andrea. 2005. *Conquest: Sexual Violence and American Indian Genocide*. Boston: South End.

Smith, Andrea. 2011–2012. "Decolonizing Anti-Rape Law and Strategizing Accountability in Native American Communities" *Social Justice* 37, no. 4 (122): 36–43.

Snauffer, Douglas. 2006. *Crime Television*. Westport, CT: Praeger.

Snorton, C. Riley. 2017. *Black on Both Sides: A Racial History of Trans Identity*. Minneapolis: University of Minnesota Press.

Snyder, Howard N. 2000. "Sexual Assault of Young Children as Reported to Law Enforcement: Victim, Incident, and Offender Characteristics." National Center for Juvenile Justice, Office of Justice Programs, U.S. Department of Justice, July.

Somerville, Siobhan B. 2000. *Queering the Color Line: Race and the Invention of Homosexuality in American Culture*. Durham, NC: Duke University Press.

Spade, Dean. 2015. *Normal Life: Administrative Violence, Critical Trans Politics, and the Limits of Law*. Durham, NC: Duke University Press.

Spinoza, Baruch. 1941. (1677). *Ethics*, translated by Andrew Boyle. New York: E. P. Dutton.

Stanley, Eric, and Nat Smith, eds. 2011. *Captive Genders: Trans Embodiment and the Prison Industrial Complex*. Chico, CA: AK Press.

Statistic Brain. 2017. "Sex Offender Statistics" StatisticBrain.com, April 1. Accessed January 2, 2018. http://www.statisticbrain.com/sex-offender-statistics.

Stead, W. T. 1885. "The Maiden Tribute to Modern Babylon." *Pall Mall Gazette*, July 6.

Stephens, Sharon, ed. 1995. *Children and the Politics of Culture*. Princeton, N.J.: Princeton University Press.

Stewart, Garrett. 2016. "Frame-Advance Modernism: The Case of Fritz Lang's *M*." In *Moving Modernisms*, edited by David Bradshaw, Laura Marcus, and Rebecca Roach, 237–55. New York: Oxford University Press.

Stillman, Sarah. 2016. "The List." *New Yorker*, March 14. https://www.newyorker.com/magazine/2016/03/14/when-kids-are-accused-of-sex-crimes. Accessed 1/3/2018.

Stockton, Kathryn Bond. 2009. *The Queer Child, or Growing Sideways in the Twentieth Century*. Durham, NC: Duke University Press.

Stoler, Ann Laura. 1995. *Race and the Education of Desire: Foucault's History of Sexuality and the Colonial Order of Things*. Durham, NC: Duke University Press.

Stoler, Ann Laura. 2002. *Carnal Knowledge and Imperial Power: Race and the Intimate in Colonial Rule*. Berkeley: University of California Press.

Strickland, Ronald, ed. 2002. *Growing Up Postmodern: Neoliberalism and the War on the Young*. Lanham, MD: Rowman and Littlefield.

Strub, Sean. 2017. "HIV: Prosecution or Prevention? HIV Is Not a Crime." In *The War on Sex*, edited by David M. Halperin and Trevor Hoppe, 347–352. Durham, NC: Duke University Press.

Stryker, Susan, and Aren Aizura. 2013. "Introduction: Transgender Studies 2.0." In *The Transgender Studies Reader 2*, edited by Susan Stryker and Aren Aizura, 1–12. New York: Routledge.

Sudbury, Julia, ed. 2004. *Global Lockdown: Race, Gender and the Prison-Industrial Complex*. New York: Routledge.

Sutherland, Edwin H. 1950a. "The Diffusion of Sexual Psychopath Laws." *American Journal of Sociology* 56, no. 2: 142–48.

Sutherland, Edwin H. 1950b. "The Sexual Psychopath Laws." *Journal of Criminal Law and Criminology (1931–1951)* 40, no. 5: 543–54.

Tadiar, Neferti. 2009. *Things Fall Away: Philippine Historical Experience and the Makings of Globalization.* Durham, NC: Duke University Press.

Tagg, John. 1988. *The Burden of Representation: Essays on Photographies and Histories.* Minneapolis: University of Minnesota Press.

Tallbear, Kim. 2013. *Native American dna: Tribal Belonging and the False Promise of Genetic Science.* Minneapolis: University of Minnesota Press.

Tappan, Paul. 1955. "Some Myths about the Sex Offender." *Federal Probation* 19: 7–12.

Taylor, Troy. 2004. "Albert Fish: The Life and Crimes of One of America's Most Deranged Killers." *Dead Men Do Tell Tales:* http://www.prairieghosts.com/fish.html. Accessed December 15, 2015.

Tchividjian, Boz. 2014. "Five Common Characteristics of Child Sexual Offenders: Eliminating the Edge." Religious News Service, June 13. Accessed January 2, 2018. http://boz.religionnews.com/2014/06/13/five-basic-characteristics-child-sexual-offenders-eliminating-edge/#sthash.k8VCkUsh.dpuf.

Terry, Don. 1998. "Mother Rages against Indifference." *New York Times,* August 24. Accessed August 14, 2018. https://www.nytimes.com/1998/08/24/us/mother-rages-against-indifference.html.

Terry, Jennifer. 1999. *An American Obsession: Science, Medicine, and Homosexuality in Modern Society.* Chicago: University of Chicago Press.

Testa, Megan, and Sara G. West. 2010. "Civil Commitment in the United States." *Psychiatry* 7, no. 10 (October): 30–40.

Thomas, Greg. 2007. *The Sexual Demon of Colonial Power: Pan-African Embodiment and Erotic Schemes of Empire.* Bloomington: Indiana University Press.

Thompson, Lisa B. 2012. *Beyond the Black Lady: Sexuality and the New African American Middle Class.* Champagne-Urbana: University of Illinois Press.

Thomson, David. 2016. *Television: A Biography.* New York: Thames and Hudson.

Thuma, Emily. 2014. "'Prison/Psychiatric State': Coalition Politics and Opposition to Institutional Violence in the Feminist 1970s." *Feminist Formations* 26, no. 2: 26–51.

Thuma, Emily. 2019. *All Our Trials: Prisons, Policing, and the Feminist Fight to End Violence.* Urbana-Champagne: University of Illinois Press.

Tibbets, John. 1993. "Clint Eastwood and the Machinery of Violence." *Literature/Film Quarterly* 21, no. 1: 10–17.

Tobin, Robert Deam. 2015. *Peripheral Desires: The German Discovery of Sex.* Philadelphia: University of Pennsylvania Press.

Tomkins, Silvan S. 1963. *Affect Imagery Consciousness, Volume 2: The Negative Affects.* New York: Springer.

Tompkins, Kyla Wazana. 2012. *Racial Indigestion: Eating Bodies in the Nineteenth Century*. New York: New York University Press.

Tomso, Gregory. 2017. "HIV Monsters: Gay Men, Criminal Law, and the New Political Economy of HIV." In *The War on Sex*, edited by David M. Halperin and Trevor Hoppe, 353–377. Durham, NC: Duke University Press.

Toumarkine, Doris. 2003. "Capturing a Controversy: Moviefone Co-founder Andrew Jarecki Makes Acclaimed Documentary Debut." *Film Journal International* (June): 20–21.

Tsang, Daniel, ed. 1981. *The Age Taboo: Gay Male Sexuality, Power, and Consent*. London: Gay Men's Press.

Turim, Maureen. 1989. *Flashbacks in Film: Memory and History*. New York: Routledge.

Turnbull, Sue. 2014. *The tv Crime Drama*. Edinburgh: Edinburgh University Press.

Turner, Frederick Jackson. (1893) 2007. *The Frontier in American History*. Gutenberg Project (October 14). Accessed January 27, 2019. http://www.gutenberg.org/files/22994/22994-h/22994-h.htm.

Vachss, Andrew. 1989. "How We Can Fight Child Abuse." *Parade Magazine*, August 20. Accessed December 15, 2015. http://www.vachss.com/av_dispatches/disp_8908_a.html.

Vachss, Andrew. 2002. "The Difference between Sick and Evil." *Parade Magazine*, July 14. Accessed December 15, 2015. http://www.vachss.com/av_dispatches/parade_071402.html.

van Dijck, José. 2008. "Future Memories: The Construction of Cinematic Hindsight" *Theory, Culture and Society* 25, no. 3: 71–87.

Vaught, Sabina E. 2017. *Compulsory: Education and Dispossession of Youth in a Prison School*. Minneapolis: University of Minnesota Press.

Villarejo, Amy. 2001. "Queer Film and Performance 'In Theory.'" GLQ 7, no. 2: 313–33.

Volpp, Leti. 1994. "(Mis)Identifying Culture: Asian Women and the 'Cultural Defense.'" *Harvard Women's Law Journal* 17: 57–101.

Volpp, Leti. 2011. "Framing Cultural Difference: Immigrant Women and Discourses of Tradition." *Differences* 22 no. 1: 90–110.

Wacquant, Loïc. 2009. *Punishing the Poor: The Neoliberal Government of Social Insecurity*. Durham, NC: Duke University Press.

Waldram, James. 2012. *Hound-Pound Narrative: Sexual Offender Habilitation and the Anthropology of Therapeutic Intervention*. Berkeley: University of California Press.

Walker, Janet. 2005. *Trauma Cinema: Documenting Incest and the Holocaust*. Berkeley: University of California Press.

Walkowitz, Judith. 1992. *City of Dreadful Delight: Narratives of Sexual Danger in Late-Victorian London*. Chicago: University of Chicago Press.

Wang, Lee Ann. 2016. "Unsettling Innocence: Rewriting the Law's Invention of Immigrant Woman as Cooperator and Immigrant Enforcer." *Scholar and Femi-*

nist Online 13, no. 2 (Spring). Accessed September 10, 2018. http://sfonline
.barnard.edu/navigating-neoliberalism-in-the-academy-nonprofits-and
-beyond/lee-ann-wang-unsettling-innocence-rewriting-the-laws-invention
-of-immigrant-woman-as-cooperator-and-criminal-enforcer.

Ward, Geoff K. 2012. *The Black Child-Savers: Racial Democracy and Juvenile Justice.* Chicago: University of Chicago Press.

Warner, Michael. 1993. *Fear of a Queer Planet: Queer Politics and Social Theory.* Minneapolis: University of Minnesota Press.

Watkins, Robert E. 2008. "Vulnerability, Vengeance, and Community: Butler's Political Thought and Eastwood's *Mystic River.*" In *Judith Butler's Precarious Politics: Critical Encounters,* edited by Terrell Carver and Samuel A. Chambers, 188–203. London: Routledge.

Weheliye, Alexander G. 2014. *Habeas Viscus: Racializing Assemblages, Biopolitics, and Black Feminist Theories of the Human.* Durham, NC: Duke University Press.

Weinbaum, Alys Eve. 2004. *Wayward Reproductions: Genealogies of Race and Nation in Transatlantic Modern Thought.* Durham, NC: Duke University Press.

Weinbaum, Alys Eve. 2007. "Racial Aura: Walter Benjamin and the Work of Art in a Biotechnological Age." *Literature and Medicine* 26, no. 1 (Spring): 206–39.

Weinbaum, Alys Eve. 2019. *The Afterlife of Reproductive Slavery: Biocapitalism and Black Feminism's Philosophy of History.* Durham, NC: Duke University Press.

Wells, Ida B. 1997a. *A Red Record* (1895). In *Southern Horrors and Other Writings: The Anti-Lynching Campaign of Ida B. Wells, 1892–1900,* edited by Jacqueline Jones Royster, 73–157. Boston: Bedford.

Wells, Ida B. 1997b. *Southern Horrors: Lynch Law in All Its Phases* (1892). In *Southern Horrors and Other Writings: The Anti-Lynching Campaign of Ida B. Wells, 1892–1900,* edited by Jacqueline Jones Royster, 49–72. Boston: Bedford.

Wexler, Laura. 2000. *Tender Violence: Domestic Visions in an Age of U.S. Imperialism.* Chapel Hill: University of North Carolina Press.

Whittier, Nancy. 2009. *The Politics of Child Sexual Abuse: Emotion, Social Movements, and the State.* New York: Oxford University Press.

Wiegman, Robyn. 1999. "Whiteness Studies and the Paradox of Particularity." *Boundary 2* 26, no. 3 (1999): 115–50.

Wiegman, Robyn. 2002. "Intimate Publics: Race, Property, and Personhood." *American Literature* 74, no. 4 (December): 859–85.

Williams, Linda. 1993. "Mirrors without Memories: Truth, History, and the New Documentary." *Film Quarterly* 46, no. 3: 9–21.

Wilson, J. Q. 2013. *Thinking about Crime.* New York: Basic.

Wiseman, Jane. 2015. "Incidence and Prevalence of Sexual Offending (Part I)." SOMAPI Research Brief (July). Accessed July 10, 2019. https://www.smart.gov /pdfs/IncidenceandPrevalenceofSexualOffending.pdf.

Wong, Stephen C. P., Mark E. Olver, and Terry P. Nicholaichuk. 2013. "Assessing Risk Change in Sexual Offender Treatment Using the Violence Risk Scale—

Sexual Offender Version: A Brief Overview." *Sexual Offender Treatment* 8, no. 1. Accessed January 13, 2019. http://www.sexual-offender-treatment.org/115.html.

Wooden, Ken. 2018. "A Profile of the Child Molester." Child Lures Prevention website. http://childluresprevention.com/research/profile.asp. Accessed 1/2/2018.

Woodman, Spencer. 2015. "Chris Hansen Is Back to Catching Predators." *New Republic*, October 18. Accessed January 2, 2018. https://newrepublic.com/article/123138/chris-hansen-back-catching-predators.

Woodward, Kathy. 2009. *Statistical Panic: Cultural Politics and Poetics of the Emotions*. Durham, NC: Duke University Press.

Wright, Richard G., ed. 2009. *Sex Offender Laws: Failed Policies, New Directions*, New York: Springer.

Wynter, Sylvia. 2001. "Towards the Sociogenic Principle: Fanon, Identity, the Puzzle of Conscious Experience, and What It Is Like to Be 'Black.'" In *National Identities and Sociopolitical Changes in Latin America*, edited by Mercedes F. Durán-Cogan and Antonio Gómez-Morian, 30–66. New York: Routledge.

Wynter, Sylvia. 2003. "Unsettling the Coloniality of Being/Power/Truth/Freedom: Towards the Human, after Man, Its Overrepresentation—An Argument." *cr: The New Centennial Review* 3, no. 3: 257–337.

Ybarra, Megan. 2017. *Green Wars: Conservation and Decolonization in the Maya Forest*. Berkeley: University of California Press.

Yudice, George. 2003. *The Expediency of Culture: Uses of Culture in the Global Era*. Durham, NC: Duke University Press.

Zelizer, Viviana. 1994. *Pricing the Priceless Child: The Changing Social Value of Children*. Princeton, NJ: Princeton University Press.

Zgoba, Kristen M., Michael Miner, Raymond Knight, Elizabeth Letourneau, Jill Levenson, and David Thornton. 2012. "A Multi-State Recidivism Study Using Static-99 and Static-2002 Risk Scores and Tier Guidelines from the Adam Walsh Act." National Criminal Justice Reference Service, November. Accessed July 10, 2019. https://www.ncjrs.gov/pdffiles1/nij/grants/240099.pdf.

Zimmer, Catherine. 2015. *Surveillance Cinema*. New York: New York University Press.

Zimmer, Catherine. 2018. "Serial Surveillance: Narrative, Television, and the End of the World." *Film Quarterly* 72, no. 2 (Winter): 12–25.

INDEX

abduction, sexually motivated examples of, 15, 65–66, 69–71, 108; in *M*, 181; in *Mystic River*, 151–53

Abnormal (Foucault), 30, 56–57

abnormality: actuarial prediction of, 83–85; child molestation discourse, 56–57; expansion of sex crime laws and, 79–81; non-harmful sexual conduct and, 63–65; racialized and gendered formations of, 45–46; sexual liberation discourse and, 55; in *The Woodsman*, 186–88

About a Boy (film), 195

Abu Ghraib Prison, 88

Ackerman, Alissa, 92, 209n6, 210n10

actuarial prediction, 12, 20–22, 72, 83–85, 88, 211n20

ACT UP, 68

Adam, Sophie, 56–57, 60

Adam Walsh Child Protection and Safety Act, 11, 71, 82–83, 89, 211n26

Adler, Amy, 76, 203

adult-child sex, 26; consensual relations and, 59; film explorations of, 128–31; Foucault's discussion of, 56–58; in *Mysterious Skin*, 166–70, 176–78; normalcy and, 54; Orientalist stereotypes of, 60–61; psychopathic framing of, 33–36, 56–61; spectaculariza-tion of, 29–33, 80–81; virtual pedophilia and, 59–61; in *The Woodsman*, 181–93

Adult Swim (television program), 101

Advanced Notification of Traveling Sex Offenders, 93, 211n26

aestheticization: in *Capturing the Friedmans*, 131–32; forensic science and, 26–27; in television crime series, 106, 121–27; in *The Woodsman*, 181–93

affect: in *Capturing the Friedmans*, 134; in *Mysterious Skin*, 164, 166–67, 173–74; virtual pedophilia and, 107; in *The Woodsman*, 164, 178–79, 185–88

African Americans: black male youth, targeting of, 68–69; in male sex offender registries, 7–8, 92–94; racialized childhood for, 43; as sex crimes victims, 70–71; sexual predator stereotypes and, 37–38, 41, 43, 212n34; sexual targeting of, 43–44, 200–201; vulnerability of women and children, 43–44, 60, 200–201, 212n34

age of consent: adult-child sexuality and, 57, 59; homosexuality and, 162; rape and, 54

Ahmed, Sara, 173

Alexander, Jace, 126

Alexander, Jacqui, 55

27, 129, 131–45; critical reception of, 131–35; family-produced footage in, 134–35; virtual memory in, 136–41; virtual pedophilia in, 142–45

Carroll, Lewis, 164

Cash, David, Jr., 71

Cassidy, Patrick, 112–14

Catholic Church, child sexual abuse and, 66

Center for Sex Offender Management (CSOM), 91, 96, 220n47

Center for Sexual Justice (CSJ), 196

Center on Youth Registration Reform (CYRR), 196

Central Park jogger case, 68–69

Chaudhary, Zahid, 203

Chen, Mel, 160, 226n24

Cherniavsky, Eva, 157, 223n28, 227n21

childhood: human capital logics and, 10; nationalist normalization of, 38–39; permanent insecurity in, 64–65; in queer theory, 170; racialization of, 43; sexuality in, 42–46, 167–70; white iconization of, 67–68

Child Lures Prevention website, 96–97

child molestation discourse, 56–61, 65; child sexual abuse in, 66; diagnostic categories and, 75–76, 217n22; in film, 129–31; in *Special Victims Unit* (SVU) (*Law and Order* television series), 108–14; whiteness of child sexual abuse and, 67–68

"child molester," cultural mediation of, 55–61

Child Molesters: A Behavioral Analysis, for Law Enforcement Officers Investigating Cases of Child Sexual Exploitation (Lanning), 76–77, 91

child pornography, 72; in *Capturing the Friedmans*, 131–32; diagnosis and treatment of pedophilia and, 83–88; televisual code and, 126–27

child sexual abuse, 66; in *Capturing the Friedmans*, 131–45; data on, 90–94; in film, 142–43; in *Mystic River*, 145–49

Chinese Exclusion Act of 1882, 38

cinematic hindsight, in *Capturing the Friedmans*, 139

cinematic surplus: in *Mysterious Skin*, 173–78; on-screen pedophiles and, 161–70, 226n2; in *The Woodsman*, 181, 188–93

civil rights: decline of white supremacy and, 55–61; sexual assault and, 46

Civil Rights Childhood (Capshaw), 67

Clarke, John, 78

class: child molestation discourse and, 56–57, 60–61; criminality and, 41–46; of suspect in *Special Victims Unit* (SVU) (*Law and Order* television series), 111–14

Cohen, Cathy, 193, 216n11, 226n1

colonization: pedophilia and, 33–36; power structures and, 203–7; sexual exploitation and, 37–38

Color of Violence, The, 16

"Combahee River Collective Statement," 69

Combined DNA Index System (CODIS), 220n47

common sense: *Capturing the Friedmans* and, 145; data analysis of sex offenders and, 93–94; feminist and queer theory approaches to, 69; normalcy of whiteness and, 20; sex panic and, 30–33, 47–54; sexual psychopathology and, 46; sexual security and, 3–4, 26–27; television audiences and, 107–14; virtual pedophilia and, 195–96

community notification practices, sexual predators and, 72–78, 211n26

Community Protection Act (Washington State), 70

Community United against Violence, 206

"complex TV," 106

constitutional exceptions, sex crime laws and, 71–72

Cooper, Rand Richards, 134

Cops (television series), 99

Corbet, Brady, 165

Corrigan, Rose, 17, 84, 210n16

counterinsurgency initiatives: cultural mediation and, 32–33; pathologization counterinsurgency initiatives (*continued*) of homosexuality and, 26; racial profiling and, 9

Creative Interventions, 206

Crenshaw, Kimberlé, 200, 216n5

crime procedural serials, virtual pedophile and, 100–106

Criminal Intent (television series), 99

criminality: cultural transformation of, 19–25; diagnostic categories and, 73–76; pedophilia and, 25–26; preventative criminalization and punishment, 72; psychopathology and, 33–36; racialized and gendered formations of, 45–46

criminalized populations: racial profiling and, 10–11, 39; white male sex offenders in, 6–8

criminal justice, sex crimes and, 196

Criminal Justice Information Services (FBI), 220n47

criminology: big data and, 88–94; emergence of, 37–38, 41

Critcher, Chas, 78

Critical Resistance, 206

CSI (television franchise), 99–100

Cuesta, Michael, 4

cultural mediation: biopolitical security and, 3–4; in *Capturing the Friedmans*, 133–34; film representations of pedophiles and, 128–31; pedophilia and, 204–7; production of pedophile and, 19–25; representational distance and, 126–27; sex panic analysis and, 16–19; of sexual psychopathology, 46; sexual security and, 26–27; source genres for, 24–25. *See also specific media*

custodial parental rights, child-snatching and, 65–66

Dade County Coalition for the Humanistic Rights of Gays, 58

Danet, Jean, 57

danger: pedophilia associated with, 78–88;

in SVP rulings, 219n38. *See also* stranger danger

Dangerous Sex Offenders (APA), 82

Daniels, Lee, 179–80

Dash, Damon, 180

data analysis of pedophilia: actuarial predictions of abnormality and, 83–85; focus on, 200–207; inconsistencies in, 85–88; information vs., 88–94; for LGBTQ, minorities, and noncitizens, 199–200; problems in, 11–12, 210nn9–10; racialization of crime and, 41, 215n29; in *Special Victims Unit* (SVU) (*Law and Order* television series), 109–14; spectacularization and, 54; vile sovereignty and, 42–46

Daughters of Bilitis, 45

Davis, Angela, 210n18, 212n34, 215n35

Davis, Lisa Selin, 166

Davis, Richard Allen, 217n14

Deer, Sarah, 16, 212n33, 213n9, 215n34

Deleuze, Gilles, 21, 179, 212n40, 223n30

deterrence of sex predation, legal initiatives for, 44–46

Diagnostic and Statistical Manual of Mental Disorders (DSM), 56, 73–78, 217n20, 217n22; in *Special Victims Unit* (SVU) (*Law and Order* television series), 108–14

"Diffusion of Sex Psychopath Laws, The" (Sutherland), 52–53

Dodd, Westley Allan, 217n14

Doom Generation, The (film), 166

Doppman, Lloyd, 132–33

Do the Right Thing (film), 68–69

Drink before the War, A (Lehane), 147–49

Dyer, Alfred, 36, 78

Dyer, Richard, 116

Eastwood, Clint, 4, 27, 129–30, 145, 149

Ebony magazine, 67

Edelman, Lee, 14, 60–61, 170, 211n25

Edholm, Charlton, 37

Edward R. Byrne Justice Assistance Grant funds, 88

future (*continued*)
  against, 6, 10; sex panic and fear of, 14;
  sexual violence impact in, 128; treatment
  of pedophilia in, 81–83

Galasso, Frances, 132
García, Inez, 215n35
Gates Foundation, 100
gateway offenses: analysis of, 197–98; sex
  crime legislation and, 79–80; sex offender
  registries and, 11
Gay Liberation Front, 59
gender: civil rights and, 55–61; criminality
  and, 41–46; non-normative practices and,
  26; pedophilia and, 17; power structures
  and, 203–7; racialization of, 69, 216n5;
  white iconization of, 67–68
"Gender Violence and the Prison Industrial
  Complex," 16
General Allotment Act (Dawes Act), 38–39
Generation Five, 207
Genre and Television (Mittell), 100
Getaway, The (film), 181–82
Gilmer, Rachel, 200
Gladwell, Malcolm, 1–2
global sex industries, children in, 215n44
Goldberg, Amy, 12, 77, 85, 218n26
Goldsby, Jacqueline, 203, 213n7
Gordon-Levitt, Joseph, 165
GPS tracking, 217n18
Grant, Hugh, 195
Greek premodern culture, pedophilia in, 32,
  35–36, 39–40, 59
Greenfeld, Lawrence A., 85–86
Greenfeld Report, 7, 85–88, 90, 210n9, 219n41
Grier, David Alan, 178, 180
Gross, Kali, 41, 210n19
Guantánamo Bay Detention Camp, 88
Guiry, Tom, 146

Hagerman, Amber, 70
Hall, Richard, 85
Hall, Ryan C. W., 85

Hall, Stuart, 78–79, 122
Hamer, Fannie Lou, 46
Hanhardt, Christina, 17
Hankin, Richard, 132
Hansen, Chris, 124–27
Hansen vs. Predator (spinoff program), 125–27
Hanson, R. Karl, 12, 219n35,
Happiness (film), 4, 128
haptic visuality, 167–71, 226n6
Hard Candy (film), 161
Harden, Marcia Gay, 146
Hargitay, Mariska, 103
Hargreaves, Allison, 16
Harmful to Minors (Levine), 4, 14
Harris, Andrew, 83
Harris, Cheryl, 213n7
Harris, Luke, 200
Harris, Neil, 106
"Have You Seen Me?" campaigns, 65–66
Hayden, Michael, 112–14
Hayes, Kelly, 199
Hayles, Katherine, 21–22, 138
Healy William, 41
Heim, Scott, 161, 164–65, 167, 171, 172, 226n4
Hendricks, Leroy, 80–81, 218n31
hetero-realism, in *The Woodsman*, 183–88
Hirsch, Foster, 225n18
History of Sexuality, Volume I, The (Foucault), 56–57
HIV/AIDS: feminist and queer activism about,
  69; racial and sexual politics of, 68–69,
  216n7
Hocquenghem, Guy, 57
Holland, Ida Mae, 43
Homeland Security Act, 88
homophile organizations, normalization
  campaigns of, 45
homosexuality: changing attitudes about,
  68–69; civil rights and, 55–61; normalization campaigns for, 45–46, 59–61; pathologization of, 26, 58, 65; sex offenders and,
  162–70; whiteness and, 68

National Association for Rational Sex
Offense Laws (NARSOL), 196
National Center for Missing and Exploited
Children (NCMEC), 7, 76, 96, 210n12
National Center for Reason and Justice
(NCRJ), 197
National Child Abuse and Neglect Data Sys-
tem (NCANDS), 90, 220n48
National College Women Sexual Victimiza-
tion Study, 90
National Crime Information Center (NCIC),
220n47
National Crime Victimization Survey
(NCVS), 86
National Incidence Studies of Missing, Ab-
ducted, Runaway, and Throwaway Chil-
dren (NISMART-1 and -2), 90, 220n48
National Incident-Based Reporting System
(NIBRS), 86, 219n40
National Intimate Partner and Sexual Vio-
lence Survey (NISVS), 90
nationalist normalization, childhood ideol-
ogy and, 38–39
National Palm Print System (NPPS), 220n47
National Security Agency, 88
National Sex Offender Database (Dept. of
Justice), 23–25
National Sex Offender Public Website
(NSOPW), 96, 220n47
National Sex Offender Targeting Center, 93
National Survey of Children's Exposure to
Violence (NatSCEV), 90, 220n48
neoliberalism, mass incarceration and, 8–10
New Queer Cinema, 166, 226n8
news media: criticism of sex offender regis-
tries in, 196–99; white child rape and mur-
der cases in, 42–43
New York Herald Tribune, 42
New York State Film Tax Credit Program, 100
New York Times, 42, 198
Ngai, Mae, 215n29
Ngai, Sianne, 107, 222n17
No Future (Edelman), 14

No More Silence database, 200
nongovernment websites, sexual predator
data on, 96–97
Noonan, Tom, 120
normalcy: actuarial prediction of abnormality and, 83–85; advocacy for, in Special
Victims Unit (SVU) (Law and Order television series), 109–14; aura of virtual pedophilia and, 117–21; gendered and racialized
divisions of, 200–207; hetero-realism in
The Woodsman and, 183–88; pedophile
identification and, 1–2, 59; predatory pedophile and, 21–25; psychopathic framing of
sexuality and, 33–36; racialized violence
and, 45–46; rape and, 63–65; white male
sexuality and, 41–42; white supremacy and,
37–38. See also abnormality
North American Man-Boy Love Association
(NAMBLA), 26, 59, 109
Nowhere (film), 166

Ocen, Priscilla, 200
Okami, Paul, 12, 77, 85, 218n26
Olguín, Ben, 88–89
Onorato, Joseph, 132
operational aesthetic, 106, 113, 116, 222n16
Orientalism: adult-child sexuality and, 59–
60; whiteness as norm vs., 38–39, 214n16;
white slavery discourse and, 41
Ossido, Salvatore, 42–43
Oz (television series), 100

padeophilia erotica, 25, 34; racial differentia-
tion and, 39–40
Page Act of 1875, 38
Pall Mall Gazette, 36
Panaro, Peter, 132–33
Parade Magazine, 20–21, 68, 77
paraphilia, pedophilia as category of, 73–75,
217nn19–20
Parker, Alison, 200, 210n11
Parks, Rosa, 46
Pasolini, Pier Paolo, 107

psychopathology: detection of pedophilia in, 73–78; deterrence of predation and, 44–46; diagnosis and treatment of pedophilia and, 83–88; homosexuality and, 26; perversion and, 40–46; popular reason and legislative power vs., 79–88; sex offender management and, 47–54; sexuality and, 33–36

Puar, Jasbir, 160, 204, 209n3, 215n38, 218n23, 220n45

Public Enemy, 68

public health, sexual psychopathology and, 41

public opinion, sexual psychopathology and, 47–48

public service announcements in *Special Victims Unit* (*svu*) (*Law and Order* television series), 109–10

Puri, Jyoti, 211n24, 219n39

Pynchon, Thomas, 103

Queen of America Goes to Washington City, The (Berlant), 14

queer studies: child sexual abuse and, 69; New Queer Cinema and, 166–67; sex offender registration and, 193; sexual security and, 27–28; social constructions of pedophilia and, 203–7; virtual pedophile and, 161–70

Quinn, Tim, 218n31

race and racism: actuarial prediction of abnormality and, 84–85; criminalization and, 41–46, 199–207, 215n29; devaluation of children and, 200–207; forensic informatics and, 88–94; gender and sexuality and, 69, 216n5; pedophilia and, 65; policing of sexuality and, 194; politics of surveillance and, 24–25; power structures and, 203–7; sex offender registration and, 6–8, 88–94, 180; sexual targeting of African American women and children and, 43–44, 60, 200–201; social Darwinism

and, 38–39; suppression of people of color and, 8–9; visualization and, 204–7; white sexual endangerment myth and, 37; in *The Woodsman*, 185–88

Racial Innocence (Bernstein), 67

racial prerequisite immigration cases, 38–39

racial slavery, sexuality and, 36–38

Rajskub, Mary Lynn, 173

rape: consensual sex and, 54; data and statistics on, 85–86, 219n40; feminist scholarship on, 63–65; increased media coverage of, 69–71; racial disparities in coverage of, 70–71

Rashomon (film), 135

reason, sex panic and, 47–54

Red Record, A (Wells), 37

Reform Sex Offender Laws (rsol), 196

Reinhardt, James M., 47–48

Religion News Service, 96

remediation in *Capturing the Friedmans*, 133–34, 136–41

respectability, 24, 46, 166, 214n27, 228n26; in *The Woodsman*, 185, 190, 193

Reyes, Kevin, 188

Rich, B. Ruby, 166, 226n5

Richie, Beth, 16–18

ridiculosity in television crime series, 102–6

Riehele, Richard, 173

risk: in *Mysterious Skin*, 173–74, 178; of pedophilia, 78–88; predation and, 3; racialization of, 88–94; sexuality of, 161–93; sorn protocols for, 89

Ritchie, Andrea, 16, 199, 200, 210n17

Rivera, Geraldo, 133

"roaming danger" of sexuality, 64, 162

Robbins, Tim, 145

Roberts, Brian, 78

Rockefeller Foundation, 47

Roe v. Wade, 55

Romeo and Juliet crimes, 11, 79, 197

Rosenberg, Jordy, 160

Rossum, Emmy, 146

Rubin, Gayle, 59, 69, 217n13

Saada Saar, Malika, 200

Sage, Bill, 165

Satan's Silence: Ritual Abuse and the Making of a Modern American Witch Hunt (Nathan & Snedeker), 132

Save Our Children campaign, 26, 58

science: vile sovereignty and, 42; whiteness norms and, 38–39

Scottsboro Boys, 43, 204

securitization: common sense dispersion of, 26–27; cultural entitlement and, 204–7; information gathering on pedophilia and, 88–94; pedophilia and, 194–207; predator identification and, 3–4; regimes for, 211n24; settler colonialism and, 6; vile sovereignty and, 26; whiteness and, 39

Sedgwick, Eve Kosofsky, 140

Sedgwick, Kyra, 178, 180

Seltzer, Mark, 155

sensory surplus: in *Mysterious Skin*, 166; on-screen pedophiles and, 161–70

sentimentalism, sex panic and, 24–25

settler colonialism, security logics and, 4–5

sex offender management: data analysis and informatics and, 88–94; incarceration rates and, 64–65; indefinite detention and, 72–78; panic and reason involving, 47–54; racialization of, 88–94, 180; reform of, 28; in *The Woodsman*, 178, 181–93

Sex Offender Management Assessment and Planning Initiative (SOMAPI), 220n47, 221n52

Sex Offender Registration and Notification Act (SORNA), 88, 93

Sex Offender Registration and Notification (SORN) system, 7–9, 11, 26; creation of, 212n26; efforts to dismantle, 28, 195–207; preventative state and, 72–78; queer outcomes and, 27–28, 193; racialization of, 89–90, 92–94; risk prioritization in, 161–62

sex offender registries, 71–77; data analysis and informatics and, 92–94; demographics of, 92–94; gateway offenses added to,

11, 79–80; map of registered offenders, 8; opposition to, 196–98; racial profiling in, 6–8

sex offenders: demographics of, 7–9; map of registered offenders, 8; pedophiles as, 6

Sex Offender Sentencing, Monitoring, Apprehending, Registering, and Tracking (SMART), 92–93, 220n47

sex offenses: language about, 209n2; new definitions of, 7; queer theory and, 162–70

Sex Offenses and Offenders (Bureau of Justice Statistics), 85–86

Sex Panic and the Punitive State (Lancaster), 14

sex panic framework: evolution of, 13–19; in film, 130–31; perceptions of vulnerability in, 6–7; predator prediction and, 3; psychopathology discourse and, 42–46; reason and, 47–54; recent trends in, 212n30; spectacularization of pedophilia and, 202–7. *See also* moral panic framework

sexual abuse (sexual harm): accountability for, 201–7; child sexual abuse and, 66, 129–31; child's vulnerability to, 36; data on child victims of, 90–94; legal reforms concerning, 63–65; opportunistic occurrences of, 201–7; pedophilia's dominance as, 6–7, 22–25; racial and gendered inflictions of, 15–16; self-defense against, 55–61; sexual freedom and, 204–7; social fabric and, 15, 212n33; in *Special Victims Unit* (*SVU*) (*Law and Order* television series), 108–14

Sexual Assault Response Team (SART) Toolkit, 96

Sexual Behavior in the Human Male (Kinsey), 47

sexuality: adult-child, 26; cultural transformation of, 19–25; Foucault's "roaming danger" of, 162; as moral threat, 13–19; psychopathological view of, 33–36; racialization of, 69, 194; research on, 47; of risk, 161–93

virtuality, 5; deviance and, 20–25; in *Mystic River*, 149–56

virtual memory in *Capturing the Friedmans*, 136–41

virtual pedophile: aura of, in film and television, 115–21, 161–62; in *Capturing the Friedmans*, 142–45; cinematic hetero-realism and, 184–88; as cultural category, 101; in cultural materials, 3–5, 19–25; emergence of, 2–4; film representations of, 128–31; genealogy of, 62–65; image regime of, 179–93; indentifiability of, 161–70; in *Mystic River*, 149–56; procedural tone of, 106–14; profiling instrumentation and, 85–88; in queer theory, 162–70; resistance politics and, 28; SORN registry and, 202–7; spectacularization of, 59–61; surveillance of, 194–95; television coding of, 121–27; in television programming, 99–106

visual images: aura of virtual pedophilia and, 116–21; in *The Woodsman*, 181–83

Volpp, Leti, 17

vulnerability, sex panic and perceptions of, 6–7, 14–15

Waldram, James B., 63, 73, 85, 222n5

Walsh, Adam, 66

Wang, Lee Ann, 17

Wanrow, Yvonne, 216n12

Warner, Michael, 212n38

"War on the Sex Criminal" campaign, 29, 42, 48

websites: pedophilia information on, 23–25, 96–98; in *Special Victims Unit* (*SVU*) (*Law and Order* television series), 109–14

Webster, George, 165

Wells, Ida B., 37–38, 212n34

Wetterling, Jacob, 68

Wexler, Laura, 203, 213n10

"What Works?" (Martinson), 56

White, Ryan, 68, 216n7

white male: adult-child sexuality and, 60–61; degeneracy discourse about, 14–46; film images of pedophiles and, 130–31; as pedophile stereotype, 2–6, 26–27, 31–33, 86–88; securitization and, 195–96; sex crimes and, 69–70; SORN registry impact on, 200–207; as suspect in *Special Victims Unit* (*SVU*) (*Law and Order* television series), 111–14

whiteness: adult-child sexuality and, 60–61; child sexual abuse and images of, 67–68; civil rights and break with, 55–61; colonialism and, 37–38; criminalized populations and, 10–11; looking and, 204–7; mask of normalcy for, 19–25; sex crimes legislation and, 70–71; sex panic as affirmation of, 29; sex trafficking and, 36–37; sexual endangerment and vulnerability linked to, 37, 212n34; sexual entitlement and, 18–19, 202–7; social Darwinism and, 38–39; white-on-white crime and, 10

white slavery: cultural mediation of, 36–37; vile sovereignty and discourse of, 40–46

Whittier, Nancy, 17, 67, 91, 206

Williams, Linda, 135, 139

Wire, The (television series), 100

Witch's Flight: The Cinematic, the Black Femme, and the Image of Common Sense, The (Keeling), 162–63

Wolf, Dick, 99

Wong, B. D., 109

Woodsman, The (film), 4, 27–28, 161–64, 178–93; hetero-realisms in, 183–88; visual regime in, 178–83

"Work of Art in the Age of Mechanical Reproduction, The" (Benjamin), 116

Zimmer, Catherine, 126, 222n16, 223n29

Zoot Suit Riots, 45